MW01250682

THE LONG PEACE PROCESS

The Long Peace Process

The United States of America and Northern Ireland, 1960–2008

ANDREW SANDERS

Liverpool University Press

This book is dedicated to
Ruairi, Imogen, and Fearghal

First published 2019 by
Liverpool University Press
4 Cambridge Street
Liverpool
L69 7ZU

British Library Cataloguing-in-Publication data
A British Library CIP record is available

ISBN 978-1-78694-044-5

Typeset by Carnegie Book Production, Lancaster
Printed and bound in Poland by BooksFactory.co.uk

Contents

List of Abbreviations		vii
Acknowledgements		xi
Introduction		1
1.	The USA and Ireland before 1968	7
2.	The Early Years of the 'Troubles'	29
3.	Jimmy Carter and the Presidential Statement on Northern Ireland	91
4.	Thatcher, Reagan, and Northern Ireland	139
5.	The Bush Administration and Northern Ireland as a Local Political Issue	185
6.	Bill Clinton and the Path to Good Friday	207
7.	George W. Bush, Barack Obama, and Post-Conflict Northern Ireland	259
Conclusion		277
Select Bibliography		289
Index		299

Abbreviations

ACIF	American Congress for Irish Freedom
AIA	Anglo-Irish Agreement
ANIA	Americans for a New Irish Agenda
AOH	Ancient Order of Hibernians
BLBC	Burns Library, Boston College
CIA	Central Intelligence Agency
CSJ	Campaign for Social Justice
DFA	Department of Foreign Affairs
DUP	Democratic Unionist Party
ECHR	European Court of Human Rights
EEC	European Economic Community
EU	European Union
FARC	Fuerzas Armadas Revolucionarias de Colombia [Revolutionary Armed Forces of Colombia]
FBI	Federal Bureau of Investigation
FCO	Foreign and Commonwealth Office
FRU	Force Research Unit
GOI	Government of Ireland
HMG	Her Majesty's Government
HMP	Her Majesty's Prison
HMSO	Her Majesty's Stationery Office
IAUC	Irish American Unity Conference
IFI	International Fund for Ireland

IICD	Independent International Commission on Decommissioning
IIRM	Irish Immigration Reform Movement
ILGO	Irish Lesbian and Gay Organization
INAC	Irish Northern Aid Committee (Noraid)
INLA	Irish National Liberation Army
INS	Immigration and Naturalization Service
IRA	Irish Republican Army
IRSP	Irish Republican Socialist Party
IT	*Irish Times*
JFK	John F. Kennedy
LBJ	Lyndon Baines Johnson
MP	Member of Parliament
NAI	National Archives of Ireland
NAIJ	National Association for Irish Justice
NARA	National Archives and Records Administration
NATO	North Atlantic Treaty Organization
NBC	National Broadcasting Corporation
NICRA	Northern Ireland Civil Rights Association
NIPA	Northern Ireland Police Authority
NSA	National Security Advisor
NSC	National Security Council
NYT	*New York Times*
PD	People's Democracy
PRONI	Public Record Office of Northern Ireland
PSNI	Police Service of Northern Ireland
RTÉ	Radio Telefís Éireann
RUC	Royal Ulster Constabulary
SALT	Strategic Arms Limitation Talks
SAS	Special Air Service
SDLP	Social Democratic and Labour Party
TD	Teachta Dála
TNA	The National Archives of the United Kingdom

UDA	Ulster Defence Association
UDR	Ulster Defence Regiment
UN	United Nations
UNGA	United Nations General Assembly
UPRG	Ulster Political Research Group
USG	United States Government
USSR	Union of Soviet Socialist Republics
UUAC	United Unionist Action Council
UUP	Ulster Unionist Party
UVF	Ulster Volunteer Force
UWC	Ulster Workers Council

Acknowledgements

This project was made possible by a generous grant from the John Moore Newman Scholar Endowment, in honour of John D.J. Moore. I wish to thank colleagues at University College Dublin for their support and assistance over the duration of my Newman Fellowship, in particular Jessica Kavanagh, Catherine Carey, and Suzanne d'Arcy. I would also like to acknowledge colleagues in the United States at Sam Houston State University, Texas A&M University–Central Texas, and Texas A&M University–San Antonio, in particular Dr Philis Barragán Goetz, who kindly read and provided feedback on an earlier draft. My father, Stuart Sanders, was also kind enough to read and comment on earlier drafts.

I am also very grateful for the continued support of my mentors, Professor Richard English, Professor Graham Walker, and Ian S. Wood. I was honoured to spend some time as a Visiting Research Fellow in what is now the School of History, Anthropology, Philosophy and Politics at Queen's University Belfast during the writing of this book. I am also very grateful to Alison Welsby and all at Liverpool University Press for their patience and assistance with this project.

The assistance of staff at the various archives that I visited for this project was invaluable, in particular those at the University of Pittsburgh Archives Center, who helped me navigate a brief visit that coincided with an interview across town.

Finally, I would like to thank my family, in particular my wife, Heather, for everything.

Introduction

Gerry Adams is long credited with masterminding the so-called long war and I don't believe that for a minute. I think what Gerry Adams was orchestrating was the long peace process and I think that started in the 70s ... They had a lot of patience and they did a lot of planning but as a republican I don't think they did it on their own, I think they had a lot of help.[1]

Marian Price, 1 July 2010

The United States will help to secure the tangible benefits of peace ... We are proud to support Northern Ireland. You have given America a very great deal ... We will stand with those who take risks for peace in Northern Ireland and around the world ... We are entering an era of possibility unparalleled in all of human history. If you enter that era determined to build a new age of peace, the United States of America will proudly stand with you.[2]

President Bill Clinton, 30 November 1995

Arriving in Belfast, one is met with the iconic image of the Harland and Wolff cranes, known locally as David and Goliath, which tower

---

[1] Marian Price, interview with author, 1/7/2010.
[2] Bill Clinton, 'Address to the Employees of the Mackie Metal Plant', 30/11/1995, Miller Center, University of Virginia, available at https://millercenter.org/the-presidency/presidential-speeches/november-30-1995-address-employees-mackie-metal-plant.

over the eastern bank of the River Lagan. Edward Harland purchased the Belfast shipyard, which was later responsible for the construction of the *Titanic*, in 1859. Two years later, Harland took Gustav Wolff on as a partner and by the turn of the century Harland and Wolff employed some 9,000 people. As was the case in other cities throughout the United Kingdom, shipbuilding was very much the iconic industry in early twentieth-century Belfast, but it was not the largest employer; that title belonged to the linen industry.[3]

Linen was synonymous with Belfast at the start of the twentieth century; mid-way through the nineteenth century, Belfast had accounted for half the linen output for all of Ireland and there were twenty-eight linen mills in the city. Just over a third of these were located on the Falls Road, which runs south-west from the city centre towards Andersonstown along the foot of the Black Mountain. Sectarian divisions in Belfast were pronounced in its two main industries: while the shipyards were the preserve of the Protestant working classes, the linen mills provided a steady source of employment to Catholics, many of whom ended up living in houses built and owned by mill owners.[4]

The local community relied on the linen industry, which provided both employment and resources for local businesses. One such business was owned by James Scrimgeour on Albert Street, in the lower Falls area, and made spinning frames. In 1858, Scrimgeour, suffering from financial difficulties, handed control to his manager James Mackie. Building up the business over the next two decades, Mackie created a successful export business where he manufactured flax cutters, bundling presses, and twisting frames, all essential cogs in the industry of late nineteenth-century Belfast. Mackie's was also adaptable: during both world wars, they manufactured armaments. As the business expanded, Mackie bought new premises on the Springfield Road.[5] His family continued to run the business until the early 1970s when the company was turned into a workers' cooperative. It retained this status, run as a cooperative by its 5,000 workers, until it was acquired by American textile firm Lummus Industries in the mid-1980s. The Georgia firm

[3]   National Archives of Ireland, 'What Was Belfast like in the Early 20th Century?', available at www.census.nationalarchives.ie/exhibition/belfast/main.html.
[4]   Culture Northern Ireland, 'The Story of Irish Linen', 6/4/2011, available at https://www.culturenorthernireland.org/features/heritage/story-irish-linen.
[5]   Culture Northern Ireland, 'The Industrial Heritage of West Belfast', 11/12/2008, available at https://www.culturenorthernireland.org/features/heritage/industrial-heritage-west-belfast.

entered bankruptcy in 1992 and Mackie's was purchased by Patrick Dougan, a former Antrim hurler, at the behest of the UK Under Secretary of State Richard Needham.[6]

In 1984, Nobel Laureate and former Irish Minister for External Affairs Sean MacBride wrote nine fair employment principles, known as the MacBride Principles, as a corporate code of conduct for American companies seeking to do business in Northern Ireland. While these did not enter law until they formed section 2811 of the 1999 Omnibus Consolidated and Emergency Supplemental Appropriations Act, they quickly became the guidelines by which American companies, such as Lummus Industries, conducted their business in Northern Ireland.[7] With Dougan's takeover, Mackie's, which had become reliant on Protestant workers, began actively to recruit Catholics and managed to increase the proportion of Catholic workers from one-fifth in 1991 to one-third in 1994.[8]

In November 1995, President of the United States Bill Clinton visited Belfast for the first time. Clinton had, over three years earlier, committed the United States to an active role in resolving the conflict in Northern Ireland that had beset the country since the late 1960s. During his trip, the President delivered a keynote address at Mackie's factory before switching on the Christmas tree lights at Belfast City Hall.

Clinton's association with Mackie's was seen as 'a triumph' for Patrick Dougan. When Dougan assumed control of the company, part of the agreement was that he would assume responsibility for the company's £13 million debt.[9] Now that the violence that had beset Northern Ireland for nearly three decades had subsided, international companies felt more secure in considering places like Belfast for investment. This opened up opportunities but also brought challenges for local businesses. This was particularly true for Mackie's, which could not compete with the strong Asian manufacturing industry.[10]

The Northern Irish economy did pick up, with millions of pounds invested across the six counties, most notably in central Belfast. There, relics of the past, previously tainted by conflict, were reimagined

---

[6]   *Guardian*, 8/3/1999.

[7]   Full information on the Bill available at https://www.congress.gov/bill/105th-congress/house-bill/4328/text.

[8]   *New York Times* (hereafter *NYT*), 8/9/1994.

[9]   *NYT*, of 8/9/1994, reported the figure as $21 million, £13 million is calculated using an approximate exchange rate of $1.65 to £1.

[10]   *Guardian*, 8/3/1999.

as pillars of the new Northern Irish community and economy. The Grand Central Hotel, for example, formerly one of the finest hotels in Ireland, which was forced to close in 1971 after violence in Belfast saw the imposition of extreme security measures around the city centre, housed British soldiers during the 1970s before it was transformed into the CastleCourt shopping centre, owned by Australian multinational Westfield. The frequently bombed Europa Hotel, where President Clinton stayed during the 1995 visit, remains a leading high-end hotel in the city.

This regeneration was aided by investment from American companies like Citigroup, Allstate, and Liberty Mutual. These investments could not have occurred without the cessation of violence. Industry had been impacted by the violence, but the bombing campaign of the Provisional Irish Republican Army particularly focused on destabilising the Northern Ireland economy, with a view to undermining its economic viability. If the cost of the conflict became too great, the theory went, then the British would withdraw and leave Ireland to reunify. In practice, however, the struggling economy reduced opportunities for young people who either left Northern Ireland or fell into patterns of long-term unemployment. Both of these outcomes resulted in the failure to establish a solid foundation for the regeneration of the Northern Irish economy once the conflict ended; engagement of external partners was essential.

The United States was one such partner, and it became particularly active after Clinton assumed the Presidency in 1993. Clinton was able to seize the momentum of the waning peace process with key moves like his appointment of former Senator George Mitchell to the role of Special Advisor to the President and Secretary of State for Economic Initiatives in Ireland in early 1995. One of Mitchell's first tasks was to coordinate a Clinton-backed investment conference on Ireland.[11]

It is true to say that the Northern Ireland peace process, an initiative driven by the British and Irish governments in the first instance, had developed without significant political or financial investment from the United States, but it is also fair to argue that Clinton and Mitchell provided a decisive intervention during their time in office. This intervention, however, could not have taken place without the years of engagement between the governments and elected representatives of

[11]   *Irish Times* (hereafter *IT*), 11/1/1995.

the United Kingdom, the Republic of Ireland, the United States, and Northern Ireland. Richard English has noted that:

> The reason for President Clinton's active involvement in the politics of the north of Ireland is more likely to be found in the complexities of his own political trajectory and interests—such as his response to a new kind of Irish–American lobbying, or his desire to be associated with international success stories in conflict resolution—than in the macropolitics of interstate power relations. Moreover, previous US presidents had been involved in Northern Irish politics to a degree that observers often forget.[12]

It is this involvement, highlighted by Professor English, that this book seeks to explore. The Northern Ireland conflict had its roots in the long and complicated histories of Ireland and the United Kingdom, and the American dimension to the conflict dated back to the arrival of Irish people in the United States. This migration took place over centuries but peaked during the era of the Great Famine of the 1850s and 1860s. This book does not seek to tackle that particular period in Irish-American history, covered as it is by an extensive existing literature.[13] The purpose of this book, rather, is to draw upon a range of primary and secondary sources and investigate the continuing relationships between the United States, the United Kingdom, the Republic of Ireland, and Northern Ireland in the context of the peculiar period of conflict known as the 'troubles'. For seven consecutive Presidents, a policy on Northern Ireland as part of their foreign policy towards either the United Kingdom or the

---

[12] English, R., *Armed Struggle: The History of the IRA* (London: Macmillan, 2003), pp. 306–307.

[13] See, among many other valuable studies, McCaffrey, L.J., *The Irish Diaspora in America* (Bloomington: Indiana University Press, 1976) and *The Irish Catholic Diaspora in America* (Washington, DC: Catholic University of America Press, 1997); Meagher, T.J., *Inventing Irish America: Generation, Class, and Ethnic Identity in a New England City, 1880–1928* (South Bend, IN: University of Notre Dame Press, 2001); Drudy, P.J. (ed.), *The Irish in America: Emigration, Assimilation, and Impact* (Cambridge: Cambridge University Press, 1985); Doyle, D.N., 'The Remaking of Irish America, 1845–1880', pp. 213–252, in Casey, M. and Lee, J.J. (eds), *Making the Irish American: History and Heritage of the Irish in the United States* (New York: NYU Press, 2007); Miller, K.A., *Emigrants and Exiles: Ireland and the Irish Exodus to North America* (Oxford: Oxford University Press, 1988) and *Ireland and Irish America: Culture, Class, and Transatlantic Migration* (Dublin: Field Day Publications, 2008); Wittke, C.F., *The Irish in America* (Baton Rouge: Louisiana State University Press, 1956); Moody, T.W., 'Irish-American Nationalism', *Irish Historical Studies* 15(60) (1967), pp. 438–445.

Republic of Ireland, or both, was a necessity. Publicly, the vast majority of these Presidents deferred to the official line that Northern Ireland was a matter of domestic concern for the United Kingdom. Many highly prominent members of Congress did not agree with this deferral. This book will explore the dynamics behind US policy towards Northern Ireland throughout the late twentieth and early twenty-first centuries.[14]

With the precise date of the start of the conflict a continuing matter of debate among scholars, this book will use the year 1968 for the purposes of drawing a line between the pre-conflict and conflict eras in US–Northern Ireland relations. That year saw a Presidential election as well as the 5 October march in Derry that led to serious violence occurring between the Royal Ulster Constabulary and civil rights protesters. The first chapter will set the scene by examining the historical ties between the United States of America and Northern Ireland. Chapter 2 will examine the ways that Presidents Nixon and Ford sought to establish US policy towards the conflict, and the initial engagements of US representatives in the conflict. Chapter 3 will focus on the Jimmy Carter administration, the first to issue an official statement on Northern Ireland. The Reagan years will be examined in Chapter 4, a period where the dynamics of the conflict changed dramatically, driven in part by an aggressive policy on the part of British Prime Minister Margaret Thatcher and her government. Chapter 5 focuses on the Presidency of George H.W. Bush, before Chapter 6 looks at the Clinton Presidency. Chapters 7 and 8 will explore the post-conflict relationship between Northern Ireland and the United States, looking at the George W. Bush Presidency in the former, and the role of Northern Ireland for President Obama and his administration in the latter. Chapter 8 will also serve as a concluding chapter, looking back at the Obama years and the waning interest in Northern Ireland on the part of the United States.

---

[14]   Two recent studies that cover the topic from different perspectives are James Cooper's *The Politics of Diplomacy: US Presidents and the Northern Ireland Conflict 1967–1998* (Edinburgh: Edinburgh University Press, 2017) and Alan MacLeod's *International Politics and the Northern Ireland Conflict: The USA, Diplomacy and the Troubles* (London: I.B. Tauris, 2016). The former of these considers the issue from the perspective of Presidents from Johnson to Clinton, while the latter focuses only on the period 1971–1974, from the introduction of internment without trial to the aftermath of the collapse of the power-sharing assembly.

CHAPTER ONE

The USA and Ireland before 1968

American political figures were intrigued by the newly partitioned Ireland from the earliest years of the two new states. In 1925, shortly before the Irish Boundary Commission concluded its work on the redrawing of the border between the Irish Free State and Northern Ireland, Senator Joe Robinson, an Arkansas Democrat, visited the two new states as part of a European tour.[1] The previous decade had seen significant unrest across Ireland, not least two major internal conflicts in the form of the Irish War of Independence and the subsequent Irish Civil War. Robinson was one of the earliest international visitors to newly partitioned Ireland and his extensive articles, published on consecutive Sundays in the *New York Times*, drew attention to the political stability that began to develop there following the end of violence and alluded to the economic opportunities for industrialists:

> Political agitation has almost ceased. Nothing sensational has occurred in Ireland during the last two years. No social upheaval is threatened. Nevertheless a new Ireland with which Americans are unfamiliar is being created ... Nothing in modern history is more striking than the quick transition under the new Irish Government from the lawlessness and guerrilla warfare which prevailed in Ireland ... to the astonishing condition of orderly peace which now exists ... It could not have occurred if Irishmen generally had not become weary of violence and agitation.[2]

[1]   Weller, Cecil E., Jr., *Joe T. Robinson: Always a Loyal Democrat* (Fayetteville: University of Arkansas Press, 1998), p. 105.
[2]   *NYT*, 11/10/1925.

He continued, at length, to extoll the virtues of post-conflict Ireland, though he was critical of the effort to restore the Irish language to Ireland: 'Inevitably it will widen the breach between Northern Ireland and the Free State and tend to perpetuate the present separation. Gaelic cannot be made the language of the new Ireland, and the sooner this is recognized the better it will be for the cause of Irish progress'.[3]

The second instalment of his report focused on Ulster. Robinson suggested that partition was 'the outgrowth of conditions that render quite improbably, in the near future, the reunion of Ireland under a single Dominion Government. The rivalry between Northern Ireland and the Free State is notable, and indicates antagonism so distinct as to seem at present irreconcilable'.[4] Robinson noted that Northern Ireland was considerably more industrialised than the Republic and observed the sectarian divisions that were already present across the province: 'there are considerable areas, particularly in the Counties of Armagh and Tyrone, Northern Ireland, where Catholics outnumber all the Protestants combined'. He concluded 'no one is justified in dreaming that complete social and political harmony will ever come between Ulstermen and the inhabitants of Southern Ireland'.[5] The Irish economy benefited little from Robinson's visits, though, and it was not until reforms brought in under Taoiseach Sean Lemass in the late 1950s that serious growth resulted.[6] Tom Garvin has suggested that Lemass, while taking credit for this growth, had actively supported the protectionist economic policies that Ireland adopted during the 1930s.[7]

In 1950, twenty-five years after Joe Robinson's trip to Ireland, Northern Irish Prime Minister Viscount Brookeborough travelled to the United States, but found its politicians less than receptive to his visit. The Republican-dominated Congresses between 1948 and 1951 proposed sixteen anti-partition resolutions, and were therefore unlikely

---

[3] Ibid.

[4] *NYT*, 18/10/1925.

[5] Ibid.

[6] Taoiseach, which translates as 'chieftain', or 'leader', is the name given to the position of Prime Minister, Chief Executive, and Head of Government of Ireland.

[7] Garvin, T., *Preventing the Future: Why Was Ireland So Poor for So Long?* (Dublin: Gill & Macmillan, 2004), pp. 45–46; also Daly, M.E., *Industrial Development and Irish National Identity, 1922–1939* (Dublin: Gill & Macmillan, 1992).

to welcome a visit from Brookeborough.[8] The Northern Irish Prime Minister also 'found President Truman "out of town"'. As the *New York Times* later observed, 'this was interpreted here as a convenient way of avoiding trouble with Irish-Americans who were members of the Democratic Party'.[9] He met with protest in New York, but the trip was, for Graham Walker, 'relatively successful' and Ulster Unionists, conscious of the Republic of Ireland's absence from NATO, took up the idea of establishing a Northern Ireland office in the United States as a means to promote North Atlantic security. Irish neutrality in international relations was seen as an opportunity for the Belfast government to curry favour with the United States.[10]

President Eisenhower, victorious in the 1952 Presidential election, was the recipient of an honorary Doctor of Laws from Queen's University in 1945, but had paid little attention to Ireland or Irish issues in his first campaign for the Presidency.[11] By the time of his campaign for re-election in 1956, however, Eisenhower faced Adlai Stevenson, and a Democratic Party that had begun to target special interest groups such as the Irish in the United States. The Democrats had first appealed to Irish America directly in 1884, endorsing Irish home rule in 1888, with the Republicans following suit in 1892. By 1956, the party platform loosely referred to favouring 'the peaceful and orderly achievement of ... legitimate aspirations towards political, geographical and ethnic integrity'. The *New York Times* noted that 'it was unspecific as to the countries where it favoured this approach', but the allusion to Ireland was very clear.[12]

---

[8]   Davis, T., *Dublin's American Policy* (Washington, DC: Catholic University of America Press, 1998), p. 77. One such resolution was proposed by Senator Herbert H. Lehman, a New York Democrat and one of the most prominent Jewish politicians of his era, ahead of St Patrick's Day 1950; see *NYT*, 17/3/1950. A vote on a resolution from Congressman John Fogarty, a Rhode Island Democrat, the following September, was defeated in the House by a vote of 206 to 139; see *NYT*, 28/9/1951.

[9]   *NYT*, 29/9/1963.

[10]   Walker, G., 'Northern Ireland, British–Irish Relations and American Concerns, 1942–1956', *Twentieth Century British History* 18(2) (2007), pp. 194–218, esp. pp. 212–214.

[11]   *IT*, 25/8/1945. In 1952, Vice-President Richard Nixon had, however, suggested applying economic pressure on the British with a view to forcing Irish unification; see *Boston Daily Globe*, 9/9/1952 and Akenson, D., *Conor: A Biography of Conor Cruise O'Brien* (Ithaca, NY: Cornell University Press, 1994), p. 134.

[12]   *NYT*, 18/8/1956; Democratic Party Platform, 1956, 13/8/1956, available at https://www.presidency.ucsb.edu/documents/1956-democratic-party-platform.

Eisenhower received a visit in March 1959 from Irish President Sean T. O'Kelly, who spent two weeks in the United States. O'Kelly's comments upon arrival, that 'there are very few Irish families without a relative somewhere or other in the United States', became a popular message for Irish dignitaries visiting the United States, particularly around St Patrick's Day, as they attempted to emphasise the shared histories of the two nations.[13] O'Kelly addressed a joint session of Congress, telling the two houses that 'one of the dangers that confront mankind is an exacerbated antagonism between the so-called colonial and anti-colonial countries. As well as being a European country, Ireland is also a country with a long and a well-known history of stubborn resistance to foreign rule', also commenting on 'the great and challenging problem of partition'.[14] In these two speeches, O'Kelly established the narrative that Irish politicians would follow for decades to come on the occasion of their visits to the United States; the implicit desire for American investment, both politically and economically, rarely far from their major concerns.

Eighteen months after leaving office, in August 1962, Eisenhower returned to Ireland and took in Dublin, Belfast, Wexford, and Cork. The now former President had lunch with President Eamon de Valera and dinner with Taoiseach Sean Lemass. He also attended a reception at the US Embassy whilst in Dublin. Cork was his last stop where he boarded a cruise liner bound for New York.[15] Relations between Ireland and the United States had strengthened significantly after the election of John F. Kennedy in 1960. In honour of his inauguration on 20 January 1961, the Irish national athletics stadium in Dublin was named the John Kennedy Stadium.[16] A mark of Kennedy's interest in Ireland was the quick appointment of his Ambassador to Ireland, businessman Edward Stockdale. The *New York Times* considered the Dublin post 'one of the most desirable appointments for a career diplomats … the Ambassador represented his government amid dignified and pleasant surroundings'.[17]

Kennedy was the second son of one of the wealthiest and most powerful Irish-American families in the United States. His great-grandparents

---

[13]   *NYT*, 17/3/1959.
[14]   *NYT*, 19/3/1959.
[15]   *IT*, 29/3/1969.
[16]   *NYT*, 24/1/1961. The stadium ran into financial difficulties in 1964 and was ultimately saved and renamed for Billy Morton, the man who led the fight to save it.
[17]   *NYT*, 8/11/1961.

had migrated from Ireland in 1849, eventually settling in Boston. His father Joseph had served as the US Ambassador to the UK between 1938 and 1940.[18] John won election to the House of Representatives for the 11th Congressional district in Massachusetts in 1946, and held the seat for six years before moving to the Senate in the 1952 midterm elections. Shortly after becoming a Senator, Kennedy started to become active in international issues and his immediate focus turned to the ancestral homeland. He pledged to support the ending of partition, in the event that a majority of the population also supported such a move, which would have raised more than a few eyebrows a few years later: 'I intend to do all within my power to have the influence and prestige of the United States used to further the unity of Ireland'.[19] Kennedy followed up on his pledge by introducing, along with Republican Senator Everett Dirksen of Illinois, a resolution in the Senate in January 1953 which called for a plebiscite on the unification of Ireland.[20] Throughout the twentieth century, Ireland remained a bipartisan political issue in the United States, and the Kennedy–Dirksen resolution was an early example of this.

The following year Kennedy appeared at a St Patrick's Day dinner at the Astor Hotel in New York. There he spoke to the Friendly Sons of St Patrick and drew an analogy between the struggle of the Irish people for freedom and that of people in Communist nations, calling on the latter to 'conspire for independence'. Kennedy continued to praise the 'unquenchable spirit of Lord Edward Fitzgerald, of Arthur O'Connor, of Oliver Bond, of Padraic Pearse, and of Robert Emmett and all the others who faced death in order that the spirit of liberty might not also die in their land'.[21] The Irish as an example for oppressed peoples internationally was a theme Kennedy continued to address in subsequent years, notably at the 1957 St Patrick's dinner where he again highlighted a parallel of the Irish with people behind the Iron Curtain, who felt 'that the United States has abandoned them to permanent captivity'.[22]

---

[18]   For more on this episode, see Nasaw, D., *The Patriarch: The Remarkable Life and Turbulent Times of Joseph P. Kennedy* (New York: Penguin, 2012).

[19]   *IT*, 15/11/1952.

[20]   *IT*, 17/1/1953. Dirksen had previously co-sponsored a similar resolution in 1949; see Keane, E., *An Irish Statesman and Revolutionary: The Nationalist and Internationalist Politics of Sean MacBride* (London: I.B. Tauris, 2006), p. 108.

[21]   *NYT*, 18/3/1954.

[22]   *NYT*, 17/3/1957.

Kennedy was also becoming increasingly vocal on France's three-year-old conflict in Algeria. In July 1957, Kennedy delivered what the *New York Times* considered 'a major speech', calling on the Eisenhower Administration to withdraw its support for France's war in Algeria and to work towards Algerian independence, which was 'coldly received' by Secretary of State John Foster Dulles. Dulles suggested that the large European population in Algeria made the problem 'one of exceptional difficulty', and went on to turn the focus to Soviet satellites which he considered were 'the most evil manifestations of colonialism'.[23] Kennedy's speech prompted journalist Harold Callender to draw an analogy between the Algerian situation and that in Ireland prior to partition, though he cautioned against the partition of Algeria. Callender emphasised that Kennedy had offered no solution for the 'pieds-noirs', the group he termed the 'Scotch-Irish' of the Algerian situation.[24] Kennedy himself neglected to compare the Irish and Algerian situations, instead making the comparison between the experiences of people in Ireland and those in Eastern Europe as his campaign for the Presidency gathered momentum in early 1960. During a stop in Gary, Indiana, he referred to the 'foreign oppression' that Ireland suffered.[25] After being confirmed as the Democratic candidate for the 1960 Presidential election, Kennedy won the endorsement of Irish playwright, and former IRA volunteer, Brendan Behan.[26]

The Border Campaign

Kennedy's campaign for the Presidency coincided with the Irish Republican Army's Border Campaign, a significant uprising in the Irish border region. The IRA had endured an unsuccessful campaign during the Second World War, where it had attempted to capitalise on British preoccupation with events in mainland Europe through collaboration with the German *Abwehr*. IRA Chief of Staff Sean Russell visited Berlin for training. Russell, who died on his return trip to Ireland, was buried at sea, wrapped in a swastika. The Irish remained neutral during the war, but continued to fight against the IRA. Effective legislation in the form

[23]   *NYT*, 7/7/1957.
[24]   *NYT*, 14/7/1957.
[25]   *NYT*, 6/2/1960.
[26]   *NYT*, 3/9/1960.

of the 1939 Offences Against the State Act and the 1940 amendment
to the Emergency Powers Act provided the Dublin government with
the power to undermine militant republicanism. The internment camp
at the Curragh, in County Kildare, became home to many prominent
IRA figures of the time.

A period of politicisation within the Irish republican movement
followed and republicans enjoyed a successful 1955 United Kingdom
general election. Philip Clarke and Tom Mitchell, both imprisoned for
IRA-related offences, won seats in Fermanagh and South Tyrone and
Mid-Ulster, respectively. The two received a combined 61,000 votes,
evidence of the popular appeal of Irish republicanism at the time.[27]
Republicans chose to test the extent of this appeal by launching their
first campaign that focused on the Northern Irish state.

Armed and strategically prepared thanks to Sean Cronin's plan
for the Border Campaign, codenamed Operation Harvest, the IRA
launched a series of attacks along the Irish border on the night of 11
December 1956.[28] These hit a variety of installations, civilian and
military, and prompted the Northern Irish government under Basil
Brooke to implement internment under the Special Powers Act. The
Dublin government, concerned that IRA activity might lead to confrontation between Ireland and Britain, followed and Taoiseach John
Costello enacted the Offences Against the State Act. Prominent IRA
figures were, once again, arrested and interned.[29]

As it had been during the Second World War, internment was highly
effective against the IRA. It was reintroduced in Northern Ireland
by mid-December 1956 and around 500 volunteers were interned by
mid-1958. The IRA struggled to continue their campaign and the
Dublin government closed the Curragh internment camp in March
1959. Internment camps in Northern Ireland closed in April 1961 and
the IRA eventually called off the campaign in February 1962. Later
that year, Cathal Goulding was appointed as IRA Chief of Staff and the
movement began to look internationally seeking strategic inspiration.
There was, at the time, some evidence of the potential for a USA-based

[27]   Both men were found ineligible to sit as MPs because of their convictions and
both seats ended up in Unionist hands.
[28]   Cronin later became a journalist for the *Irish Times* and was their correspondent
in Washington, DC.
[29]   Flynn, B., *Soldiers of Folly: The IRA Border Campaign, 1956–1962* (Cork: Collins
Press 2009), p. 83. The expectation of attacks throughout 1956 was even noted by
NYT, on 8/1/1956.

support network. In November 1958, rookie New York police officer Robert Crowley was shown a bullet by his younger brother, a pupil at St Helena's Roman Catholic School in the Bronx. The brother reported that a classmate had given him the bullet and Crowley's subsequent inquiries led him to a private residence in East Bronx where he discovered an arms cache that was reportedly destined for the IRA. The property owner, Henry Barrett, a native of County Cork, confessed to being an IRA sympathiser and was arrested.[30]

It is, of course, inaccurate to talk up the prospects of a significant US support network evolving for Irish republicans at this time, but Barrett was one of a handful of Irish natives in the United States who were both active and supportive of the IRA's armed campaign. Another, and perhaps the most famous, was Mayo native George Harrison, who migrated to New York in 1938 where he joined Clan Na Gael.[31] There he met Liam Cotter who became the IRA's representative in New York during the 1950s. The two men, working with local gun dealer George De Meo, began to supply weapons to Ireland using Irish sailors stopped off at Brooklyn docks. By the late 1950s, they had sourced and supplied machine guns to the IRA. When Brendan Behan visited New York in 1960, he was reported to have met the two men who sent him back to Ireland with guns and ammunition.[32] Harrison became so prolific that at his 1982 weapons trial he took objection to the prosecution's assertion that he had been running guns for six months: his lawyer protested to the court 'Mr Harrison is insulted … he wants the court to know that there has not been a weapon sent to Northern Ireland in the last 25 years without Mr. Harrison'.[33]

JFK in Ireland

By 1963, Kennedy had begun looking ahead to his campaign for re-election the following year. One section of the electorate that Kennedy had polled particularly well with in 1960 was, perhaps unsurprisingly, Irish Catholics. Kennedy won 80 per cent of Catholic

[30] *NYT*, 20/11/1958.
[31] The successor to the Fenian Brotherhood which formed in New York in 1867.
[32] Holland, J., *The American Connection: U.S. Guns, Money and Influence in Northern Ireland* (Dublin: Poolbeg, 1989), pp. 70–74.
[33] *NYT*, 16/3/2000.

votes, noteworthy mainly because he only achieved 38 per cent of the Protestant vote, and his support within the Irish-Catholic community was probably even higher.[34] Kennedy marked his first St Patrick's Day in office with a visit from Irish Ambassador Thomas Kiernan. Kiernan presented the new President with a parchment scroll with the Kennedy coat of arms.[35] The following year, his gift was two porcelain pots of shamrocks.[36] John Joseph Hearn had first sent a gift to the White House on the occasion of St Patrick's Day when he sent President Truman a box of shamrocks in 1952, and these visits became an annual tradition.[37]

After two volatile years in office, which saw, among other events, the Bay of Pigs invasion, the construction of the Berlin Wall, the troubled introduction of desegregation, and the Cuban Missile Crisis, Kennedy's third year in office gave him the opportunity to put his statesman skills on show with a European tour. His visit to partitioned Berlin yielded one of the most iconic speeches of his political career, the 'Ich bin ein Berliner' address, before he travelled from Germany to Ireland.

In travelling to Ireland ahead of an election, John Kennedy was following in the footsteps of his younger brother Edward (Ted), who visited in February 1962 as he campaigned for election to the Senate seat that John had vacated.[38] The *Irish Independent* said of Edward Kennedy's visit that 'he is coming because later this year he is due to be involved in a political fight back home in Massachusetts. He is playing the political game in what has now come to be known as the Kennedy method'.[39] The *New York Times* was rather kinder about the elder Kennedy's trip in

[34]   Smith, R.C., *John F. Kennedy, Barack Obama and the Politics of Ethnic Incorporation and Avoidance* (Albany: SUNY Press, 2013), p. 136.

[35]   *NYT*, 18/3/1961.

[36]   *NYT*, 18/3/1962.

[37]   White House, 'St Patrick's Day and Irish Heritage in American History', 14/3/2018, available at https://www.whitehouse.gov/articles/st-patricks-day-irish-heritage-american-history/.

[38]   Ellis, S., 'The Historical Significance of President Kennedy's Visit to Ireland in June 1963', *Irish Studies Review* 16(2) (2000), pp. 113–130, esp. pp. 115–117; also Fair, J.D., 'The Intellectual JFK: Lessons in Statesmanship from British History', *Diplomatic History* 30 (2006), pp. 119–142; Mitchell, *JFK and his Irish Heritage*, p. 48. Kennedy family friend and JFK's college roommate, Benjamin Smith, filled the seat until Ted turned thirty.

[39]   *Irish Independent*, 25/2/1962. Sherrill has contested that Ted Kennedy, much like his brother, was trying to enhance his reputation as an internationalist. Sherrill, R., *The Last Kennedy* (New York: The Dial Press, 1976), p. 36.

1963, suggesting it was 'a sentimental interlude that figured to do him no harm among the Irish-American voters back home'.[40] Ted spent some time at New Ross, the Kennedy family homestead in County Wexford, before dinner at the American Embassy and a lunch hosted by President de Valera.[41]

The genesis of President Kennedy's 1963 visit to Ireland was the decision to build a new American Embassy in Dublin. The Embassy would move from its Merrion Square location to a larger site in Ballsbridge in south Dublin and Ambassador Stockdale announced plans for President Kennedy to dedicate the new building upon its completion.[42] These plans were announced soon after Kennedy's inauguration but construction was slow, and Kennedy would not live to witness its completion.[43]

North of the border in Belfast, Captain Terence O'Neill had recently succeeded Viscount Brookeborough as the Prime Minister of Northern Ireland and immediately targeted the Kennedy visit to Ireland as an opportunity to promote Northern Ireland on the international stage. O'Neill invited the President to open a national park at the Giant's Causeway, but found Kennedy reluctant.[44] In May it was confirmed that Kennedy would not visit Northern Ireland, though it was not because of a lack of time, with the trip extended to three days to allow the President to visit Cork and Galway.[45] A northern trip was deemed too risky and lacked the political benefits of a southern tour, which would resonate far more significantly with Irish voters in the United States. O'Neill continued to seek out Kennedy and later in the year travelled to Washington, DC to attend the meeting of the International Bank for Reconstruction and Development with the hope that he might be able to meet with President Kennedy, 'if the President's engagements permitted'.[46] Such a meeting was still unlikely, as it could have hindered Kennedy's attempts to secure another large majority of the Irish Catholic vote in 1964. President Truman had adopted a similar strategy during the visit of Viscount

---

[40] *NYT*, 30/6/1963.
[41] *IT*, 27/2/1962.
[42] *NYT*, 19/6/1961. Construction began in July 1962; see *NYT*, 2/7/1962.
[43] *NYT*, 16/4/1963 and 21/4/1963.
[44] Walker, G., *A History of the Ulster Unionist Party: Protest, Pragmatism and Pessimism* (Manchester: Manchester University Press, 2004), p. 151.
[45] *NYT*, 6/5/1963.
[46] *NYT*, 29/9/1963.

Brookeborough to the United States in 1950.[47] McGeorge Bundy, National Security Advisor to both Kennedy and Lyndon Baines Johnson, later confirmed that the decision to avoid O'Neill was for 'tactical reasons'.[48]

Air Force One landed in Dublin on the evening of Wednesday, 26 June 1963. Irish President Eamon de Valera welcomed Kennedy, telling him 'we are proud of you' before the Presidential motorcade travelled through Dublin to the Irish Presidential residence, Aras an Uachtarain, in Phoenix Park.[49] Kennedy spent some time at New Ross before addressing a joint session of the Oireachtas.[50] Television cameras were, unusually, permitted inside to film the event. Kennedy's twenty-five-minute address mentioned the role of the Irish in the American Civil War, before recalling his pre-Presidential rhetoric and commenting that he was 'deeply honored to be your guest in a Free Parliament in a free Ireland'.[51] He later returned to the theme of freedom and self-determination, stating that 'for knowing the meaning of foreign domination, Ireland is the example and inspiration to those enduring endless years of oppression'. Along with De Valera, Kennedy used the occasion of his visit to found the American Irish Foundation, with the Irish government making an inaugural donation of £10,000.[52] Later Kennedy was given the freedom of the city of Dublin and awarded two honorary degrees: from the National University of Ireland and Trinity College. The President visited Galway and Limerick before returning to Air Force One at Shannon Airport where he boarded the plane to a twenty-one-gun salute and flew to London.

[47]   Ibid.

[48]   Memorandum for the President from McGeorge Bundy, 17/3/1964. 'Your meeting with Captain O'Neill', Papers of Lyndon Baines Johnson, President, 1963–1969, National Security File, Country Files, Europe, Box 195, LBJ Library.

[49]   *NYT*, 27/6/1963.

[50]   William Shannon, who was later appointed as US Ambassador to Ireland by President Carter, wrote Kennedy's address to the Oireachtas; see Edward M. Kennedy Institute, Oral History, 'Interview with Elizabeth Shannon', available at https://www.emkinstitute.org/resources/elizabeth-shannon.

[51]   'Address before the Irish Parliament, June 28, 1963', John F. Kennedy Presidential Library and Museum, available at https://www.jfklibrary.org/learn/about-jfk/historic-speeches/address-before-the-irish-parliament.

[52]   House of the Oireachtas, Oireachtas Business, Ceisteanna—Questions. Oral Answers—American–Irish Foundation, Tuesday, 16/7/1963, available at https://www.oireachtas.ie/en/debates/debate/dail/1963-07-16/.

The Presidential motorcade travelled with a heavy police presence and many of those officers present were armed with submachine guns. Heightened security is explained by declassified Irish state papers which suggested that three separate death threats were made against the President.[53] The *New York Times* considered Kennedy's 'sentimental journey', to have been 'a week of extraordinary personal triumph', but added that 'for John F. Kennedy the President it was a week of testing, the outcome of which remains to be seen'.[54]

Kennedy pointedly did not make any mention of Great Britain during his speeches in Ireland, noting only in his departure speech at Limerick that: 'This is the last place I go, and then I am going to another country, and then I am going to Italy and then I am going back home to the United States'.[55] Interestingly, his attitude towards the place he referred to as 'another country' was actually rather warm and the importance Kennedy placed in America's relationship with this 'other country' is obvious from comments he made later that same day, at London's Gatwick Airport.[56] These remarks reflected the strategic importance of the UK for the United States during the tension of the Cold War.[57]

In October, Irish Taoiseach Sean Lemass travelled to the United States where he met Kennedy and dined at the White House.[58] In reciprocating Kennedy's visit, Lemass wanted to reflect and return in kind 'the pleasure that Mr. Kennedy himself experienced when he visited this country earlier in the year'.[59] The Taoiseach's trip began in Philadelphia and although Lemass had claimed that the trip was not to seek trade talks, he did publicise the Irish economy throughout his time in the United States, a move that drew praise from nationalist

[53]   *NYT,* 29/12/2006.
[54]   *NYT,* 27/6/1963 and 30/6/1963.
[55]   Remarks at a Reception at Green Park Race Course, Limerick, Ireland, 29/6/63, The Papers of President Kennedy, Pre-Presidential Papers, Senate Files, Holborn Research Materials, 1958–1960, JFK Library.
[56]   Remarks Upon Arrival at Gatwick Airport, England, 29/6/63, The Papers of President Kennedy, Pre-Presidential Papers, Senate Files, Holborn, Research Materials, 1958–1960, JFK Library.
[57]   For details of the Kennedy–Harold Macmillan relationship, see Bradlee, B.C., *Conversations with Kennedy* (New York: W.W. Norton & Company, 1975).
[58]   *NYT,* 15/10/1963; *IT,* 11/10/1963.
[59]   *IT,* 12/10/1963.

politicians in the Northern Ireland government.[60] The Taoiseach also met Senator Ted Kennedy and was received by the Boston Irish Societies before returning to Ireland.[61] The Lemass visit frustrated Terence O'Neill: 'it is notable that when President Kennedy came to Dublin he was a model of circumspection; not a mention of Northern Ireland came from his lips … yet now on a return visit we have Mr. Lemass in an address to the press calling on Britain to end partition'.[62]

Following Kennedy's death on 22 November 1963, Jackie Kennedy sent a request, via the State Department, for a unit of the Irish Army to attend his funeral. Within an hour, over two dozen members of the Cadet School of the Military College, who had performed for the President in June, had begun making plans for their trip to Washington.[63] Less than a month later, it was reported that Jacqueline Kennedy was planning to take her children to Ireland for a vacation, evidence of the affection that the Kennedy family had for Ireland.[64] This trip eventually took place in 1967, when the three spent six weeks in Ireland, arriving to large crowds at Shannon Airport. Mrs Kennedy remarked, 'I am so happy to be here in this land my husband loved so much. For myself and the children it is a little bit like coming home and we are looking forward to it dearly'.[65]

The Johnson Presidency

Lyndon Baines Johnson was sworn in aboard Air Force One at Love Field in Dallas on 22 November 1963, a matter of minutes after the death of John F. Kennedy. The former Senate Majority Leader from Texas served a five-year tenure as President, winning the 1964 Presidential election in a landslide. His time in office saw tension overseas as the Vietnam War escalated, paired with a rising anti-war movement at home, but significant progress on anti-discrimination legislation such as the Civil Rights Act of 1964 and the Voting Rights Act of 1965. He was not, however, particularly engaged in Irish affairs, other than the

[60] *IT*, 12/10/1963 and 23/10/1963.
[61] *IT*, 21/10/1963.
[62] *NYT*, 18/10/1963.
[63] *IT*, 25/11/1963.
[64] *NYT*, 20/12/1963.
[65] *NYT*, 16/6/1967.

issue of landing rights for US airlines in Dublin, and his ambivalence on Ireland was reflected in the delay in replacing Matthew McCloskey as US Ambassador to Ireland.[66]

The slow process behind the reappointment of an Ambassador in Dublin, a recurring theme among Presidents with little interest in Ireland, did not necessarily reflect a complete disregard for Irish issues, though. Northern Irish Prime Minister Captain Terence O'Neill was finally able to secure a visit to the White House, and became one of the new President's first international visitors when he arrived in Washington on St Patrick's Day, 1964. O'Neill has come to personify the problems of Northern Ireland in the late 1960s, rather out of touch with political realities and caught unprepared for the developing conflict. This is reflected in accounts of his arrival in Washington:

> Captain O'Neill entered the White House last year about this time when he sent a most cordial invitation to President Kennedy to open the Giant's Causeway in Northern Ireland. President Kennedy refused for tactical reasons, but a very friendly exchange of letters followed and the Captain has always since then had a sort of half confirmed date to call on the President when he came to Washington. How he has arrived on St. Patrick's Day, of all things … He has paid a personal call on Mrs. Kennedy, and I incautiously promised the same with you before learning of Larry O'Brien's concern. He has undertaken to keep this off the record, and it may not last more than a minute or two with a picture. If you simply speak of President Kennedy's warm feeling toward him, the job is done.[67]

That neither Kennedy nor Johnson wanted very much to do with Northern Ireland or the Northern Irish Prime Minister was all too

---

[66]   *NYT*, 19/1/1964 and 12/2/1965. Though the delay was not untypical of the passage of time between a US Ambassador in Ireland ending their mission and a new appointment arriving, six months passed between the departure of Francis Matthews in September 1952 and the arrival of William Taft III in March 1953. For further details on the issue of landing rights in Dublin, see Sanders, A., 'Landing Rights in Dublin: Relations between Ireland and the United States, 1945–72', *Irish Studies in International Affairs*, 28 (2017), pp. 147–171.

[67]   Memorandum for the President from McGeorge Bundy, 17/3/1964, 'Your meeting with Captain O'Neill', Papers of Lyndon Baines Johnson, President, 1963–1969, National Security File, Country Files, Europe, Box 195, LBJ Library.

clear, but Johnson nonetheless provided O'Neill with a few minutes of his time. Despite Kennedy's concerns over appearing with O'Neill, the meeting with Johnson was well received:

> It was so very good of you to receive me and those personal gifts from the people of Northern Ireland. I fear that owing to my haste in leaving to catch my plane I omitted to let you know that I have ordered two banqueting cloths to be woven, suitable for official use at the White House. They will take at least six months to weave and will have engraved upon them the Presidential Seal ... As relations between the North of Ireland and the South of Ireland improve I do so hope that the Irish Question can be removed from American politics as it has been from English politics for the past 40 years ... With renewed thanks and all good wishes for the election. Your magnificent T.V. appearance, which I saw in Washington, should stand you in good stead.[68]

Perhaps only partially hidden within an otherwise painfully polite and formal letter was O'Neill's mention of the 'Irish Question' and its role in American politics. The Irish issue was, of course, a relatively small one for Johnson, even less so than it had been for Kennedy. O'Neill also wrote to McGeorge Bundy, suggesting that Bundy's role in arranging his meeting with Johnson might have been 'responsible for changing the course of Irish history!' He continued to express his regret that he had not been able to meet Kennedy: 'If I could have paid my respects to the South of Ireland's most distinguished son it might have had an even greater effect on Southern Irish opinion and consequently improved relations between North and South'. When Sean Lemass had visited Kennedy and spoken publicly against partition, O'Neill's tone had been somewhat different. O'Neill ended the letter on a humble note: 'I enclose a letter for the President as you alone can judge whether you should bother him with it'.[69] Johnson's reply was short, thanking O'Neill for the gift of an 'interesting and beautifully bound volume on

---

[68]   Letter from Terence O'Neill to Johnson, 26/3/1964, Papers of Lyndon Baines Johnson, President, 1963–1969, National Security File, Country Files, Europe, Box 195, LBJ Library.

[69]   Letter from Terence O'Neill to McGeorge Bundy, 26/3/1964, Papers of Lyndon Baines Johnson, President, 1963–1969, National Security File, Country Files, Europe, Box 195, LBJ Library.

the Scotch-Irish in the United States'.[70] The letter was remarkable if
only for its brevity and similarity to the letters that Johnson would send
to the members of the public who wrote to him during his Presidency.
O'Neill met with Jacqueline Kennedy, also briefly, and presented her
with gifts of Irish linen.[71]

In the way they handled Captain O'Neill, both Kennedy and
Johnson betrayed their wariness of becoming embroiled in the issue of
Northern Ireland. Neither would contest a second election and therefore
neither would have to engage with the issue in the context of appeasing
the Irish-American vote. Even in the years before the Northern Ireland
conflict dramatically changed international perceptions of the Irish
question, the Irish question remained confined to its relevance to
Irish-American voters, at least in the eyes of the White House.

One positive bilateral development of Captain O'Neill's trip to
Washington was that it prompted a meeting between the Northern
Irish Prime Minister and Taoiseach Sean Lemass. The two men
discussed trade and tourism as well as the Dublin to Belfast railway.[72]
The Northern Irish economy around this time was still relatively
healthy, with manufacturing employment rising slightly between 1964
and 1965, though levels remained lower than in the UK or the
Republic of Ireland.[73] Among those companies invested in Northern
Ireland were several US firms, with 1964 investment totalling approximately $75 million, and roughly 7,000 jobs. Two thousand of those
were employed by Standard Telephones and Cables at its Monkstown
facility.[74] The company also operated locations in Belfast, Larne, and
Enniskillen. Du Pont chemicals and Chemstrand were also considered
major contributors to the Northern Irish economy, with Du Pont's
investment particularly significant as the company continued to develop
its plant in Derry at a time when Northern Irish Minister of Commerce
Brian Faulkner predicted an imminent economic downturn. The Du
Pont investment would help the city of Derry weather the storm as the

---

[70]   Letter from Johnson to O'Neill, 31/3/1964, Papers of Lyndon Baines Johnson,
President, 1963–1969, White House Central Files, Box 41, CO125 Ireland, LBJ
Library.
[71]   *NYT*, 17/3/1964.
[72]   *NYT*, 15/1/1965.
[73]   Rowthorn, B. and Wayne, N., *Northern Ireland: The Political Economy of Conflict*
(Cambridge: Polity Press, 1988).
[74]   *NYT*, 10/1/1964.

British economy dipped over the course of 1966.[75] Du Pont had set up in Maydown near the city in 1957, eventually opening in 1960, and one of its earliest projects was the manufacture of Neoprene, used to make conveyor belts, window seals, tyres, paints and high-insulation foam.[76] Later, as violence began to spread across Northern Ireland, Prime Minister O'Neill paid tribute to the role of the DuPont plant, which employed a mainly Catholic workforce, in reducing unemployment in the north-west of Northern Ireland.[77]

Other American companies with investments in Northern Ireland included Worcester Valve Company, which had a plant at Armagh, Wisconsin's Walker Manufacturing Company in Belfast, and Centralab Ltd, a subsidiary of Globe-Union of Milwaukee. Autolite Motor Products, part of the Ford Group, employed 700 in Belfast, and there was also a branch of Ames Textile Corporation of Lowell, Massachusetts, 'which is building Britain's most advanced cotton-spinning mill at Ballymoney'.[78] The *New York Times* ran an article in April 1966 that emphasised the role of economic development in fostering conciliation in Ireland, recalling the views of Senator Joe Robinson, made after his 1925 visit.[79] This point was underlined by a series of attacks by a group styling itself the Ulster Volunteer Force in April, May, and June of 1966. These attacks resulted in the deaths of three civilians.

The fact that President Kennedy had neglected to visit Northern Ireland, even with such significant US investment there, emphasised the problems that Unionist Northern Irish figures would have in pressing their case to an American audience. There were, however, attempts at building important cultural ties between the United States and Northern Ireland during this time. For example, in June 1966, the Very Revd Francis B. Sayre, Dean of Washington Cathedral, dedicated the ancestral home of his grandfather, President Woodrow Wilson, near the village of Strabane. Speaking at the ceremony, Captain O'Neill commented, 'we are proud that Ulster, this small part of the world, should have had such an undying influence on the great American people'. Ancestral homesteads for Presidents Arthur,

---

[75]   *IT*, 25/5/1966 and 29/8/1966.
[76]   *Belfast Telegraph*, 14/12/2010.
[77]   Meeting at 10 Downing Street, 4/11/1968, PRONI, CAB/4/1413.
[78]   *NYT*, 21/1/1966.
[79]   *NYT*, 16/4/1966.

McKinley, Grant, and Jackson were also advertised in brochures for Northern Ireland.[80]

On 31 March 1968, President Johnson announced that he would not run for re-election. His concerns over his failing health and the divisions that had arisen within the Democratic Party lay behind his decision, but there were many domestic and international political obstacles that stood in his way as well. Lining up to replace Johnson as the Democratic candidate were figures such as Minnesota Senator Eugene McCarthy, Vice-President Hubert Humphrey, and New York Senator Robert Kennedy, the younger brother of the slain President. Kennedy, who had served as Attorney General in his brother's administration, was less willing or able to play up to Irish supporters and lacked the broad popularity that John had enjoyed, both within Irish America, and in Ireland itself. Donal Foley, in the *Irish Times*, emphasised that Robert Kennedy would struggle to capture the Irish vote, arguing that 'the Irish vote as such does not exist anymore to any extent, but Irishmen are still very much a political force in the Democratic Party and Kennedy dare not ignore them'.[81] For his part, Robert Kennedy had not shown the same interest in Ireland as had his brother. He cancelled a scheduled visit to Ireland in 1964, though he did take part in a charity Gaelic Athletic Association event in New York that same year.[82] He was invited to open the John Kennedy Memorial Forest near the Kennedy homestead of New Ross in 1968, funded in part by Irish-American societies, but the trip was placed in doubt after he announced his candidacy for the Presidency, an announcement made shortly before he took part in the New York St Patrick's Day march.[83] It was clear that Robert Kennedy was aware of how Irish America could work to his advantage, but less clear on his strategy for engagement with Irish issues. In the event, Kennedy was fatally shot in Los Angeles on 6 June 1968, shortly after he won the California primary. Captain Terence O'Neill was among his well-wishers as news broke of his shooting:

[80] *Washington Post*, 18/6/1966.
[81] *IT*, 16/4/1968.
[82] *IT*, 23/6/1964 and 13/4/1965.
[83] *IT*, 12/1/1968 and 18/3/1968. Eunice Shriver ultimately opened the park in May 1968; see *IT*, 30/5/1968. See also Schlesinger, A., *Robert Kennedy and His Times* (New York: Houghton Mifflin, 2002), p. 849. On funding for the park, see Memorandum from George Springsteen, 8/6/1968, 'Meeting with the Irish Prime Minister, Mr. John M. Lynch', Papers of Lyndon Baines Johnson, President, 1963–1969, National Security File, Country Files, Europe, Box 195, LBJ Library.

Both because I have a deep affection for the United States—a country which I visited again only last week—and a high regard for the remarkable qualities of Senator Robert Kennedy, who, as Attorney General, entertained me on an earlier visit to America, I am most shocked and grieved that a further senseless act of violence should have cast another shadow upon a family whose great achievements have been matched only by their ill fortunes. Let us hope Mr. Kennedy's great physical endurance and fighting spirit will pull him through.[84]

Jack Lynch was the only head of government to attend Kennedy's funeral and paid a visit to the White House on this trip.[85] The two nations retained largely positive relations at this time, and Johnson's briefing for his meeting with the Taoiseach noted that the only tensions in their bilateral relationship remained the issue of tourism and 'the persistent Irish refusal to grant an American carrier landing rights in Dublin'.[86] Lynch invited Johnson to visit Ireland, but 'the President's response to this invitation was appreciative but noncommittal'.[87] This was predictable for a newly installed President, but Johnson was already well aware of the rising political and social unrest across Northern Ireland at this time.

Northern Irish Civil Rights and American Concerns

A number of Northern Irish groups had already reached out to President Johnson to make him aware of the situation in Northern Ireland, among them the Campaign for Social Justice. Instead of replying directly, a reply was sent from the State Department, an early

[84] *IT*, 6/6/1968.
[85] Memorandum from W.W. Rostow to the President, 8/6/1968, Papers of Lyndon Baines Johnson, President, 1963–1969, National Security File, Country Files, Europe, Box 195, LBJ Library.
[86] Memorandum from George Springsteen, 8/6/1968, 'Meeting with the Irish Prime Minister, Mr John M. Lynch', Papers of Lyndon Baines Johnson, President, 1963–1969, National Security File, Country Files, Europe, Box 195, LBJ Library. For details, see Sanders, A., 'Landing Rights in Dublin: Relations between Ireland and the United States 1945–72', *Irish Studies in International Affairs* 28 (2017), pp. 147–171.
[87] Department of State, Memorandum of Conversation, 6/6/1968, Papers of Lyndon Baines Johnson, President, 1963–1969, National Security File, Country Files, Europe, Box 195, LBJ Library.

indication that the White House would be keeping Northern Ireland at a relatively safe distance. It emphasised that 'The Government of the United States does not, of course, accept the premise that a state of occupation exists in Northern Ireland nor the contention that an authoritarian regime has deprived the people of Northern Ireland of their freedom'.[88] This remained the position of the United States for years to come.

The Campaign for Social Justice (CSJ) had been founded in Dungannon in early 1964, only a few months before President Johnson signed the Civil Rights Act into law. The Northern Ireland Civil Rights Association (NICRA) then followed in January 1967.[89] These groups were part of the wider civil rights movement in Northern Ireland and drew the attention of Irish America. Andrew Wilson has noted the existence of 'a network of fraternal organizations [in the United States], ranging from IRA veterans groups to the Loyal League of Yiddish Sons of Erin' prior to the onset of the conflict in the late 1960s, at which point a number of smaller NICRA support groups developed. These included the Committee for Justice in Northern Ireland, which sent more than $6,000 to Northern Ireland by the end of 1969. Larger and more active was the American Congress for Irish Freedom, which was founded on 26 February 1967 by James Heaney, a lawyer from Buffalo. It had twenty-five chapters and 3,000 members nationwide by 1969.[90] Other groups of the era included the National Association for Irish Justice, which was founded by Brian Heron, who was a grandson of Easter 1916 martyr James Connolly, the Irish Republican Clubs of the United States and Canada, and the Irish Northern Aid Committee.

NICRA started to gather momentum during a sit-in protest in the County Tyrone town of Caledon. Dungannon Rural District

---

[88]   Letter from J. Harold Shullaw, Country Director for United Kingdom, Ireland, and Malta Affairs to Patricia McCluskey, Campaign for Social Justice in Northern Ireland, 29/5/1967, RG59, General Records of the Department of State, Bureau of European Affairs, Office of Northern European Affairs, Records Relating to Ireland, 1963–1975, AGR-Gen-1971 to AV-15 Charters 7.D, Box 1, National Archives and Records Administration, College Park, MD (hereafter NARA).

[89]   Prince, S., *Northern Ireland's '68: Civil Rights, Global Revolt and the Origins of the Troubles* (Dublin: Irish Academic Press, 2007), p. 116; see also pp. 115–118.

[90]   Kenny, K., 'American-Irish Nationalism', in Lee, J.J. and Casey, M. (eds), *Making the Irish American: History and Heritage of the Irish in the United States* (New York: NYU Press, 2006), pp. 289–301 at p. 297; Wilson, A.J., *Irish America and the Ulster Conflict 1968–1995* (Belfast: Blackstaff Press 1995), pp. 22–24.

Council, responsible for housing allocation in the area, had allocated a house to a nineteen-year-old unmarried Protestant woman ahead of several Catholic families. The young woman worked as a secretary for a local Unionist politician, prompting accusations of preferential treatment. Led by Nationalist MP Austin Currie, the Caledon Protest was an important stage in the escalation of the civil rights campaign in Northern Ireland, leading towards the first civil rights march in August. The march was organised by the CSJ and NICRA and was supported by the Nationalist Party, the National Democratic Party, the Liberal Party, and the Northern Ireland Labour Party. Nearly 2,000 protesters marched for four miles from Coalisland to Dungannon.[91]

The Ministry of Home Affairs was particularly concerned about this march. It decided to re-route it 'in the interests of law and order', contending that 'had the organisers of the march been allowed to carry out their original intentions, there would have been a large scale riot with consequential injury to persons and damage to property'.[92] With a second march planned for Derry on 5 October, Minister of Home Affairs, William Craig, issued an order banning 'all public processions or meetings'.[93]

Defying the order, the march took place and was almost immediately stopped by the RUC who broke up the march by baton-charging the protesters. Widespread coverage of the violence drew international attention, and the response of the O'Neill government, which emphasised that they supported the actions of the police 'in a firm way', meant that 'we have now become a focus of world opinion'. British representatives in the United States were reported to 'have been under intense pressure from the American press'.[94] The *New York Times* report betrayed the Unionist influence of their source, stating that 'the trouble began when more than 500 members of the Londonderry Catholic Civil Rights Committee and their supporters paraded into a Protestant area of the city'.[95]

A flurry of meetings between representatives from London, Dublin, and Belfast followed, and all failed to yield any significant progress

---

[91]   *IT*, 15/8/1968 and 17/8/1968.

[92]   Northern Ireland Information Service Press Release, 26/8/1968, CAB/9/B/205/7, Public Record Office of Northern Ireland (hereafter PRONI).

[93]   Letter from John McAnerney, NICRA, to RUC Strand Road, 8/9/1968, HA/32/2/28, PRONI, and Public Order Act (Northern Ireland) 1951, statement by William Craig, 3/10/1968, HA/32/2/30, PRONI.

[94]   Memorandum by the Prime Minister, 14/10/1968, CAB/4/1406, PRONI.

[95]   *NYT*, 3/11/1968.

on the Northern Irish question. Taoiseach Jack Lynch travelled to London to meet Harold Wilson and called for the ending of partition as a means to resolve the unrest in Northern Ireland. Wilson 'dissented from this view and expressed the opinion that "banging of the drum" would only make conditions worse than they were'.[96] At a meeting the following week between Wilson and Captain Terence O'Neill, the British PM emphasised 'Northern Ireland's responsibility for its own internal affairs', implicitly threatening to reduce London's financial contributions to Northern Ireland should the UK government need 'to bring pressure to bear'. Wilson did note that he felt that 'a great deal of liberalisation had been accomplished under Captain O'Neill despite the agitation of pressure groups', and that while he would not press O'Neill too hard for reforms it was important that the process of reform accelerate.

As the conflict in Northern Ireland escalated over the course of 1969, the new administration, led by President Richard Nixon, was forced to establish formal US policy on the matter. Civil rights issues overshadowed both the 1968 US Presidential election and the 1969 election to the Stormont assembly in Northern Ireland, but while segregationist George Wallace, standing as an independent candidate, only carried five states in the 1968 Presidential election, Captain Terence O'Neill's victory in the 1969 Northern Ireland general election was a narrow one and left the Prime Minister without a strong mandate for his reforms. It was, in any case, already too late to save Northern Ireland from violence.

---

[96]   Note of a meeting between Jack Lynch and Harold Wilson in London on 30/10/1968, TAOIS/2000/6/657, National Archives of Ireland (hereafter NAI).

CHAPTER TWO

The Early Years of the 'Troubles'

We trust that both the British and Irish Governments are doing all they can to avoid a civil war.[1]

Henry Kissinger to Gerald Ford, January 1975

President Nixon appointed Henry Kissinger as his National Security Advisor in January 1969. Part of his remit in this role was to keep the President informed on events in Northern Ireland. Working alongside Kissinger were a number of senior officials who followed the developing conflict and offered insight as to how it might impact the United States and its relations with the UK and the Republic of Ireland. Kissinger was later appointed as Secretary of State by Nixon in 1973.[2]

The eight years between the election of Richard Nixon and that of Jimmy Carter bore witness to the worst years of the Northern Ireland conflict. By the time of Carter's election on 2 November 1976, 1,831 people had been killed in Northern Ireland. Yet eight years previously only small signs of the trouble that lay ahead for Northern Ireland were evident. Three Ulster Volunteer Force murders in mid-1966 had been the only significant violence until the emergence of, and particularly the violent resistance that met, the Northern Ireland Civil Rights Association two years later. The situation escalated rapidly, however, to

[1] Memorandum for the President from Henry Kissinger, 'Official Visit of UK Prime Minister Harold Wilson, January 30–31, 1975', White House Central Files, Subject File, CO 70 Ireland, Box 25, Gerald R. Ford Presidential Library (hereafter Ford Library).
[2] Mount, G., *895 Days that Changed the World: The Presidency of Gerald Ford* (Montreal: Black Rose Books, 2006), p. 11.

the extent that by the mid-point of Nixon's first term in office Northern Ireland sat on the brink of a bloody sectarian civil war.

Throughout Nixon's time in office, there were repeated attempts on the part of political figures both internationally, from the United Kingdom and the Republic of Ireland, and domestically, in the form of members of Congress, to engage his administration in the conflict. Nixon considered that any official intervention would be a violation of UK sovereignty and was determined that this would not happen, and the US position was consistently that a solution could only come through the engagement of all domestic parties.[3] This did not stop figures such as Senator Edward Kennedy and Thomas P. 'Tip' O'Neill, Jr. from taking a keen interest in both the conflict and the US response to it. O'Neill began the Nixon Administration as a Representative and served as House Majority Whip and House Majority Leader before becoming the Speaker of the House in January 1977. Kennedy and O'Neill would lead Congressional efforts to engage the United States in the Northern Ireland conflict that endured far longer than either Nixon or Ford.

The Origins of the Northern Ireland Troubles

On Monday, 4 November 1968, Captain Terence O'Neill, the Prime Minister of Northern Ireland, travelled to London with his Home Affairs Minister William Craig and Minister of Commerce Brian Faulkner to meet with British Prime Minister Harold Wilson and Home Secretary James Callaghan. Wilson told the Northern Irish contingent that 'there was now great concern at Westminster over many aspects of the Northern Ireland scene' and that 'the United Kingdom did not need to get involved in a constitutional crisis in order to exert its will over Northern Ireland'. Wilson also highlighted that:

> The United Kingdom Government were responsible for overseas relationships and it was a matter of regret that when they entered into an international agreement on the observance of Human Rights a derogation had to be made in respect of the Special Powers Acts in Northern Ireland. This weakened the

---

[3]   James Cooper has argued that pressure from within Irish America on Nixon made some form of intervention necessary; see Cooper, *The Politics of Diplomacy*, p. 16.

United Kingdom's standing abroad and gave other countries an excuse to criticise.[4]

The following day, the US Presidential election was held. Ahead of the election, Richard Nixon, who defeated Hubert Humphrey to secure the Presidency, had spent some time travelling internationally to assert his foreign policy credentials. Included on his 1967 trip was a stop in London, where he met Harold Wilson as well as former Prime Ministers Harold Macmillan and Sir Alec Douglas-Home.[5] Like the majority of late twentieth-century Presidents, Nixon was of Irish stock; his Quaker ancestor Thomas Milhous left Ireland for the United States in the eighteenth century and had two great-great-great-great grandfathers from County Antrim, one of whom, James Moore, was from Ballymoney.[6] Nixon had, however, been unable to engage the Irish vote, with two-thirds of Irish Catholic voters choosing Humphrey.[7] Nixon had cited Northern Ireland during a 1957 speech in San Francisco as an example for other governments seeking to set up 'active and efficient bureaus and hospitable policies to promote and welcome foreign capital'.[8] A decade later, however, things had changed substantially.

The escalation of NICRA protests, most notably that on 5 October 1968, drew attention in the US media.[9] Northern Ireland Home Affairs Minister William Craig banned civil rights marches in the aftermath of 5 October, prompting further, larger-scale marches on the part

---

[4]   Meeting at 10 Downing Street, 4/11/1968, CAB/4/1413, PRONI.

[5]   President's Meetings with Foreign Statesmen, Foreign Affairs File, 1969–1974, Box 167, President's Personal File, Richard Nixon Presidential Library (hereafter Nixon Library).

[6]   Letter from Harry Hollingsworth of Inglewood California to Ronald Ziegler, Press Secretary White House, 22/9/1970 and Letter from Noble Melencamp, Staff Assistant to the President to Miss Josephine McGirr, Drumcondra, 6/10/1970, White House Central Files, Subject Files, Trips Box 45, Nixon Library.

[7]   Dolan, J.P., *The Irish Americans: A History* (New York: Bloomsbury Press, 2008), p. 293. The Irish Catholic vote was, at the time, resolutely Democratic, and 78 per cent of Irish voters had voted for Lyndon Johnson four years earlier.

[8]   *NYT*, 16/10/1957.

[9]   There was some coverage, notably NBC *Nightly News*, 15/8/1969 and Robert Korengald, 'The White Negroes', *Newsweek*, 2/12/1968. Other news reports often linked the civil rights struggles in Northern Ireland and the USA; see Ward, K., 'Ulster Terrorism: The US Network News Coverage of Northern Ireland, 1968–1979', in Alexander, Y. and O'Day, A. (eds), *Terrorism in Ireland* (London, 1984), p. 204; Dooley, B., *Black and Green: The Fight for Civil Rights in Northern Ireland and Black America* (London: Pluto Press), p. 76.

of the Derry Citizens Action Committee. One march on Saturday, 16 November, which saw an estimated 15,000 people take part in a sit-down demonstration in the Diamond area of Derry, was given extensive coverage in the *New York Times*, which emphasised the lack of major violence during the protest.[10]

By the end of the week, Captain O'Neill announced a package of reforms that sought to tackle disenfranchisement. It included a points system for public housing allocation, an ombudsman to investigate complaints against government departments, the abolishment of the Special Powers Act as soon as practicable, the establishment of a development commission to run Londonderry Corporation, and ending company votes. This last point was emphasised in the 1968 Electoral Law Act (Northern Ireland).[11] Inter-communal tension was still evident across Northern Ireland, however, exemplified in a counter-demonstration in Armagh on Saturday, 28 November, organised by Reverend Ian Paisley's Ulster Constitution Defence Committee.[12] Paisley, who would bookend his political career by sharing power with a Sinn Féin party that featured former IRA volunteers, was sentenced to three months in prison in January 1969 for organising this illegal counter-demonstration.[13] At the end of 1968, Captain O'Neill described the situation in Northern Ireland, leading with the assertion that 'Ulster stands at the cross roads'. He continued:

> In Londonderry and other places recently a minority of agitators determined to subvert lawful authority played a part in setting light to highly inflammatory material. But the tinder for that fire in the form of grievances real or imaginary had been piling up for years … it is our duty to … be firm in the maintenance of law and order and in resisting those elements which seek to profit from any disturbances … it is simple-minded to imagine that problems such as these can be solved by repression. I for one am not willing to expose our Police Force to indefinite insult and injury.[14]

[10] *NYT*, 17/11/1968.
[11] Electoral Law Act (Northern Ireland) 1968, available at https://cain.ulster.ac.uk/hmso/ela1968.htm.
[12] *IT*, 28/11/1968.
[13] *IT*, 28/1/1969.
[14] Television Broadcast by Captain Terence O'Neill, Prime Minister of Northern Ireland on B.B.C. (Northern Ireland) and Ulster Television, Monday, 9 December, at 6.0 p.m., PRONI, CAB/9/B/205/8.

O'Neill continued to highlight his 'genuine and far-reaching changes', which his 'Government as a whole is totally committed to'. He was, of course, 'totally committed' to them only after protests had emerged. Two days later, William Craig was sacked as Home Affairs Minister. One matter Craig and O'Neill disagreed on was the legality of Westminster intervention on devolved matters. This was, in the view of the United States Consulate General in Belfast, a move that was likely to yield an increase in public support for O'Neill's moderate reforms and, in turn, support for his five-point programme. A memorandum to the State Department on the issue also noted the presence of Communists in the Civil Rights movement who 'may disturb the balance or provoke Protestant extremists'.[15] There were indeed communists present within NICRA and the wider civil rights movement, although the extent to which the Protestant extremists required provocation was much less obvious.[16]

On Friday, 20 December, the People's Democracy (PD) announced that it would undertake a protest march from Belfast to Derry starting on New Year's Day 1969, demanding the immediate implementation of one man, one vote in local elections and the total repeal of the Special Powers Act. Despite pleas from Captain Herbert Long, the new Northern Ireland Minister of Home Affairs, to cancel the march, it went ahead.[17] Kevin Boyle, a PD committee member noted that:

> In planning this march, we had in mind a similar march between Selma and Montgomery in Alabama in March, 1965, led by Dr. Martin Luther King. There the march was banned and beaten back by the order of George Wallace, Alabama's racist Governor. Federal courts upheld the right to march, Federal marshals protected the marchers and the march produced the Voting Rights Bill, giving the vote to the Negroes in the Southern States.[18]

---

[15]   Airgram to Department of State from Amconsul Belfast, 3/2/1969, 'Northern Ireland Reforms—Londonderry Commission Names' and Airgram to Department of State from AmConsul Belfast, 11/12/1968, NARA, RG 59, General Records of the Department of State, Central Foreign Policy Files, 1967–1969, Political & Defense, POL 29 IRAQ to POL 15 IRE Box 2222.

[16]   The most authoritative account on loyalism in the early years of the conflict is Gareth Mulvenna's *Tartan Gangs and Paramilitaries: The Loyalist Backlash* (Liverpool: Liverpool University Press, 2016).

[17]   *IT*, 21/12/1968 and 28/12/1968.

[18]   *IT*, 31/12/1968.

The analogy, regrettably, went deeper than Boyle might have liked. On Saturday, 4 January, the march passed Burntollet Bridge, roughly seven miles from its destination. There they suffered a vicious ambush by loyalists led by Major Ronald Bunting, an ally of Ian Paisley, and a number of off-duty members of the Ulster Special Constabulary.[19] The following day, O'Neill's statement criticised the march, labelling it a 'foolhardy and irresponsible undertaking'.[20]

O'Neill still lacked total support within his own government, though, and the resignation of Brian Faulkner on 24 January over a lack of 'strong government' was evidence of this. One month after Faulkner's resignation, O'Neill called an election. This attempt to strengthen support for political reform was considered a political gamble, but it was a gamble that paid off, with the majority of Unionists returned in the election in support of O'Neill's reforms. The US Consulate had predicted this outcome, although the Irish government in Dublin was cynical as to his ability to retain power in the longer term.[21] Among the challenges to mainstream Unionism, the spectre of the Reverend Ian Paisley, branded an 'extremist' by the US Consulate in Belfast, loomed large.[22]

Amidst this uncertainty in Northern Ireland, emerging Irish-American organisations such as the American Congress for Irish Freedom sought to engage President Nixon on Northern Irish matters. Nixon's advisers recommended that he avoid the group, but suggested that a government official could meet with a group that had sent 'innumerable, often identical, and sometimes intemperate, letters to the White House, Congress, and the Department, calling upon the United States Government to become involved, indirectly or directly, in the "partition" issue or the Protestant–Catholic problems of Ulster'.[23] Nixon's major preoccupation at this time was the 'strengthening and

---

[19]   *IT*, 6/1/1969.

[20]   *Belfast Telegraph*, 6/1/1969.

[21]   *IT*, 26/2/1969.

[22]   Airgram to Department of State from Amconsul Belfast, 30/1/1969, 'Northern Ireland: "Extremists" Sentenced to Prison', NARA, RG 59, General Records of the Department of State, Central Foreign Policy Files, 1967–1969, Political & Defense, POL 17 IRE to POL IRE-US Box 2223.

[23]   Memorandum to Under Secretary from John M. Leddy, 20/2/1969, 'Meeting with Representatives of the American Congress for Irish Freedom', NARA, RG 59, General Records of the Department of State, Central Foreign Policy Files, 1967–1969, Political & Defense, POL 17 IRE to POL IRE-US Box 2223.

revitalizing' of the North Atlantic community and his European trip of February 1969 was geared at doing precisely this.[24] Prior to this trip, he met with newly appointed United Kingdom Ambassador to the United States, John Freeman, a former MP and editor of the *New Statesman* magazine who had previously called Nixon 'a man of no principle'.[25]

Nixon's deliberate lack of engagement on Northern Ireland was not reflective of the US government as a whole; whilst he avoided the issue as far as possible, members of Congress debated the idea of possible United Nations intervention in Northern Ireland in March 1969. It was an idea that was quickly shot down. In a letter to Thomas E. Morgan, the Chairman of the House Committee on Foreign Affairs, William Macomber, the Assistant Secretary for Congressional Relations, noted that anyone seeking to inscribe the issue of Northern Ireland, or indeed the partition of Ireland, on the agendas of the Security Council or General Assembly, would be 'vulnerable to the charge of interfering in the internal affairs of others, a matter specifically excluded by the UN Charter'. The United Nations had intervened in the Congo, New Guinea, and Yemen during the 1960s, situations that were scarcely analogous with Northern Ireland. Indeed, Article 2(7) of the United Nations Charter precluded the UN from intervening in 'matters which are essentially within the domestic jurisdiction of any state'.[26] Macomber continued to note that US attempts to engage the UN would be ill received in both Dublin and London: 'both governments would be likely to resent what they would regard as interference'.[27]

[24] *NYT*, 21/1/1969 and 7/2/1969; President's Meetings with Foreign Statesmen, United Kingdom, President's Personal File, Foreign Affairs File, Box 167, Nixon Library.
[25] *NYT*, 5/2/1969; *New Statesman*, 7/3/2013. He apologised to the President upon his assignment to Washington and, reportedly, the two would later become friends.
[26] Charter of the United Nations: Chapter I: Purposes and Principles, available at https://www.un.org/en/sections/un-charter/chapter-i/index.html.
[27] Letter from William B. Macomber, Assistant Secretary for Congressional Relations to Thomas E. Morgan, Chairman, Committee on Foreign Affairs, House of Representatives, 19/3/1969, NARA, RG 59, General Records of the Department of State, Central Foreign Policy Files, 1967–1969, Political & Defense, POL 29 IRAQ to POL 15 IRE Box 2222.

Summer, 1969: The Army Arrives

The resignation of Terence O'Neill as Northern Ireland Prime Minister on 28 April 1969 was the second blow to Ulster Unionism that month. Following the death of Unionist MP for Mid-Ulster George Forrest in December 1968, a by-election was held in April and the seat was won by independent Unity candidate, and prominent PD leader, Bernadette Devlin. At twenty-one, she became the 'baby of the house' and was the youngest woman ever to be elected as an MP.[28] After losing one of their Westminster seats, the Ulster Unionists were then forced to find O'Neill's successor. James Chichester-Clark, the Northern Ireland MP for South Londonderry, was narrowly elected to the Ulster Unionist Party leadership. One of his first acts in office was to announce an amnesty for all offences associated with demonstrations since 5 October 1968, an announcement which saw Ian Paisley released from prison. Two weeks after leaving office, O'Neill was interviewed by the *Belfast Telegraph* and his comments betrayed just how out of touch he actually was with the realities of Northern Ireland in 1969:

> It is frightfully hard to explain to Protestants that if you give Roman Catholics a good job and a good house, they will live like Protestants because they will see neighbours with cars and television sets; they will refuse to have eighteen children. But if a Roman Catholic is jobless, and lives in the most ghastly hovel, he will rear eighteen children on National Assistance. If you treat Roman Catholics with due consideration and kindness, they will live like Protestants in spite of the authoritative nature of their Church.[29]

That same month in Dublin, a new US Ambassador was appointed. As a recipient of the American Irish Historical Society Gold Medal in 1966, and the founder of the Ireland–US Council for Commerce and Industry, John Moore was well equipped for the post.[30] His counterpart, the Irish Ambassador to the United States, William Fay, was already working on

[28] She remained so until Mhairi Black was elected as Scottish National Party MP for Paisley and Renfrewshire South in May 2015 at the age of twenty years.
[29] *Belfast Telegraph*, 10/5/1969.
[30] Memorandum for the President From Henry Kissinger, Nixon Presidential Materials, National Security Council Files, President's Trip Files, Box 469, Nixon Library.

developing US–Irish relations at this time and invited President Nixon to become the Honorary Co-Chairman, with Irish President Eamon de Valera, of the American Irish Foundation.[31] Nixon's rejection, even to the offer of an honorary role in a relatively benign foundation, betrayed his reluctance to engage on the Irish situation. Nixon explained that the decision was 'in accordance with his policy of avoiding private affiliations while in office', but his reluctance was particularly helpful to the British government.[32] A letter from Presidential Assistant Bryce Harlow to Tip O'Neill, then a Congressman for Massachusetts's 8th district, clarified the administration's position a little further. Harlow emphasised that 'the U.S. Government has no effective basis to intervene in internal political controversies or civil disorders in other sovereign countries', continuing that:

> Northern Ireland is part of the United Kingdom. At the same time, in a manner unique within the United Kingdom, it has been given broad powers of self government with regard to local affairs. We continue to believe that any problems concerning Northern Ireland can best be resolved by the governments directly concerned, i.e., the Government of Northern Ireland and the British Government. The Government of the United States is outside the area of constructive influence as well as sovereign responsibility.[33]

Later, in a letter to Representative John Murphy, Henry Kissinger echoed these comments: 'The United Kingdom certainly would react to official United States intervention in those problems in the same way as we would react to foreign intervention in our efforts to resolve problems of civil rights and equality of opportunity in the United States'.[34] The

[31]   House of the Oireachtas, Oireachtas Business, Ceisteanna—Questions. Oral Answers—American–Irish Foundation, Tuesday, 16/7/1963, available at https://www.oireachtas.ie/en/debates/debate/dail/1963-07-16/.
[32]   Memorandum, Department of State, 12/9/1969, NARA, RG 59, General Records of the Department of State, Central Foreign Policy Files, 1967–1969, Political & Defense, POL 29 IRAQ to POL 15 IRE Box 2223.
[33]   Letter to Thomas P. O'Neill, Jr from Bryce Harlow, Assistant to the President, 7/7/1969, White House Central Files, Subject Files, Countries, CO160, United Kingdom, Nixon Library.
[34]   Letter from Henry Kissinger to John Murphy, House of Representatives, 29/9/1969, White House Central Files, Subject Files, Countries, CO160, United Kingdom, Nixon Library.

situation in Northern Ireland continued to deteriorate and mid-July 1969 saw two Catholics suffer fatal injuries at the hands of the Royal Ulster Constabulary. The first, sixty-seven-year-old Francis McCloskey, was injured when the RUC charged a crowd throwing stones at Dungiven Orange Hall. He died in hospital the following day.[35] He was considered by Mr Justice Scarman, during his report into the violence of the summer of 1969, to have been a bystander who had been unlucky to have suffered a fatal injury, but 'the indications in the evidence are against the inference of excessive use of force'.[36] Two days later, Samuel Devenney died after suffering injuries in a brutal attack from RUC officers in his home in William Street, a short distance from the historic walled city. The role of the police in these deaths raised serious questions about their ability to maintain control over Northern Irish security.

In a Cabinet Security Committee meeting at Stormont Castle on Tuesday, 15 July, the day after McCloskey's death, Chichester-Clark 'expressed his concern at the reporting of this death by the *Irish News* and thought that this could not do other than exacerbate the situation'.[37] In an attempt to seize control of the security situation, Chichester-Clark mobilised the Ulster Special Constabulary.[38] With the deaths of McCloskey and Devenney confirming for many in the nationalist community that the police were not only institutionally biased against them, but prepared to use lethal force to suppress their protests, the wisdom of mobilising the notoriously aggressive and overwhelmingly Protestant USC casts serious doubt upon Chichester-Clark's judgement. The Cameron and Hunt Reports of September and October 1969 rather proved the case that there were serious institutional issues in the police and, particularly the USC. The Hunt Report went so far as to recommend the disbandment of the B-Specials.[39]

---

[35]   The UVF killings of 1966 represent the first three attributed to the conflict. See McKittrick et al., *Lost Lives*, p. 32; also University of Ulster, 'Conflict Archive on the Internet', 'Violence: Significant Violent Incidents During the Conflict', available at https://cain.ulster.ac.uk/issues/violence/majinc.htm.

[36]   McKittrick et al., *Lost Lives*, p. 32.

[37]   Conclusions of a meeting of the Cabinet Security Committee held in Stormont Castle on Tuesday, 15th July 1969, at 2.30 p.m., PRONI, HA/32/3/1.

[38]   *IT*, 15/7/1969.

[39]   Disturbances in Northern Ireland, Report of the Commission Appointed by the Governor of Northern Ireland (Belfast: HMSO, 1969), Cmd (Series) (NI) 532. Copy at https://cain.ulster.ac.uk/hmso/cameron.htm; Report of the Advisory Committee on Police in Northern Ireland (Belfast: HMSO, 1969), Cmd (Series) (NI) 535. Copy at https://cain.ulster.ac.uk/hmso/hunt.htm.

Amidst all the tension in Northern Ireland, Nixon met with Prime Minister Harold Wilson at Mildenhall Air Force Base, taking the opportunity to discuss issues of mutual concern during a stop on his way to the Far East on 3 August 1969.[40] Nixon alluded to the situation in Northern Ireland during his comments at Mildenhall: 'the path to peace may seem very difficult, and preserving the peace is, of course, a task which we have found to be tremendously arduous and hazardous over these past few years, that the people of the world deep in their hearts want peace'.[41] The path to peace in Northern Ireland became even more difficult in August when serious violence decisively overwhelmed the RUC and the British Army were deployed in aid to the civil power. The British government was consistent in their position that 'Northern Ireland should not cease to be a part of the United Kingdom without the consent of the people of Northern Ireland'.[42] Further complicating the path to peace at this time, were the actions of Irish Minister for External Affairs, Dr Patrick Hillery.

A Teachta Dála (TD) for Clare, Hillery qualified as a medical doctor before embarking upon a political career after encouragement from Eamon de Valera, his Fianna Fáil constituency colleague.[43] Hillery was one of a number of Irish political figures who visited the United States over the summer of 1969 as the conflict in Northern Ireland began to develop, and would regularly find himself in the United States at times of serious crisis in Ireland. In August 1969, with the RUC beleaguered and the British Army on the streets of Northern Ireland, Hillery visited New York, taking the opportunity while there to announce his plans to return the following month to attend the opening of the United Nations General Assembly. There, he planned to address the situation in Northern Ireland, claiming that there was a possibility that the Secretary General, U Thant, would send a representative and an observer corps to Northern Ireland. Further, according to a State

[40] President's Meetings with Foreign Statesmen, United Kingdom, President's Personal File, Foreign Affairs File, Box 167, Nixon Library.

[41] Remarks on Arrival at Mildenhall Air Force Base, England, 3/8/1969, the American Presidency Project, available at https://www.presidency.ucsb.edu/documents/remarks-arrival-mildenhall-air-force-base-england.

[42] Northern Ireland, Text of a Communiqué and Declaration Issued after a Meeting at 10 Downing Street on 19 August 1969 (London: HMSO, 1969), available at https://cain.ulster.ac.uk/hmso/bni190869.htm.

[43] Teachta Dala, a member of Dáil Éireann.

Department telegram, 'he had left to U Thant and his staff to devise a mutually acceptable formula for UN intervention'.[44] The idea of UN intervention in Northern Ireland, which had earlier been raised in Congress in March 1969, would remain popular among Irish-American politicians.

Bernadette in the USA

A series of leading Northern Irish political figures visited the United States over the summer of 1969, but none more famously than Bernadette Devlin. The newly elected MP for Mid-Ulster arrived on 21 August 1969 for a tour organised by the National Association for Irish Justice in which she would attempt to raise $1 million for refugee families.[45] Devlin's exhausting schedule, which saw her hold meetings and attend events from 7 a.m. until 4 a.m., began minutes after her arrival in New York, speaking that evening in front of 600 Irish and Irish Americans who began arriving for her talk two hours early. She was clear on the social problems that existed in Northern Ireland: 'the Catholics are not fighting the Protestants because they're Protestants. Nor vice-versa. It's the poor against the government'. She continued:

> We need money. I've come for a million dollars. You don't need to be told about the British. You know them. They're the models of democracy to the world and the devils of slavery to the Irish. They beat us down last week, but they know we're rising. The 500 families who were burned out by the Ulster police need help. They asked me to come to America to find it. I told them I'd get a million dollars. I'm starting tonight. Are you going to help me?[46]

She reportedly raised $1,000 that evening. The following day she visited Mayor Lindsay and was presented with a key to the city of New York, going on to picket the New York offices of the British Overseas Airways Corporation, before moving on to Philadelphia where a crowd

---

[44] Department of State telegram, 23/8/1969, RG 59, General Records of the Department of State, Central Foreign Policy Files, 1967–1969, Political & Defense, POL 29 IRAQ to POL 15 IRE, Box 2222, NARA.

[45] *NYT*, 22/8/1969, *Harper's Magazine*, January 1970.

[46] *Washington Post*, 23/8/1969.

of 350 people met her at Penn Station.[47] On 26 August, she visited the United Nations and met with Secretary General Thant, reportedly impressing the Burmese diplomat.[48] The Irish nationalist case being pressed upon diplomats at the very highest level drew concern among Ulster Unionists, who immediately planned a trip to 'counter the Catholic propaganda campaign'.[49] W. Stratton Mills, Unionist MP for Belfast North, travelled to the United States with Robin Bailie, the Northern Irish MP for Newtonabbey.[50] Their agenda was obvious from their comments upon arrival when Mills labelled Devlin as 'Castro in a miniskirt'. Devlin commented acerbically, 'they've probably been sitting around for six weeks trying to think up a cute phrase about me, and that must be it'.[51]

Devlin's trip also drew concern from US representatives in the UK, with Wayne Fisher, a First Secretary in the London Embassy, writing to Bryce Harlow to describe her as a 'self-styled Joan of Arc', encouraging Harlow that Devlin's 'remarks should be taken with a grain of salt, Bryce. There are real grievances, but she has some fuzzy approaches to them'.[52] Away from these attempts to reassure Ulster Unionists, and possibly British diplomats, that Devlin should not be taken seriously, her trip began to run into serious issues whilst she was in Los Angeles on 27 August. There, Devlin overheard a telephone call taken by Brian Heron of the National Association for Irish Justice in which a friend of Heron's complained that the money raised was to be used for relief purposes. The following day at San Francisco airport, Devlin said, 'I specifically do not want money for guns. If I were to discover that one dollar was spent on violence, I would immediately disassociate myself from the entire collection and insist that all money collected under false pretences be returned'.[53] Then, in Chicago a few days later, she criticised Mayor Richard Daley's idea of sending aid to the Irish Red Cross.[54] In a stab at Daley, Devlin commented, 'I cannot understand the mental conflict

[47]   *NYT*, 23/8/1969 and 24/8/1969; *Washington Post*, 26/8/1969.
[48]   *NYT*, 27/8/1969.
[49]   *Washington Post*, 27/8/1969.
[50]   *NYT*, 30/8/1969.
[51]   *Washington Post*, 31/8/1969.
[52]   Letter from Wayne Fisher, Consul General, American Embassy London, to Bryce Harlow, 29/8/1969, White House Central Files, Subject Files, Countries, CO160, United Kingdom, Nixon Library.
[53]   *Harper's Magazine*, January 1970.
[54]   *Washington Post*, 31/8/1969.

of some of our Irish Americans who will fight forever for the struggle for justice in Ireland, and yet who play the role of oppressor and will not stand shoulder to shoulder with their fellow black Americans'.[55]

Her visit then ended abruptly on 2 September, when she left a party in West Orange, New Jersey and returned to Northern Ireland despite having scheduled meetings in Washington the following day. Among those on her schedule was House Speaker John McCormack. The Federal Bureau of Investigation, who had been monitoring her trip, suggested that she cut the visit short once she received confirmation that the NAIJ was involved in fundraising for the IRA.[56] The *New York Times* estimated that her trip had raised $200,000 but Devlin commented upon her return that she wasn't sure how much was raised, with money placed in a variety of accounts across the United States to be sent to a single bank in New York and then transferred to Belfast.[57] A televised debate, entitled 'The Battle of Belfast', between Devlin and Mills, was shown at 10 p.m. the day after she left.[58]

Ian Paisley, uncharacteristically late to take an opportunity to engage a wide audience with his bombastic rhetoric, followed Mills and Bailie to the United States. Upon his arrival in Philadelphia, it was clear that the Devlin trip had raised awareness of some of the major political issues in Northern Ireland and Paisley had to deflect questions about gerrymandering and civil rights from reporters.[59] He described Devlin as 'the nearest thing to a Communist in the Roman Catholic Church that I can see'.[60] At what point Devlin became a representative of the Catholic Church remains unclear. Paisley moved on to Los Angeles and accused Devlin of seeking the 'destruction of the state'.[61] Later, Paisley would claim that he had raised $20,000. This figure was entirely feasible, but would have represented significantly less than that raised by Devlin.[62]

---

[55]   *Harper's Magazine*, January 1970.
[56]   FBI memo, 11/9/1969, The Papers of Frank Durkan, Box 8, Archives of Irish America (hereafter AIA), Tamiment Library, New York University. Mary Holland in the *Observer* also reported this; see *Observer*, 6/9/1969.
[57]   *NYT*, 3/9/1969 and 4/9/1969.
[58]   *Washington Post*, 3/9/1969. Mills and Bailie also debated with Paul O'Dwyer on their trip; *NYT*, 6/9/1969.
[59]   *NYT*, 7/9/1969.
[60]   *Washington Post*, 7/9/1969.
[61]   *Washington Post*, 11/9/1969.
[62]   *Washington Post*, 14/9/1969.

As peace walls were constructed in Belfast, and prospects of a quick end to hostilities began to fade, political leaders in both Belfast and Dublin arranged their own visits to the United States.[63] Prime Minister James Chichester-Clark's planned September visit was postponed but Northern Ireland Minister of Commerce Roy Bradford visited in his place for a trip that was 'generally regarded as an image-building tour on behalf of Northern Ireland'.[64] The fact that Chichester-Clark had been forced to postpone his own trip told its own story as to the image of Northern Ireland at the time. Bradford returned to the United States in January 1970, addressing several groups of businessmen on the merits of investment in the Northern Irish economy.[65] Meanwhile, Taoiseach Jack Lynch declared his intention to travel to the United States, and during a speech entitled 'The Situation in the Six Counties of North-East Ireland … The Basis of Our Thinking and Policy', delivered to an audience in Tralee, he emphasised that:

> it was and has been the Government's policy to seek the re-unification of the country by peaceful means … It will remain our most earnest aim and hope to win the consent of the majority of the people in the Six Counties to means by which North and South can come together in a re-united and sovereign Ireland earning international respect both for the fairness and efficiency with which it is administered and for its contribution to world peace and progress.[66]

Despite Lynch endorsing the 'principle of consent', US figures were reluctant to commit to a visit from the Taoiseach.[67] Lynch spoke privately

[63] Conclusions of a meeting of the Joint Security Committee held on Tuesday, 9th September 1969, at Stormont Castle, HA/32/3/2, PRONI.

[64] *IT*, 13/8/1969.

[65] Speech by the Rt. Hon. Roy Bradford, M.P., Minister for Comerce for Northern Ireland at a Wall Street Luncheon for Bankers, etc., in New York on Monday, January 12, 1970, at 12.30 p.m., in RG 59, General Records of the Department of State, Bureau of European Affairs, Records Relating to Ireland, 1962–1975, Box 3, NARA.

[66] Jack Lynch, *The Situation in the Six Counties of North-East Ireland … the Basis of Our Thinking and Policy*, 20/9/1969, available at https://cain.ulster.ac.uk/othelem/docs/lynch/lynch69.htm.

[67] Memorandum for Charles A. Fagan III, Deputy Assistant Secretary for Economic Development from Henry Kissinger, 29/11/1969, Nixon Presidential Materials, National Security Council Files, Country Files, Europe, Box 694, Nixon Library.

about the idea of a trip with Ambassador John Moore, who in turn consulted Kissinger aide Helmut Sonnenfeldt. Sonnenfeldt suggested that the visit should be postponed: 'I see no particular foreign policy reason favoring a visit by the Prime Minister. If there were other reasons supporting a visit, I think it would be best to delay it at least until the problems in Belfast were a bit closer to resolution than they now appear'.[68]

This hypothetical resolution seemed ever distant as 1969 wore on. The first RUC officer was killed by loyalists in October, and friction within the Irish republican movement led to a split in the IRA in late 1969, followed by a split in Sinn Féin on 11 January 1970 at the party's Ard Fheis. The split was over a number of issues, notably the failure of the IRA to defend the Catholic communities during the summer of 1969, but politically there were concerns over the growing socialist influence over leaders of the movement.[69] Ambassador Moore was particularly wary that 'Communist activity in Ireland, long of negligible proportions, is now increasing in significance' and noted that 'communists have been making determined efforts to infiltrate the Irish Republican Movement and expand their front activities'.[70]

With loyalist paramilitaries active throughout the winter of 1969–1970, pressure grew on the IRA to protect the nationalist communities of Northern Ireland. The Irish government developed contingency plans to intervene in Northern Ireland, plans that have become popularly known as 'Exercise Armageddon'.[71] Amidst this tension, it was alleged that two Irish ministers, Charles Haughey and Neil Blaney, had become involved in illegal arms importation to Irish republicans in Northern Ireland. The two were sacked from office on 6 May 1970 and on the twenty-eighth of that month stood trial. Both were found not guilty. The US Consulate in Belfast was somewhat dismissive of the crisis, reporting that 'smuggling of guns and other things, such as pigs, butter, and eels, is not novel and therefore is viewed

[68]   Memorandum for Henry Kissinger from Sonnenfeldt, 15/11/1969, Nixon Presidential Materials, National Security Council Files, Country Files, Europe, Box 694, Nixon Library.
[69]   Sanders, A., *Inside the IRA: Dissident Republicans and the War for Legitimacy* (Edinburgh: Edinburgh University Press, 2011), p. 45.
[70]   Letter from Ambassador Moore to Elliot L. Richardson, Under Secretary of State, 26/2/1970 and Telegram from Amembassy Dublin to Secretary of State, 3/2/1970, RG59, General Records of the Department of State, Subject Numerical Files, 1970–1973, Political & Defense, POL12 IRAQ-POL IRE, Box 2383, NARA.
[71]   See *IT*, 31/8/2009.

with anxiety but not wild alarm', also noting that 'militant socialist' Bernadette Devlin 'condemned Blaney, Haughey etc. as irresponsible trouble-makers who had no regard for workers of the north and south'. They added, 'Miss Devlin further criticized Lynch for playing politics only to perpetuate "Green Toryism" in the Republic and to extend his Fianna Fáil administration to the north'.[72]

The situation escalated further over the summer of 1970, with Devlin, newly re-elected in the June 1970 UK general election, imprisoned for incitement to riot. On 3 July, the British Army imposed a curfew on the Lower Falls area of west Belfast. The Falls Curfew deeply exacerbated existing tensions and four civilians were killed in the violence that followed. On Monday, 6 July, the day after the curfew was lifted, Dr Patrick Hillery decided to pay a visit to Belfast to gather information on the situation.[73]

Nixon Visits

Nixon's September 1970 visit to Europe was designed to reassert US influence in the Mediterranean, where Soviet naval capabilities had been enlarged, as well as to reassert his diplomatic skills ahead of the mid-term elections of November 1970.[74] These diplomatic skills had not previously extended as far as the emerging conflict in Northern Ireland, and Nixon neglected to raise the issue during his meeting with British Prime Minister Edward Heath on 3 October at Chequers. Heath's Principal Private Secretary Robert Armstrong, present at the meeting, recalled the awkwardness of the meeting between the two.[75] Henry Kissinger was present on the trip, and his advance notes for the trip alluded to the uncomfortable relationship that Armstrong perceived:

> Despite ... the fact that Britain, as a power factor, will continue to decline, our relations with the UK will undoubtedly retain a special quality of intimacy and informality; our peoples

---

[72] Airgram to Department of State from Amconsul Belfast, 15/5/1970, 'Northern Ireland Reaction to Dublin Political Crisis', RG59, General Records of the Department of State, Subject Numerical Files, 1970–1973, Political & Defense, POL12 IRAQ-POL IRE, Box 2382, NARA.

[73] *NYT*, 27/6/1970 and 9/7/1970.

[74] *NYT*, 4/10/1970.

[75] Lord Armstrong, interview with author, 9/10/2013.

will continue to have extensive contacts and connections and our communications at all levels will be frequent, diverse and essentially frank. Your good personal relationship with Heath will undoubtedly continue to prove an asset.[76]

In Ireland, however, he would be forced to utilise a more diplomatic approach. This was the first trip that a US President had made to Ireland since the onset of the conflict in the north and whatever course Nixon adopted would establish US policy towards the issue. Kissinger was acutely aware of this:

> We have made clear repeatedly that we consider Northern Ireland under British sovereignty, and so a domestic concern of the UK. Stressing your desire to have good relations with our friends, the UK and Ireland, you should express the hope that the conciliatory Irish policy together with the efforts of the British and Northern Ireland governments will continue to help reduce tensions.[77]

Kissinger added that Lynch's 'moderate and conciliatory policy toward the disturbances in the north, although elements within the governing party (and nationalist extremists) contend that more militancy is required'. He encouraged Nixon to 'delicately demonstrate tacit support for Prime Minister Lynch's moderate policy toward Northern Ireland'.[78] Kissinger's notes make it very clear that the United States viewed Ireland as subordinate to the UK when it came to Northern Ireland; Northern Ireland was, after all, legally a part of the United Kingdom. This concerned John Moore, who cautioned, 'we should avoid giving the impression to the Irish that our relationship with the UK overrides our policy considerations affecting Ireland'.[79]

---

[76] Memorandum for the President from Henry Kissinger, 'Your Visit to England, Saturday, October 3, 1970', Nixon Presidential Materials, National Security Council Files, President's Trip Files, Box 470, Nixon Library.

[77] Memorandum for the President from Henry Kissinger, Nixon Presidential Materials, National Security Council Files, President's Trip Files, Box 469, Nixon Library.

[78] Memorandum for the President from Henry Kissinger, Nixon Presidential Materials, National Security Council Files, President's Trip Files, Box 469, Nixon Library.

[79] Airgram from Amembassy Dublin to Department of State, 17/9/1970, RG59, General Records of the Department of State, Subject Numerical Files, 1970–1973, Political & Defense, POL32 IRE-POL7 ISR, Box 2384, NARA.

Moore was among the welcoming party for Nixon at Shannon airport, along with Lynch and Dr Patrick Hillery. Nixon stayed in Dromoland Castle in County Clare before travelling to Timahoe, the Quaker burial site where his ancestors lay, where he met with Ambassador Moore and representatives of the Quaker Community of Ireland. The party then drove to Dublin and visited the Ambassador's residence in Phoenix Park.[80] The group met President Eamon de Valera before their departure to Dublin Airport. Pointedly, Nixon, much like Kennedy seven years previously, avoided travelling to Northern Ireland and also avoided any mention of his northern ties in any of his public statements. Instead, his arrival statement established something of a pattern for future Presidential visits and noted both personal ancestral ties and national friendships. Nixon opened by joking that 'I would have been honored to be the first U.S. President to visit Ireland in office, but as you know there was a slight hitch in 1960. I am glad that I can be the second'. He continued:

> As is true for millions of American families, there are close and abiding Nixon family connections with Ireland. My paternal fourth great grandfather, James Nixon, emigrated to Delaware from Ireland around 1740, while my maternal fourth great grandparents, the Milhouses, came to New Jersey from County Kildare in 1729 … I hope that my visit will underscore the great warmth, closeness, and the non-partisanship of American-Irish ties, rooted in our Irish ancestry, in our admiration for Irish traditions, and our dedication in common to work for a democratic and peaceful world.[81]

In a toast at lunch on 5 October, Nixon commented on the contributions of Irish Americans to American society and praised Ireland's commitments to the United Nations, particularly, echoing Kennedy, their role in peace-keeping operations in the Congo.[82]

Lynch paid a reciprocal visit to the United States in early 1971, following an invitation from the Friendly Sons of St Patrick in Philadelphia to attend the St Patrick's Day celebrations in the city

---

[80]   The Nixons' pet Irish setter dog was called King Timahoe.

[81]   Ireland Arrival Statement, Nixon Presidential Materials, National Security Council Files, President's Trip Files, Box 469, Nixon Library.

[82]   Toast at lunch, October 5, Nixon Presidential Materials, National Security Council Files, President's Trip Files, Box 469, Nixon Library.

in 1971. Also planning a visit at this time was J.P. Liddy, the Mayor of Limerick, who would attend the Limerickman's Association in Chicago. Liddy was one of several relatively minor Irish political figures to seek an audience with the President on the occasion of their visit to the United States. Ambassador John Moore suggested that Nixon might wish to consider receiving Liddy to help warm relations with south-west Ireland in light of the ongoing landing rights issue.[83] As General Haig decisively pointed out, however: 'From a foreign relations standpoint, there is no reason for the President to receive the Mayor. Indeed, for him to do so (perhaps for domestic reasons) might very well cause some embarrassment to other foreign leaders, including some Foreign Ministers, whom the President has recently declined to receive'.[84]

James Chichester-Clark also planned an early 1971 trip to the United States, where he would visit Washington, New York, and Chicago, speaking at a National Press Club lunch in the capital and giving media interviews.[85] As had been the case in September 1969, events in Northern Ireland precluded the trip and Chichester-Clark instead travelled to London to meet British Home Secretary Reginald Maudling about the security situation in Northern Ireland.[86] Irish-American groups, led by James Heaney of the ACIF, threatened to picket the White House to protest against Chichester-Clark's visit, although he was informed that there had, in fact, never been any plans for such a visit.[87] There had been some embarrassment over the visit of Captain O'Neill to President Johnson in 1964 and now there was concern that being seen to receive the Unionist leader of Northern Ireland would be to establish US policy on Irish partition. In the way that the Nixon administration handled the proposed visits by Chichester-Clark and J.P. Liddy, they betrayed

[83]   Letter from J.P. Liddy, Mayor of Limerick to Nixon, 25/2/1971, White House Central Files, Subject Files, Countries, Ireland, Nixon Library. See Sanders, 'Landing Rights'.
[84]   Memorandum for Henry Cashen from General Haig, 28/12/1970, White House Central Files, Subject Files, Countries, Ireland, Nixon Library.
[85]   *IT*, 13/1/1971.
[86]   *IT*, 18/1/1971.
[87]   Letter from James Heaney, President American Congress for Irish Freedom to Nixon, 5/2/1971, White House Central Files, Subject Files, Countries, CO160, United Kingdom, Nixon Library; Letter from Helmut Sonnenfeld to Heaney, 24/2/1971, White House Central Files, Subject Files, Countries, CO160, United Kingdom, Nixon Library.

their reluctance to engage on any matters Northern Irish, while the perception was that southern politics remained relatively benign.

As implicit in the urgency of the meeting between Chichester-Clark and Maudling, the security situation in Northern Ireland had deteriorated further. On Saturday, 6 February, Robert Curtis became the first soldier killed, shot by an IRA sniper in north Belfast. One month later, three young soldiers were found dead at the side of a road in north-west Belfast, apparently lured from a city centre bar into an IRA ambush with the promise of a party. Almost immediately, demands for the reintroduction of internment without trial began.[88] This was the context in which Lynch and Nixon met, with the President again praising the Taoiseach's 'conciliatory policy' towards Northern Ireland and the 'continuing dialogue between Ireland and the United Kingdom'.[89] Nevertheless, domestic pressure on Nixon to intervene in Northern Ireland persisted, with House Resolutions calling for either formal intervention or to seek the inscription of the issue on the agenda of the UN Security Council and General Assembly. Similar pressure came from Ireland, in the form of requests from Patrick Hillery. The State Department continued to recommend that no action be taken in either case.[90]

One of those figures putting pressure on Nixon from within Congress was Representative Mario Biaggi, a Democrat from New York's 24th District. Biaggi had served as a New York Police officer, claiming to have been the recipient of twenty-six medals during his tenure.[91] Over the course of his political career, which ended abruptly after he was convicted of corruption in 1987, Biaggi was a constant thorn in the side of the British government thanks to the prominent and often radical positions he adopted on Northern Irish issues. Biaggi, who represented a largely Italian area of New York, claimed that it was hearing stories of the situation in Ireland from an Irish colleague named

[88]   Sanders, A. and Wood, I.S., *Times of Troubles: Britain's War in Northern Ireland* (Edinburgh: Edinburgh University Press, 2012), pp. 45–50.
[89]   William Rogers Memorandum for the President, 12/3/1971, 'The Lynch Visit: Perspectives', RG59, General Records of the Department of State, Subject Numerical Files, 1970–1973, Political & Defense, POL7 IRE-POL23 IRE, Box 2383, NARA.
[90]   Draft Letter, White House Central Files, Subject Files, Countries, Ireland, Nixon Library.
[91]   See 'Beyond the Line of Duty: Lieutenant Mario Biaggi', available at www.beyondthelineofduty.com/HeroBiaggi.html.

Pat McMahon that had prompted his interest in the Irish situation, rather than any constituent pressure.[92] Among Biaggi's early endeavours was an unsuccessful attempt to organise an international investment conference for Northern Ireland.[93]

Internment without Trial and the US Response

Pressure on James Chichester-Clark, who found himself both unable to solve the political unrest in Northern Ireland and unable to elicit a satisfactory security response from London, prompted his resignation on Saturday, 20 March. The resignation emphasised the problems facing Northern Irish politicians at the time, with control of the security operation resting in London, but political accountability firmly in the laps of those in Belfast. He was replaced, three days later, by Brian Faulkner. The rising violence also put pressure on the Irish Government to crack down on the IRA, though the Dublin Embassy considered such a move to be unlikely.[94] As events escalated towards the introduction of internment without trial in early August, however, an Irish response became necessary.

Tension continued to build and the deaths of two Catholic civilians, both shot by the army during rioting in Derry on 8 July, prompted

[92]   Holland, *The American Connection*, pp. 118–119. He had also spoken on a *Panorama* television programme in early 1979 about his time in the NYPD; see *Panorama*, 12/2/1979, transcript, in Ireland and US Policy on Northern Ireland, TAOIS/2009/135/745, NAI.

[93]   Letter from Mario Biaggi to Martin Hillenbrand, 31/3/1971, RG59, General Records of the Department of State, Subject Numerical Files, 1970–1973, Political & Defense, POL7 IRE-POL23 IRE, Box 2383, NARA; Telegram from Amembassy Dublin to Secretary of State, 13/4/1971, 'Congressman Biaggi letter', RG59, General Records of the Department of State Subject, Numerical Files, 1970–1973, Political & Defense, POL7 IRE-POL23 IRE, Box 2383, NARA. Also Letter from Jeffrey Ling, British Embassy Washington, DC to Robert DuBose, State Department, 8/11/1972, 'Financial Assistance to Industry in Northern Ireland', RG59, General Records of the Department of State, Bureau of European Affairs, Office of Northern European Affairs, Records Relating to Ireland, 1963–1975, AGR-Gen-1971 to AV-15 Charters 7.D, Box 1, NARA.

[94]   Telegram from Amembassy Dublin to Secretary of State, 21/7/1971, 'Lynch Government likely to fail to crack down on IRA', RG59, General Records of the Department of State, Subject Numerical Files, 1970–1973, Political & Defense, POL7 IRE-POL23 IRE, Box 2383, NARA.

the withdrawal of the SDLP from Stormont after the government failed to announce an inquiry into the shootings. Talks at Stormont were, however, still focused on security and Faulkner reported in his memoirs that 'the message was beginning to come through that there was only one major unused weapon in the government's anti-terrorist arsenal—internment'.[95] This would prove to be a disastrous decision. Even the General Officer Commanding of the British Army in Northern Ireland, Sir Harry Tuzo, had recommended against using internment without trial.[96] On the morning of 9 August 1971, Faulkner announced to the media that 'a number of men have been arrested by the security forces at various places in Northern Ireland this morning. I will be making internment orders in respect of any of these men who constitute a serious and continuing threat to public order and safety'. All police leave was cancelled as a result of the move.[97] The aggression of the internment policy was matched by the conduct of those enforcing it.[98] As a result, internment has remained arguably the decisive break between the nationalist community and the British state, particularly its security forces. Former IRA volunteer Richard O'Rawe recalled:

> The campaign was really starting to kick off in 1971, prior to internment coming in. There was the bombing campaign, particularly in the town, [which] was gathering pace and the ambush campaign was also starting to increase but it was really internment that was the catalyst for a huge upsurge in activity and it was internment that gave the IRA a sort of political cover. Prior to internment there was an IRA campaign going on, but I'm not so sure it had the widespread support that it needed to endure for any sustained period but internment gave it that. Internment was so obnoxious to the psyche of nationalists that they sort of rallied against the state—not necessarily into the arms of the IRA, more of a broad republican support base.[99]

[95]   Faulkner, B., *Memoirs of a Statesman* (London: Weidenfeld & Nicolson, 1978), pp. 115–116.
[96]   *Irish News*, 13/3/1971.
[97]   *Belfast Telegraph*, 9/8/1971.
[98]   McCleery, M., *Operation Demetrius and its Aftermath: A New History of the Use of Internment without Trial in Northern Ireland 1971–1975* (Manchester: Manchester University Press, 2015).
[99]   Richard O'Rawe, interview with author, 15/2/2010.

Later, the Compton Inquiry issued a critical report in response to allegations against the security forces in November 1971, although it stopped short of describing the highly controversial methods used, like hooding and sleep-deprivation, as either brutality or torture.[100] Some of the worst cases ultimately went to the European Court of Human Rights. Significantly, internment without trial had serious implications within the United States as well.

The State Department considered that internment could mark a turning point for Northern Ireland, and while they were quite correct in this assessment, it was not the positive turning point that they had envisioned. Merely three weeks after the introduction of the policy, they noted that violence had increased and cooperation between London and Dublin had been undermined. Still, the view was that if IRA activity was curtailed it would present Prime Minister Edward Heath with an opportunity to implement longer-range policies, with the significant caveat of 'if, as now appears more likely, violence cannot be contained in this way for very long, a new policy will be required for dealing with the Ulster problem'.[101]

Perhaps part of the State Department's cynicism as to the value of internment stemmed from a May 1971 report produced by the US Embassy in Dublin which considered the IRA to be of limited threat. This report stated that 'The IRA's career has been marked by internal disputes, bad luck, missed opportunities, poor judgment, worse planning, ill-chosen tactics, blunders, and bitter failure'. It considered its recruits to be 'dedicated would-be patriots and martyrs whose IRA activities seem to combine a tradition of revolution and force with the ideal of unselfish and puritanical service to Ireland' and that these recruits tended to come from 'unemployed or under-employed rural, rather poorly-educated but Irish-speaking, idealistic youths from homes with a marked religious and nationalist atmosphere'.[102]

[100] Report of the Enquiry into Allegations against the Security Forces of Physical Brutality in Northern Ireland Arising out of Events on the 9th August, 1971 (London: HMSO, 1971).

[101] Intelligence Note, 27/8/1971, 'UK: What Next for Northern Ireland?', RG59, General Records of the Department of State, Subject Numerical Files, 1970–1973, Political & Defense, POL7 IRE-POL23 IRE, Box 2383, NARA.

[102] Telegram from Amembassy Dublin to Secretary of State, 18/5/1971, 'The IRA: An Assessment', RG59, General Records of the Department of State, Subject Numerical Files, 1970–1973, Political & Defense, POL7 IRE-POL23, IRE, Box 2383, NARA.

The IRA was, in fact, quickly developing as an armed movement in Ireland, a fact that should have been of concern to the US government. Across the United States, a network of highly organised and effective support organisations began to develop, most notably the Irish Northern Aid Committee, also known as Noraid. Irish Civil War veteran Michael Flannery, who had been living in the United States since 1927, had returned to Ireland in December 1969 and met with the leadership of the nascent Provisional IRA, agreeing to establish a support network in the United States.[103] In September 1971, they sponsored a visit by IRA volunteer Joe Cahill. Cahill flew to the United States, only to find that the four-year visa he had been issued the previous year had been abruptly cancelled as he was mid-flight, following an urgent protest by the British government to the State Department.[104] Cahill was detained upon arrived and Noraid quickly dispatched lawyer Frank Durkan, of New York firm O'Dwyer and Bernstein, to the US Immigration Service's Lower Manhattan detention centre where Cahill was held. Durkan, a native of County Mayo who had lived in the United States since 1947, stated that Cahill 'categorically denied statements attributed to him that he was coming out here to get money to buy guns to shoot British soldiers', with Cahill supporters claiming his visit was to conduct a lecture tour.[105] Cahill had, however, openly stated that the purpose of his visit was 'to raise money, guns and ammunition to fight the British Army in Northern Ireland'.[106]

Cahill's detention predictably generated publicity and reaction from supporters in the United States. The State Department was wary of the situation escalating to the point where other prominent Irish republican figures decided to visit the United States to raise the profile of their cause. They issued a telegram that stated: 'we want posts to do everything possible to determine whether other prominent IRA leaders or supporters have received visas, and want notification by immediate telegram if known IRA members or supporters make application'.[107]

[103] Wilson, *Irish America*, pp. 42–43.
[104] *The Times*, 2/9/1971; Wilson, *Irish America*, pp. 53–54. *IT*, 7/9/1971 also reported that the British had supplied information about Cahill's 1942 conviction for murder.
[105] *IT*, 4/9/1971.
[106] *IT*, 2/9/1971.
[107] Telegram from Department of State, 3/9/1971, 'Visit to U.S. by IRA leaders and supporters', RG59, General Records of the Department of State, Subject Numerical Files, 1970–1973, Political & Defense, POL7 IRE-POL23 IRE, Box 2383, NARA; *Independent*, 10/5/1999 on Kennedy.

Threats were made on the American Embassy in Dublin, too, with one phone call stating, 'this is the Irish Republican Army and if Joe Cahill isn't allowed into the United States we declare total war on the American government and on all its buildings and property'.[108]

At a hearing in New York on 7 September, Cahill made no secret of his contempt for the British security forces, claiming that killing British soldiers was necessary for the defence of the Irish people. Crucial to the case for deportation, however, was Cahill's failure to declare his conviction for the 1942 murder of a police officer on his 1970 visa application. He was duly sent back to Ireland the following day and banned from the United States. Upon arrival in Dublin he was again detained, under the Offences Against the State Act, and held for twelve hours without charge. Despite his ban, Noraid retained Cahill as the registered recipient of their remittances until January 1972.[109]

Frustration began to grow within the US administration at the lack of progress on the situation in Northern Ireland. A late September meeting between Heath, Faulkner, and Lynch was considered by Henry Kissinger to have yielded 'no appreciable results' on Northern Ireland.[110] This agitation was obvious, too, in Congress, and in October 1971 a resolution was co-sponsored by Senator Edward Kennedy and Connecticut Senator Abraham Ribicoff in the Senate, and Representative Hugh Carey of New York in the House, which called for the withdrawal of British troops from Northern Ireland. Kennedy commented that 'Ulster is becoming Britain's Vietnam', a statement that provoked outrage from the United Kingdom and one that he later came to regret, although he would reprise it.[111]

Kennedy had returned to Ireland in early 1970 following an invitation from the Trinity College Historical Society to visit Dublin

---

[108] Telegram from Amembassy Dublin to Secretary of State, 4/9/1971, RG59, General Records of the Department of State, Subject Numerical Files, 1970–1973, Political & Defense, POL7 IRE-POL23 IRE, Box 2383, NARA. Cathal Goulding was also denied entry to the USA in September 1972; see Telegram from Department of State, 16/9/1972.

[109] Summary of Noraid Returns to the US Department of Justice, in Ireland and US Policy on Northern Ireland, TAOIS/2009/135/745, NAI.

[110] Memorandum for the President from Henry Kissinger, 29/9/1971, 'Your meeting with Sir Alec Douglas-Home, 30/9/1971', Nixon Presidential Materials, National Security Council Files, Country Files, Europe, Box 729, Nixon Library.

[111] *Time*, 1/11/1971, *Boston Globe*, 28/8/2009. On comparing Bloody Sunday to My Lai, see Wilson, *Irish America*, p. 64.

and deliver an address during its bicentennial celebrations.[112] He arrived in Dublin on 2 March and visited what had become Kennedy Memorial Park in County Wexford before a lunch at Iveagh House the following day.[113] His speech at Trinity met with protest from left-wing student groups. In a letter to the *Irish Times* after the visit, the American Congress for Irish Freedom's James Heaney explained that 'Senator Kennedy was instrumental in enacting the 1965 Immigration Act which now keeps the Irish out of the United States … Kennedy is a great anglophile'.[114] Kennedy neglected to comment on the political situation in Ireland, which undoubtedly helped Taoiseach Jack Lynch given the sensitive nature of the issue at the time. On US soil, however, he felt more at ease with strong sentiments—rhetoric that was swiftly and strongly criticised by those in the United Kingdom—although Kennedy aide Carey Parker argued that a more extreme resolution would probably have been tabled without Kennedy's input.[115]

Northern Irish Prime Minister Brian Faulkner stated that Kennedy had 'shown himself willing to swallow hook, line and sinker the hoary old propaganda that I.R.A. atrocities are carried out as part of a freedom fight on behalf of the Northern Irish people'. Others alluded to Chappaquiddick, with an unnamed Conservative MP claiming that Kennedy was not in a position to 'express moral judgements on anything'.[116] British Prime Minister Edward Heath was reported to have described the statement as 'an ignorant outburst'.[117] Various commentators have since highlighted the flaw of the Vietnam analogy, even though Kennedy's aim was ostensibly to provide a frame of reference for the American public.[118] Kennedy himself wrote to *The Times* of London and suggested that the reaction to his statement might be a product of Britain's 'guilty conscience over Ulster'.[119] Perhaps more damaging was Kennedy's assertion that

---

[112]   *IT*, 10/1/1970.

[113]   *IT*, 2/3/1970.

[114]   *IT*, 4/3/1970 and 15/3/1970.

[115]   Memorandum to R Haugh, Private Secretary to Lord Widgery, from DS Cape, Embassy Washington, 18/1/1973, on attitude of citizens of USA towards situation in Northern Ireland, FCO 87/238, The National Archives of the United Kingdom (hereafter TNA).

[116]   *Time*, 1/11/1971.

[117]   *Christian Science Monitor*, 28/8/2009.

[118]   English, *Armed Struggle*, pp 122–124; Campbell, B., 'Northern Ireland Needs Truth Not Money', *Guardian*, 28/1/2009; Ward, 'Ulster Terrorism'.

[119]   *The Times*, 25/10/1971.

Ulster Protestants who were unwilling to accept a unified Ireland 'should be given a decent opportunity to go back to Britain'.[120]

Congressional Hearings on Northern Ireland and Bloody Sunday

The Kennedy–Ribicoff resolution eventually led to congressional hearings in February 1972 and from the perspective of the British the timing could scarcely have been worse. The intervening period had seen a series of events that raised the temperature of these hearings considerably. First was the publication of the Compton Report into allegations of security force brutality during the introduction of internment without trial on 16 November 1971. The American Embassy in Dublin noted Irish anger at the report: 'Official described Compton report as "complete whitewash" and said that the evidence of torture "however delicately described by English gentlemen, was irrefutable"'.[121] A later telegram noted that the Irish government might seek 'short-term measures of confrontation with British, such as appeal to European human rights commission on brutality/tortures issue'.[122] Later that year, a further Senate Resolution on Northern Ireland followed, proposing that the United States offer its assistance in the peaceful resolution of the problems in Northern Ireland.[123]

Kennedy had maintained a strong line on Northern Ireland and a December meeting with TD Charles Haughey left the future Taoiseach under the impression that Kennedy was 'very anxious that some form of United Nations intervention should take place in Northern Ireland'. Haughey proposed placing British troops under UN control as a first

---

[120] *The Times*, 27/8/2009.

[121] Telegram from Amembassy Dublin to Secretary of State, 19/11/1971, 'GOI Probably to take Torture Allegations to Strasbourg', RG59, General Records of the Department of State, Subject Numerical Files, 1970–1973, Political & Defense, POL7 IRE-POL23 IRE, Box 2383, NARA.

[122] Telegram from Amembassy Dublin to Secretary of State, 30/11/1971, 'The New Goal: Irish Unity', RG59, General Records of the Department of State, Subject Numerical Files, 1970–1973, Political & Defense, POL7 IRE-POL23 IRE, Box 2383, NARA.

[123] Senate Resolution 221, 'To Extend the Good Offices of the US in Resolving the Northern Ireland Crisis', 17/12/1971, White House Central Files, Subject Files, Countries, CO160, United Kingdom, Nixon Library.

step, which Kennedy agreed with. Haughey then asked that Kennedy attempt to convince Nixon to raise the issue of Northern Ireland during talks with Edward Heath, continuing to suggest that the Democratic Party platform for the 1972 election could refer to a peaceful solution to the conflict and the reunification of Ireland.[124] The US Embassy in Dublin noted Haughey's involvement in the 1970 arms trial, a matter of concern given their observation that 'in press reports, it is difficult [to] separate Haughey's opinions from Kennedy's'. They did highlight, however, that 'Senator [Kennedy] is opposed to violence'.[125]

The introduction of internment had brought this renewed focus on the situation in Northern Ireland from the United States, but had also reinvigorated the protest movement within Northern Ireland itself. Prime Minister Brian Faulkner banned parades and marches on 18 January 1972, but this ban was largely ignored and therefore highly ineffective. A significant protest march took place at an internment centre at Magilligan strand in County Derry on 22 January. British troops blocked the march, reportedly a thousand people strong, and deployed CS gas. A further march was announced for the following weekend. Despite the request from the Chief Superintendent of the RUC that the march be allowed to take place without military intervention, soldiers from the British Army were on duty in Derry and ultimately opened fired on protesters. Fourteen people died as a result of the violence on what became known as Bloody Sunday. The day after the march Edward Heath appointed Lord Chief Justice Widgery to head an inquiry into the deaths.[126]

For the British government, the presence of Irish Minister of External Affairs, Patrick Hillery, in New York at this time could scarcely have been more problematic. Hillery was in the United States to address the United Nations and took the opportunity to call on Secretary of

---

[124]   *IT*, 20/12/1971.

[125]   Telegram from Amembassy Dublin to Secretary of State, 20/12/1971, Haughey's Report on Talks with Senator Kennedy, RG59, General Records of the Department of State, Subject Numerical Files, 1970–1973, Political & Defense, POL7 IRE-POL23 IRE, Box 2383, NARA.

[126]   Report of the Tribunal Appointed to Inquire into the Events on Sunday, 30th January 1972, available at https://cain.ulster.ac.uk/hmso/widgery.htm. It should be noted that in 2010 the inquiry under Lord Saville ruled the killings unjustified and effectively rendered the Widgery report obsolete. See 'The Bloody Sunday Inquiry', available at https://www.gov.uk/government/publications/report-of-the-bloody-sunday-inquiry.

State Rogers 'to see this as a problem for the U.S. and not just for the Dublin Government'. The United States was aware that the Irish had become frustrated at US reluctance to involve themselves in the issue:

> We have been told by [a] variety of sources that resentment continues over USG unwillingness to support Irish efforts to have Northern Ireland matter inscribed on UNSC and UNGA agendas in 1969. Presumably there is also bitterness re our refusal to intervene with British re internment this summer … We believe therefore that Irish will not [repeat] not be satisfied by polite expressions of sympathy and they will expect at least a U.S. commitment to approach British and ask them to take steps to relieve tensions in north. Irish may suggest we urge end to internment, withdrawal of British troops from Catholic ghetto areas, direct rule, talks, etc … If we are to avoid serious damage to U.S.–Irish relations in this tense situation, given sensitivities already aroused by landing rights issue, we strongly believe U.S. should be forthcoming on this issue, that cost to U.S. relations with Ireland of not doing anything considerably outweigh possibility that U.S. relations with Britain will suffer very much if we approach HMG.[127]

International tensions were high and Hillery's appearance at the UN could scarcely have come at a more delicate moment. Two days after Bloody Sunday, a protest at the British Embassy in Dublin led to the building being burnt to the ground. Alec Douglas-Home declared to the House of Commons:

> No doubt there are strong feelings in Ireland, but they cannot possibly justify the outrage perpetrated in Dublin yesterday. I feel I must give warning to the Irish Government that if they were to maintain the attitude they have taken—as in Mr. Hillery's speech, for instance, in New York yesterday—they could do most serious and lasting damage to relationships between our two countries.[128]

---

[127]   Telegram from Amembassy Dublin to Secretary of State, 2/2/1972, RG59, General Records of the Department of State, Subject Numerical Files, 1970–1973, Political & Defense, POL7 IRE-POL23 IRE, Box 2383, NARA.

[128]   Sir Alec Douglas-Home, British Embassy Dublin, Hansard, HC vol. 830, cols 692–696 (3 February 1972), available at https://api.parliament.uk/historic-hansard/commons/1972/feb/03/british-embassy-dublin.

The American Embassy in London communicated this statement to Rogers, adding that Douglas-Home was cynical as to the intensity of Irish attempts to protect the British Embassy. For their part, the Irish chargé d'affaires in London had accepted full responsibility on behalf of his government, who were accountable for the security of the Embassy.[129] The controversy around the entire situation, exacerbated by Hillery's comments, meant that plans for Taoiseach Jack Lynch to visit the United States had to be shelved.[130]

The popular media were cautious in their coverage of Bloody Sunday, the *New York Times* writing of 'an awful slaughter' in its editorial two days later, but also observing that 'the brief clips of the Catholic demonstration shown on American television prove beyond doubt that the provocation for the troops was deliberate and great'.[131] The *Los Angeles Times* highlighted what it perceived as British intransigence on issues of discrimination and proposed the implementation of an international inquiry, although it did also note the confrontational nature of the IRA.[132] These events set the context in which the Kennedy- and Ribicoff-led hearings took place in February, heard by the House of Representatives Committee on Foreign Affairs Sub-Committee on Europe.

Kennedy led the proceedings, declaring Bloody Sunday to have been an act of 'terrible death and destruction', a product of 'Britain's inability to deal fairly and justly with the people of Ireland', to begin a dramatic address. He continued to speak of 'a new chapter of violence and terror … being written in this history of Ireland … written in the blood of a new generation of Irish men and woman and children'. He suggested that a US Naval Communications Station near Londonderry might provide the government with the rationale for some form of intervention.[133] Kennedy was also quick to criticise the 'repressive

---

[129] Ibid. Also Telegram from Amembassy London to Secretary of State, 4/2/1972, 'Anglo-Irish Relations', RG59, General Records of the Department of State, Subject Numerical Files, 1970–1973, Political & Defense, POL7 IRE-POL23 IRE, Box 2383, NARA.

[130] Memorandum for Gordon Strachan from Charles Colson, 18/2/1972, Nixon Presidential Materials, National Security Council Files, Country Files, Europe, Box 694, Nixon Library.

[131] *NYT*, 1/2/1972.

[132] *Los Angeles Times*, 1/2/1972.

[133] Hearings on Northern Ireland, Testimony of Senator Edward Kennedy, House of Representatives Committee on Foreign Affairs, Subcommittee on

policy of internment': 'the soaring daily toll of bloodshed, bullets, and bombing in Ulster is a continuing awful reminder of how wrong that policy was', claiming that 'internment has brought British justice to her knees'.[134] The British review of the hearings described his speech as 'demagogic'.[135]

Michigan Representative James O'Hara followed Kennedy and also focused on internment, arguing 'these internments are barbarous acts, reminiscent of the worst features of totalitarianism, and totally at odds with the posture of a country that professes to be part of the Free World'. O'Hara described Ireland as being 'brutally colonized by the systematic and deliberate discrimination in housing, employment, political representation and educational opportunities ... The government of Northern Ireland has been either unwilling or unable to resolve the problem in peaceful fashion', considering the Northern Irish parliament to be 'simply an instrument of colonial suppression'.[136]

New York Congressman Jonathan Bingham said that 'even before Bloody Sunday in Derry, it was clear that British policies in Northern Ireland—policies based on official discrimination, internment and attempted repression by armed force—were doomed to fail, indeed were only making matters worse'. He continued to compare Bloody Sunday to the 1961 Sharpeville massacre in South Africa, where sixty-seven were killed, and the Algerian civil war, contending that

Europe, 28/2/1972, in Attitude of Government and Citizens of the United States of America towards Political Situation in Northern Ireland, FCO 87/102, TNA. Also available in Cormac K.H. O'Malley Papers, 1957–1981, Subseries 2:B, New York University Library, the Archives of Irish America, AIA 019. Andrew Wilson also notes that Ted Kennedy made a comparison between the situations in Vietnam and Ulster, something that was condemned by both NI Prime Minister Brian Faulkner and Edward Heath. Wilson, *Irish America*, pp. 59–60.

[134] Hearings on Northern Ireland, Testimony of Senator Edward Kennedy, House of Representatives Committee on Foreign Affairs, Subcommittee on Europe, 28/2/1972, in Attitude of Government and Citizens of the United States of America towards Political Situation in Northern Ireland, FCO 87/102, TNA.

[135] Telegram on Congressional Hearings on Northern Ireland, March 1, 1972, in Attitude of Government and Citizens of the United States of America towards Political Situation in Northern Ireland, FCO 87/102, TNA.

[136] Testimony of Representative James G. O'Hara before the subcommittee on Europe, House Committee on Foreign Affairs on H Res. 745—Calling for Peace in Northern Ireland (undated), in Attitude of Government and Citizens of the United States of America towards Political Situation in Northern Ireland, FCO 87/102, TNA.

'the British must recognize that it is their policies which lead to such acts'.[137]

The British Foreign and Commonwealth Office closely monitored proceedings, concerned at the prospect of Congress passing the Kennedy- and Ribicoff-led resolution and recommending United Nation intervention in Northern Ireland, even though this remained an unlikely prospect.[138] Reviewing the hearings, there was a palpable sense of relief that, in the media, Kennedy's call for intervention 'attracted a good deal of adverse editorial comment and was highly unpopular with the press and general public opinion'.[139] Nevertheless, the idea had been raised on a prominent platform and the British Prime Minister, Edward Heath, saw fit to comment to the *New York Times* that:

> there is much misunderstanding of the situation there [Northern Ireland] even in some of the highest quarters in the United States, though not I hasten to add, the President. It seems not to be understood that the great majority of people in Northern Ireland are Protestants, that Northern Ireland is part of the United Kingdom and that the majority wish to stay in the United Kingdom.[140]

Secretary Rogers, in a note added to the briefings file ahead of the hearings, placed emphasis on one form that US intervention in Northern Ireland could take:

> if I were a private citizen. I would be asking leading members of the Irish-American community for the funds to pay for a comprehensive survey of industrial investment prospects in

---

[137] Remarks of Congressman Jonathan B. Bingham before the Subcommittee on Europe, Committee on Foreign Affairs, House of Representatives, Washington, DC, 29/2/1972, in Attitude of Government and Citizens of the United States of America towards Political Situation in Northern Ireland, FCO 87/102, TNA. Bingham would later lobby on behalf of the Fort Worth Five, but was somewhat inconsistent in his support for Irish issues; see *IT*, 17/7/1972.

[138] Memorandum, 'Analysis of Pending Legislation Dealing with the Situation in Northern Ireland, February 14, 1972', in Attitude of Government and Citizens of the United States of America towards Political Situation in Northern Ireland, FCO 87/101, TNA.

[139] Unclassified Memorandum, March 17, 1972, in Attitude of Government and Citizens of the United States of America towards Political Situation in Northern Ireland, FCO 87/102, TNA.

[140] *NYT*, 6/3/1972.

the most depressed areas of Northern Ireland. When I had
the results in hand, I would then go to American firms which
are already planning to make investments in the European
Community area. I would point out that Britain and Ireland are
both expected to enter the Community soon, and I would do my
best to persuade them to include Northern Ireland's economically depressed areas among the sites for their planned future
investment. I would do this in the knowledge that no one could
take exception to this effort, and in the confident expectation
that this might be one of the most important contributions that
Americans could possibly make to the long-term welfare of the
people of the North.[141]

The Irish government was also angry at having been 'placed in [an]
embarrassing political position by published statements made by Irish
political figures returning from U.S. Congressional hearings'. The
hearings afforded Irish political opposition the opportunity for point-
scoring and claims were made that Patrick Hillery had neglected to
request any assistance from the United States. Speaking to Secretary
Rogers, Hillery said: 'it is being assumed here that I asked for nothing
whatever with the implication that if I had asked for something short
of intervention the US would have given it ... it is being suggested that
I crossed the Atlantic and did not ask you for anything, which is not
true'.[142]

The State Department noted that Hillery had not asked for formal
US intervention in Northern Ireland, rather that he suggested 'that the
US go to the British and advise them in a friendly fashion that they
should change their policy toward Northern Ireland'. Hillery also 'made
it clear that he did not expect us to adopt a hostile attitude toward Great
Britain'. Rogers, for his part, noted US concern over the situation but
that the United States could not 'go to the British and tell them that
their policy is wrong and that they should change it. Such an approach
to the British would be taking sides'.[143]

[141] Ibid.
[142] Telegram from Amembassy Dublin to Secretary of State, 6/3/1972, RG59,
General Records of the Department of State, Subject Numerical Files, 1970–1973,
Political & Defense, POL7 IRE-POL23 IRE, Box 2383, NARA.
[143] Department of State telegram, 7/3/1972, RG59, General Records of the
Department of State, Subject Numerical Files, 1970–1973, Political & Defense,
POL7 IRE-POL23 IRE, Box 2383, NARA.

The Irish were keen that there be no misunderstanding, and Irish Ambassador Warnock contacted the State Department to emphasise that the Irish 'had made no attempt [to] influence [the] course of recent hearings and he had no intention of "lobbying" in US for GOI [Government of Ireland] point of view'. Martin Hillenbrand, on behalf of the State Department, in turn, emphasised that 'We had in no way rebuffed Hillery. Hillery meeting with the Secretary on very short notice, was friendly and useful although we could not accede to request that we weigh in with British. The USG [US Government] obviously very unhappy and concerned about situation and we hope that moderation and reason will soon prevail. Terrorism and violence accomplish nothing'. Of particular significance was the State Department's view that Warnock's 'presentation reinforces Dublin's assessment that [the Irish government is] in considerable political difficulty as he was most anxious to grasp any straws that might help answer critics'.[144] The State Department seemed keen to drop the issue quickly, suggesting that any misunderstandings were on a semantic basis.[145]

It is worth noting that at the time the State Department was advising US citizens against travel to Northern Ireland, 'except for strong and urgent reasons'. With around 1,500 US citizens in Northern Ireland at the time, it also noted that, 'with the indiscriminate nature of the violence in the last few months there is no way that travellers' safety can be assured, and with our small staff (presently two officers) at Belfast we cannot offer protection to American citizens'. Further, it emphasised, 'there is absolutely no reason why persons should not travel to the Irish Republic. Things are normal there'.[146]

Spurred on by the Sub-Committee hearings, Kennedy wrote directly to Nixon:

[144] Department of State telegram, 8/3/1972, RG59, General Records of the Department of State, Subject Numerical Files, 1970–1973, Political & Defense, POL7 IRE-POL23 IRE, Box 2383, NARA.

[145] Telegram from Department of State, 9/3/1972, 'Hillery–Rogers Feb 3 Meeting and Hillenbrand's Testimony', RG59, General Records of the Department of State, Subject Numerical Files, 1970–1973, Political & Defense, POL7 IRE-POL23 IRE, Box 2383, NARA.

[146] Hearings Working File, February 1972, Questions and Answers, in RG59, General Records of the Department of State, Bureau of European Affairs, Office of Northern European Affairs, Records Relating to Ireland, 1963–1975, Aviation Negotiations to FT-13 Foreign Trade: Duties, Tariffs, Surcharges 1969, Box 3, NARA.

The continuing reign of killing and violence in Ulster is a source of deep concern to millions of citizens in America and peoples throughout the world. The recent hearings on Northern Ireland by the House Subcommittee on Europe have focused new attention on the inexorable tragedy now unfolding in that land, and have brought home to people in this country a new awareness of the horror of the violence taking place. In the face of the constant terror and brutality, I believe that the Administration has a greater responsibility to speak and act than it has shown so far. Tragically, in its foreign policy, the Administration gives the appearance of being quick to speak and act when great power issues or military affairs are at stake, but slow to respond when the issue is one of basic human rights.

He continued to encourage the White House to do more than simply adopt 'a passive official role that publicly declines to use our good offices unless the Irish and British Governments actually request us to do so'. Kennedy cited the precedent of Walter Page, the American Ambassador in London during the First World War, who was instructed by President Wilson to ask British Prime Minister David Lloyd George to take steps to settle the Irish question.[147] Of course, at that time, the British would introduce conscription in Ireland following the German Spring Offensive of 1918.

In response, Nixon lobbyist William Timmons wrote to Kennedy, advising him of the various exchanges that Nixon had held with British officials. He highlighted a meeting with Edward Heath in Bermuda in December 1971 where Nixon 'told Mr. Heath of the concern of the American people over this tragic situation and assured Prime Minister of our support for efforts to put Northern Ireland on the road to peace with justice'.[148] This clearly fell short of Kennedy's expectations, but a fuller response was not perceived to be possible within the administration.

[147] Letter from Kennedy to Nixon, 14/3/1972, White House Central Files, Subject Files, Countries, CO160, United Kingdom, Nixon Library. Other representatives pressuring Nixon to act included Congressman Michael Harrington from Massachusetts who sat on the House Armed Services Committee. See Letter to Nixon from Michael J. Harrington, House of Representatives Armed Services Committee, 15/3/1972, White House Central Files, Subject Files, Countries, CO160, United Kingdom, Nixon Library.
[148] Letter to Kennedy from Timmons, 20/3/1972, White House Central Files, Subject Files, Countries, CO160, United Kingdom, Nixon Library.

White House Chief of Staff General Alexander Haig told Timmons to avoid quoting from or referring to statements made by either Patrick Hillery or Jack Lynch, and emphasised that 'This is a very sensitive issue with the Irish leaders'.[149]

Sean Donlon, who served as Consul General to the Irish Consulate in Boston in the late 1960s, and later became Ireland's Ambassador in Washington, recalled of Kennedy:

> I suppose there were two phases in Kennedy's involvement in Ireland. Up to and including Bloody Sunday, he almost took the instinctive, old-fashioned Irish-American approach because he didn't really, well, first of all, he didn't have Carey Parker and he didn't really have much knowledge about what was happening in Ireland. There was a huge emotional link going back probably to President Kennedy's visit in 1963 and he had visited Ireland pretty regularly, but he was not in touch with what I would call the Irish political situation. His conversion— and I can be very specific—he met John Hume in Germany; there were Congressional hearings immediately after Bloody Sunday, the House Sub-Committee on Europe in the Foreign Affairs Committee held hearings on Northern Ireland, and even though Kennedy was in the Senate, Senators are allowed to sit in on House hearings. They're not allowed to participate but they're allowed to sit in. Kennedy was hoping to meet John Hume. John didn't leave Northern Ireland because the situation after Bloody Sunday was so volatile; he didn't want to be out of the place. Kennedy asked the Irish Embassy in Washington to set up a meeting for him with John Hume the next time he, Kennedy, was in Europe. The following March, that would be March '72, Kennedy was going to a NATO gathering in Bonn, so we arranged for John Hume to travel to Bonn and to meet Ted Kennedy. That was, in my view, the crucial meeting which brought Kennedy on to what I would call an informed interest in Ireland. From then on Carey Parker kept in touch with people; Kennedy was kept briefed. If you look at statements after March of '73 you would find Kennedy very close to the, what I would

---

[149] Memorandum for William E. Timmons from General Haig, 20/3/1972, White House Central Files, Subject Files, Countries, CO160, United Kingdom, Nixon Library.

call, the Dublin hymn sheet, or the John Hume hymn sheet, whereas the statements made before March '73 were pretty emotive and not particularly constructive.[150]

The resolution and the Congressional hearings raised Kennedy's profile as an interested party within Congress, drawing the attention of John Hume. Kennedy later reflected on the role that Hume, referred to by one biographer as the 'fifth horseman', played in his increasingly moderate stance on Northern Ireland:

> My understanding of the situation in Northern Ireland really began to evolve after I met John Hume, a brilliant young member of Parliament from Northern Ireland. We had met briefly in 1972, after I co-sponsored a resolution with Abe Ribicoff calling for the withdrawal of the British troops from Northern Ireland and establishing a united Ireland. But it was really in late 1972 that John began the great education of Edward Kennedy about Northern Ireland and established the seeds that grew into a wonderful relationship.[151]

Hume had been elected as an Independent Nationalist Member of the Northern Ireland Parliament in early 1969 and served until the imposition of Direct Rule from London in March 1972, the British government's response to the rising violence in Northern Ireland. In late 1969, he was invited to address the Donegal Men's Association of Boston, but it was not until later that he and Kennedy met.[152] The first substantive meeting between the two took place in Bonn, then the capital of West Germany, and Hume's ability to express his case for constitutional reform as the most effective manner of resolving the conflict convincingly was crucial in persuading Kennedy to approach the issue of Northern Ireland in a more sensitive manner.[153] Hume explained to Kennedy that, rather than simply exposing

---

[150] Sean Donlon, interview with author, 24/2/2012.
[151] Kennedy, *True Compass*, p. 355. Maurice Fitzpatrick used the 'fifth horseman' title, a reference to the 'four horsemen' of Kennedy: Tip O'Neill, Daniel Patrick Moynihan, and Hugh Carey. See *John Hume in America: From Derry to DC* (Newbridge: Irish Academic Press, 2017), Preface.
[152] Fitzpatrick, *John Hume in America*, p. 31.
[153] Fitzpatrick points out that the two had been in contact, and met briefly, prior to this. See ibid., p. 34.

British intransigence on Irish unity, his previous stance on Northern Ireland had served to legitimise the cause of those who supported the nationalist cause through violence. As the *Boston Globe* noted, 'having lost two brothers to assassination, Kennedy became outspoken against IRA violence, even as he criticized British policies he said drove young Catholics to join the IRA'.[154] The engagement of those who opposed British policy in Northern Ireland and the ability to draw them into a far more constitutional, politicised, protest agenda, was central to the international appeal of the SDLP.

Nixon's Campaign for Re-election

With Nixon focused on the election of November 1972, California Governor Ronald Reagan travelled across the Atlantic on his behalf. Nixon's letter of introduction to Irish President Eamon de Valera described Reagan as 'both an American and a son of Ireland', Nixon adding, 'I know that he has particularly looked forward to visiting Ireland and making your acquaintance'.[155] Northern Ireland remained a thorny issue for Nixon given the sensitivity required in an election year. General Haig was advised that even 'inclusion of a reference [to Northern Ireland] in a Presidential speech ... would be interpreted as taking sides'.[156] In July, Haig wrote to Bruce Kehrli, a special assistant to Nixon, clearly stating the situation as he perceived it:

> Thus far, we have avoided a hornets' nest by confining ourselves to saying that we are concerned about the Ulster tragedy, welcome all responsible efforts to stop the violence, and would consider playing a 'useful role' if asked, at the same time emphasizing that it would be 'inappropriate and counter-productive' to intervene in any way ... The wisdom of this course is that it keeps us on good terms with the British who insist Ulster is an internal affair and, perhaps even more importantly, keeps us on

---

[154]   *Boston Globe*, 28/8/2009.
[155]   Letter from Nixon to de Valera, 30/6/1972, White House Central Files, Subject Files, Countries, Ireland, Nixon Library.
[156]   Memorandum for General Haig from Robert Livingston, 28/7/1972, Nixon Presidential Materials, National Security Council Files, Country Files, Europe, Box 694, Nixon Library.

good terms with the Irish Government which also has no desire to benefit from U.S. meddling.[157]

In August, Lord Chief Justice Widgery, the author of a controversial government report on Bloody Sunday, visited Washington. British Ambassador Lord Cromer had mentioned to Nixon that the Lord Chief Justice would be in Washington during an earlier meeting, to which Nixon, seemingly absent-mindedly, replied, 'We'll have to have him over for a meal'. Charles Powell, assistant to Cromer, talked with an assistant in the National Security Council (NSC), and agreed not to push the meeting on Nixon, with the NSC noting that the 'meeting might cause possible domestic political trouble'.[158]

Nixon met Alec Douglas-Home in September and the two discussed a range of topics, notably US–European relations, Strategic Arms Limitation Talks (SALT), the Middle East and Japan, China and Vietnam. On Northern Ireland, Kissinger advised the President that despite Prime Minister Heath's 'continuing efforts to find a peaceful solution … There has, in fact, been little progress'. Kissinger referenced the establishment of Diplock Courts, where judges sat without juries, as well as the Darlington Conference of 25 September where Ulster Unionists, Northern Ireland Labour Party members, and the Alliance Party met William Whitelaw to discuss the political future of Northern Ireland. Kissinger emphasised to Nixon that, 'Should the subject arise, you should reaffirm your policy of non-involvement by the United States and of support for the UKs efforts to work out a peaceful solution'.[159]

This non-involvement policy was stretched somewhat by a State Department review of its own policy regarding the issuance of visas for members of the IRA. In a draft cable, following communication from Belfast Consul General Grover Penberthy, the Department communicated that:

[157] Memorandum for Bruce Kehrli from Al Haig, 31/7/1972, Nixon Presidential Materials, National Security Council Files, Country Files, Europe, Box 694, Nixon Library.
[158] Memorandum for General Haig from Dick Campbell, 31/7/1972, Possible Presidential Meeting with British Chief Justice, Meeting with Sir Alec Douglas-Home, 29/9/1972, Nixon Presidential Materials, National Security Council Files, Country Files, Europe, Box 729, Nixon Library.
[159] Memorandum for the President from Henry Kissinger, 28/9/1972, Meeting with Sir Alec Douglas-Home, 29/9/1972, Nixon Presidential Materials, National Security Council Files, Country Files, Europe, Box 729, Nixon Library.

Any visa applicant who is suspected of being a member of either wing of the I.R.A. or of the Ulster Volunteer Force (UVF) will be read section 212 (a)(28) (F) and asked if that section applies to him ... If answer is affirmative, whether signed statement is obtained or not the visa should be refused. All such refusals should be reported to the Dept. graphically. If applicant replies in negative and consular officer has reason to believe applicant is a member of or affiliated with IRA or UVF case should be referred to Dept. for guidance with full particular.[160]

Joseph Thompson has suggested that Penberthy's views might have been somewhat favourable to the British, notably the view that detention or internment by the British was sufficient proof of IRA affiliation.[161] The reciprocal ban for UVF members was, of course, an obvious and politically consistent move, and it was hardly atypical of a diplomat to share views with a major political and strategic ally such as the government of the United Kingdom. Further, Penberthy's superiors in the State Department also questioned the reliability of the RUC and the Army, considering that 'we do not believe Government intelligence is all that good', preferring to rely on 'a public statement of affiliation by an applicant as recorded in a reputable media would, in Dept'.s view, constitute sufficient proof of affiliation to deny visa'. The British authorities could also present documentary proof of affiliation, but the United States was conscious that 'Many if not all cases will come under intense public scrutiny'.[162]

Patrick Hillery made yet another trip to New York in late 1972 where he met Secretary Rogers and again addressed the United Nations. His speech at the UN made, for the Belfast Consul General, 'no helpful contribution to peace in Northern Ireland, or even to discussion of problem'. Penberthy was especially critical: 'Hillery's claim

[160] Draft Cable, 'Visas for the I.R.A.' (undated), Arms to Ireland 1972, RG59, General Records of the Department of State, Bureau of European Affairs, Office of Northern European Affairs, Records Relating to Ireland, 1963–1975, AGR-Gen-1971 to AV-15 Charters 7.D, Box 1, NARA.
[161] Thompson, J.E., *American Policy and Northern Ireland: A Saga of Peacebuilding* (Westport, CT: Praeger, 2001), pp. 35–36.
[162] Arms to Ireland 1972, Draft Cable, 'Visas for the I.R.A.', in RG59, General Records of the Department of State, Bureau of European Affairs, Office of Northern European Affairs, Records Relating to Ireland, 1963–1975, AGR-Gen-1971 to AV-15 Charters 7.D, Box 1, NARA.

that Irish Government "will act, by every constitutional means open to them, to work towards a reasoned political settlement" rang somewhat hollow. It contrasts with his government's failure to propose changes in constitution and laws of Republic that would make new Ireland less unpalatable to northern Protestants'.[163]

Hillery also requested a meeting with the President. Despite Secretary Rogers's reluctance, Helmut Sonnenfeldt considered that 'the Irish would see it as balancing the President's meeting with Sir Alec Douglas-Home', and that such a meeting could alleviate Irish-American concerns over Northern Ireland.[164] Nixon used the meeting to express 'his profound sadness at the continuing bitterness and strife in Northern Ireland … he had a keen interest in finding a peaceful solution'. Hillery explained to Nixon that 'his government did not seek open or public declarations by the United States Government but hoped in our private discussions with the British we would make our views known', to which Nixon assured him that Northern Ireland was constantly on the agenda of high-level discussions with the British.[165] The American Embassy in Dublin considered that this meeting had 'already yielded diplomatic pay-offs and promises more benefits to come if the atmosphere that was generated by the President's meeting can be maintained'.[166]

The Second Nixon Administration

Ahead of the 1972 Presidential election, General Haig expressed concern about the administration's 'lack of do-goodism on the Ulster

[163]   Telegram from Amconsul Belfast to Secretary of State, 13/10/1972, 'Comment on Hillery UN Speech', RG59, General Records of the Department of State, Subject Numerical Files, 1970–1973, Political & Defense, POL12 IRAQ-POL IRE, Box 2383, NARA.

[164]   Memorandum for Henry Kissinger from Sonnenfeldt, 21/9/1972 and Memorandum for Henry Kissinger from Sonnenfeldt, 2/9/1972, Presidential Meeting with Irish Foreign Minister, Nixon Presidential Materials, National Security Council Files, Country Files, Europe, Box 694, Nixon Library.

[165]   Memorandum of Conversation, 'President's Meeting with Irish Foreign Minister, 6/10/1972', Nixon Presidential Materials, National Security Council Files, Country Files, Europe, Box 694, Nixon Library.

[166]   Telegram from Amembassy Dublin to Secretary of State, 17/11/1972, 'Diplomatic Dividends of President Nixon's Meeting with Foreign Minister Hillery', RG59, General Records of the Department of State, Subject Numerical Files, 1970–1973, Political & Defense, POL12 IRAQ-POL IRE, Box 2383, NARA.

problem'.[167] Nixon's second term in office, completed by Vice-President Gerald Ford, saw little change in US policy towards Northern Ireland. Similarly, there was no perceptible positive change in the 'Ulster problem' itself. In the words of Ambassador John Moore: 'Attitude change takes a long time … Reforms will hardly come in time to influence outcome of current stage in NI conflict'.[168]

At the end of 1972, the Irish government was in the process of tightening legislation against the Irish Republican Army, exemplified by the Offences Against the State (Amendment) Act, 1972, introduced in December.[169] This bill amended and extended the existing acts from 1939 and 1940, enabling court action to be taken against persons suspected of being members of an illegal organisation.[170] The US Embassy in Dublin noted the timing of Lynch's new stance against the IRA, positing that this was an electoral strategy rather than the Taoiseach 'seizing opportunity to undertake tightening he has long wanted'.[171] These moves were important with the Taoiseach scheduled to travel to the United States in early 1973.[172] During this visit, Lynch would seek to encourage US investment in Ireland, but it was also hoped that he could 'dampen private U.S. support for the IRA'. With Edward Heath scheduled to visit Washington later in the month, Nixon could receive both British and Irish perspectives on Northern Ireland in quick succession.[173] For their part, the British were concerned about the possibility that Lynch

---

[167]   Memorandum for Bruce Kehrli from Al Haig, 31/7/1972, Nixon Presidential Materials, National Security Council Files, Country Files, Europe, Box 694, Nixon Library. See also *NYT*, 25/9/1972, which reported Nixon as having a 62 per cent to 23 per cent lead over McGovern in polls.

[168]   Telegram from Amembassy Dublin to Secretary of State, 20/11/1972, 'Reforms for Unity?', RG59, General Records of the Department of State, Subject Numerical Files, 1970–1973, Political & Defense, POL12 IRAQ-POL IRE, Box 2383, NARA.

[169]   Irish Statute Book, Offences Against the State (Amendment) Act, 1972, available at www.irishstatutebook.ie/eli/1972/act/26/enacted/en/html.

[170]   *IT*, 23/11/1972 and 5/12/1972. The first prosecutions under the new act took place on 14 December; see *IT*, 15/12/1972.

[171]   Telegram from Amembassy Dublin to Secretary of State, 30/11/1972, RG59, General Records of the Department of State, Subject Numerical Files, 1970–1973, Political & Defense, POL12 IRAQ-POL IRE, Box 2383, NARA.

[172]   Memorandum to Peter Flanigan from David Gunning, 22/12/1972, White House Central Files, Subject Files, Countries, Ireland, Nixon Library.

[173]   Schedule Proposal From Henry Kissinger Meeting with Prime Minister of Ireland John Lynch, Monday, January 8, 1973, 23/12/1972, White House Central Files, Subject Files, Countries, Ireland, Nixon Library.

'would not support any arrangements for Northern Ireland "in which the possibility of the reunification of Ireland was not a very important feature"', and might express these views to Nixon so soon before Heath's visit to the President.[174]

Lynch's cabinet saw significant changes in 1973, with Brian Lenihan replacing Patrick Hillery in the renamed role of Minister for Foreign Affairs. The Americans welcomed the move, noting that they expected Lenihan to be easier to work with, given Hillery's tendency to be 'cold, inaccessible, and not especially interested in relations with the U.S.— except when he had something to ask'. It was clear that Hillery's repeated visits to the United States had rankled with some in the administration, particularly those who sought strong cooperation between London and Dublin on all Northern Irish issues.[175]

Officials at the Dublin Embassy recommended a stronger line on Northern Ireland for Nixon's second term in office, suggesting that because of the impact of violence in Ireland on US interests, 'the U.S. should contribute in any appropriate way to a diminution of Irish political violence'. Further: 'we must maintain good contacts with all parties to the problem, exercise our influence for peace quietly in the normal course of these contacts, and use the information we derive to search for other opportunities'. Not insignificant was the fact that 'American investment and tourism have been affected'.[176] Lynch's comments on the misuse of funds raised in the United States drew praise from the British, who intended to press that very issue during Heath's meeting with Nixon. Heath, in turn, was aware that the United States had been active 'against the smuggling of arms destined for Northern Ireland', and in 'refusing visas to IRA members and sympathisers'.[177]

Heath's visit also saw him meet with the Senate Foreign Relations Committee. There, Oregon Senator Mark Hatfield asked for Heath's

[174]   Prime Minister's Meeting with President Nixon, Brief on Item 12—Northern Ireland, 17/1/1973, in Prime Minister's Visit to President Nixon, CJ 4/350, TNA.
[175]   Telegram from Amembassy Dublin to Secretary of State, 3/1/1973, RG59, General Records of the Department of State, Subject Numerical Files, 1970–1973, Political & Defense, POL7 IRE-POL23 IRE, Box 2383, NARA.
[176]   Airgram from Amembassy Dublin to Department of State, 9/1/1973, 'U.S. Policy Assessment: Ireland', RG59, General Records of the Department of State, Subject Numerical Files, 1970–1973, Political & Defense, POL32 IRE-POL7 ISR, Box 2384, NARA.
[177]   Prime Minister's Meeting with President Nixon, Brief on Item 12—Northern Ireland, 17/1/1973, in Prime Minister's Visit to President Nixon, CJ 4/350, TNA.

views on Ireland, which elicited a lengthy explanation of the situation there. The Prime Minister underlined that 'Ulster was part of the United Kingdom', and commented on the complicated patterns of migration that gave Ireland sectarian diversity. He emphasised the importance of the principle of consent and added that 'it was important to decide in Northern Ireland whether unification should be sought by creating tension, as the IRA and others wished, or (as the British Government believed) by relaxing it'.[178] What is clear from the minutes of this meeting is that very few of the assembled members of Congress had much knowledge of the situation in Ireland, though their willingness to learn is also apparent.

Lynch returned to Ireland and faced a general election, which saw Liam Cosgrave elected Taoiseach. The transition to the Fine Gael–Labour Party coalition brought, in the words of Henry Kissinger, 'no significant differences between the old government and the new in the fields of foreign affairs, Ireland's relations with the EC, or on Northern Ireland'.[179] Kissinger added, in a note to Nixon, that Cosgrave was 'generally well disposed toward the United States and has visited here on several occasions'.[180] As it turned out, rather than Cosgrave, Minister for Foreign Affairs Garret FitzGerald would take a leading role in developing Irish–American relations during the Cosgrave government. John Moore described FitzGerald as 'very brilliant and interesting'.[181]

FitzGerald was forced to confront the issue of US support for the IRA, which persisted throughout the period, and news of an October 1973 visit to Capitol Hill by Ruairí Ó Brádaigh did little to quieten British and Irish concerns. Ó Brádaigh met with Tip O'Neill and

[178] Record of a meeting between the Prime Minister and the Senate Foreign Relations Committee at the Capitol, Washington, DC, at 3 p.m. on Thursday, 1 February 1973: Importance of US relationship now Britain in EEC, in Prime Minister's Visit to President Nixon, CJ 4/350, TNA.
[179] Memorandum for Henry Kissinger, the White House, 3/3/1973, 'The Irish Election', RG59, General Records of the Department of State, Subject Numerical Files, 1970–1973, Political & Defense, POL7 IRE-POL23 IRE, Box 2383, NARA.
[180] Memorandum for the President from Henry Kissinger, 3/3/1973, Nixon Presidential Materials, National Security Council Files, Country Files, Europe, Box 694, Nixon Library. The issue was indeed resolved during the Cosgrave Government and the first Trans Western Airways flight landed in Dublin on 2/5/1974.
[181] Letter from John Moore to Henry Kissinger, 15/8/1973, White House Central Files, Subject Files, Countries, Ireland, Nixon Library.

Silvio Conte in a reception at the Rayburn House Office Building, though there was some confusion as to how Ó Brádaigh had entered the country: 'INS was never able to locate any record of O Bradaigh's entry or exit from the US; neither do we have any record of visa issuance'.[182] Rosemary O'Neill, an official in the State Department and daughter of Tip, recalled that her father was unaware of exactly whom he was meeting prior to attending.[183] Ó Brádaigh later attempted to visit the United States in 1974, unsuccessful in his application for a visa under the anglicised version of his name, Peter R. Brady.[184] On this occasion, he had been expected to attend a reception for some 1,400 Irish Northern Aid supporters in Queens, New York, which would also be attended by New York Congressman Ogden Reid.[185]

According to FBI reports, by this point Noraid had already raised $1.5 million. This clearly provided a valid reason to block the Ó Brádaigh visit but the Nixon administration still anticipated resistance from Congress. As officials noted, 'intense Congressional scrutiny of the Administration's position on Northern Ireland … eventually dies down since our actions are based on US law and our policy of non-involvement, not requests from the British Government'.[186] This was not necessarily true for Senator Ted Kennedy, however, who visited London in November 1974 to meet Prime Minister Wilson and raised concerns about cross-party cooperation on the issue of Northern

[182] Memorandum from William A. Buell to Assistant Secretary Stoessel, 20/11/1973, 'US Support for the IRA', in RG59, General Records of the Department of State, Bureau of European Affairs, Office of Northern European Affairs, Records Relating to Ireland, 1963–1975, Aviation Negotiations to FT-13 Foreign Trade: Duties, Tariffs, Surcharges 1969, Box 3, IRA Misc., NARA. The Ó Brádaigh visit was also discussed in a background paper provided to Gerald Ford; see Briefing Memorandum, 3/1/1975, 'Your Meeting with Irish Foreign Minister FitzGerald, Wednesday, January 8, 3.00 p.m.', National Security Adviser, NSC Europe, Canada, and Ocean Affairs Staff, Files 1974–1977, Country Files, Ireland, 1974, NSC, Box 12, Ford Library. This document suggests that O'Neill was angry at having been associated with the meeting.
[183] Rosemary O'Neill, interview with author, 3/5/2012.
[184] *IT*, 17/1/1974.
[185] *IT*, 21/1/1974.
[186] Memorandum from William A. Buell to Assistant Secretary Stoessel, 20/11/1973, 'US Support for the IRA', in RG59, General Records of the Department of State, Bureau of European Affairs, Office of Northern European Affairs, Records Relating to Ireland, 1963–1975, Aviation Negotiations to FT-13 Foreign Trade: Duties, Tariffs, Surcharges 1969, Box 3, IRA Misc., NARA.

Ireland. A briefing note ahead of the visit advised Wilson that Kennedy 'continues to be interested in Northern Ireland but has refrained from unhelpful criticism in the last few months'.[187]

In Dublin, the Fine Gael government followed the lead of the British and sought to challenge the United States on the issue of American-sourced weapons for the IRA, informing the Nixon Administration that they believed that roughly three-quarters of the IRA's resources came from US sources. Garret FitzGerald had emphasised the issue in a meeting with Congressman Joshua Eilberg, noting that 'NI violence could never have been sustained at such a high level over past three years except for American contributions'. He added:

> Irish-American groups should stop and consider how they would like it if Irish organizations were making contributions to militants bent on destruction of US society. He was aware that Americans collecting money for 'Irish Aid' said funds would be used for charitable purposes, but he thought that contributors would have to be extremely naïve to accept such assurances when it was well known that money was going to Provisional Sinn Féin/IRA.[188]

New ideas were forthcoming in an attempt to bring about significant and meaningful constitutional change to Northern Ireland. A White Paper, entitled, 'Northern Ireland Constitutional Proposals', was published which proposed the creation of an Assembly that would be elected by proportional representation. This led to a conference at Sunningdale Park, near London, in December 1973, which saw the British and Irish plans for Northern Ireland develop into a strategy that would ultimately underpin the far more successful Good Friday Agreement of 1998. The most crucial aspect of the so-called Sunningdale Agreement was its attempt to establish a power-sharing Executive in Belfast along with a cross-border Council of Ireland.

---

[187] Briefing Memorandum, FCO, 11/11/1974, 'US Senators: Calls on the Prime Minister and Record of a Conversation between the Prime Minister and Senator Edward Kennedy at 11.20 a.m. on Tuesday 12 November 1974 at 10 Downing Street', in Visits to London of Senators Bentsen, Humphrey, Jackson and Kennedy—November 1974, PREM 16/1152, TNA.

[188] Telegram from Amembassy Dublin to Secretary of State, 21/6/1973, 'American Contributions to Irish Violence', RG59, General Records of the Department of State, Subject Numerical Files, 1970–1973, Political & Defense, POL7 IRE-POL23 IRE, Box 2383, NARA.

In a memo to Kissinger, Theodore Eliot astutely predicted that '[William] Craig and Paisley will probably continue to call on their supporters to make the whole system unworkable', but also noted that the British had been successful in splitting the Unionist Party and would now seek a successful outcome to the negotiations between Faulkner and the SDLP.[189] There was evidence that Catholic voters in Northern Ireland favoured cooperation with Unionist parties, with the SDLP polling well in areas where the IRA had demanded spoiled ballots.[190] An intelligence note about the elections raised questions as to whether or not 'Protestants who support [a power-sharing assembly] will now be able to cooperate effectively with the moderate Catholic deputies—a sine qua non for the formation of a majority in the new Assembly—is an open question'.[191] The problem of the IRA was, of course, trickier to solve, as Eliot noted, 'in any event, violence at some level will in all probability continue since the IRA can point to its "successes"—the downfall of the old Parliament, Stormont; the disarming of the Royal Ulster Constabulary; the disbanding of the "B Specials"'.[192]

The Northern Ireland Executive took power on Tuesday, 1 January 1974.[193] Within a week, Brian Faulkner had resigned as the leader of the Ulster Unionist Party and the Ulster Unionist Council had voted, 427 to 374, to reject the Council of Ireland. A large-scale strike followed in May which Kissinger noted had 'paralyzed the economy, produced

[189]   Memorandum for Henry Kissinger from Theodore Eliot, Executive Secretary, Department of State, 3/7/1973, Nixon Presidential Materials, National Security Council Files, Country Files, Europe, Box 694, Nixon Library.
[190]   Memorandum for Henry Kissinger, the White House, 3/7/1973, 'Northern Ireland Elections', RG59, General Records of the Department of State, Subject Numerical Files, 1970–1973, Political & Defense, POL7 IRE-POL23 IRE, Box 2383, NARA.
[191]   Intelligence Note, 3/7/1973, 'Northern Ireland: Election of New Assembly Creates Great Uncertainty', RG59, General Records of the Department of State, Subject Numerical Files, 1970–1973, Political & Defense, POL7 IRE-POL23 IRE, Box 2383, NARA. The 1973 Assembly election returned a huge majority of Unionists, with the UUP winning twenty-four seats. The SDLP, Alliance Party, and Northern Ireland Labour Party won twenty-three seats, representing the only non-Unionist victories.
[192]   Memorandum for Henry Kissinger from Theodore Eliot, Executive Secretary, Department of State, 3/7/1973, Nixon Presidential Materials, National Security Council Files, Country Files, Europe, Box 694, Nixon Library.
[193]   *Belfast Telegraph*, 30/1/2013; *Daily Mail*, 12/4/2010.

near-anarchy, and toppled the provincial government'.[194] Attempts to restore power to Stormont followed over the summer of 1974, including a July White Paper entitled, 'The Northern Ireland Constitution', which sought to establish a Constitutional Convention to work towards an agreed political settlement.[195] Kissinger appeared pessimistic as to the likelihood of their success, particularly given the requirement for some form of power sharing that remained at the core of these proposals.[196]

Vice-President Gerald Ford Takes Over

As Nixon's time in the White House neared its end, the advice from National Security Council experts remained that 'U.S. interests are still best served by our policy of strict nonintervention in the Northern Ireland situation'.[197] The possibility of US intervention on Northern Ireland, very clearly a remote prospect under President Nixon, reduced further with the domestic upheaval that occurred over the summer of 1974. News broke of a 1972 break-in at the Watergate complex in Washington, and the scandal ultimately prompted Nixon's resignation on 9 August. Vice-President Gerald Ford, who was appointed to replace Spiro Agnew, took the oath of office that same day. Existing literature details how Ford's Foreign Policy was merely a continuation of Nixon's, facilitated by the retention of Nixon's foreign policy team, and his approach towards Northern Ireland would provide similar continuity.[198] Indeed, a briefing ahead of a meeting with Irish Foreign Minister Garret FitzGerald emphasised 'we would also want to avoid a suggestion

[194]   Memorandum for the President from Henry Kissinger, 'Your Visit to England, Saturday, October 3, 1970', Nixon Presidential Materials, National Security Council Files, President's Trip Files, Box 470, Nixon Library.
[195]   The fourteen-day Ulster Workers Council strike demanded the dissolution of the power-sharing assembly. On Friday, 17 May, at the height of the strike, the Ulster Volunteer Force exploded a series of bombs in Dublin and Monaghan, killing thirty-three.
[196]   Memorandum for the President from Henry Kissinger, 're New UK White Paper on Northern Ireland', Nixon Presidential Materials, National Security Council Files, Country Files, Europe, Box 694, Nixon Library.
[197]   Memorandum for Major General Brent Scowcroft from George Springsteen, Department of State, 8/7/1974, Nixon Presidential Materials, National Security Council Files, Country Files, Europe, Box 694, Nixon Library.
[198]   Thompson, *American Policy and Northern Ireland*, p. 49.

that we are considering any change in our policy of deliberate and strict non-intervention in the Northern Ireland problem'.

This briefing suggested to Ford that the Irish feared a British withdrawal from Northern Ireland but could not say so publicly. It also highlighted US efforts against IRA fundraising and gun-running and noted that 'we have offered moral support to those moderates who seek to break the circle of violence'.[199] Ford met Harold Wilson on 30 January to discuss the ongoing Bureau of Alcohol, Tobacco and Firearms investigation into IRA gunrunning. ATF intelligence suggested that up to half the IRA's weapons of American origin were actually acquired from the international military surplus market and that the IRA did not possess modern US military firearms, rather the commercial versions of US military weapons.[200] This sat uneasily with a report produced by Representative Les Aspin of Wisconsin which suggested that the IRA had stolen 6,900 weapons and 1.2 million rounds of ammunition between 1971 and 1974, and attempted to recruit members of the Marine Corps.[201]

Meanwhile, Garret FitzGerald sought additional US investment in Ireland, and made a return trip to the United States in early 1975 with a view to increasing the $400 million of US money that was invested in Ireland at the time. It was suggested to Ford that the successful development of the Republic of Ireland economy could facilitate the ultimate Irish goal of reunification, though there was no implication that the United States should adjust its non-interventionist policy on Northern Ireland.[202] Ford's advisers did, however, note that Ireland could be more cooperative with the British government on the extradition of suspects and border security, and perceptions of Irish intransigence over the issue of intelligence sharing exacerbated US concern that 'the Irish

[199] Bilateral Talks during UNGA Ireland, Foreign Minister FitzGerald, 11/9/1974, National Security Adviser, NSC Europe, Canada, and Ocean Affairs Staff, Files 1974–1977, Country Files, Ireland, 1974, NSC, Box 12, Ford Library.
[200] Office of the Secretary of the Treasury, 30/1/1975, Information Memorandum for the meeting of the President with the Prime Minister of the United Kingdom, National Security Adviser, NSC Europe, Canada, and Ocean Affairs Staff, Files 1974–1977, Country Files, Ireland, 1974, NSC, Box 12, Ford Library.
[201] *NYT*, 2/9/1975.
[202] Briefing Memorandum, 3/1/1975, 'Your Meeting with Irish Foreign Minister FitzGerald, Wednesday, January 8, 3.00 p.m.', National Security Adviser, NSC Europe, Canada, and Ocean Affairs Staff, Files 1974–1977, Country Files, Ireland, 1974, NSC, Box 12, Ford Library.

have been unwilling to share their own intelligence information on this subject with us, probably because they doubt our ability to protect it from IRA sympathizers within the USG'. Further, the briefing noted that 'a serious problem for US law enforcement agencies is IRA sympathizers within its own ranks'. Most significant, however, was 'The danger for the US ... that we could be dragged into this situation against our better judgment and our national interest by domestic political pressure to step in and save the Irish Catholics of Ulster. Particularly at election time'. Among the possible solutions to the conflict that were offered in this paper was the deployment of a UN Peace Force.[203]

The Balcombe Street Gang

The IRA's bombing campaign on the UK mainland included two high-profile attacks in Guildford and Birmingham on 5 October and 21 November 1974, respectively. These attacks led to the arrest and imprisonment of three groups: the Guildford Four, who were accused of the Guildford bombings; the Maguire Seven, who were accused of providing support to the Guildford bombers; and the Birmingham Six, accused of the attacks in Birmingham. All of those convicted in these cases were ultimately exonerated. Those actually responsible for the Guildford attack were a group known as the Balcombe Street Gang. The gang was also responsible for a series of bomb attacks in London, including a bombing at the Hilton Hotel in Park Lane, which killed two civilians.[204] The activities of the gang are important in the context of a discussion of the role of the United States in the conflict for two reasons.

The first of these was the involvement of the group in the murder of off-duty police officer Stephen Tibble, who joined in the chase of a suspect through the streets of London. That suspect was US citizen William Quinn. Quinn fled immediately to Dublin where he was arrested and jailed for IRA membership, serving nine months of a year-long sentence before returning to his native San Francisco. Six years after he fled to the United States, Quinn would become the subject of tense court proceedings as he appealed against his extradition to the UK on the grounds that his crime was political in nature.[205]

---

[203]   Ibid.
[204]   See McKittrick et al., *Lost Lives*, pp. 574–575.
[205]   Ibid., p. 521.

The second of these actions took place eight months after Tibble's murder. At around nine o'clock on the morning of 23 October 1975, Gordon Hamilton-Fairley, a renowned cancer expert, was walking his dogs near his home in Campden Hill Square, London. As he walked past the car of his neighbour, Sir Hugh Fraser, the Conservative Member of Parliament for Stafford and Stone, he noticed a device planted on the underside of the vehicle. He bent down to investigate it and accidentally triggered one of the anti-tampering switches, detonating the bomb. Hamilton-Fairley and his two dogs were killed instantly. The bomb had been intended for Sir Hugh, whose regular morning routine would have seen him depart before his neighbour passed by but on the morning in question, he had been delayed by a telephone call.[206] The attack had particular international significance because an intended passenger in Sir Hugh's car that morning was Caroline Kennedy, the daughter of the late President John F. Kennedy. She had been staying with the Fraser family whilst taking an art appreciation course at Sotheby's auction house.

Caroline Kennedy had experienced what the *New York Times* described as a 'narrow escape', and the *Boston Globe* considered that 'this brings the tragedy much closer to most Americans than have most other terrorist acts'.[207] The British government spotted an opportunity to publicise the attack in an attempt to undermine the IRA's credibility within the United States. Elliott Richardson, the US Ambassador to the UK, was asked to approach Ted Kennedy, Caroline's uncle, to ask the Senator to issue a statement condemning IRA fundraising in the United States. Time was of the essence, as the Foreign Office noted: 'we have to recognise that it is most unlikely that he will speak out during an election year'.[208] Others within the Foreign Office felt that Kennedy 'had been reluctant earlier to say anything in case it had been interpreted as the consequence in some way of his daughter's [*sic*] escape from the bombing attack in London'.[209]

---

[206] *The Times*, 24/10/1975. During his much later public downfall, it was revealed that Aitken had been having an affair with Sir Hugh's wife, Antonia; see *Independent*, 20/1/1999.
[207] *NYT*, October 24, 1975; *Boston Globe*, 27/10/1975; McKittrick et al., *Lost Lives*, p. 588.
[208] Letter from J Hartland-Swann, FCO, Republic of Ireland Dept to Sykes, 8/3/1976, IRA Fundraising in the USA, FCO 87/577, TNA.
[209] Note for the Record on Meeting with Ambassador Elliott Richardson, 15/1/1976, IRA Fund-raising in the USA, FCO 87/575, TNA.

The Balcombe Street Gang was captured a few weeks later after they were spotted opening fire at Scott's, a Mayfair restaurant. The restaurant had been bombed three weeks earlier. After a chase, the IRA volunteers were cornered in a flat in Balcombe Street in the Marylebone area of London, where they took two residents hostage. Following a five-day siege, they surrendered, and in February 1977 were given forty-seven life sentences at the Old Bailey.[210]

After seeking Kennedy's support and finding the Senator reluctant to speak out against IRA fundraising in the United States, the British government had to navigate the issue themselves. Irish Northern Aid was still active in fundraising, though remittances began to drop in early 1975.[211] The group featured in a December 1975 piece in the *New York Times*, and were described by Bernard Weinraub as 'a relief organization for Roman Catholic women and children in Ulster ... which operates out of a storefront at 273 East 194th Street'.[212] Two days later, the same newspaper reported the speech delivered by British Prime Minister Harold Wilson at the annual dinner of the Association of American Correspondents in London:

> Those who subscribe to the Irish Northern Aid Committee are not financing the welfare of the Irish people, as they might delude themselves. They are financing murder. When they contribute their dollars for the old country, they are not helping their much-loved shamrock to flower. They are splashing blood on it. Nor are they helping the minority Catholic population.[213]

He continued that this money had 'directly financed these murders, this maiming, this indiscriminate bombing' in what Weinraub considered to be the 'strongest denunciation by a British Prime Minister of the American group and of support among Americans for the I.R.A.'.[214] By coincidence, that same month a group of Irish Americans were indicted on charges of smuggling 378 rifles and 140,000 rounds of ammunition to the IRA from August 1970. They were also charged with attempting

---

[210]   *Guardian*, 10/4/1999. They were released under the terms of the Good Friday Agreement in April 1999.
[211]   Summary of Noraid Returns to the US Department of Justice, in Ireland and US Policy on Northern Ireland, TAOIS/2009/135/745, NAI.
[212]   *NYT*, 16/12/1975.
[213]   *NYT*, 18/12/1975.
[214]   Ibid.

to purchase rocket-launchers, mortars, and machine guns.[215] These high-capacity weapons were an important part in the IRA's strategy to escalate their campaign after their ceasefire officially ended in 1976.

The IRA remained officially on ceasefire in the early days of the New Year, but the murders of six Catholics and ten Protestants in blatantly sectarian attacks on consecutive nights signalled that this would soon end.[216] With Northern Ireland seemingly on the brink of an all-out sectarian civil war, the British Government deployed the Special Air Service to South Armagh.[217] Sean Donlon, formerly the Irish Consul General in New York but now a Department of Foreign Affairs adviser to FitzGerald, communicated concerns to the US Embassy in Dublin that the Wilson statement and the fact that the UK had deployed the SAS to South Armagh were implicitly critical of Dublin's attitude towards border security and an indication of bilateral tension over the issue of border security in Ireland.[218]

These attacks had drawn international attention, with the Kingsmill massacre making front-page news in the *New York Times* and the *Washington Post*. Around this time, Northern Ireland Minister of State Stanley Orme flew to the United States on an industrial promotion tour where he would visit Chicago, Dallas, and New York to talk with senior executives about investing in Northern Ireland.[219] The message he delivered was to 'invest in jobs, not in guns'.[220] The issue of gun-running still troubled officials from the United States, UK, and the Republic of Ireland, and Orme's trip drew the attention of both the Attorney General Edward Levi and National Security Advisor Brent Scowcroft.[221] The American figures prepared for engagement on 'the illicit gun-running', which Scowcroft was advised 'clearly

[215]   *NYT*, 23/12/1975.
[216]   McKittrick et al., *Lost Lives*, pp. 609–614.
[217]   Sanders and Wood, *Times of Troubles*, pp. 151–152.
[218]   Briefing item (undated), Irish Government's Assessment of Developments in Northern Ireland, National Security Adviser, NSC Europe, Canada, and Ocean Affairs Staff, Files 1974–1977, Country Files, Ireland, 1974, NSC, Box 12, Ford Library.
[219]   *IT*, 6/1/1976.
[220]   *IT*, 7/1/1976.
[221]   Memorandum for the Attorney General, 15/1/1976, Foreign Policy Implications of Use of American-Supplied Weapons in Northern Ireland, National Security Adviser, NSC Europe, Canada, and Ocean Affairs Staff, Files 1974–1977, Country Files, Ireland, 1974, NSC, Box 12, Ford Library.

adversely affects our bilateral relations with both Ireland and the UK. The problem is not decreasing. It is possible that it may spring up in a presidential press conference'.[222]

Taoiseach Liam Cosgrave spent St Patrick's Day 1976 in Washington, also marking the US bicentennial on his visit. Cosgrave addressed a joint session of Congress on St Patrick's Day, giving what the *New York Times* called 'an unusually timely and relevant speech'.[223] The report added that 'the true significance of the Taoiseach's speech lay in his eloquent condemnation of violence as an instrument for advancing Irish unity and his warning to Americans of the terrible folly of assisting the Ulster terrorists'. Cosgrave, who had visited Harold Wilson in London before travelling to the United States, emphasised that 'what [groups such as Noraid] are doing ... with every penny, dime or dollar they give thoughtlessly for such purposes, is helping to kill or maim Irish men and women of every religious persuasion in Ireland'.[224] This was also the theme of a joint communiqué issued by the Taoiseach and President Ford.[225] Cosgrave left Washington and travelled to Philadelphia, Chicago, and New York, all major business centres with large Irish populations, with a view to spurring economic investment in Ireland.[226] The Irish considered the visit to be an 'unqualified success and significant contribution to US–Irish relations'.[227]

The State Department had identified increased US investment in Northern Ireland as a possibly useful strategy that could 'provide more jobs and thus combat high unemployment and general depressed

---

[222] Memorandum for Brent Scowcroft from Clift, 13/1/1976, National Security Adviser, NSC Europe, Canada, and Ocean Affairs Staff, Files 1974–1977, Country Files, Ireland, 1974, NSC, Box 12, Ford Library.

[223] *NYT*, 19/3/1976.

[224] *NYT*, 17/3/1976 and 19/3/1976.

[225] Communiqué by the President of the United States and the Prime Minister of Ireland, following discussions held in Washington, DC, 17/3/1976, National Security Adviser, NSC Europe, Canada, and Ocean Affairs Staff, Files 1974–1977, Country Files, Ireland, 1974, NSC, Box 12, Ford Library.

[226] Meeting with Liam Cosgrave, Prime Minister of the Republic of Ireland, 17/3/1976, draft notes, 15/3/1976, National Security Adviser, NSC Europe, Canada, and Ocean Affairs Staff, Files 1974–1977, Country Files, Ireland, 1974, NSC, Box 12, Ford Library.

[227] Telegram from State Department to American Embassy, Dublin, 24/3/1976, National Security Adviser, NSC Europe, Canada, and Ocean Affairs Staff, Files 1974–1977, Country Files, Ireland, 1974, NSC, Box 12, Ford Library.

economic conditions on which political instability and terrorism feed'.[228] To this end, the impact of the Ireland Funds, an organisation that held its first annual dinner on 26 May 1976, was significant.

The first annual Ireland Funds dinner was hosted by former Irish rugby international and Chief Operating Officer of Heinz, Anthony O'Reilly, and Dan Rooney, the owner of the Pittsburgh Steelers, at the Waldorf Astoria hotel in New York. Despite the prominence of the two men, in particular Rooney, whose team had just won the second of back-to-back Super Bowl titles, they could not muster a significant crowd for their event. Rooney and O'Reilly would both later joke that the second dinner, held in May 1977, was only held to pay for the first.[229] Rooney recalled that, despite the relative struggles of the first dinner, 'we just kept going. We started off with our papers in a shoebox and graduated to a file box once we started to do half way decent'.[230] Their second annual dinner enjoyed a higher profile and featured speeches from Edward Kennedy and John Hume. Hume's speech focused on the issue of IRA fundraising within the United States: 'while the killing in Northern Ireland goes on, let no American have it on his conscience that his efforts or his dollars helped to make the violence worse'.[231] The funds raised at this event were part of a half-million-dollar contribution sent to Ireland during the first three years of The Ireland Fund's existence. From there, the fund went from strength to strength and in 1978 raised nearly half a million dollars in a single event, a dinner in honour of Tip O'Neill. This was evidence both of their rapid growth and the power of O'Neill, who had just been elected Speaker of the House of Representatives.[232]

Irish America and the H-Blocks Campaign

The introduction of the 1976 Prevention of Terrorism Act began to reshape the conflict in Northern Ireland. In a speech to the House of

---

[228] Memorandum from State Department to Clift, 10/3/1976, 'US Interests and Policy Objectives for Ireland 1976', National Security Adviser, NSC Europe, Canada, and Ocean Affairs Staff, Files 1974–1977, Country Files, Ireland, 1974, NSC, Box 12, Ford Library.

[229] Rooney, D., *My 75 Years with the Pittsburgh Steelers and the NFL* (Philadelphia: Da Capo, 2007), p. 177.

[230] Dan Rooney, interview with author, 21/10/2013.

[231] *NYT*, 19/5/1977.

[232] *NYT*, 21/5/1978.

Commons on 25 March 1976, Secretary of State for Northern Ireland Merlyn Rees spoke of the need to achieve 'the primacy of the police'.[233] Police primacy was a significant part of the 'Ulsterisation' strategy that was designed to create a security solution appropriate to the Northern Ireland conflict. A further dimension was the abolition of special category status for paramilitary prisoners, which had been introduced in 1972 and heavily criticised in the 1975 Gardiner Report. As it was phased out, all newly convicted prisoners were subject to treatment as ordinary prisoners: made to wear prison uniform, conduct prison work, and serve their sentences in the recently constructed Maze prison at Long Kesh. This new prison facility had caught the attention of New York lawyer Paul O'Dwyer, who wrote to President Ford appealing for an intervention.[234]

The ending of special category status also prompted a response inside the prisons of Northern Ireland. IRA volunteer Kieran Nugent arrived in prison on 14 September 1976 and refused to wear the prison issue uniform, thereby launching the blanket protest. This escalated into a no-wash 'dirty' protest, at which point the protest began to attract the attention of figures in the United States.[235] Irish America had previously rallied round IRA prisoner Frank Stagg, who died on a hunger strike in Wakefield Prison in England in February 1976, prompting a large protest march in Manhattan.[236]

A wider culture of protest emerged over the summer of 1976, with a major peace group evolving out of yet another tragedy in the litany of tragedies that had become life in Northern Ireland during the 1970s. It stemmed from an incident where an IRA volunteer was shot dead by a British soldier during a car chase in west Belfast. The car being driven by the IRA man ran out of control and drove into the Maguire family, killing three children. Betty Williams, who witnessed the incident, went on to form a group called The Peace People, with Mairead Corrigan, the aunt of the three children.[237] The Peace People quickly garnered

[233] Northern Ireland, Hansard HC vol. 908, cols 641–674 (25 March 1976), available at https://api.parliament.uk/historic-hansard/commons/1976/mar/25/northern-ireland.
[234] Telegram from Paul O'Dwyer, New York City Council President, to Gerald R. Ford, 16/10/1975, White House Central Files, Subject Files, ND18/CO 40–ND18/CO160, Box 35, Ford Library.
[235] *NYT*, 22/5/1978.
[236] *NYT*, 1/3/1976.
[237] McKittrick et al., *Lost Lives*, pp. 669–670.

international attention, and an article in the *New York Times*, merely two weeks after their foundation, detailed the multiple death threats that Williams had received.

The actions of the troops involved in the incident drew the scrutiny of the European Commission on Human Rights, which was also conscious of the fatal shooting of a twelve-year-old girl in South Armagh that same month.[238] The ECHR published an 8,400-page report on allegations of torture made against the British security forces, accusing them of 'torture and inhuman and degrading treatment' against internees. It discussed the use of the so-called 'five techniques' of interrogation and concluded that these were in contravention of the 1950 European Convention on Human Rights.[239] Peter Kilborn, writing in the *New York Times*, suggested that the findings were 'likely to aggravate the ill-concealed bitterness of relations between the British and the Irish Governments'.[240] As the United States moved towards the Presidential election of November 1976, it was perhaps inevitable that the issue of Northern Ireland would feature on an electoral platform.

The 1976 Presidential Election

"We have not, since 1968 when the present Irish troubles began, had a Democratic President and we have no experience of how Democratic Party pressure may cause him to act on Ireland."[241] These were the words of one British civil servant, writing to a colleague, as the inauguration of President Jimmy Carter approached. The possibility of a Democratic President dramatically altering the US approach to the conflict in Northern Ireland had become a matter of concern when reports emerged in the British media that Senator Daniel Patrick Moynihan, during the drafting of the party's election platform, had suggested the inclusion of a line that declared that 'the United States should encourage the formation of a united Ireland'.[242] It was noted

---

[238]   *NYT*, 22/8/1976.
[239]   The five techniques were hooding of prisoners, enforced wall-standing, loud noise, starvation, and sleep deprivation. *Washington Post*, 27/8/1976.
[240]   *NYT*, 28/8/1976.
[241]   Letter from I.M. Burns to P.L.V. Mallet, RID, FCO, 13/1/1977, in US Presidential Election and Northern Ireland, CJ 4/1835, TNA.
[242]   *Guardian*, 17/6/1976.

that 'there was laughter round the table when Mr Moynihan proposed the plank [but] no one, including Jimmy Carter's representatives, opposed it'.[243] The Foreign Office investigated these claims and noted that another proposed inclusion was for a call for British withdrawal from Northern Ireland.[244] The official finalised platform, predictably, contained no such language.

There was a series of incidents during the run-up to the election that gave the British cause for concern, however. On St Patrick's Day 1976, a photograph was taken of Georgia Governor Jimmy Carter as he marched in the New York City parade. At this parade, Carter, who at the time had won five of the six Democratic primary contests, was photographed wearing a badge that read 'England get out of Ireland', an approved slogan for the parade.[245] The photograph was first published in *The Economist* of 17 April 1976 and captioned, 'A man with God on his mind', with both the magazine and the candidate seemingly totally oblivious to the message on the badge. A few weeks later, the same magazine published an article which described Carter's view on the situation in Northern Ireland as being 'apparently ... that the British and Irish should solve the problem of Ulster together'.[246]

There is little evidence of the photograph creating any political unrest in either the United Kingdom or the United States until late October, long after the nomination had been secured, when Carter's campaign team became aware that London's *Daily Express* newspaper was set to republish the photograph. Carter had just appeared at an event in Pittsburgh which was organised by the Irish National Caucus. *The Irish People*, the newspaper of Irish Northern Aid, reported him as having commented that 'it is a mistake for our country's Government to stand quiet on the struggle of the Irish for peace and for the respect

---

[243]   *Guardian*, 15/6/1976.

[244]   Attachments to letter from J. Davidson to M. Hodge, RID, FCO, 17/6/1976, Amendments on Ireland Proposed and Rejected at Democratic Party Platform Meeting, in US Presidential Election and Northern Ireland, CJ 4/1835, TNA.

[245]   *NYT*, 15/3/1976. The *Irish Times* reported Carter as wearing a badge reading, 'I love New York', 18/3/1976.

[246]   *The Economist*, 17/4/1976, p. 31, and 8/5/1976. See also Draft Minute, President-Elect Carter and Northern Ireland, in US Presidential Election and Northern Ireland, CJ 4/1835, TNA.

of human rights and for unifying Ireland'.[247] The British were somewhat consoled by reports that the Irish government 'had been furious', about the meeting.[248]

A 'nervous' member of Carter's team made contact with the Foreign Office's information department to assure them that, rather than having worn such a badge at the event in Pittsburgh, 'one had been pinned to his lapel in New York in the St Patrick's Day parade and that a photograph had been taken before he was able to take it off'.[249] There are, however, two very distinct photographs of Carter wearing the badge, the one published in *The Economist* and a second photograph which was taken by the Associated Press photographer Richard Drew. The pictures seem to have been taken at different times and neither gives the impression that Carter was even aware of the fact that the badge was neatly positioned on his lapel.

These events prompted the publication of a statement as well as a personal memo to Irish Minister for Foreign Affairs Garret FitzGerald. In both, Carter emphasised that, 'I do not favour violence as part of a solution to the Irish question. I favour negotiations and peaceful means for finding a just solution which involves the two communities of Northern Ireland and protects human rights which have been threatened'.[250] The statements suggested to the British that 'Carter must realise that he stirred up a hornet's nest at Pittsburgh (whatever he actually said there)'.[251] His campaign team strongly emphasised that 'Governor Carter has never advocated violence as part of the solution to the tragic problems of Northern Ireland. He has never endorsed the tactics of organisations which either implicitly or explicitly advocate such a solution'.[252] The British were unconcerned by the prospects of Carter advocating for Irish nationalism:

Despite the fact that there are pockets of Irish-American

[247]   *Irish People*, 6/11/1976.
[248]   Memorandum from R.M. Russell to G.W. Harding, RID, FCO, 5/11/1976, in US Presidential Election and Northern Ireland, CJ 4/1835, TNA.
[249]   Telegram from Ramsbotham to FCO, 29/10/1976, in US Presidential Election and Northern Ireland, CJ 4/1835, TNA.
[250]   Telegram from Ramsbotham Washington to FCO, 28/10/1976; Carter message to Fitzgerald, in US Presidential Election and Northern Ireland, CJ 4/1835, TNA.
[251]   Letter from I.M. Burns to P.L.V. Mallet, RID, FCO, 13/1/1977 in US Presidential Election and Northern Ireland, CJ 4/1835, TNA.
[252]   Telegram from Ramsbotham Washington to FCO, 28/10/1976; Carter message to Fitzgerald, in US Presidential Election and Northern Ireland, CJ 4/1835, TNA.

sympathisers in the State Department, it seems unlikely that we have anything to fear from President Carter, at least for the time being. The constraints of the office of the President are likely to prevent him from making any further potentially controversial remarks on Northern Ireland, even should he wish to. The Pittsburgh speech must be looked at in its correct context, as part of the final run-in at the end of a long and close-fought election campaign and at a stage when, with opinion polls suggesting a very close result, every vote was important. Furthermore, it is unlikely that Carter will wish to indulge in unnecessary polemic when, even as a lame duck, he will be assuming the complicated reins of government.[253]

Despite claims that 'Northern Ireland is of little importance in the whole gamut of American domestic and foreign policy issues', made within the UK government over the weeks following Carter's election in November 1976, the new President nevertheless felt compelled to issue an unprecedented statement on Northern Ireland in August 1977.[254]

[253]   Draft Minute, President-Elect Carter and Northern Ireland, in US Presidential Election and Northern Ireland, CJ 4/1835, TNA.
[254]   Memorandum from D.A. Hill, 24/11/1976, and Memorandum from E.J. Hughes, 3/12/1976; Governor Carter and Northern Ireland, in US Presidential Election and Northern Ireland, CJ 4/1835, TNA.

CHAPTER THREE

Jimmy Carter and the Presidential Statement on Northern Ireland

On Saturday, 1 January 1977, Graeme Dougan was sat on his mother's knee in his family car, ready to evacuate his home in Harmin Park, Glengormley, on the northern outskirts of Belfast. A car bomb alert had been raised for the area and the Royal Ulster Constabulary were going door to door to warn residents to leave until the alert was over. The bomb exploded nearby, and debris struck and killed the fifteen-month-old child who became one of the youngest victims of the troubles.[1] A little over a year later, in May of 1978, John Bateson, Rory O'Connor, and John Watson were sentenced for the murder. Bateson received six life sentences, whilst O'Connor and Watson received sixteen years for manslaughter.[2]

Dougan may not have been the target of the IRA's bomb but one must question who, in a residential area of Belfast, really was. Dougan is listed in *Lost Lives*, the most authoritative account of the victims of the Northern Ireland troubles, as the 1,867th victim. He was, according to the Sutton Index of Deaths, the 1,030th civilian victim. The criminal indifference to the lives of innocent civilians, a mark of all sides throughout the Northern Ireland troubles, was heavily present on New Year's Day 1977 in North Belfast.

On 20 January 1977, James Earl Carter, Jr., the former Governor of Georgia, was inaugurated as the 39th President of the United States. Carter's election brought another President to the White House with Irish roots; in his case, Scots-Irish.[3] During his Presidency, the United

---

[1]   McKittrick et al., *Lost Lives*, p. 698.
[2]   *IT*, 27/5/1978.
[3]   *Time*, 22/8/1977 and *Irish America*, April/May 2009. He also has English heritage.

States would take great steps towards formalising its role as a partner in the Northern Irish peace process. The changing patterns of the conflict in the mid-1970s facilitated what became a significant, if often overlooked, intervention from an American President. The mid to late 1970s, in particular 1976, was a pivotal time in the Northern Irish conflict. Police primacy was reintroduced as the British government attempted to redefine the dynamics of their security operation in Northern Ireland. Special Category Status for paramilitary prisoners was abolished as part of a normalisation strategy, a move which would provoke a protest within the prisons of the province that would culminate in the 1981 hunger strike.

The improving security operation had become increasingly effective against the Provisional Irish Republican Army. Richard English has observed that this was a 'difficult [period] for the Provisional movement: Volunteers were being imprisoned in large numbers and military momentum was stalling'.[4] Power within the movement had shifted northwards in 1976 with the Ulster-based Northern Command taking control of overall Provisional strategy. With the six counties of Northern Ireland representing the focus of the campaign, this was a logical move on the part of the republican leadership. As a volunteer, imprisoned at the time for her role in the bombing of the Old Bailey, Marian Price later reflected, 'we're not designed for a long war we're designed for a short sharp hit and then retreat'.[5] The reaction to Bloody Sunday, which had driven young people towards republican paramilitarism, had somewhat dissipated and the British security forces had managed to avoid any further provocative actions. The 'short sharp hit', which Price refers to, by 1977 had become a full five years long for the volunteers who signed up in the aftermath of Bloody Sunday.

Part of the new strategy devised by northern leaders was the creation of a cell structure for the organisation. The old brigade and company structure, which mirrored that of a traditional army, had compromised the movement as the security forces developed more effective intelligence-gathering techniques, notably the use of informers. Under the new structure, volunteers were only familiar with the members and operations of their own cell, thereby limiting the damage that informers could inflict on the movement. The IRA also completed its 'Green Book' around this time, a manual which detailed the aims

---

[4]   English, *Armed Struggle*, p. 212.
[5]   Marian Price, interview with author, 1/7/2010.

and objectives of the movement.[6] The military campaign would become considerably more focused on British security targets after the killing of the infant in Glengormley on New Year's Day, but no less brutal. By the end of January, the IRA had killed three soldiers and two RUC officers in a series of gun and bomb attacks across Northern Ireland.

There was significant political upheaval in the United States, United Kingdom, and Republic of Ireland during this period, with all three seeing significant changes in administration. Carter, the first Democratic President since the outbreak of the troubles in Northern Ireland, would also be the last Democratic President until the 1992 election of Bill Clinton. He would serve only a single term and was soundly beaten by the Republican Ronald Reagan in the 1980 Presidential election. In the UK, the Conservatives under Margaret Thatcher succeeded the Labour government of Jim Callaghan. Thatcher's famously close relationship with Ronald Reagan heavily influenced White House policy towards Northern Ireland throughout the 1980s. Meanwhile, in the Republic of Ireland, Jack Lynch brought Fianna Fáil back to power before a dramatic resignation saw the controversial Charles Haughey succeed him as Taoiseach.

During the early years of the decade, Irish-American organisations had established themselves as major sources of moral and financial support for military Irish republicanism. This began to change, largely thanks to the interventions of Senator Edward Kennedy and Speaker Tip O'Neill and their group of like-minded Irish-American politicians, which evolved into the Congressional Friends of Ireland in 1981. Through their emergence as leaders of substance for the Irish-American communities, particularly in the north-eastern United States, they were effective in cutting support for radical groups such as the Irish Northern Aid Committee and the Irish National Caucus.

Northern Ireland during the Carter Years

President Jimmy Carter was inaugurated at noon on Thursday, 20 January 1977. His commitment to civil and human rights would be a mark of his Presidency, as well as his post-Presidential career, and was emphasised in his inaugural address:

---

[6]   See English, *Armed Struggle*, pp. 213–214.

The passion for freedom is on the rise. Tapping this new spirit, there can be no nobler nor more ambitious task for America to undertake on this day of a new beginning than to help shape a just and peaceful world that is truly humane … Because we are free we can never be indifferent to the fate of freedom elsewhere. Our moral sense dictates a clearcut preference for these societies which share with us an abiding respect for individual human rights. We do not seek to intimidate, but it is clear that a world which others can dominate with impunity would be inhospitable to decency and a threat to the well-being of all people.[7]

A few hours later in Northern Ireland, the Irish Republican Army planted three incendiary devices in John Frazer's clothes store in Castle Street in Belfast. A fire was spotted in the store at 1.30 a.m. The owner arrived at the store and attempted to enter the building to locate his security officer, fifty-three-year-old Catholic James McColgan, but was unable to do so. Firemen with respiratory equipment managed to find McColgan but were unable to resuscitate him. Later that day, Catholic lorry driver Michael McHugh, a prominent member of the local Sinn Féin party, was shot dead by the Ulster Freedom Fighters near his farmhouse in County Tyrone.[8] A further six people were killed before the end of January 1977, two of whom were members of the security forces. The toll of civilian deaths had passed through the one thousand barrier in 1976.[9]

With control of Northern Irish security passing to the Royal Ulster Constabulary in March 1976, the British Army returned to a support role more akin to its original Northern Ireland objective of 'aid to the civil power'. The increased presence of police officers on the streets of Northern Ireland brought an increase in attacks on police personnel. Twenty-one RUC officers were killed in 1976, an increase of eleven from the previous year, but that figure dropped in 1977 as the IRA's new cell structure brought with it a more focused campaign of violence. It had long targeted the Northern Irish economy, but the New Year brought with it a new dimension to the economic campaign in the form of the assassinations of prominent businessmen. This began on 2 February when English businessman Jeffrey Agate, the Managing Director of the

---

[7]   Inaugural Address of Jimmy Carter, 20/1/1977, Yale Law School, the Avalon Project, available at http://avalon.law.yale.edu/20th_century/carter.asp.
[8]   McKittrick et al., pp. 699–700.
[9]   Security force deaths at the time stood at 463.

Du Pont factory in Derry, was shot dead by the IRA outside his home in Talbot Park, Derry as he arrived home from work.

Du Pont, an American petrochemical company, was a significant source of employment in the Derry area. In 1966, it built its fourth plant in Derry, bringing their total payroll up to approximately 1,500 employees. At the time, Agate announced that the United States-based company would have to expand its apprenticeship training scheme.[10] The creation of these jobs was particularly significant because it occurred just as Minister of Commerce Brian Faulkner forecast a downturn in British industry.[11] By mid-1975, Du Pont was responsible for nearly 2,000 employees across its four factories.[12]

Agate was well known and well respected in the local business community. He had been awarded an OBE in the Queen's birthday honours list in 1968.[13] In early 1969, he was appointed to the Derry Commission, a nine-person board which included four Catholics, a decision which drew protest from nationalists like Republican Labour Party member of the Stormont Parliament, Harry Diamond.[14] In September 1970, Prime Minister James Chichester-Clark appointed him to the Northern Ireland Economic Council and in February 1971 he joined the new Derry Development Commission.[15] After Agate's killing, Brian Faulkner said, 'it is unrewarding simply to condemn this callous outrage. Those of us who remain can still hope that it may help to produce the ultimate revulsion'. Alderman James Hegarty, the nationalist mayor of Derry, described Agate as a 'true friend of Derry'.[16] Despite the murder of Agate, DuPont did not withdraw from Derry.

One week later, Provisional IRA volunteer Raymond McCartney appeared at Belfast Magistrates Court charged with the murder, along with that of Detective Constable Liam McNulty on 27 January. McCartney had been held in Castlereagh police station and complained about his treatment whilst in custody.[17] He was convicted of both murders and sentenced to two life sentences, with the recommendation

---

[10]   *IT*, 25/5/1966.
[11]   *IT*, 29/8/1966.
[12]   *IT*, 21/8/1975.
[13]   *IT*, 8/6/1968.
[14]   *IT*, 31/1/1969.
[15]   *IT*, 11/9/1970 and 5/2/1971.
[16]   *IT*, 7/2/1977.
[17]   *IT*, 9/2/1977.

that he serve at least twenty-five years.[18] He was released from prison
in 1994 and in 2004 was elected as a Member of the Northern Ireland
Assembly for the Foyle constituency. His convictions were overturned
in February 2007.[19]

Agate's murder marked the start of an IRA murder campaign
against prominent businessmen. The IRA argued: 'they represent and
maintain economic interests which make the war necessary'.[20] The
logic of the assassination campaign was not far removed from that of
the bombing campaign which began in central Belfast in 1971: if local
business and services were undermined, then Northern Ireland would
struggle to maintain economic viability and eventually the United
Kingdom would grow tired of the unending expense of maintaining
the state and withdraw.

There were, however, issues of purpose inherent in the IRA's
campaign against economic targets. It was essential that the IRA
maintain discipline in order to adhere to a longer-term strategy,
something that was all the more difficult when the thirst for violence
among volunteers grew strong, as was often the case in the aftermath of
a controversial action on the part of the security forces. The Provisional
IRA took a long time to realise that, rather than convincing the public
to pressure the government to cede to their demands, the endangering,
injuring, and killing of innocent civilians had the opposite effect.
Even in cases where their bombing targets were large businesses, the
inevitably imprecise nature of a bomb attack tended to put the public in
danger of death or serious injury. The IRA had not learned these lessons
from the backlash following two of their most notorious bombings: the
Abercorn restaurant on 4 March 1972 and Bloody Friday, 21 July 1972.
These attacks killed two and eleven, respectively.

The assassination of leading industrialists offered the IRA more
strategic precision but depended on the perception that the people
they killed were representatives of industry, and not relatively ordinary
people with families. On 23 November 1976, Joseph Glover, a chartered
accountant and former president of the Londonderry Chamber of
Commerce, was shot nine times by the IRA at the timber yard where
he worked in a very clear case of assassination.[21] After Jeffrey Agate

18 *IT*, 27/10/1980.
19 *IT*, 12/5/2011.
20 McKittrick et al., *Lost Lives*, p. 702.
21 Ibid., p. 690.

was killed, Peter Hill, a forty-five-year-old businessman who worked in a Derry furniture and drapery firm, was shot dead by the IRA as he returned home from work on 23 February. He was still listed as a member of the UDR at the time of his death, even though he had retired the day before he was killed.[22]

The murders of prominent businessmen was exclusively the purview of the Derry Brigade of the IRA until retired businessman Robert Mitchell was shot dead on 26 February by the IRA at his home near Newry.[23] Soon after, on 2 March, Donald Robinson, the managing director of a ceilings firm was shot dead in his Belfast office by the IRA.[24] On 14 March, English businessman James Nicholson was shot dead by the IRA as he left the premises of Strathearn Audio in Belfast. Paddy Devlin of the SDLP commented that 'the clear intention of the organisation behind the killing is to sabotage the efforts of those who have been striving to bring industry to west Belfast'.[25] Seamus Twomey, the IRA's Chief of Staff, commented:

> One of the major reasons for the attacks on British businessmen is what is happening to our prisoners who are being brutalized in jails in England and Ireland. We hit a type of person that can bring pressure on the British Government. I would like to state clearly that is one of the major reasons for the hitting [*sic*] of businessmen. Irrespective of what politicians say or what they don't say these sort of people are part and parcel of the British establishment and can bring pressure to bear on the British Government.[26]

The IRA had previously attempted to kidnap businesspeople and demand ransoms in exchange for their safe return during the early 1970s. This tactic ended disastrously with the death of German industrialist Thomas Niedermayer in December 1973 who died whilst being held captive. His remains were found in a wood on the outskirts

---

[22] Ibid., p. 704.
[23] Ibid., pp. 705–706.
[24] Ibid., p. 707.
[25] Ibid., p. 709.
[26] *Hibernia*, 1/4/1977, cited in Ross, F.S., *Smashing H Block: The Popular Campaign against Criminalization and the Irish Hunger Strikes, 1976–1982* (Liverpool: Liverpool University Press, 2011), p. 36 n. 14. See also Moloney, E., *A Secret History of the IRA* (London: Penguin, 2003), p. 185.

of Belfast in March 1980.[27] Their kidnapping of Tiede Herrema in Limerick in October 1975 was somewhat more successful in that the Dutch businessman survived his ordeal but the IRA demands for the release of prisoners were not met and Herrema was freed after a siege in Monaleen.[28] The financial merits of a kidnap and ransom campaign began to dwindle after the IRA became the recipients of financial assistance and armaments from the United States and Libya.[29]

The strategic changes within the IRA at this time were reflective of the internal changes that the movement was experiencing, some of which were a matter of necessity. On 3 December, Seamus Twomey was arrested by Gardaí in Dun Laoghaire. During a search of the flat in which he had been staying, an IRA document was found which suggested that the IRA was debating the role of the army within the movement.[30] Twomey had, a few months previously, given an interview on French television in which he claimed that the IRA campaign could endure for decades.[31] The document discovered by Gardaí, however, suggested that the movement was in the process of shifting control from the military wing to Sinn Féin. As if to underline Twomey's defiance, the IRA ended the year with a series of firebomb attacks on hotels across Northern Ireland.

With Twomey again incarcerated, control of the movement passed to Gerry Adams, who had been released from prison earlier that year.[32] The time was ripe for the Provisional republican movement to make political advances and, under the Adams leadership, the transition discussed in the documents found at Twomey's flat began to take shape. Within this transition was the change in direction of the IRA's economic campaign. It was still, however, focused on driving industry from Northern Ireland, where unemployment rose to 60,000 in June 1977, the highest June figure since 1940.[33]

---

[27]   McKittrick et al., *Lost Lives*, pp. 410–411.
[28]   *Time*, 20/10/1975.
[29]   *An Phoblacht*, 21/7/2005.
[30]   English, *Armed Struggle*, p. 244.
[31]   Wharton, K., *Wasted Years, Wasted Lives Volume 1: The British Army in Northern Ireland 1975–1977* (Solihull: Helion, 2013), p. 394.
[32]   English, *Armed Struggle*, p. 110.
[33]   Northern Ireland (Emergency Provisions), Hansard, HC vol. 934, cols 633–683 (30 June 1977), available at https://api.parliament.uk/historic-hansard/commons/1977/jun/30/northern-ireland-emergency-provisions.

By killing businesspeople instead of kidnapping them, the IRA's 'economic' strategy had developed from one that attempted to exploit the presence of international industry in Northern Ireland to one that sought to intimidate it out of existence. The move also spoke to the lack of success that the IRA had enjoyed with its kidnapping strategy. The lack of financial demands for the release of Herrema and Niedermayer, whose freedom was reportedly offered in exchange for that of the Price sisters, was further evidence that the IRA enjoyed sufficient financial support, a significant proportion of which came from Irish-American benefactors. This meant that the economic campaign could focus on damaging the viability of Northern Ireland; in essence to make Northern Ireland too costly for Britain to support and force withdrawal.

Interestingly, the IRA was not the only organisation attempting to undermine Northern Irish industry in early 1977. Ian Paisley's United Unionist Action Council announced that it would hold a region-wide strike in May 1977 in order to demand tougher security responses from the British government, along with a return to Stormont rule. The strike lasted for thirteen days but largely failed in its goals of disrupting industry and commerce. Indeed, two days after the UUAC announced its strike, Secretary of State Roy Mason announced that the Harland and Wolff shipyard in Belfast was to receive an order to construct two liquid gas carriers worth roughly £70 million.

The Carter Statement, the Four Horsemen, and US Policy towards Northern Ireland

As noted in the previous chapter, the British government had carefully watched the 1976 Presidential election campaign, particularly the contest for the Democratic candidacy. Following Carter's narrow victory over Gerald Ford, they began to establish more formal ties with the new administration. Secretary of State for Northern Ireland Roy Mason, who had replaced Merlyn Rees in September 1976, reached out to American political figures as part of a move to establish common ground between the Callaghan and Carter governments over the issue of Northern Ireland. Over the course of 1977, he met Senator Edward Kennedy twice, once in May during Kennedy's visit to the United Kingdom and again in October during his own visit to Washington. The Speaker of the House of Representatives, Tip O'Neill, also attended the latter meeting. The record of the meeting noted:

Mr Mason expressed his gratitude on behalf of HMG [Her Majesty's Government] and the people of Northern Ireland for the responsible lead taken by [Kennedy, O'Neill, Governor Hugh Carey, and Senator Daniel Patrick Moynihan]. Partly as a result of this lead the terrorists were finding it increasingly difficult to find safe havens. He recognised the need to maintain the credibility of the responsibly leaders of the Irish American community on the issues of Northern Ireland and he did not wish in any way to contribute to the tarnishing of their political reputations.[34]

The so-called Four Horsemen—Kennedy, O'Neill, Carey, and Moynihan—all supported Irish unity but had been outspoken in their support for a non-violent solution to the Northern Ireland conflict and had been very helpful, from the UK perspective, in terms of undermining support for violent Irish republicans within the United States.[35] They did, however, seek to influence British policy on Northern Ireland and were frequently frustrated by the perceived inaction of the London government over Northern Irish issues. For their part, the UK welcomed their support for a non-violent solution but were frustrated by what they saw as attempts to interfere in British domestic policy. Retaining the support of the four without losing support for Northern Irish policy at home was a tricky task for Britain throughout the late 1970s. The Carter statement, which he issued on 30 August 1977, helped considerably:

It is natural that Americans are deeply concerned about the continuing conflict and violence in Northern Ireland. We know the overwhelming majority of people there reject the bomb and the bullet. The United States wholeheartedly supports peaceful means for finding a just solution that involves both parts of the community of Northern Ireland, protects human rights and guarantees freedom from discrimination—a solution that the people in Northern Ireland, as well as the Governments of Great Britain and Ireland can support. Violence cannot resolve Northern

[34] Record of Meeting between Secretary of State for Northern Ireland and Speaker O'Neill and Senator Kennedy, 17 October 1977 at 10.45 a.m. at the Capitol, in Senator Edward Kennedy interest in Northern Ireland, Foreign and Commonwealth/Political Matters, CJ 4/2389, TNA.
[35] In April 1977, Governor Carey visited Ireland where he met with Taoiseach Liam Cosgrave and addressed the Royal College of Surgeons in Dublin, condemning the 'killers' and 'Marxists' of the IRA. See *NYT*, 23/4/1977.

Ireland's problems: it only increases them, and solves nothing ... We hope that all those engaged in violence will renounce this course and commit themselves to the peaceful pursuit of legitimate goals. The path of reconciliation, co-operation and peace is the only course that can end the human suffering and lead to a better future for all the people of Northern Ireland. I ask all Americans to refrain from supporting, with financial or other aid, organisations whose involvement, direct or indirect, in this violence delays the day when the people of Northern Ireland can live and work together in harmony, free from fear. Federal law enforcement agencies will continue to apprehend and prosecute any who violates US laws in this regard ... US Government policy on the Northern Ireland has long been one of impartiality, and that is how it will remain.[36]

Relatively benign in substance, the statement nevertheless ran somewhat contrary to the previous US position of non-intervention. It was hardly what could reasonably be termed an official statement of intervention, but it established a precedent for future statements and offers of assistance that was hugely significant. British Ambassador Peter Jay noted that the British view of the possibility of United States Government aid to Northern Ireland was based 'on the exact words which the President used which were carefully chosen words', and focused more on the issue of private investment, which 'we welcome very much'.[37] The British had been aware that a statement was imminent, as were the Irish media, and were consulted by a number of figures within the US administration prior to its release.[38] It has been suggested that British officials, notably Secretary of State for Northern Ireland Roy Mason, were troubled by the statement and considered the utility of speaking out again in the context of continued investment in Northern Ireland from companies like Du Pont.[39]

Significantly, the Carter statement filled a void which had hitherto existed in terms of the official US policy towards Northern Ireland. This void had allowed more radical thinking to emerge within the structures

[36] Statement by President Carter, 30/8/1977, the US ban on the sale of arms for the Royal Ulster Constabulary, FCO 87/1219, TNA.
[37] *IT*, 20/1/1978.
[38] *Irish Independent*, 10/6/1977.
[39] *Times*, 20/11/1977; Dumbrell, J., *A Special Relationship: Anglo-American Relations in the Cold War and After* (Basingstoke: Macmillan, 2001), p. 202.

of American government and thereby legitimise the groups which adopted a far more radical stance on the Irish question in both Ireland and the United States, such as Noraid and the Irish National Caucus. The lack of concern within the British government at the possibility of Carter releasing a statement on Northern Ireland reflected the increased trust between the new President and the British after the missteps by Carter during his campaign for the presidency. Diplomats on either side worked together on the drafting of the statement and Carter's National Security Advisor, Zbigniew Brzezinski, was constantly briefed on the development of the statement, which was first passed through the offices of Senator Kennedy and Speaker O'Neill.[40]

The Carter statement might have been poorly received by some in London, but the cordial relationship between Carter and Callaghan was evident during their March 1977 meeting. Carter commented on Callaghan's 'superb leadership capability' while Callaghan noted his 'excitement' at the prospect of 'sharing your new hopes, your new aspirations, your intentions, your new policies, being here at the beginning of a new administration'.[41] Peter Jay, Callaghan's former son-in-law and his Ambassador to the United States, recalled:

> Callaghan and Carter really did have a special relationship, no doubt about that. Callaghan worked very hard to exploit [it], some of the foundations of it: that they had the same initials, that they both had a Methodist upbringing, etc, etc, were maybe a bit artificial if you like, but the truth of the matter was that they got on and the trusted each other. When Callaghan wandered across the Garden in Corsica where they had the meeting with the group of five and Callaghan made a basic deal with Carter about Trident and all that which was extremely important. They undoubtedly liked and trusted each other, the relationship was good.[42]

[40] Memorandum for Zbigniew Brzezinski, 19/7/1977, NLC-10-4-1-16-8, United Kingdom, Prime Minister Thatcher, 12/11/79: Briefing Book II, Jimmy Carter Presidential Library (hereafter Carter Library).
[41] Visit of Prime Minister James Callaghan of Great Britain, Remarks of the President and the Prime Minister at the Welcoming Ceremony, 10/3/1977, the American Presidency Project, available at https://www.presidency.ucsb.edu/ws?pid=7143.%20Peter%20Jay%2C%20interview%20with%20author%2C%20 7/12/2011.
[42] Peter Jay, interview with author, 7/12/2011.

The summer months saw the political landscape change once again with the election of Jack Lynch as Taoiseach, bringing Fianna Fáil back to power with a considerable majority. The importance of Irish issues to Callaghan was evident from the speed with which a meeting with the new Taoiseach was arranged; the two men meeting in London on 28 September 1977 to discuss Northern Ireland with a focus on economic co-operation across the Irish border. Early in 1977, the Northern Ireland office had expressed concern that:

> if a Fianna Fáil government were to be returned at the next Irish general election, it would seek to encourage Carter to adopt a less aloof stance than recent American governments, perhaps leading to American attempts (such as Fianna Fáil made in 1969) to internationalise the Northern Ireland situation; or even to pressure Carter to endorse a policy of British withdrawal from Northern Ireland.[43]

Journalist Mary Holland also noted that Edward 'Kennedy views it as a major breakthrough in his campaign, which he began by bringing pressure to bear on Henry Kissinger at the State Department, to "internationalise the issue" of Northern Ireland, by declaring a United States interest and position on the problem'.[44] Holland was, however, pessimistic about the prospect that the statement might have any significant impact on the issue of American intervention in Northern Ireland. Early versions of the statement included the proposal of a US pledge of $100 million which would have been submitted on the basis that a political solution to the conflict was imminent. It was omitted from the final statement. She also noted the hostility from the British Foreign and Commonwealth Office towards what it considered to be an unwarranted intrusion in the internal affairs of an ally by the United States.[45]

Roy Mason visited Washington in mid-October 1977, where he met with Speaker O'Neill and Senator Kennedy. During this meeting, O'Neill emphasised that:

> Many Irish thinking people had already been turned around. The flow of guns and money had been greatly reduced. These

[43] Letter from I.M. Burns to P.L.V. Mallet, RID, FCO, 13/1/1977, in US Presidential Election and Northern Ireland, CJ 4/1835, TNA.
[44] *Magill*, 2/10/1977. Holland also emphasises the influence of John Hume on the statement.
[45] *Magill*, 2/10/1977.

efforts of the Irish American leaders, however, had been at
some cost to their own political reputations, and they now felt
the need for some strong action from Britain to demonstrate
to the Irish American community that a responsible, moderate
stand was a better route to a settlement of the problems than
militancy or violence. It was not easy for the Four to 'keep the
lid on'.[46]

Around the same time, Mairead Corrigan and Betty Williams,
the founding members of the Peace People, were awarded the Nobel
Peace Prize.[47] Belfast City Corporation refused to hold a civic reception
in their honour, but Speaker O'Neill wrote to congratulate the Peace
People on their work which he considered to be a 'driving force for peace
and justice'.[48]

The Role of Jack Lynch and the Irish Government

New Year 1978 brought new challenges for the United Kingdom as
several prominent figures in the Republic of Ireland attempted to press
the British government, publicly, to act more decisively on Northern
Ireland. On 8 January, Taoiseach Jack Lynch appeared on RTÉ
and spoke about the possibility of an amnesty for Provisional IRA
volunteers as well as his desire for a British declaration in favour of
Irish unity. Eight days later, Tomas O Fiaich, the Catholic Primate
of Ireland, offered similar comment to the *Irish Press*.[49] Thirdly, on 18
January, the European Court of Human Rights ruled that internees
had been subjected to 'inhuman and degrading treatment' by British

---

[46] Record of Meeting between Secretary of State for Northern Ireland and
Speaker O'Neill and Senator Kennedy, 17 October 1977 at 10.45 a.m. at the
Capitol, in Senator Edward Kennedy interest in Northern Ireland, Foreign and
Commonwealth/Political Matters, CJ 4/2389, TNA.
[47] *NYT*, Biographical Service, vol. 8 (New York: NYT Press, 1977). Corrigan's
sister, Anne Maguire, took her own life four years later; see McKittrick et al.,
Lost Lives, p. 669.
[48] Telegram from O'Neill to Betty Williams and Mairead Corrigan, 14/10/1977,
in Congressional Archives, Thomas P. O'Neill Papers, Series II: Staff Files,
Subseries A: Kirk O'Donnell Files, Sub-Subseries 19-20: Box 21, 21/15 Ireland—
Community of the Peace People, 1979–1980 and 1977, John J. Burns Library,
Boston College (hereafter, BLBC).
[49] *Irish Press*, 16/1/1978.

security forces during 1971. It was careful, however, to note that it did not support the use of the word 'torture' to describe their treatment.

Lynch's comments, which some within the Northern Ireland Office considered 'extraordinary', were in fact rather more in line with official Irish government policy than many might have realised.[50] Sean Donlon, who would become Ireland's Ambassador in Washington later that year, commented to British representatives that they should not have been surprised by Lynch's remarks and that he had warned them that, after playing 'Northern Ireland in the low key for the first few months he was in office, he would have to make his position clear sooner or later'.[51]

Michael O'Kennedy, Lynch's Minister for Foreign Affairs, had twice spoken publicly towards the end of 1977, in the Dáil in October and at the Kings Inns Debating Society in November, and attacked the constitutional guarantee that Northern Ireland would not cease to be part of the United Kingdom without the consent of the majority of Northern Irish citizens. O'Kennedy described this as 'the negative British guarantee to the Unionists, which we believed to be unhelpful in the solution of the problem of Northern Ireland and in the establishment there of a lasting peace'.[52]

Misinterpretation of Lynch's comments was rather more striking in the United States, where Congressman Mario Biaggi, the head of the Ad Hoc Congressional Committee on Irish Affairs, was moved to write to the Taoiseach, offering his commendation 'on your recent call for a declaration of intent from Great Britain to withdraw her troops from Ireland. This action represents an important initiative toward establishing a peace which the people in the North of Ireland long for'.[53] Lynch responded:

> One of the obstacles to progress is violence which, though it has time and time again been rejected by the overwhelming

[50]   Brief for the Prime Minister, 'The Political Situation in Northern Ireland', The Situation in Northern Ireland: The US Initiative in Northern Ireland, PREM 16/1721, TNA.
[51]   Ford Conversation with Sean Donlon, 2/2/1978, in Irish Republic Relations with USA, CJ4/2257, TNA.
[52]   *Sunday Independent*, 29/1/1978.
[53]   Letter from Congressman Mario Biaggi to Lynch, 24/1/1978, in Ireland and US Policy on Northern Ireland, TAOIS/2009/135/745, National Archives of Ireland (NAI).

majority of the Irish people, emanates from extremists of both
political traditions and, in both cases, derives support and
encouragement from small groups outside the country. One
such group is the Irish National Caucus which, whatever its
recent pretensions to the contrary has been closely associated
with the cause of violence in Northern Ireland. It has been noted
in media reports that the Irish National Caucus termed the
establishment of your Ad Hoc Committee as a victory for itself
and that you yourself have visited Ireland at the request of the
Caucus. We in Ireland have also noted your public identification
when here with supporters of violence who have no democratic
mandate from our people.[54]

This response was well received by many, particularly Edward Kennedy
who wrote to Roy Mason in April to highlight that he believed that
'Prime Minister Lynch's letter to Congressman Biaggi has helped …
and we intend to do all we can to reduce the activities in this country
that encourage the violence'.[55] Kennedy's letter came quickly after
another St Patrick's Day statement from the Four Horsemen in support
of a peaceful solution in Northern Ireland.

Tip O'Neill did express concern that Lynch's criticism of Biaggi
might be counter-productive, but 'Mr Lynch apparently replied that
he considered it essential that he should have written as he had in his
letter to the Congressman and that he should continue to speak on those
lines'.[56] There was also concern within the British Foreign Office; one
letter to the Washington Embassy noted: 'The letter from the Taoiseach
may have checked Congressman Biaggi but it may not have entirely
stopped him from making headway with his ad hoc committee'.[57] The
committee was over one hundred members strong before the end of the

[54] Letter from Lynch to Biaggi, 17/2/1978, in Ireland and US Policy on Northern Ireland, TAOIS/2009/135/745, NAI.
[55] Letter from Kennedy to Roy Mason, 3/4/1978, in Senator Edward Kennedy interest in Northern Ireland, Foreign and Commonwealth/Political Matters, CJ 4/2389, TNA.
[56] Letter from W.R. Hayden, Embassy Dublin to P.L.V. Mallet, FCO, 6/6/1978, 'Lynch visit to USA', United States Congressional Hearings on Northern Ireland, FCO 87/779, TNA.
[57] Letter from P.L.V. Mallet, FCO to R.M. Russell, Embassy Washington, 23/2/1978, in Senator Edward Kennedy interest in Northern Ireland, Foreign and Commonwealth/Political Matters, CJ 4/2389, TNA.

year.[58] The Lynch–Biaggi exchange offered some hope that politicians might be able to reach agreement on the way forward for Northern Ireland, but events in the early weeks of 1978 served as a reminder that a cessation of violence was still some distance away.

On 17 February, the Irish Collie Club and the Northern Ireland Junior Motorcycle Club were holding functions at the La Mon House Hotel near Belfast. Just before 9.00 p.m. the hotel received a warning that three bombs had been left on the premises. The warning was received at the precise moment of the detonation of the first device. This device was primed with petrol, causing many of those inside the hotel to be doused in burning fuel. Detectives added that 'such explosive devices often included an amount of adhesive to make burning petrol stick on whatever it splashed. It must therefore have had a napalm like effect'.[59]

So grotesque was the scene at La Mon that Ted Kennedy described it as 'one of the worst atrocities committed in the entire eight years of violence in Northern Ireland'. Kennedy added that all Americans should ensure that 'no involvement of our own—neither our actions, nor our dollars, nor our words—contributes in any way to the violence in Northern Ireland'.[60] Anger within Protestant communities was visceral. Jean Coulter, the former Official Unionist Convention member, said that 'the Republican ghettoes should be bombed from the air. There were no innocent people in them'.[61] The IRA later admitted responsibility for the bombing in a statement:

> The Irish Republican Army admits responsibility for the bombing operation in the La Mon House in which twelve innocent people died. There is nothing we can offer in mitigation bar that our inquiries have established that a nine-minute warning was given to the RUC: This was proved totally inadequate given the disastrous consequences. We accept condemnation and criticism from only two sources: from the relatives and friends of those who were killed, and from our supporters who have rightly and severely criticised us. Abroad and at home the

[58]   Dossier on Visit of US Congressional Delegation, April 1979, in Ireland and US Policy on Northern Ireland, TAOIS/2009/135/745, NAI.
[59]   *IT*, 18/2/1978.
[60]   Statement of Senator Edward M. Kennedy on the Belfast Bombing, 21/2/1978, in Senator Edward Kennedy interest in Northern Ireland, Foreign and Commonwealth/Political Matters, CJ 4/2389, TNA.
[61]   *IT*, 18/2/1978.

British Government have had a field day with its unchallenged version of events, and that peace lies in the destruction of Irish Republicanism.[62]

A month after La Mon, Callaghan and Carter met in Washington. High on the agenda were the shared economic difficulties that the two nations were experiencing, difficulties which would ultimately contribute to their respective political downfalls. The tension of the period was not evident from the record of the meeting and Callaghan's Ambassador, and son-in-law, Peter Jay recalled the favourable impression of the President that existed within the UK Government at the time:

> I had a very high opinion of Jimmy Carter in that he was, in my experience and my perception, exceptionally intelligent, astonishingly hard-working and totally willing to engage with the changing realities of the world and the changing realities of the American power, based on a recognition of a number of important and fundamental issues of principle ... The frustration about being a Jimmy Carter admirer, and it seems an extraordinary thing to say about a man who had been elected President of the United States, was that he loathed politics. He not only loathed it, he disapproved of it.[63]

Congressional Hearings on Ireland

One potential problem that went unaddressed in the meeting between the President and the Taoiseach was the possibility of further Congressional hearings on Northern Ireland, sought by the Irish National Caucus through Lester Wolff's International Relations Sub-Committee.[64] In a letter to senior Northern Ireland Office civil servant Brian Cubbon, who was then still recovering from injuries suffered in the July 1976 bombing

---

[62]   *IT*, 20/2/1978.
[63]   Note for the Record, Meeting with the President of the United States in the Cabinet Room of the White House, Thursday, 23 March at 1100 hours, Freedom of Information Release 248745, TNA; Peter Jay, interview with author, 7/12/2011.
[64]   Wolff had proposed these in late 1974, see Letter from D.C. Walker, Embassy Washington, DC to J.P.B. Simon, Republic of Ireland Department, 9/12/1974 in FCO 87/363, Visits from United States of America to Northern Ireland and Republic of Ireland, TNA.

which killed British Ambassador to the Republic of Ireland Christopher Ewart-Biggs, Jay noted that:

> The Provisional front groups have been busy seeking to dissociate themselves in American minds from the terrorists and to associate themselves with the Irish Government and with the human rights stand of the Carter Administration. They have been quietly gathering support in Congress. Zablocki told us that there was nothing to worry about—but in the same breath added that the Biaggi Ad Hoc Committee on Ireland now had nearly a hundred members of Congress on its books, which was, he said, 'a problem'.[65]

The emergence of the Ad Hoc Congressional Committee for Irish Affairs created a new problem for both the British and American governments. Congressman Mario Biaggi founded this group in September 1977 at the request of Jack Keane, the President of the Ancient Order of Hibernians (AOH). Keane wrote to Biaggi asking him to head up a committee 'Because of your service to the Irish-American community, we know you share our concern about the tragic situation in Ireland today'.[66]

While the 'ad hoc' nature of the group meant that Representatives did not need to maintain any official allegiance to the group, it listed some 122 affiliated representatives, roughly a quarter of Congress, by November 1978.[67] The Ad Hoc Committee, along with Biaggi himself, would continue to trouble the British administration in the United States over the remainder of the conflict and, at the time of writing, persists with a significant membership. In his introductory letter, Biaggi explained that it would tackle the issue of 'human rights violations employed by Britain' in Northern Ireland, investigate the denial of visas to 'leading Irish political figures' such as Ruairí Ó Brádaigh, the issue of

---

[65]   Letter to Brian Cubbon, NIO, from Peter Jay, 14/2/1978, in Senator Edward Kennedy interest in Northern Ireland, Foreign and Commonwealth/Political Matters, CJ 4/2389, TNA.

[66]   Letter from John M. 'Jack' Keane, National President, Ancient Order of Hibernians to Biaggi, 31/8/1977, in Congressional Archives, Thomas P. O'Neill Papers, Series II: Staff Files, Subseries A: Kirk O'Donnell Files, Sub-Subseries 19-20, 21/21 Ireland-Ad Hoc Congressional Committee for Irish Affairs, 1977–1983, BLBC.

[67]   Dossier on Visit of US Congressional Delegation, April 1979, in Ireland and US Policy on Northern Ireland, TAOIS/2009/135/745, NAI.

Irish self-determination, as well as a discussion of the Carter statement and the possibility of US economic aid for Ireland.[68] The Biaggi Committee would pose significant problems for the three governments over the issue of Northern Ireland throughout 1978 as it pushed for a congressional hearings on Northern Ireland to take place, particularly as they would do so in the context of the continuing protest inside the H-Blocks of HMP Maze.[69] Much of the evidence from state papers seems to suggest that the threat of Congressional hearings, particularly during the Carter administration, was used as a means to prompt the British government into action on the Northern Ireland situation.[70]

The issue of Congressional hearings was a major concern for both the British and Irish governments throughout 1978. They had survived hearings in 1972, but renewed pressure from within Congress, which was approaching midterm elections, as the prison protest continued to escalate was a problem they would have rather not encountered. The driving force this time around was Democratic Congressman Lester T. Wolff, who was, according to the Foreign Office, motivated by both electoral reasons and because of his 'unshakeable belief that human rights continue to be violated in Northern Ireland'. In October 1975, he held what he termed 'unofficial pre-hearings' in New York, which included Father Sean McManus of the Irish National Caucus. At the event, the Maze prison was compared to Dachau concentration camp. Predictable for such an event was the absence of UK or Irish government officials: 'Dr FitzGerald sent a strongly-worded letter criticising the whole proceeding. These pre-hearings may have achieved some spurious recognition when Wolff managed to get the transcript printed in the record of the House of Representatives on 4 December 1975'.[71]

---

[68]   Letter from Biaggi to O'Neill, 16/9/1977, in Congressional Archives, Thomas P. O'Neill Papers, Series II: Staff Files, Subseries A: Kirk O'Donnell Files, Sub-Subseries 19-20, 21/21 Ireland-Ad Hoc Congressional Committee for Irish Affairs, 1977–1983, BLBC.

[69]   Letter from R.G. Jones, NIO, to M.J. Newington, FCO, 20/12/1978, Possibility of Congressional Hearings in 1979 in United States Congressional Hearings on Northern Ireland, FCO 87/779, TNA.

[70]   See United States Congressional Hearings on Northern Ireland, FCO 87/779, TNA, particularly two telegrams from Ambassador Peter Jay to the FCO on 14 and 15 December 1978 which report Speaker O'Neill as considering hearings 'inevitable' without progress on the prison protest.

[71]   Memorandum Congressional hearings on Northern Ireland, 4/5/1977, in Senator Edward Kennedy interest in Northern Ireland, Foreign and Commonwealth/Political Matters, CJ 4/2389, TNA.

With the threat of congressional hearings hanging over them, it was imperative that the British and Irish governments develop a more cohesive strategy to deal with the situation in Northern Ireland. There was, however, much ground to cover. The Anglo-Irish Agreement, which secured Irish involvement in the Northern Irish peace process, was still seven years away and the distance between the governments, particularly in the early months of 1978, was striking. Conor O'Clery, writing in the *Irish Times*, noted that 'there are signs that the British Government may at last be awakening to the fact that its lack of policy on Northern Ireland, and its shabby attempts to deflect blame for violence on to the Republic', and how this had 'caused a dangerous diplomatic rift with the Republic which should now be repaired'.[72] Diplomatic relations between the UK and Ireland were complicated by their joint membership of the European Economic Community. During a summit in Copenhagen in early 1977, British Foreign Minister David Owen and his counterpart Michael O'Kennedy, the Irish Minister for Foreign Affairs, met to discuss the issue of border control. Owen asked the Irish to tone down their statements on the north, but found O'Kennedy to be 'pretty unrepentant'.[73] The mood of the British was somewhat tempered by the fact that Taoiseach Lynch had condemned radical Irish-American groups during his speech at the Fianna Fáil Ard Fheis, after pressure from the AOH.[74]

Lynch visited the United States in May, a visit that Sean Donlon was integral in organising. Donlon explained that Lynch intended to focus on three major issues: the UN, encouraging investment from the United States to the Republic, and contacts with the Irish-American community. The visit was considered by the British to be based on a desire to meet one particular individual:

> The reason that the Irish went to Washington at all was, according to Donlon, to have breakfast with Tip O'Neill who was unable to meet them in New York. Donlon's impression was that while O'Neill had plenty of goodwill towards the Irish Government and their aims, he was not completely involved

---

[72]   *IT*, 28/3/1978.
[73]   Letter from W.K. Prendergast, FCO to M. Hopkins, NIO, 17/2/1978 in The Situation in Northern Ireland: The US Initiative in Northern Ireland, PREM 16/1721, TNA.
[74]   Letter from J. Davidson to M. Hodge, 23/2/1978, in The United States Congressional Hearings on Northern Ireland, FCO 87/778, TNA.

though he would be as helpful as possible within certain limitations. He had given the Taoiseach, and later said this publicly, an assurance that the Biaggi hearings would not take place.[75]

Donlon was an important contact for the British during this period, a contact which helped to establish a productive relationship between the two nations after his appointment as Irish Ambassador to the United States. Lynch also met Governor Hugh Carey and Senator Daniel Patrick Moynihan, the two less-prominent members of the Four Horsemen group, during his visit. The British Embassy in Dublin, which clearly had a very low estimation of the two American figures, reported to the Foreign Office:

> the meeting with Carey took place fairly late at night and was not all that satisfactory. Carey drank a great deal of Irish Coffee and has, in any case, according to Donlon, a 'drinking problem'. He was preoccupied by New York City's finances and made it clear that while he supported the Irish Government he did not want to be distracted by secondary or tertiary issues which he considered Ireland was. Donlon also appeared unimpressed by Moynihan who, he said, spent most of his time describing why British socialism was failing.

The issue of how much effort the American administration was making to halt the exportation of arms from the United States to Northern Ireland was broached in the aftermath of Lynch's visit.[76] O'Neill again raised the prospect of Congressional hearings during his meeting with Lynch. He told the Taoiseach that while 'he was privately opposed to hearings and that they would not be held in the current Congress', he remained concerned that the mid-term elections that November would increase pressure for hearings, particularly if a British general election took place and no new Northern Ireland initiative was forthcoming. Peter Jay, in a letter to Brian Cubbon, wrote: 'I am hoping to get in to see O'Neill to do what I can to stiffen his resolve. But I fear that Kennedy and O'Neill may simply

[75] Letter from W.R. Hayden to P.L.V. Mallet, FCO, 6/6/1978, 'Lynch visit to USA 23–27 May', in Irish Republic Relations with USA, CJ4/2257, TNA.
[76] Letter from W.R. Hayden, Embassy Dublin to P.L.V. Mallet, FCO, 6/6/1978, re Lynch visit to USA, in United States Congressional Hearings on Northern Ireland, FCO 87/779, TNA.

not be able, for understandable political reasons, to keep the lid on indefinitely'.[77]

In late August, it was reported that Donlon had been earmarked to replace John Molloy, the Irish Ambassador in Washington.[78] As well as being a well-known and respected figure within British circles, Donlon was 'one of the foremost authorities on Northern Ireland in the Department of Foreign Affairs, having been attached to the Northern Ireland Affairs Section since 1972'.[79] During a meeting with British Ambassador Peter Jay, Donlon 'made it clear that he was disposed to be as helpful as possible to us in dealing with the Irish National Caucus and similar bodies, but hoped that he would not be diverted from his main task of investment promotion'.[80]

The issue of attracting inward American investment was important for both parties and there was an element of competition between the North and the Republic for this investment. In early August, the building of the DeLorean car factory was announced, which would create 2,000 new jobs in west Belfast.[81] The total £65 million investment, however, included British investment of £56 million. Northern Ireland was a perennial drain on British financial resources, and it was therefore important to try to attract inward investment, particularly from the United States. Following Jay's meeting with Donlon, however, staff at the British Embassy were suspicious of his exact intentions:

> We were also struck by Donlon's labouring of the point that his main function in Washington will be economic. As you will recall, he went out of his way to make the same point to our Ambassador. I have heard that he gave the same message to Irish and British journalists before leaving here. I have a (perhaps uncharitable) suspicion that Donlon has a purpose in all this. It may be simply that he wishes to disarm suspicion

---

[77] Letter from Jay to Brian Cubbon, NIO, 6/6/1978, in Relations and meetings with the Irish Republic Foreign Minister (Mr O. Kennedy) Irish Republic/ Political Activity, CJ4/2259, TNA.

[78] *Daily Telegraph*, 21/8/1978.

[79] *Irish Independent*, 16/8/1978.

[80] Letter from C.W. Squire to E.A.J. Fergusson, 13/10/1978, re Jay lunch with Donlon, in Irish Republic Relations with USA, CJ4/2257, TNA.

[81] After DeLorean went bankrupt in 1982, French company Montupet took over the plant and won a huge manufacturing contract in 2016; see *Belfast Telegraph*, 29/5/2016.

that he has been sent to Washington, as the Irish Government's expert on Northern Ireland, in order to help Fianna Fáil to 'play the American card'. That would be understandable if the Irish Government actually did hope at a later date to play the American card. We have no clinching evidence either way, but I personally suspect that Donlon is protesting too much. If he has been sent principally on an economic mission, it is odd that Mr Lynch and Mr O'Kennedy selected the senior official at the DFA with the least financial and commercial experience. At the time of his posting, Donlon made much of his need to get away from Northern Ireland affairs.[82]

Despite this early suspicion, Donlon had a very cordial relationship with his counterpart in the British Embassy, Peter Jay. Jay recalled of their relationship:

> It was extremely good, probably closer than maybe some of my Embassy colleagues would have thought was entirely appropriate. I liked the guy. It was obvious to me that his mission and his purpose was highly constructive and coincided with British interests—it wasn't done because it coincided with British interests, but it did coincide with British interests. Moving Irish-Americans away from supporting terrorism, which of course wasn't what they thought they were doing anyway, but it was what they were doing, and to support the legitimate elected government of the Republic of Ireland and the Government of the United Kingdom was very important and the success of violence and terrorism was a disaster for democracy in Ireland, whatever its consequences in Britain might have been. In my opinion there was a high degree of common interest here. Secondly, Sean and I just liked each other, we got on very well, we were always in and out of each other's houses, we had social and informal meals together and the families got on. I valued that greatly, I thought he was a great guy, a very skilled professional.[83]

Most significantly, the close relationship between the two reflected that of the British and Irish Embassies when it came to Northern Irish

[82] Letter from P.J. Goulden, Embassy Dublin to J. Davidson, Embassy Washington, 26/10/1978, re Sean Donlon, in Irish Republic Relations with USA, CJ4/2257, TNA.

[83] Peter Jay, interview with author, 7/12/2011.

affairs in the United States. This was important because congressional interest in Northern Ireland showed no signs of slowing and the threat of congressional hearings on the situation in Northern Ireland loomed over much of the late 1970s. On 28 September, Joshua Eilberg and Hamilton Fish paid a five-day visit to Northern Ireland and in mid-November Congressman Mario Biaggi visited Ireland on a fact-finding mission.[84] Ahead of the trip, Biaggi was boosted by a joint press conference which he held with New York Governor Hugh Carey. In this press conference, Carey broke with the Four Horsemen's convention of distancing themselves from Biaggi to praise the controversial congressman:

> He has specially worked long and hard to secure peace and justice in Northern Ireland—and I greatly appreciate his efforts in that direction. Mario's leadership in Congress has helped focus attention on this issue—and I look forward to working with him to see whether hearings can be arranged to further the cause of peace. His current efforts towards establishing peace can contribute to the elusive peace we all pray for. Certainly any efforts which are undertaken will have Mario Biaggi in a prominent role.[85]

Peter Jay reported that Carey's remarks, geared at courting the Italian vote in the 1978 gubernatorial election, received little publicity thanks to a New York newspaper strike.[86] Carey also took to Biaggi's idea of a Northern Ireland peace forum and later invited Secretary of State for Northern Ireland Humphrey Atkins and Irish Foreign Minister Michael O'Kennedy to a summit in New York in order to discuss Northern Ireland, an invitation which was politely declined: 'The Prime Minister [Margaret Thatcher] made it clear that there could, in her view, be no question of discussing Northern Ireland with Governor Carey in New York. If Governor Carey wished to

---

[84]   Dossier on Visit of US Congressional Delegation, April 1979, in Ireland and US Policy on Northern Ireland, TAOIS/2009/135/745, NAI.

[85]   Telegram from Washington to FCO, 6/11/1978, re Governor Carey joint press conference with Biaggi, 31/10/1978, in Irish Republic Relations with USA, CJ4/2257, TNA.

[86]   Telegram from Washington to FCO, 6/11/1978, re Governor Carey joint press conference with Biaggi, 31/10/1978, in Irish Republic Relations with USA, CJ4/2257, TNA.

engage in such discussions, he should come to London'.[87] It was also noted within the Foreign Office that 'We recognise Governor Carey's good intentions in inviting Mr Atkins and Mr O'Kennedy to talks in New York. Both UK and Irish Governments have no difficulty about talking to one another at all levels and on any subject. No need for intermediary'.[88]

Biaggi's attempts to engage Northern Irish figures in his peace forum failed to engage any of the major parties, and even the Alliance Party, who did agree to a meeting, were firm in their statement that they would not participate in a forum.[89] Biaggi had, on a previous trip to Ireland in 1975, met Irish republican leaders like Ruairí Ó Brádaigh, Maire Drumm, and Joe Cahill. Having been denied access to Portlaoise Prison on that trip, the British felt it wise to allow Biaggi to visit the Maze prison in 1978, if only to avoid Biaggi exploiting a refusal.[90] Biaggi's account spoke to a far more significant trip than declassified British state papers suggested:

> The trip commenced in Belfast on the morning of November 14. Before that day was over, we had consumed some 14 hours in meetings with at least 12 groups. Our meetings were conducted with leading political parties, paramilitary groups, church, peace, and labor leaders. One of the most important things we learned was of the growing sentiment among all levels in the North in favor of a British declaration of intent to withdraw its presence from the North ... Perhaps the most dramatic moment of the entire trip occurred on the first day when we met with approximately 75 relatives of prisoners incarcerated in various prisons in Northern Ireland.[91]

---

[87]   Letter from Private Secretary, 10 Downing Street to Northern Ireland Office, 23/8/1979, in Weapons used by security forces in N. Ireland, FCO 87/958, TNA.

[88]   Paragraphs for inclusion in brief for Lord Privy Seal's visit to UNGA, 1–6 October, Essential Facts, Northern Ireland, in Weapons used by security forces in N. Ireland, FCO 87/958, TNA.

[89]   Telex from NIO to Washington, 20/11/1978, re Biaggi and Gilman, accompanied by Blancato, Bateman, and O'Brien, visited Northern Ireland on 14/15 November, in Irish Republic Relations with USA, CJ4/2257, TNA.

[90]   Letter from R.G. Jones, Visit of Congressman Biaggi, 10/11/1978 and Letter from J.A. Marshall re Visit of Congressman Biaggi to HMP Maze, 13/11/1978, in Irish Republic Relations with USA, CJ4/2257, TNA.

[91]   Congressional Record Extension of Remarks, February 13, 1979, Trip to Ireland—November 14–17, 1978 Part I, Hon. Mario Biaggi of New York.

The Problems of the Late Callaghan Years and the Start of the Thatcher Administration

Prospects of an economic solution to the Northern Ireland conflict took a hit in late 1978 after a series of redundancies were announced at the Harland and Wolff shipyard in Belfast.[92] What international economic investment there was in Northern Ireland was insufficient to save these jobs. Violence continued apace, too, and the Northern Ireland (Emergency Provisions) Act was set for renewal and a series of IRA attacks towards the end 1978 were, in the view of Lord Melchett, 'an attempt by the Provisional IRA to restore its waning credibility and to stampede the smaller towns in Northern Ireland into calling for the reintroduction of the old security restrictions which have been lifted'. He added, 'these attacks should be seen against an overall continuing decline in the level of violence'.[93] There remained some hope for political progress, with a February 1979 meeting between Northern Ireland Secretary Roy Mason and Irish Minister for Foreign Affairs Michael O'Kennedy focusing on the issue of British withdrawal from Northern Ireland. O'Kennedy underlined that the Lynch government 'accepted that there was no move to integration', but emphasised the importance of some form of political progress. Mason highlighted the problems that the prospect of Irish unification created for the British in terms of Ulster Unionist resistance: 'Even a hint from Her Majesty's Government supporting Irish unity would destroy any prospect of devolution in Northern Ireland. It would just feed Protestant fears and lead Ian Paisley and Harry West to stand together. Talk of Irish unity and all-Ireland Councils in the long term made it difficult to make progress on devolution in the short term'.[94]

The Irish accepted that, with the UK general election looming, a major political initiative on Northern Ireland was unlikely. The Irish

[92] Shipbuilding (Redundancy Payments), Hansard, HC vol. 960, cols 393–394W (15 December 1978), available at https://api.parliament.uk/ historic-hansard/written-answers/1978/dec/15/shipbuilding-redundancy-payments#S5CV0960P0_19781215_CWA_31.

[93] Northern Ireland (Emergency Provisions) Act 1978 (Continuance) (No. 2) Order 1978, Hansard, HL vol. 397, cols 826–837 (14 December 1978), available at https://api.parliament.uk/historic-hansard/lords/1978/dec/14/northern-ireland-emergency-provisions#S5LV0397P0_19781214_HOL_218.

[94] Note of a meeting with Mr O'Kennedy at 11.00 a.m. on Wednesday, 14 February 1979 at 1 Carlton Gardens, NIO/12/138, PRONI.

maintained that they would still like to see some recognition on the part of the British Government as to the improving economy of the Republic. The two discussed the evolving prison protests, particularly as they might impact the possibility of Congressional hearings being held in the United States. O'Kennedy maintained that the Irish government remained opposed to these hearings but that the lack of movement on the prison situation continued to frustrate their friends and supporters in the United States, notably Tip O'Neill. Mason accepted that the Maze protest was an issue, especially in the context of the United States, but argued that 'We were being as humane as possible but could not afford to show any signs of weakness'.[95]

O'Neill was scheduled to visit Ireland in April 1979, following an invitation from Sean Donlon in late 1978.[96] O'Neill's own interest in the conflict had developed and he had recently received a delegation in Washington from the UDA-aligned Ulster Political Research Group (UPRG), an attempt on the part of the group to present their case to the Speaker.[97] The UPRG later wrote to O'Neill's aide, Kirk O'Donnell, saying that they thought the trip had been very successful.[98] Still, violence in Northern Ireland posed problems and following the IRA's assassination of British Ambassador to the Netherlands Richard Sykes, and the INLA's assassination of Shadow Secretary of State for Northern Ireland, and Thatcher ally, Airey Neave, preparations for O'Neill's visit took place amidst heightened security.[99]

O'Neill described Neave's assassination as 'another outrageous act by those who think they promote the cause of Irish nationalism

[95]   Ibid.
[96]   Telegram from Jay to FCO, 15/12/1978, in United States Congressional Hearings on Northern Ireland, FCO 87/779, TNA.
[97]   See Wood, I.S., *Crimes of Loyalty: A History of the UDA* (Edinburgh: Edinburgh University Press 2006).
[98]   Letter from Glen Barr to Kirk O'Donnell, January 31, 1979. Congressional Archives, Thomas P. O'Neill Papers, Series II: Staff Files, Subseries A: Kirk O'Donnell Files, Sub-subseries 20: Box 24, Ireland—Violence, 1977–1979, 1981–1982, BLBC. On the UDA and UPRG, see Wood, *Crimes of Loyalty*.
[99]   Margaret Thatcher Speech at Airey Neave's Memorial Service, 16/5/1979, available at https://www.margaretthatcher.org/document/104085; Jimmy Carter: 'Airey Neave Message to Prime Minister James Callaghan of the United Kingdom on the Death of the Conservative Party Member of Parliament', March 31, 1979, online by Gerhard Peters and John T. Wooley, the American Presidency Project, available at https://www.presidency.ucsb.edu/documents/airey-neave-message-prime-minister-james-callaghan-the-united-kingdom-the-death-the.

by killing and maiming', also emphasising that 'The murder of Mr. Neave is a stark reminder to Irish Americans that we must be careful to avoid encouraging in any way those who seek to impose their will in Northern Ireland through the use of violence'.[100] The State Department conducted a threat assessment ahead of O'Neill's visit and concluded that 'even though the speaker has made numerous speeches in the United States against Irish-American support (an important financial source) for the IRA, any actions by Irish terrorists against the Speaker would only alienate this Irish-American support base'.[101]

During the visit a dinner was held in O'Neill's honour at Dublin Castle. Delivering remarks at the dinner, Jack Lynch joked that 'the Speaker's position is one of great importance and influence in the U.S. In fact it is said of the present incumbent in Washington that the nickname "TIP" is really short for the phrase "To Influence Presidents"'.[102] Those present at the dinner certainly enjoyed the full extent of Irish hospitality, the bill for the dinner totalling over £5,000, and a receipt from the Royal Hibernian Hotel also indicates that the O'Neill-led delegation had a celebratory time, with more than 150 bottles of liquor consumed during their stay.[103] During his own remarks, O'Neill took the opportunity to criticise both the British and Irish governments for the lack of progress in Northern Ireland:

> Together with other American politicians of Irish descent, notably Senator Kennedy, Senator Moynihan and Governor Carey of New York, I have been deeply concerned for the lack of political progress in recent years. It is not for Americans to say to the parties involved: this is the solution or here is the way

[100] Comments by Speaker Thomas P. O'Neill, Jr. on the death of Mr Airey Neave, Member of Parliament, 2/4/1979, Congressional Archives, Thomas P. O'Neill Papers, Series II: Staff Files, Subseries A: Kirk O'Donnell Files, Sub-subseries 20: Box 24, Ireland—Violence, 1977–1979, 1981–1982, BLBC.

[101] Department of State Memorandum, Threat Assessment for Congressional Visit of Speaker O'Neill to the United Kingdom, Belgium, Hungary and Ireland, April 12–23, 1979, Congressional Archives, Thomas P. O'Neill Papers, Series II: Staff Files, Subseries A: Kirk O'Donnell Files, Sub-subseries 20: Box 24, Ireland—Violence, 1977–1979, 1981–1982, BLBC.

[102] Speech by the Taoiseach, Mr J. Lynch, T.D. at the dinner for Speaker and Mrs O'Neill and American Congressmen, Dublin Castle, 19 April 1979, at 10.00 p.m., in Ireland and US Policy on Northern Ireland, TAOIS/2009/135/745, NAI.

[103] Letter to Accounts Branch, Department of Finance, 12/6/1979, in Speaker Tip O'Neill visit to Ireland, April 1979, TAOIS/2009/135/751, NAI.

forward. But together with all sides in Ireland we insist that Britain bears a very heavy responsibility for the failures of recent years on the political front. We have been concerned that the problem has been treated as a political football in London or has otherwise been given a low priority. So far as I am concerned, there is no more serious problem on the agenda of British politics than a crisis which has claimed 2,000 lives and caused almost 20,000 serious injuries. Nothing mars the credibility of political leadership than brutality in the name of the law. It is for this reason that together with my colleagues I called on the British Government to root out this evil practice and see to it that those who are responsible are punished.[104]

The 'political football' comment angered many in the United Kingdom and Ireland, not least the Peace People organisation, whose founder Ciaran McKeown released a statement which accused O'Neill of indulging in 'third generation Irish nationalism', also noting that:

> while Speaker Tip O'Neill is a powerful domestic politician, he is no expert on Foreign Affairs, nor is he unduly influential on such matters … His opinions on Ireland are a combination of sentimental Irish Americanism, a calculated interest in the Irish American vote, and the persistent line by John Hume and the more gullible members of the Irish Foreign staff in Washington.[105]

McKeown's co-founder Mairead Corrigan was also vocal in her deep disappointment that O'Neill 'should have blundered into our politics'.[106] This rift would later prompt a letter of apology from Corrigan to O'Neill in August 1980.[107] Significantly, it was not the first

[104] Speech by Speaker 'Tip' O'Neill on the occasion of a dinner in his honour in Dublin Castle, 19 April 1979, in Ireland and US Policy on Northern Ireland, TAOIS/2009/135/745, NAI.

[105] Statement by Ciaran McKeown, 20/4/1979, in Congressional Archives, Thomas P. O'Neill Papers, Series II: Staff Files, Subseries A: Kirk O'Donnell Files, Sub-subseries 21/15, Ireland—Community of the Peace People, 1979–1980 and 1977, BLBC.

[106] Statement by Mairead Corrigan, 20/4/1979, in Congressional Archives, Thomas P. O'Neill Papers, Series II: Staff Files, Subseries A: Kirk O'Donnell Files, Sub-subseries 21/15, Ireland—Community of the Peace People, 1979–1980 and 1977, BLBC.

[107] Letter from Mairead Corrigan to O'Neill, 22/8/1980, ibid.

time O'Neill had used the expression, having commented in a May 1978 address to The Ireland Fund in New York:

> I would appeal to the British Government to reexamine seriously its own role in Northern Ireland. The problem of Northern Ireland will not be solved if it is permitted to become a football in British politics. Nor will it be solved if the British Government gives to one side or the other in the political conflict a basis to assume that concessions are not necessary. I must say that the evidence of the past few years would suggest the problem of Northern Ireland has sometimes become a pawn in British political calculations. At other times it has been forgotten when British political priorities were assessed.[108]

Elected as Speaker of the House of Representatives in 1977, O'Neill became increasingly comfortable inserting himself into US foreign policy as it pertained to the Northern Ireland conflict. A few months after his Dublin trip, this opportunity presented itself in the form of an order for weapons which was placed with an American company on the behalf of the Royal Ulster Constabulary.

Guns for the RUC

Following a vote of no confidence in the Labour Government of Jim Callaghan in March 1979, the United Kingdom general election of 3 May brought the Conservative Party back to power under Prime Minister Margaret Thatcher. Thatcher had developed relationships with international leaders during her time as leader of the opposition Conservative Party which gave her a strong foothold to begin her time as Prime Minister, particularly on the issue of Northern Ireland and the US role in Irish affairs. This was important because almost immediately after her election she was faced with a serious challenge when the Department of State decided to block a shipment of weapons to the Royal Ulster Constabulary.

---

[108]   Remarks of Thomas P. O'Neill, Jr. The Speaker, US House of Representatives before The Ireland Fund, Wednesday, May 10, 1978, The Waldorf Astoria, New York, New York, Congressional Archives, Thomas P. O'Neill Papers, Series II: Staff Files, Subseries A: Kirk O'Donnell Files, Sub-subseries 21/16, Ireland—Ireland Fund, 1977–1980, 1982, BLBC.

On 31 January 1979, the State Department approved export licences which entitled Sturm Ruger of Connecticut to send 3,000 .357 magnum revolvers and 500 .223 rifles to the Viking Arms Limited company in Harrogate, Yorkshire, where they would be transported to the Police Authority of Northern Ireland and employed in the RUC's training programme for ultimate use in security operations.[109] The department justified this decision on the basis that:

> the Royal Ulster Constabulary is the legally-constituted police force in Northern Ireland … this police force continues to face a very serious terrorist threat from the Provisional Irish Republican Army … most moderate observers of the Northern Irish scene support the British policy of turning responsibility for security in Northern Ireland over to the Police and withdrawing U.K. army units … in order to achieve this policy goal the British have been modernizing the Royal Ulster Constabulary including its equipment.[110]

For four months, the sale of weapons went unnoticed until journalist Jimmy Breslin reported it in the *New York Daily News* on 31 May. The first tranche of weapons had, by this stage, already arrived in Northern Ireland, but the *Boston Globe* suggested that, thanks to the Breslin article, Speaker Tip O'Neill had been alerted to the fact that a second delivery was imminent.[111] Speaker O'Neill delivered the following comment the same day as the Breslin article was published:

> Shipments of arms to anyone in Northern Ireland by anyone in the United States should not be sanctioned by the State Department. The Department's action in this matter undermines efforts by U.S. political leaders to reduce support by U.S. citizens for the forces that seek to unify Ireland through violence. Despite

---

[109] I'm grateful to the editors and reviewers at the *Journal of Transatlantic Studies* for their comments which shaped the article upon which much of the following is based; see 'The Role of Northern Ireland in Modern Anglo-American Relations: The United States Department of State and the Royal Ulster Constabulary, 1979', *Journal of Transatlantic Studies* 12(2) (2014), pp. 163–181.

[110] The Department of State's Response to the Committee's inquiry about the approval of sales of U.S. munitions list items for use by the police of Northern Ireland, in Ireland and US Policy on Northern Ireland, TAOIS/2009/135/745, NAI.

[111] *Boston Globe* of 1/6/1979 suggested that O'Neill found out about the sale as a result of Breslin's article.

recent reforms, the past record of the Royal Ulster Constabulary is not one of impartiality in maintaining law and order and the sale will therefore be viewed by many here as U.S. Government support for a particular faction in Northern Ireland. I appreciate the difficulty of maintaining peace in Northern Ireland and I condemn the recent series of murders of police and security officials there, but the U.S. Government promotes peace best by preventing, rather than permitting, arms shipments to Northern Ireland. I am notifying the State Department of my views and I am recommending that the Department not authorize such shipments in the future.[112]

It was interesting that O'Neill felt the RUC represented a 'faction' in Northern Ireland, as this was certainly the view of Irish nationalists and certainly not the view of Unionists. His prejudice against the RUC was based largely on criticism the force had received in the Bennett Report of March 1979, which indicated that its methods, particularly in relation to the interrogation of suspects, required closer monitoring. This followed criticisms made of the force in the 1978 Amnesty International report.[113]

These were cited on 12 July by Bronx Congressman Mario Biaggi when he raised the issue of the gun sale in Congress, claiming that the RUC had violated human rights in their treatment of suspects and that the sale of weapons was, in turn, a violation of Section 502 (B) of the Foreign Assistance Act of 1961. The pertinent section of this act declares:

[112] Statement by Speaker Thomas P. O'Neill, Jr on State Department Authorization of Shipment of US Manufactured Arms to Northern Ireland Police, 31/5/1979, in Congressional Archives, Thomas P. O'Neill Papers, Series II: Staff Files, Subseries A: Kirk O'Donnell Files, Sub-subseries 24/11, Ireland—US Gun Sales to R.U.C., 1979–1980, BLBC.

[113] His Honour Judge H.G. Bennett, QC, Report of the Committee of Inquiry into Police Interrogation Procedures in Northern Ireland, Presented to Parliament by the Secretary of State for Northern Ireland by Command of Her Majesty, March 1979 (London: HMSO, 1979); Amnesty International, *Northern Ireland: Report of an Amnesty International Mission to Northern Ireland (28 November 1977–6 December 1977)* (London: Amnesty International, 1978). See also Record of Meeting between Secretary of State for Northern Ireland and Speaker O'Neill and Senator Kennedy, 17 October 1977 at 10.45 a.m. at the Capitol, in Senator Edward Kennedy interest in Northern Ireland, Foreign and Commonwealth/Political Matters, CJ 4/2389, TNA.

No security assistance may be provided to any country the government of which engages in a consistent pattern of gross violations of internationally recognized human rights. Security assistance may not be provided to the police, domestic intelligence, or similar law enforcement forces of a country, and licences may not be issued under the Export Administration Act of 1979.[114]

At O'Neill's behest, Congressman Clement Zablocki, then the head of Congressional International Relations Committee, launched an investigation of the policy.[115] Congressman Hamilton Fish, an occasional opponent of British policy in Ireland from his Congressional seat in upstate New York, wrote to Matthew Nimetz to detail his outrage at the sale, claiming that it did 'violence to the President's position of August 1977 on the resolution of the tragedy in Northern Ireland and makes a mockery of United States policy which forbids military aid to a country which violates human rights'.[116] Nimetz, of the State Department, announced that arms sales would be suspended pending the report of the Zablocki-led review.[117]

Those in London were as excited as Fish on the issue. Nicholas Henderson, newly installed as Peter Jay's successor as UK Ambassador in Washington, wrote in his diary: 'London is as worked up as is the USA on the subject of the sales of arms to the RUC and I foresee much bitterness. The PM feels particularly strongly after the murder of Airey Neave'.[118] The timing of the blockade, just after an election and at a time when significant political upheaval was taking place, and significant diplomatic upheaval with it, was unfortunate. Outgoing Ambassador Peter Jay spoke to O'Neill, expressing his 'surprise and regret' over the Speaker's position on the gun sale. O'Neill, however, was determined

---

[114] The Foreign Assistance Act of 1961 (P.L. 87-195), Section 502B, available at https://legcounsel.house.gov/Comps/Foreign%20Assistance%20Act%20Of%201961.pdf.

[115] *IT*, 3/8/1979.

[116] Telegram from Hamilton Fish, Jr., to Matthew Nimetz, 1/6/1979, Congressional Archives, Thomas P. O'Neill Papers, Series II: Staff Files, Subseries A: Kirk O'Donnell Files, Sub-subseries 24/11, Ireland—US Gun Sales to R.U.C., 1979–1980, BLBC.

[117] *IT*, 3/8/1979.

[118] Henderson, N., *Mandarin: The Diaries of Nicholas Henderson* (London: Phoenix Press, 1994), p. 284.

that 'this will not be swept under the rug as far as the Irish in this country are concerned'.[119] Jay later reflected that:

> we began to realise that the role of Irish politics in the United States was not about what was happening in Ireland, it was about the glue that held together an important constituency in American politics. It was held together by its folk memories. Whether they were true or out of date, or right or wrong in Ireland was no longer the point, the point was that they were useful because they supplied the cohesion of these constituencies which enabled usually Democrats, in fact almost invariably Democrats, to get support and votes on election day in the US and if some of the myths were indeed myths, it didn't matter, they worked, they did their job.[120]

O'Neill's papers reveal that the Speaker did receive criticism from within the United States for his role in the gun embargo, with one letter writer accusing him of 'support, tacit and otherwise, for the IRA'. There is also, however, significant evidence that his position drew favour from within the United States.[121] Among those very much in favour of the embargo was Mario Biaggi, who seized the opportunity presented by the embargo to propose an amendment to the State, Commerce and Judiciary 1980 Appropriations Bill. In a letter from his Ad Hoc Committee to Congress, he noted:

> the RUC had been cited by Amnesty International, among others, for human rights violations in their treatment of suspects and prisoners in Northern Ireland. This action is clearly against the intent of Section 502 (B) of the Foreign Assistance Act of 1961 which prohibits licenses from being issued under the Export Administration Act for 'crime control and detection instruments and equipment to a country, the government of

---

[119] *Boston Globe*, 6/6/1979.
[120] Peter Jay, interview with author, 7/12/2011.
[121] See, for example, Letter from John T. Maltsberger to O'Neill, 3/6/1980; Letter from John J. Finuncan, Chairman, Irish Justice Committee (letter headed Emerald Society, Fire Department of New York) to O'Neill, 4/6/1979, both in Congressional Archives, Thomas P. O'Neill Papers, Series II: Staff Files, Subseries A: Kirk O'Donnell Files, Sub-subseries 24/11, Ireland—US Gun Sales to R.U.C., 1979–1980, BLBC.

which engages in a consistent pattern of gross violations of internationally recognized human rights'.[122]

The situation was unresolved when the 1979 summer recess at Westminster began on 27 July and remained on the agenda when parliament reconvened in October. Ian Paisley, fresh from his typically vociferous objections to the visit of Pope John Paul II to Ireland in September, described 'a disgraceful situation in which a friendly power is refusing to supply arms to the legal police force of another friendly power'.[123] Paisley's rage was reflective of serious IRA violence over the summer of 1979.

On the morning of Monday, 27 August 1979, Lord Louis Mountbatten, the former Governor General of India and a cousin of both Queen Elizabeth II and Prince Phillip, was sat in his boat at Mullaghmore harbour in County Sligo along with his fourteen-year-old grandson, Nicholas Knatchbull, Lady Bradbourne, and fifteen-year-old Paul Maxwell, who had a summer job at a boatman. Sat a short distance away was Provisional IRA volunteer Thomas McMahon who had planted a remote-control bomb in the boat. McMahon detonated the device and the four occupants of the boat were all killed instantly. McMahon was arrested after being stopped at a police checkpoint and received a life sentence, from which he was released under the terms of the Good Friday Agreement in August 1998. Later that day, the IRA killed eighteen soldiers in a dual bomb attack at Narrow Water Castle outside Newry. The victims included Lt Col. David Blair, the most senior soldier to die in the Northern Ireland troubles, and Michael Hudson, a birdwatcher who happened to be employed as a coachman at Buckingham Palace. The IRA volunteers responsible for the attack, Brendan Burns and Joe Brennan, were arrested shortly afterwards by the Irish security forces, but released because of a lack of evidence.

The following day, Tip O'Neill issued a statement expressing his shock and sadness at 'these reprehensible acts' and again called for

[122] Letter from Ad Hoc Committee to Congress, 28/6/1979, Congressional Archives, Thomas P. O'Neill Papers, Series II: Staff Files, Subseries A: Kirk O'Donnell Files, Sub-subseries 21/21, Ireland-Ad Hoc Congressional Committee for Irish Affairs, 1977–1983, BLBC.
[123] On the Papal visit, see *IT*, 24/7/1979 and 29/9/1979; Royal Ulster Constabulary (Arms Supply), Hansard, HC vol. 972, cols 608–610 (25 October 1979), available at https://api.parliament.uk/historic-hansard/commons/1979/oct/25/royal-ulster-constabulary-arms-supply.

Irish Americans to renounce violence.[124] The American media were also highly critical of the IRA after the attacks. For the *Boston Globe*, the 'hideous murders ... the provisional army's action against Mountbatten and the others engenders no sympathy for their cause. The murders only strengthen arguments for the use of strong-armed tactics in the already ravaged countryside'.[125] The *New York Times* carried an article entitled, 'How to Punish the I.R.A.' and the *Baltimore Sun* discussed the possibility of British army withdrawal from Northern Ireland, predicting 'Sectarian civil warfare with mass suffering and initial "victory" for Protestants' in the event of such a withdrawal.[126] Meanwhile, the *Belfast Telegraph* commented:

> The view in Whitehall is that both domestic and international pressure may now persuade the Dublin Government that they would have public support for tackling the crucial question of how to bring fugitive terrorists, operating from the Irish Republic to justice. And, it was felt today that the response in the United States to the murder of Lord Mountbatten—a distinguished Second World War commander—will reduce attempts by Irish American politicians to muscle in on British policies towards Ulster.[127]

In her memoirs, Margaret Thatcher recalled that she 'lost no opportunity to use the revulsion the killings provoked in the United States to inform public opinion there about the realities of life in Ulster'. She considered that 'The emotions and loyalties of millions of decent Irish-Americans are manipulated by Irish Republican extremists, who have been able to give a romantic respectability to terrorism that its sordid reality belies'. She was also deeply critical of Speaker O'Neill for the blockade on guns for the RUC, an 'absurd situation' in which she felt the Speaker's intransigence offered legitimacy to radical Irish Americans.[128] This perception was not helped by Mario Biaggi's

---

[124] 24/10 Ireland—Mountbatten killing, August 1979, Statement by Speaker Thomas P. O'Neill, Jr. 28/8/1979, in Congressional Archives, Thomas P. O'Neill Papers, Series II: Staff Files, Subseries A: Kirk O'Donnell Files, Sub-subseries 20: Box 24, BLBC.

[125] *Boston Globe*, 29/8/1979.

[126] *NYT*, 29/8/1979; *The Sun (Baltimore)*, 30/8/1979.

[127] *Belfast Telegraph*, 28/9/1979.

[128] Thatcher, M., *The Downing Street Years* (London: HarperCollins, 1993), p. 58.

statement which claimed a significant portion of the credit for the blockade.[129]

November 1979 saw Jack Lynch visit the United States. The purpose of his visit was fourfold: the reaffirmation of Irish-American links; the issue of Northern Ireland; the relationship between the United States and the European Economic Community; and the development of industrial relations and tourism.[130] The issue of investment in Ireland was emphasised during an address in Washington:

> Their stress on peace and reconciliation and on the value of stability in encouraging investment in Northern Ireland is particularly welcome. There are parts of the area where over 30% of the labour force is unemployed—and have been for generations. Deprivation at that level breeds violence just as violence in turn, breeds deprivation. And only the most determined efforts involving a massive investment both of finance and of goodwill can break into that festering cycle of degradation and death.[131]

Lynch also gave an address to the National Press Club in which he praised the Carter administration for its commitment to providing economic aid.[132] Carter had a keen understanding of the problems facing Northern Ireland and his support for this particular measure provides an early indication that economic development would be crucial to political reconciliation. Sean Donlon later reflected on how attuned Carter had been to the situation in Northern Ireland:

> The day Jack Lynch arrived, the American Embassy and its occupants were taken hostage in Tehran. So Jack Lynch being an old hand at politics said 'look, get in touch with the White

---

[129]   Congressional Record Extensions of Remarks, December 18, 1979, Amnesty International 1979 Report on Human Rights in Northern Ireland, Hon. Mario Biaggi of New York, in Congressional Archives, Thomas P. O'Neill Papers, Series II: Staff Files, Subseries A: Kirk O'Donnell Files, Sub-subseries 21/21, Ireland-Ad Hoc Congressional Committee for Irish Affairs, 1977–1983, BLBC.

[130]   Letter to Department of Foreign Affairs, 26/9/1979, Taoiseach Mr. J. Lynch visit to USA, November 1979, TAOIS 2009/135/716, NAI.

[131]   Address by the Taoiseach, Mr. J. Lynch, T.D., at the dinner in honour of Vice-President Mondale, Anderson House, Washington, DC, on Friday, 9th November, 1979, in Taoiseach Mr. J. Lynch visit to USA, November 1979, TAOIS 2009/135/716, NAI.

[132]   Ibid.

House and tell them we don't expect the President to devote half a day tomorrow to Ireland'. The plan was that there would be a meeting from ten to midday then there would be a joint press conference and then there would be a lunch hosted by the President. Jack said 'look, he'll have more on his plate than dealing with Ireland, tell him we'll just do a press appearance and a lunch and leave him free to deal with this appalling situation in Tehran'. The answer came back 'the President will stick to his schedule'. We started the meeting with Jimmy Carter opening a book, a briefing book which he had obviously studied the previous night about patterns of discrimination in Fermanagh. I mean, he floored us. First of all, Jack Lynch hadn't a clue about patterns of discrimination in Fermanagh ... but Carter was fascinated by it. And here was the President of the United States, his Embassy in Tehran besieged, his employees taken hostage and he had obviously spent half the night studying patterns of discrimination in Fermanagh.[133]

Soon after Lynch departed, attention turned to the upcoming visit of Margaret Thatcher, her inaugural visit to Washington as Prime Minister. Biaggi and others were concerned that Thatcher would attempt to use the visit to end the arms embargo.[134] Speaker O'Neill was also wary of this, as a memo from his aide Kirk O'Donnell emphasised that he could 'expect intense pressure' over the issue.[135] The issue had caused some embarrassment for the Carter Administration; the State Department emphasised that 'our impartiality on Northern Ireland does not mean that we are impartial as between a legally constituted police force of a democratic government such as the United Kingdom, and armed terrorist groups. There is no impartiality as far as that goes'.[136]

---

[133] Sean Donlon, interview with author, 24/2/2012.
[134] Letter from Michael Waldron, Chairman Democratic City Committee, Malden MA to O'Neill, 18/12/1979, Congressional Archives, Thomas P. O'Neill Papers, Series II: Staff Files, Subseries A: Kirk O'Donnell Files, Sub-subseries 24/11, Ireland—US Gun Sales to R.U.C., 1979–1980, BLBC.
[135] Memorandum to O'Neill from Kirk O'Donnell, 're Mrs. Thatcher's Visit—Irish update, 17/12/1979', Congressional Archives, Thomas P. O'Neill Papers, Series II: Staff Files, Subseries A: Kirk O'Donnell Files, Sub-subseries 24/6 Ireland—Thatcher Political Initiative and Visit, 1979–1980, BLBC.
[136] Cited in Letter from A.L. Free-Gore, Republic of Ireland Department to P.W.J. Buxton NIO, 5/10/1979, in Weapons used by security forces in N. Ireland, FCO 87/958, TNA.

Confrontation between Congress and the White House over US foreign policy had also been evident ahead of Harold Wilson's 1975 visit to Washington, with the former keen to curb Presidential power ahead of the 1976 Presidential election.[137] This was again an issue in 1979.

Before the Prime Minister's visit, Foreign Secretary Lord Carrington spoke to Secretary of State Cyrus Vance and 'made plain his dissatisfaction with American decisions on arms for the RUC, and warned Mr Vance that public opinion in the United Kingdom would get increasingly upset about the American attitude'.[138] The meeting had clearly rankled Vance to the extent that he contacted Ambassador Nicholas Henderson to ask if the British could refrain from repeating requests for RUC arms during what was termed a period of 'political liability'. No specific date was given for the point at which a request would be welcomed, but Henderson was left 'in no doubt that it would be until after the Presidential elections. It remained his view that any precise action would create serious political difficulties: the clear message the State Department had received from Speaker O'Neill and other moderates in congress'.[139] This was problematic for the British given that the Presidential election was, at the time, still a full year away.

Carter was becoming increasingly preoccupied with the approaching election, not least because he faced the serious challenge, from within his own party, of Senator Edward Kennedy. On 9 December 1978, during a speech at the Democratic Party's midterm conference, Kennedy challenged Carter on the issue of domestic spending. Kennedy insisted that the speech was not an indication that he would challenge Carter for the Democratic Party's nomination for the 1980 Presidential election. Carter was less convinced: 'I presume he'll run, he'll win the nomination and I'll back him'.[140] The following September, it was reported that Kennedy had told Carter that he was seriously considering challenging

---

[137] Visit of the Prime Minister to Washington, 7–8 May 1975, Steering Brief by the Foreign and Commonwealth Office, in Prime Minister's visit to Washington, 7/5/1975, PREM 16/730, TNA.

[138] GGH Walden minute to Mr Newington, Republic of Ireland department, 27/9/1979, in Weapons used by security forces in N. Ireland, FCO 87/958, TNA.

[139] Telegram from Henderson, Embassy in Washington to FCO, 3/10/1979, in Weapons used by security forces in N. Ireland, FCO 87/958, TNA.

[140] *NYT*, 10/12/1978.

him for the nomination.[141] Carter eventually secured the nomination at the Democratic Party Convention in August 1980.[142]

The run-up to the election provided Mario Biaggi with the opportunity to reinsert himself firmly into national political discourse. After supporting Carter's campaign for election in 1976, Biaggi also spoke in favour of his campaign for re-election.[143] His vocal support for the President drew concern from the UK and prompted Nicholas Henderson to consider that Biaggi was 'playing a major role as a Congressional strategist in Carter's renomination campaign. He thus has access to Carter's inner circle'.[144] Journalist Jack Anderson suggested that the ever-cunning Biaggi had in fact developed a close relationship with Vice-President Walter Mondale.[145]

Before the end of 1979, Carter's international problems had swollen to include concerns over the Strategic Arms Limitation Treaty II, signed by Carter and Soviet premier Leonid Brezhnev on 18 June 1979. Shortly after this, Carter signed the first directive for secret aid to opponents of the pro-USSR regime in Kabul on 3 July.[146] Sixteen days later, the Sandinistas seized power in Nicaragua. In November, Iranian students seized the American Embassy in Tehran.

It was in the context of the Iranian Embassy occupation that Margaret Thatcher arrived in Washington for her first meeting with Carter since her election. The UK Ambassador to the United States, Nicholas Henderson, recalled of the meeting that 'the two hours of talks went well. The President was quiet, but clear and well briefed. There was only one subject about which he obviously did not wish to speak— arms for the RUC. He admitted to Mrs T that he agreed with her: the licence for the export of the arms should be granted by the USA, but the

[141]   *NYT*, 12/9/1978.
[142]   *NYT*, 15/8/1980.
[143]   Prime Minister's Visit to Washington, 17–18 December 1979, brief by the Northern Ireland Office, in Weapons used by security forces in N. Ireland, FCO 87/958, TNA.
[144]   Telegram from Henderson to FCO, 11/12/1979, in Weapons used by security forces in N. Ireland, FCO 87/958, TNA.
[145]   Jack Anderson's European Column, 28/4/1980, copy in Congressional Archives, Thomas P. O'Neill Papers, Series II: Staff Files, Subseries A: Kirk O'Donnell Files, Sub-subseries 21/21, Ireland-Ad Hoc Congressional Committee for Irish Affairs, 1977–1983, BLBC.
[146]   Zbigniew Brzezinski, interview with *Le Nouvel Observateur*, 15–21/1/1998.

trouble was that the Congress would not allow it'.[147] Carter emphasised to the British that:

> the difficulty was one of timing. The administration was consulting the Congress: the approval of Congress would be necessary if the sale was to take place. Mr Vance said at the moment the administration did not have the votes to secure the approval of Congress. The Speaker, Mr O'Neill, had sufficient votes to prevent approval going through and was prepared to use them. The Prime Minister asked how long this situation was likely to obtain. The President suggested that she should talk to Speaker O'Neill later in the day. Mr O'Neill had drafted a resolution on the subject and had already collected enough signatures to ensure that approval would be blocked. The President said that he himself would like to approve the sale but did not wish to be defeated in Congress or to have a major altercation with them. The political problem of handling the Northern Ireland issue in the United States would be exacerbated if he took on Congress and lost. Speaker O'Neill rarely became personally involved in policy issues. But this problem was a personal one for him.[148]

Later that same day, Thatcher met Speaker O'Neill. O'Neill thanked Thatcher for British support over the occupation of the Iranian Embassy, without making reference to the ongoing blockade of weapons for the RUC.[149] The British Embassy in Tehran had also been attacked and Embassy staff were held under armed guard for a short period of time, estimated to be roughly five hours.[150] The American response was the issuance of Executive Order 12170 on 14 November, which involved

---

[147] Henderson, *Mandarin*, p. 318.

[148] Record of a Conversation between the Prime Minister and the President of the United States, at the White House, on 17 December 1979 at 10.30, in Weapons used by the security forces in N. Ireland, FCO 87/959, TNA.

[149] Remarks by Speaker Thomas P. O'Neill, Jr. welcoming Prime Minister Margaret Thatcher, December 17, 1979, Congressional Archives, Thomas P. O'Neill Papers, Series II: Staff Files, Subseries A: Kirk O'Donnell Files, Sub-subseries 24/6, Ireland—Thatcher Political Initiative and Visit, 1979–1980, BLBC.

[150] Tehran (British Embassy), Hansard, HC vol. 973, cols 225–228 (6 November 1979), available at https://api.parliament.uk/historic-hansard/commons/1979/nov/06/tehran-british-embassy.

the freezing of Iranian assets.[151] There was an expectation that the British would follow suit, despite both Thatcher and Henderson noting the problems inherent in doing so.[152] The media were quick to pick up a perceived inconsistency in the US position. As the *New York Times* noted, 'while Washington has been pressing the British to punish terrorism in Iran—by cancelling contracts signed since the hostages were seized— the United States has been refusing to approve a perfectly proper British purchase of Ruger revolvers to counter terrorism in Northern Ireland'.[153] Lord Carrington, quoted in the same article, commented that 'you, who we think are our friends, are unable to supply us with the pistols we need for the R.U.C. because of opposition in Congress. It's rather the same thing, isn't it?'[154] Mario Biaggi, for one, did not agree. In the same newspaper, he commented that Carrington's

> analogy about Iran constitutes more of a fault than a triumph. Our position in Iran is wholly consistent with our policy in Ireland. In both instances, we are motivated by a high sense of morality. Guns should not be sold to police organizations which do not respect human rights. We consider it morally right to ask our allies to impose sanctions on the Government of Iran for their illegal and immoral holding of our citizens for some 200 days. It is the British—in both cases—who are engaging in selective morality.[155]

The Chicago Tribune was also critical of Carrington, suggesting that 'Britain's normally sensible and wise foreign secretary, was neither sensible nor wise the other day when he defended the British Parliament's decision to renege on agreed European commercial sanctions against Iran … The difference is that the British Parliament was wrong, and the U.S. Congress was right'.[156] Carrington, who

---

[151] Executive Order 12170—Blocking Iranian Government property, 14/11/1979, 44 FR 65729, National Archives and Records Administration, available at www. archives.gov/federal-register/codification/executive-order/12170.html.

[152] Prime Minister (Engagements), Hansard, HC vol. 976, cols 868–72 (20 November 1979), available at https://api.parliament.uk/historic-hansard/commons/1979/ nov/20/prime-minister-engagements#S5CV0976P1_19791120_HOC_135. Also Henderson, *Mandarin*, p. 312.

[153] *NYT*, 28/5/1980.

[154] Ibid.

[155] *NYT*, 7/6/1980.

[156] *Chicago Tribune*, 30/5/1980.

served as Thatcher's Foreign Secretary until his resignation following the Argentinian invasion of the Falkland Islands, would later reflect: 'Like most of my fellow-countrymen, I found the attitude of foreigners the most irritating facet of the Northern Ireland situation, be they American or European ... it was hard to sit down under the ignorant criticism of outsiders'.[157]

With British support for the Americans over the Iranian issue failing to meet the expectations of some, a resolution to the RUC gun embargo became less likely. A briefing for the Permanent Under Secretary at the Foreign Office noted that 'If we are too beastly about Northern Ireland, the Americans might get difficult over Iran, where we are unable to help them over the freezing of Iranian assets. I certainly do not think (as Sir N Henderson appears to) that we have a great deal of credit over Iran which can be deployed in the arms for the RUC context'.[158] Henderson himself observed that 'the present is a bad moment in which to hope that we can get our way on what seems to us an unanswerable case. What indeed makes it even more unanswerable is that we are giving the USA a lot of help over Iran and they recognise this'.[159]

The RUC gun blockade quickly became more about political principle than security needs. A memo from the Foreign Office captured the British attitude toward the issue concisely:

> the RUC were not, in fact, much fussed on this issue; they could get arms elsewhere. At the same time we should doubtless tell the Embassy that they should keep up pressure on the Americans on this subject as a matter of principle. American denial of arms for the RUC looks like a condemnation of their methods and indeed a vote for HMG's opponents on Northern Ireland, including the terrorists. Presumably, therefore, our official stance should remain the same; but, given the RUC attitude, we might perhaps give the Embassy latitude to press the Americans a little less hard than they might otherwise have done.[160]

[157] Lord Carrington, *Reflect on Things Past* (Glasgow: William Collins, 1988), p. 249; on his resignation, pp. 370–372.
[158] Briefing for the PUS, Arms for the RUC, 12/12/1979, in Weapons used by security forces in N. Ireland, FCO 87/959, TNA.
[159] Telegram from Henderson to FCO, 11/12/1979, in Weapons used by security forces in N. Ireland, FCO 87/959, TNA.
[160] Memorandum from MS Berthoud, North American Department to Mr Newington, 5/9/1979, in Weapons used by security forces in N. Ireland, FCO 87/958, TNA.

The recipient of this memo annotated on it that 'I don't believe we can afford to let up: the PM is interested'. The issue was particularly sore for the British given the inability of the American authorities to stem the flow of weaponry to the IRA from American sources. On 1 November, the Irish security forces seized a quantity of arms at Dublin docks which were believed to have been in transit from the USA to the IRA. It contained 156 weapons and included a M60 machine gun.

The Lynch Resignation

A matter of days after returning from his trip to the United States, Jack Lynch resigned as Taoiseach and was replaced by Charles Haughey. His resignation angered Speaker O'Neill, who had helped organise the official visit the previous month. Sean Donlon recalled:

> The visit itself worked well but Tip was very cross because within days of concluding the visit, Jack Lynch stepped down. Tip was very, very cross about that, never forgave Jack. I didn't want him to come for a lap of honour and if … he knew beforehand that he was about to offer his resignation, then [O'Neill] wouldn't have tolerated it. So he never forgave Lynch, I don't think they had any contact after that because Tip had put a lot of his own credibility on the line. They have lots of American visitors in Washington. It is very rare to have what's called a full state visit or a full official visit because if the United States started doing that for every country, they'd do nothing else but entertain foreign visitors, so they're very restrictive of foreign state visits or foreign official visits. So, it was a huge thing to get and then, as I say, Tip took the view that Jack had abused it by not making it clear beforehand that it was his lap of honour, so the visit went well, but the aftermath was not happy.[161]

The return of Charles Haughey, who had stood accused of supplying weapons to the Provisional IRA in 1970, brought with it significant distrust within the British establishment. In her memoirs, Margaret Thatcher commented that, despite his acquittal, 'Haughey had throughout his career been associated with the most Republican strand

---

[161]   Sean Donlon, interview with author, 24/2/2012.

in respectable Irish politics. How 'respectable' was a subject of some controversy'.[162] Sherard Cowper-Coles later recalled the tension of the time: 'Haughey ... was regarded as having strong green sympathies', which was problematic given that 'Christopher-Ewart-Biggs had been assassinated, and there wasn't really a proper Anglo-Irish process yet'.[163] Haughey sought to create collaboration between the Irish Government and groups such as Noraid and the Irish National Caucus and was quickly discouraged from doing so by Sean Donlon, the Ambassador in Washington. Haughey's response was to seek Donlon's removal from the post in order to install a more cooperative figure in his stead. This move drew quick and vocal condemnation from both John Hume and figures like Ted Kennedy and Tip O'Neill. The new Taoiseach was forced to backtrack.[164]

With Carter focused on the 1980 Presidential election, the vast majority of talks on the issue of Northern Ireland that took place that year were between the British and Irish Governments. In early 1980, Secretary of State for Northern Ireland Humphrey Atkins reintroduced the idea of a Constitutional Convention, which Harold Wilson's Labour Government had organised in 1975. Merlyn Rees announced the closure of the Convention in March 1976 after the parties in Northern Ireland failed to reach agreement. The same fate befell Atkins's Convention, although the latter attempt failed even to secure participation, let alone anything resembling consensus.[165] Significantly, through its failure to secure agreement between the communities of Northern Ireland, Constitutional Convention did help to establish the context for later peace agreements and the absolute necessity of consensus in the form of a devolved power-sharing assembly form of government. There was also some movement in terms of cooperation between the British and Irish governments. In February, Haughey had asked the British government to join the Republic in the search for a lasting solution, one which would involve the EEC and the United States.[166] There was a generally positive mood, reflected in reports emerging that both Haughey and Thatcher had 'agreed that

---

[162] Thatcher, *Downing Street Years*, p. 388.
[163] Sir Sherard Cowper-Coles, interview with author, 29/4/2013.
[164] See Fitzpatrick, *John Hume in America*, pp. 77–82.
[165] McEvoy, J., *The Politics of Northern Ireland* (Edinburgh: Edinburgh University Press, 2008), p. 77.
[166] *IT*, 18/2/1980.

they wished to develop new and closer political cooperation between the two Governments'.[167]

This cooperation would be tested over the coming months as the Irish republican paramilitary prisoner campaigns, ongoing since 1976, reached a dramatic climax in the form of two hunger strikes. The first of these began on 27 October 1980.[168] One month into the strike, four Congressmen—Mario Biaggi, Hamilton Fish, Ben Gilman, and Lester Wolff—appealed to the United Nations to mediate in the dispute.[169] A few days later, Senator-elect Alfonse D'Amato used the occasion of one of his first official trips to visit the Maze prison. D'Amato said: 'Long Kesh has become a symbol to the Catholic minority of British misrule in Northern Ireland'.[170] Of course, many Protestants also found themselves incarcerated in the Lisburn facility.

One week later, the 1980 United States Presidential election saw Republican Ronald Reagan carry forty-four states and the highest number of electoral votes ever won by a non-incumbent President when he defeated Jimmy Carter. The election of Reagan provided an opportunity for Britain to redefine its Northern Irish policy, at least as it pertained to the American dimension of the conflict, bringing in an administration that was highly sympathetic to the Conservative Party government in London. The relationship between the Thatcher and Carter governments had been uneasy, never more so than over the issue of Northern Ireland; according to her Personal Private Secretary Charles Powell, now Lord Powell, 'she regarded Carter as a weak man, who would not stand up to political pressures, people on the left, the Kennedys and so on'.[171] Lord Armstrong, Thatcher's key negotiator on the Anglo-Irish Agreement, also recalled, 'she had no respect for Carter, really. Reagan, she did have respect for: Reagan for his beliefs and his convictions'.[172]

Carter had enjoyed a very cordial relationship with Jim Callaghan during the two years they shared as leaders of their respective nations. Significantly, Thatcher's great domestic opponent, Neil Kinnock, who served as Labour Party leader and Leader of the Opposition for

---

[167] *IT*, 22/5/1980.
[168] It ended on 18 December with no deaths.
[169] *NYT*, 28/11/1980.
[170] *NYT*, 30/11/1980.
[171] Lord Powell, interview with author, 25/4/2013.
[172] Lord Armstrong, interview with author, 9/10/2013.

most of Thatcher's premiership, recalled his affection for Carter: 'my inclination was to sympathise with Carter's innate decency and attempts at progressive policies but to regard his defeat as almost inevitable'. Kinnock recalled the relationship between the Reagan administration and the UK Labour Party as 'a mixture of farcical and toxic'.[173]

Certainly there is much evidence that both Senator Edward Kennedy and Speaker Tip O'Neill had exerted considerable influence over Carter's Northern Ireland policy, but this should be considered in the context of the early 1970s, the early period of the conflict. At this time, many elected representatives became interested and outspoken on the issue of Northern Ireland and the role of Kennedy and O'Neill as well as, to a lesser extent, Daniel Moynihan and Hugh Carey, as a conduit for the issue within the United States was valuable. The Four Horsemen helped to channel US interest in Northern Ireland into a more constructive role, exemplified in the August 1977 Carter Statement. The role of the Carter administration in helping to lead Irish America away from radical groups like Noraid and the Irish National Caucus should not be underestimated.

Jimmy Carter's final day in office was 20 January 1981. The IRA marked the occasion by killing suspected informer Maurice Gilvarry in South Armagh and Private Christopher Shenton in Derry. The following day, they shot dead eighty-six-year-old Sir Norman Stronge and his son at their home.[174]

In December 2010, DuPont marked fifty years in Derry. Former plant manager, Professor Peter McKie, spoke to the *Belfast Telegraph* about the challenges the plant had faced in its earliest years, with a lack of skilled labour available to man the chemical processes that were an integral part of the daily operations of the factories. McKie remarked that 'chemical engineers were few and far between in Derry, so we had to take young farmers and train them to be chemical engineers'. He also noted that the plant depended on the skills of former members of the British military who had married locally and remained in the area. Both McKie and former financial and service support manager Bertie Faulkner poignantly paid tribute to their mentor, Jeffrey Agate.[175]

[173]   Lord Kinnock, correspondence with author, 21/3/2012.
[174]   McKittrick et al., *Lost Lives*, pp. 848–849.
[175]   *Belfast Telegraph*, 14/12/2010.

CHAPTER FOUR

Thatcher, Reagan, and Northern Ireland

Ireland was not really in the geopolitical thick of things in Washington and, despite what US census surveys might suggest, there were not 40 million Americans—or indeed any sizeable political community in the US—with any interest in what was happening in Ireland.[1]

> Sean Donlon, former Ambassador of the Republic of Ireland to the United States of America

I think from the middle of the decade onwards, the increasing American awareness of international terrorism as an issue with Libya, with the Berlin bombing, Leon Klinghoffer, all of those events in the mid-1980s alerted America to international terrorism in way that they perhaps hadn't been alerted before and made them at least wiser to what was going on in Northern Ireland and less sympathetic to the IRA as a result.[2]

> Sir Nigel Sheinwald, former Ambassador of the United Kingdom to the United States of America

On 14 January 1989, as Ronald Reagan prepared to leave office, the *Irish Times* carried an article by the former Ambassador of the Republic of Ireland to the United States, Sean Donlon, entitled 'Reagan's Irish

---

[1]   *IT*, 14/1/1989.
[2]   Sir Nigel Sheinwald, interview with author, 26/4/2013.

Connection'. This article chronicled the relationship that outgoing President Ronald Reagan had with Ireland. This relationship stretched back to the 1940s when Reagan, in his capacity as a Hollywood representative, first visited Ireland.[3] Later, as Governor of California in the 1970s, Reagan visited Ireland on behalf of President Nixon and travelled the south and west of the country, stopping at the Rock of Cashel.[4] Donlon suggested that Reagan's 'interest in Ireland went deeper than sentiment and story. The challenge for Ireland was to channel that interest to advantage, knowing that there was likely to be an especially close relationship with his ideological soul-mate at No 10 Downing Street'.[5] Later, Donlon recalled his own role in Reagan's relationship with Ireland: 'During the campaign I went to see Reagan to ask him what part of Ireland he came from, where his family came from. 'No, no', he said, 'my people were not Irish, we're English'. He believed it and he was absolutely right, he got his brother, who was a doctor, to give me copies of family papers and, right enough, it showed, as far back as they were able to go was to the UK'. Donlon continued:

> What had happened was the family had left Ballyporeen in Tipperary to travel to the United States. [The] mother went into premature labour before she boarded the ship in London to the States, but they stayed in London only long enough to catch the next sailing of the same line because they didn't have money to buy a new ticket and whatever the arrangement was, about six weeks later they were able to get another ship from the same line and continue their journey to the States. So it was in fact through the Mormons in Salt Lake City that we established all of that because they had the shipping records and they were extremely helpful. So that October, the election was November, I asked to see Reagan and I told him, 'We've established you are Irish, not British', and showed him the documentation. Interestingly, he asked me to keep it secret and said, 'I'm not going to play that card at this stage in the campaign'. I think frankly he also preferred and in particular Nancy Reagan preferred that he would be portrayed as a WASP not as an Irish-American Catholic. If you look back on the campaign that

---

[3]   See also *Public Papers of the Presidents of the United States—Ronald Reagan, 1981* (Washington, DC: United States Government Printing Office 1984), p. 259.
[4]   *IT*, 15/6/1972.
[5]   *IT*, 14/1/1989.

all the time he played that Protestant card, kind of concealing the Irish-American bit. He did say, 'if you keep it quiet, if I'm elected President, on St Patrick's Day, you can have a party and present me with my Irish roots'. And that's what I did, on St Patrick's Day [1981], Reagan came to the Embassy, we had a great lunch and I presented him with the family tree, linking him back to Ballyporeen in Tipperary and then he visited Ballyporeen … So he was eventually actually quite funny about his Irish roots, but Nancy was never comfortable with it; she much preferred the WASP bit.[6]

The statecraft evident in Donlon's approaches to Reagan, pre-election, helped to influence the President throughout his administration, though a great deal was also owed to the Speaker of the House, Tip O'Neill. Internationally, Reagan's close relationship with Thatcher would define the political relationship between the two states over the eight years that they shared in office, but it is worth noting that despite Thatcher's existing fondness for Reagan, Lord Carrington and the Foreign Office were more cautious about the incoming President. Robin Renwick, then working in the Rhodesia department of the Foreign Office but appointed as the UK Ambassador to the United States in 1991, later recalled that Carrington was 'alarmed by his anti-Soviet rhetoric'.[7]

For her part, although Margaret Thatcher remarked in her memoirs that she 'liked Jimmy Carter; he was a good friend to me and to Britain', Lord Powell, Thatcher's Personal Private Secretary, recalled her saying Carter was 'weak'.[8] Her account of her first meeting with Reagan, on the other hand, noted: 'I had been immediately struck by his warmth, charm and complete lack of affectation'.[9] For his part, in his diary, Reagan noted that 'Margaret Thatcher is a tower of strength and a solid friend of the U.S.'[10]

[6]   Sean Donlon, interview with author, 24/2/2012. WASP—White Anglo Saxon Protestant.

[7]   Renwick, R., *A Journey with Margaret Thatcher: Foreign Policy Under the Iron Lady* (London: Biteback, 2013), p. 96.

[8]   Thatcher, *Downing Street Years*, pp. 68–69; Lord Powell, interview with author, 25/4/2013.

[9]   Thatcher, *Downing Street Years*, p. 157.

[10]   Reagan, R., with Brinkley, D., *The Reagan Diaries* (New York: HarperCollins, 2007), p. 32.

Donlon, who served as the Irish Ambassador in Washington until 1984, had seen major shifts in government in each of the United States, United Kingdom, and Republic of Ireland. This latter change nearly forced Donlon's departure from Washington until the intervention of powerful friends in the US Congress, or, in Donlon's own words, a 'small number of very well-placed US politicians of Irish ancestry who, throughout the Seventies had responded very generously to suggestions to take an interest in Ireland'.[11] This group of politicians led by Senator Edward Kennedy and Speaker Tip O'Neill formed the Congressional Friends of Ireland in 1981 and helped to change the dynamic of the US relationship with the Northern Ireland conflict. Official Noraid remittances to Ireland for the period July 1971 to January 1979, which stood at a little over $1.5 million,[12] began to drop and the introduction of US government contributions to the International Fund for Ireland, created in 1986 by the British and Irish Governments, totalled $130 million by the end of Reagan's Presidency.[13]

Much as changes were ongoing in Irish America during the 1980s, so too did the dynamics of the Northern Ireland conflict change, substantially. In 1976, the Irish Republican Army had revised its strategy, which brought a reduction in the volume of violence. This is not to say that there was a significant drop in bloodshed, of course: of the 778 people who died in the conflict during the Reagan administration, 492 were killed by republican paramilitaries. The IRA may have claimed more lives than any other republican group, but the role of the Irish National Liberation Army should not be understated. The INLA had been responsible for the murder of Airey Neave, a close ally of Margaret Thatcher, a murder that shaped Thatcher's views on the Northern Ireland conflict. As noted by Simon Hoggart, 'knowing her deep attachment to Airey Neave, it was thought intolerable that she should face this crucial start to the election campaign so soon after the tragedy'.[14] Thatcher's remarks that 'we must carry on for the things he fought for and not let the people who got him triumph',

[11] *IT*, 14/1/1989.

[12] Summary of Noraid Returns to the US Department of Justice, in Ireland and US Policy on Northern Ireland, National Archives of Ireland, TAOIS/2009/135/745, NAI.

[13] The International Fund for Ireland, available at www.internationalfundfor-ireland.com/about-the-fund.

[14] *Guardian*, 31/3/1979; Holland, J. and McDonald, H., *INLA* (Dublin: Torc, 1994), pp. 131–139.

would define her attitude towards Irish republicanism throughout her time in office.[15]

Thatcher had some popularity within the United States prior to Reagan's election. She travelled extensively throughout the country in 1967 after being selected by the American Embassy in London to take part in the Foreign Leader Program. The trip between 20 February and 31 March 1967 saw Thatcher meet political and business figures as well as representatives of the International Monetary Fund.[16] Jean Lashly of the Bureau of Educational and Cultural Affairs at the State Department noted that Thatcher was 'undoubtedly one of the most delightful and competent visitors we have had. She has charmed and impressed local sponsors from coast to coast'.[17] She met California Governor Ronald Reagan in 1972 when Reagan visited Europe as an emissary of President Nixon. In her role as Secretary of State for Education and Sciences, Thatcher was present at a lunch at Downing Street in Reagan's honour. She was first introduced to Reagan's ideas by her husband Denis, who attended a talk delivered by Governor Reagan to the Institute of Directors at the Royal Albert Hall in November 1969.[18] Reagan spoke in the context of the recent deployment of British troops to Northern Ireland as someone who had himself recently deployed the National Guard to tackle student unrest at the University of California, Berkeley.[19] Thatcher and Reagan were in contact frequently and met in both 1975 and 1978, the latter meeting involving an 'exchange [of] ideas', as Reagan travelled internationally to develop his foreign policy credentials ahead of his bid for the Presidency in 1980.[20] On this trip, the US Ambassador in London Kingman Brewster refused to meet Reagan, but the Labour government afforded him a visit with Foreign Secretary David Owen.[21]

[15]   A video of Thatcher's comments is available at https://www.youtube.com/watch?v=IAgMR_gC9IY.

[16]   State Department Program for Margaret Thatcher's 1967 US tour (20 Feb.–31 Mar.), Archives of the Department of State, Washington, DC, available at www.margaretthatcher.org/document/109473.

[17]   Letter from Jean Lashly to Natalie Greening, 29/3/1967, University of Arkansas Libraries, Fayetteville, Special Collections, Group IV, CU Collection, Box 155; Folder 26, 'Margaret Thatcher'.

[18]   Thatcher, M., *The Path to Power* (London: HarperCollins, 1995), p. 372.

[19]   'Forty Years Ago Today: Governor Reagan at the Royal Albert Hall', *Wall Street Journal*, 5/11/2009.

[20]   Letter from Reagan to Thatcher, 29/12/1978, available at http://margaret thatcher.org/document/111687.

[21]   Aldous, R., *Reagan and Thatcher* (London: Hutchinson, 2012), p. 15.

Resolving the RUC Guns Embargo

Reagan's immediate focus upon his inauguration was that of improving the US economy. Unemployment leapt from 5.8 per cent in 1979 to 7.1 per cent in 1980, and would continue to rise, not dropping below 6 per cent until 1988.[22] The British, however, were interested in attempting to persuade the President to lift the embargo on weapons for the Royal Ulster Constabulary. The Foreign Office noted that the inauguration 'requires us to revert in Washington to the ban on the export of Ruger revolvers from the US for use by the RUC'. They considered that: 'As long as the ban remains opponents of UK Government policy can plausibly say to the US public that the RUC is not regarded by the US Government as a legitimate or trustworthy police force'.[23]

How best to resolve the issue remained a matter of contention. In Belfast, civil servants suggested obtaining a British-made weapon, whilst those in London were keen to avoid doing this so as not to allow the move to be interpreted as 'an apparent victory for the Irish-American lobby [which] would not be welcome at present.[24] In the event, such a course of action was not necessary because the RUC had continued to obtain Sturm Ruger weapons despite the embargo. They had done so by simply acquiring them from Vikings Arms Limited, the Harrogate company that the Northern Ireland Police Authority used to purchase its weapons. Sturm Ruger's export licence to send the second tranche of 3,000 revolvers to Vikings Arms had been blocked but they were still permitted to send a regular shipment of between fifty and seventy revolvers to Yorkshire each month; the NIPA simply purchased every revolver. The Northern Ireland Office was eventually made aware of the situation in June of 1980, though

---

[22]   The hostages in the US Embassy in Tehran were pointedly released on Reagan's first day in office. Ronald Reagan, 'Address to the Nation', February 5, 1981, text available at https://www.reaganlibrary.gov/research/speeches/20581c; Bureau of Labor Statistics, Labor Force Statistics from the Current Population Survey, available at http://data.bls.gov/timeseries/LNU04000000?years_option =all_years&periods_option=specific_periods&periods=Annual+Data.
[23]   Draft Letter for Signature by I.M. Burns, 9/12/1980, National Archives, The US ban on the sale of arms to the Royal Ulster Constabulary (RUC), FCO 87/1048, TNA.
[24]   Memorandum from D.A. Hill, Police Division 'B', Stormont House, 9/12/1980, National Archives, The US ban on the sale of arms to the Royal Ulster Constabulary, FCO 87/1048, TNA.

state papers from the time make it very obvious that the Foreign Office remained in the dark.[25] Practically, the resolution of the issue was easily accomplished, but politically the issue remained how to move past the embargo with all the inherent diplomatic and symbolic conflicts that it had caused. Here, it was important that neither side be seen to be making a concession.

RUC Deputy Chief Constable Jack Hermon was promoted to Chief Constable on 1 January 1980. A year later, Hermon wrote to the Northern Ireland office to explain that 'a quiet resolution of the [RUC gun blockade] problem is what I would really like as it has been a source of constant annoyance to me that the supply of these weapons to the RUC has become an emotive political issue and one that reflects an unfair judgement on the integrity of the Force'. The slow trickle of new weapons, obtained from Viking Arms on a monthly basis, were in fact still arriving at a quicker rate than they could be implemented into the RUC's training programme. Further, the new weapons were found to be too bulky for officers on specialist or plain-clothes duty. By way of official statement on the issue, he concluded the letter: 'I do not wish to proceed with our current request for an additional 3,000 Rugers … I will be content if the existing, unnecessary pressure surrounding the Ruger issue can be relieved and if it is clearly understood that I do not wish to have any more Rugers once the current order of 3,000 revolvers is fulfilled'.[26]

Meanwhile, Sir Nicholas Henderson, who had appeared unaware of the de facto resolution of the situation as late as December, stated 'we should prefer to limit ourselves to saying simply that the guns were acquired legally in the UK through normal commercial channels'.[27] A Foreign Office memo noted the danger of angering Tip O'Neill and offering Mario Biaggi 'a ready-made propaganda theme which

[25]   Memorandum from P.W.J. Buxton to Secretary of State, 2/7/1980, and Letter from D.C. Thomas to M.J. Newington, 16/6/1980, The US ban on the sale of arms to the Royal Ulster Constabulary, FCO 87/1048, TNA, and Letter from S.W. Boys-Smith to M. Alexander, 10 Downing Street, 2/12/1981, The US ban on the sale of arms for the Royal Ulster Constabulary, FCO 87/1220, TNA.
[26]   Letter from Jack Hermon to J.M. Burns, NIO, 26/1/1981, The US ban on the sale of arms for the Royal Ulster Constabulary, FCO 87/1219, TNA.
[27]   Telegram from Henderson to FCO, 16/6/1981, The US ban on the sale of arms for the Royal Ulster Constabulary, FCO 87/1220, and Telegram from Washington to FCO, 19/12/1980, in Weapons used by security forces in N. Ireland, FCO 87/959, TNA.

they could be counted on to exploit to the full; and NORAID and the gunrunners could expect an upsurge in contributions'.[28] Biaggi persisted with the issue, writing to the *New York Times* in May 1980 to observe, 'hope is that there will come a time when the R.U.C. will again be able to receive United States arms'.[29] The New York Congressman had derived significant political capital from his role in the blockade and wrote to Reagan, on behalf of his ad hoc committee, in early 1981 to demand the retention of the embargo.[30] Presidential Assistant Max Frieresdorf confirmed that the administration was 'holding to the policy of not approving licensing for sale of hand-guns to the RUC' but added little else.[31] By this stage, of course, all parties in both the British government and Northern Irish security had moved on. Nicholas Henderson later reflected on the episode:

> My own view is that discretion is the better part of valour on this subject of arms sales. They should never have been ordered specifically by the RUC in the first place but by HMG or the British Army. As it is, the aim should be to avoid giving the IRA the chance to say that they have won a famous victory and one which shows that the USA are on their side. It would be expedient therefore to withdraw the order in return for a promise that there will be no publicity about it and nothing to suggest that we have been turned down. However, I do not think that Mrs Thatcher in her fighting mood is likely to play it that way.[32]

[28] Letter from D.C. Thomas to M.J. Newington, 16/6/1980, The US ban on the sale of arms to the Royal Ulster Constabulary, FCO 87/1048, TNA. See also Sanders, A., 'The Role of Northern Ireland in Modern Anglo-American Relations: The US Department of State and the Royal Ulster Constabulary, 1979', *Journal of Transatlantic Studies* 12(2) (2014), pp. 163–181.

[29] *NYT*, 7/6/1980.

[30] Letter from Ad Hoc Committee for Irish Affairs to President Reagan, 24/2/1981, National Archives, The US ban on the sale of arms for the Royal Ulster Constabulary, FCO 87/1219.

[31] Letter from Max Friedersdorf, Assistant to the President to Bernard Dwyer, 5/3/1981, National Archives, The US ban on the sale of arms for the Royal Ulster Constabulary, FCO 87/1219, TNA.

[32] Henderson, *Mandarin*, p. 284.

The 1981 Hunger Strikes

On 1 March 1981, the IRA's Officer Commanding in the Maze prison, Bobby Sands, began a hunger strike. Four days later, the Member of Parliament for Fermanagh and South Tyrone, Frank Maguire, suffered a fatal heart attack. The decision was made that a hunger striker would stand in the by-election to replace him and the 9 April contest saw Sands defeat Ulster Unionist Harry West by just over 1,000 votes. There was significant American interest in the election, and particularly among the so-called Four Horsemen of Senator Edward Kennedy, Speaker Tip O'Neill, Senator Daniel Patrick Moynihan, and Governor Hugh Carey, now part of a new congressional group that focused on Irish issues. Describing themselves as the 'Congressional Friends of Ireland', they issued a declaration on St Patrick's Day urging 'all Americans to join us in condemning the violence in Northern Ireland, and to forswear any word or deed that fosters further violence'.[33] The same day, President Reagan used the occasion of his first St Patrick's Day to issue a similar statement, calling on 'all Americans to question closely any appeal for financial or other aid from groups involved in the Northern Ireland conflict to ensure that contributions do not end up in the hands of those who perpetuate violence, either directly or indirectly'.[34] These coinciding statements reflected the emerging alignment that Reagan and Speaker O'Neill shared on Irish issues, but reaction from the UK and Ireland was mixed.[35] Irish Taoiseach Charles Haughey welcomed the news of the formation of the group, but the British were cautious. A comment from the Embassy noted that the group sought support from a presumed majority of Irish Americans, who shared their 'commitment to peace, non-violence and unity by agreement', but, significantly, 'this majority is neither organized nor vocal'. In particular, the Irish National

[33]   Friends of Ireland Joint St Patrick's Day Statement 1981, in Congressional Archives, Thomas P. O'Neill Papers, Series II: Staff Files, Subseries A: Kirk O'Donnell Files, Sub-subseries 21/15, Ireland, BLBC.
[34]   Press Guidance (If Asked), Northern Ireland Hunger Strike, WHORM Subject File CO167 United Kingdom, Box 214, Ronald Reagan Presidential Library (hereafter Reagan Library). Cooper notes that Sean Donlon attempted, unsuccessfully, to elicit a more decisive statement from Reagan; see Cooper, *The Politics of Diplomacy*, p. 142.
[35]   *Public Papers of the Presidents of the United States—Ronald Reagan, 1983* (Washington, DC: United States Government Printing Office 1984), p. 405.

Caucus still sought 'to exercise control over Irish affairs in Congress'.[36] To this end, the formation of the Friends of Ireland could scarcely have come at a better time.

The hunger strikes had given a new platform to Irish republicans, not least in the United States. Anti-hunger-strike demonstrations took place in eighteen cities across the United States, and the British Embassy was concerned at reports that the Irish Embassy had reached out to Reagan seeking his assistance in ending the hunger strike.[37] The death of Bobby Sands on 5 May, after sixty-six days on hunger strike, predictably exacerbated these tensions and prompted a letter from the Friends of Ireland to Thatcher, criticising 'a posture of inflexibility that must lead inevitably to more senseless violence and more needless deaths in Northern Ireland'.[38] They warned the Prime Minister that the IRA's US lobby was 'stronger than ever'.[39] There was pressure, too, from state legislatures, notably in the north-east.

The Massachusetts House of Representatives offered a resolution demanding that the British Consulate in Boston be withdrawn until the demands of the prisoners were met and a timetable for the withdrawal of British troops was set. They also suggested additional political and economic sanctions.[40] Meanwhile, the State of Connecticut's General

[36]　Statement by Mr Charles J. Haughey, T.D. Taoiseach (Prime Minister of Ireland) in response to the announcement of proposed Friends of Ireland group in the US Congress, 16/3/1981. Kirk O'Donnell Papers, Boston College Burns Library; Memorandum on 'Friends of Ireland' organization (undated) (c.1981), in Congressional Archives, Thomas P. O'Neill Papers, Series II: Staff Files, Subseries A: Kirk O'Donnell Files, Sub-subseries 21/15, Ireland, BLBC.

[37]　Telegram from UK Embassy Washington to Foreign Office, 15/7/1981, PREM 19/506, TNA.

[38]　Letter from O'Neill, Kennedy, Carey, and Moynihan to Margaret Thatcher, 06/05/1981, in Congressional Archives, Thomas P. O'Neill Papers, Series II: Staff Files, Subseries A: Kirk O'Donnell Files, Sub-subseries 21/15, Ireland, BLBC.

[39]　Telex, 'British Press Coverage of Today, 15 May 1981, of Prime Minister Thatcher's response to Telegram from Senators Kennedy and Moynihan, Speaker O'Neill and New York Governor Carey', 15/05/1981, in Congressional Archives, Thomas P. O'Neill Papers, Series II: Staff Files, Subseries A: Kirk O'Donnell Files, Sub-subseries 21/15, Ireland, BLBC.

[40]　Resolution offered by Representatives Marie Howe (D-Somerville), Charles Doyle (D-Boston), and John McNeil (D-Malden) Adopted Unanimously by the Massachusetts House of Representatives, June 15, 1981—Demanding the Recall and Withdrawal of the British Consulate, in Congressional Archives, Thomas P. O'Neill Papers, Series II: Staff Files, Subseries A: Kirk O'Donnell Files, Sub-subseries 21/15, Ireland, BLBC.

Assembly 'bitterly' condemned 'the actions of the British government in their handling of this affair and call[ed] upon that government to reverse its decision immediately', offering their 'unyielding support' to the hunger strikers.[41]

Tension spread to New York, where British-owned offices in New York City took down the national flag, 'due to protesters ... the British don't want to give the protesters a chance to tear it down'.[42] The escalation of the hunger strike saw further pressure placed on both the British government and their US counterparts.

On 19 May, a week after the death of second hunger striker, Frank Hughes, Speaker O'Neill wrote a lengthy letter to President Reagan about what he termed to be 'a profoundly disturbing development'. He noted that the Thatcher–Haughey discussions of earlier in the year had offered hope of progress, but 'now as a result of the I.R.A. hunger strike and a succession of hunger strikers' deaths, the sectarian divisions in Northern Ireland have intensified, Anglo-Irish political dialogue has ceased and the moderate political leaders in Northern Ireland have been pre-empted by the extremist paramilitary groups'. He added that media coverage of the hunger strike had 'improved the image of the Provisional I.R.A. among thirty million Irish-Americans and reversed a five-year trend of declining financial support of the I.R.A.' O'Neill emphasised:

> This is most unfortunate and deeply upsets me. Senators Kennedy and Moynihan, Governor Carey and I sent Mrs Thatcher a telegram recently asking that she take a more flexible position regarding the prison rules the strikers are protesting. Mrs Thatcher incorrectly interpreted this as seeking political status for the strikers; something we do not seek. Members of the I.R.A. are terrorists and should be treated as such. But by refusing to negotiate regarding prison rules, Mrs Thatcher is permitting the terrorists to undo significant political progress made as a result of her recent talks with Mr Haughey, and the strike is rapidly escalating violence in Northern Ireland. Nineteen people have been killed in this latest round of violence. The United Kingdom is our most trusted and faithful ally. We

---

[41]   State of Connecticut General Assembly Press Release, WHORM Subject File CO167 United Kingdom, Box 213, Reagan Library.
[42]   *NYT*, 2/5/1982.

just cannot afford to ignore a situation such as this one which threatens to measurably damage the image of Britain among many Americans and which has the potential to raise a number of sensitive problems and issues between two old and close allies.

Crucially, O'Neill called for 'a private and discreet expression of concern by you and Secretary Haig concerning the situation in Northern Ireland [which] would help direct [Thatcher] towards a posture that would end the current impasse', adding: 'I assure you that if you agree to address the matter with her I will treat it with the utmost confidentiality'.[43] Thatcher, predictably, stood firm.

Clear from the attempted interventions of O'Neill and others was the idea that the hunger strike might provoke a rise in remittances to IRA support organisations in the United States. They were quite correct: Noraid remittances had been dwindling from the mid-1972 peak of $312,700 to only $39,000 at the start of 1978.[44] They raised nearly half a million dollars in the first half of 1981, with the three months of the hunger strike bringing in more money than most calendar years.[45] These remittances brought the Noraid contribution to 'the struggle' to roughly $5 million since 1970.[46]

Paul Bremer, then working at the State Department, wrote to National Security Advisor Richard Allen to emphasise this and to float the idea of a 'discreet intervention by the President or Secretary Haig would help move the Prime Minister toward a posture that would end the current deadlock'.[47] Clearly this was not a move that President Reagan, who was still relatively new in office, was keen on and Dennis Blair wrote to Allen to note that:

The State Department has come up with an imaginative plan to deal with the Speaker's letter. They propose that we show

[43] Letter from O'Neill to President Reagan, 19/5/1981, WHORM Subject File CO167 United Kingdom, Box 213, Reagan Library.
[44] Summary of Noraid Returns to the US Department of Justice, in Ireland and US Policy on Northern Ireland, TAOIS/2009/135/745, NAI.
[45] Holland, *The American Connection*, p. 57. Irish Northern Aid Briefing note (undated), New York University Library, Archives of Irish America, AIA 9: The Papers of George Harrison, Box 1, Series A, Organisations.
[46] *Staten Island Advance*, 18/12/1985.
[47] Memorandum for Richard V. Allen from L. Paul Bremer, State Department, 6/6/1981, WHORM Subject File CO167 United Kingdom, Box 213, Reagan Library.

O'Neill's letter to the Brits without formally endorsing its recommendation, and that we tell O'Neill we have done so. By this action we let the Brits know that, although we are not telling them what to do in Northern Ireland, we are letting them know that they are losing the media campaign here in the United States, to the point that responsible Americans such as O'Neill, who have been supporting the moderates for years, and discouraging American contributions to the IRA, are concerned. We can count on O'Neill's discretion in this matter. Unlike Biaggi and others, O'Neill has on several occasions been helpful in the Northern Ireland situation, with no publicity or leaks.[48]

The British were duly shown the O'Neill letter, though Allen was keen to stress that 'we are not formally pressing Mrs Thatcher to take any particular action in Northern Ireland'.[49] Reagan contacted the Speaker to inform him of this, adding: 'I greatly appreciate the efforts you have made to discourage Irish-American support for the IRA and will count on your continued role as an advocate of peace and reconciliation in Northern Ireland'.[50] British Ambassador Nicholas Henderson commented that the letter received via the White House had been toned down when compared to 'an earlier draft which we saw'.[51]

On 20 August, Michael Devine died. The INLA volunteer from Derry was the tenth and final hunger striker to die on the protest. On Saturday 3 October, the hunger strike formally ended. Six prisoners remained on hunger strike: Hugh Carville, James Devine, Gerard Hodgins, Jackie McMullan, John Pickering, and Pat Sheehan. Sheehan was fifty-five days into his hunger strike at this point. Three days later, Secretary of State for Northern Ireland James Prior announced changes to prison policy which included four of the five demands of the protesters. As Sean Cronin observed in the *Irish Times*, Irish America

[48] Memorandum for Richard V. Allen from Dennis C. Blair, 10/6/1981, WHORM Subject File CO167 United Kingdom, Box 213, Reagan Library.
[49] Memorandum for the President from Richard V. Allen, 15/6/1981, WHORM Subject File CO167 United Kingdom, Box 213, Reagan Library.
[50] Letter from Reagan to Speaker O'Neill, 18/6/1981, WHORM Subject File CO167 United Kingdom, Box 213, Reagan Library.
[51] Telegram from UK Embassy Washington to Foreign Office, 5/8/1981, PREM 19/506, TNA.

ended 1981 as galvanised as it had been since the onset of the troubles in Northern Ireland.[52] Unionist politicians recognised this and sought to rectify the perceived imbalance in the information that was available to those in the United States. This was the genesis of Operation USA.

Operation USA

Throughout the conflict, Ulster Unionists had struggled to find a receptive audience in the United States. The White House ignored trips by, and invitations from, Northern Irish Prime Ministers as successive administrations saw little benefit in entertaining representatives from Stormont. Washington continued to listen to both London and Dublin on all matters Northern Ireland, and only figures such as John Hume provided a northern perspective to proceedings in the United States. This remained the case once the Friends of Ireland formed, even though Tip O'Neill had received visitors from the Ulster Political Research Group.[53] The UPRG was aligned with the Ulster Defence Association, a large loyalist paramilitary group that had evaded prorogation by using a cover name for its acts of violence. The Ulster Freedom Fighters are thought to have been responsible for over 100 murders, predominantly of Catholics, by the end of the 1970s. In 1982, Ted Kennedy proposed a resolution calling for the British to ban the UDA.[54]

With a view to improving perception of Unionism generally in the United States, Reverend Ian Paisley, by now both a Member of the European Parliament and the MP for North Antrim, set about planning one of his most ambitious international endeavours: Operation USA. The plan was to lead a group of Unionist politicians to the United States to counter the significant increase in support for Irish republicanism across the country. A book, *Ulster: The Facts*, was published ahead of the trip.[55]

---

[52]   *IT*, 12/12/1981.
[53]   Letter from Glen Barr to Kirk O'Donnell, 31/1/1979, in Congressional Archives, Thomas P. O'Neill Papers, Series II: Staff Files, Subseries A: Kirk O'Donnell Files, Sub-subseries 21/15, Ireland, BLBC.
[54]   Statement of Senator Edward M. Kennedy opposing the use of plastic bullets in Northern Ireland and calling for a ban on the Ulster Defence Association, 15/7/1982, in Congressional Archives, Thomas P. O'Neill Papers, Series II: Staff Files, Subseries A: Kirk O'Donnell Files, Sub-subseries 21/15, Ireland, BLBC.
[55]   Paisley, I.R.K., Robinson, P.D., and Taylor, J.D., *Ulster: The Facts* (Belfast: Crown Publishing, 1982).

Paisley planned a speaking and fundraising tour across the south, with stops scheduled in Atlanta, Dallas, Houston, and Birmingham, Alabama. One of the first hurdles was the fact that he had been subject to visa revocation as recently as 1981. A 1979 meeting with Tip O'Neill, at the recommendation of John Hume, did little to persuade the Speaker to support Paisley's case two years later and over 100 members of Congress, including Ted Kennedy and Daniel Moynihan, had signed a letter urging the State Department to revoke the visa.[56] One unusual supporter was Paul O'Dwyer, who argued in Paisley's favour. O'Dwyer was, at the time, attempting to secure a similar visa for Owen Carron, the newly elected MP for Fermanagh and South Tyrone.[57]

Dean Fischer, a department spokesman, contended that 'Mr. Paisley's presence in the United States is prejudicial to U.S. public interests'. Paisley called the move a 'denial of free speech', criticising the 'treatment meted out to a member of the British House of Commons and the European Parliament [which] contrasts sharply with the absolute freedom with which Irish-American supporters of the I.R.A. come and go from this country without hindrance' also adding that it was part of 'the conspiracy between the Thatcher Government and the U.S.A. Government to sell out Ulster'.[58] Paisley wrote in the *Washington Post* complaining about this 'denial of freedom', citing the comments of Deputy Secretary of State William Clark as evidence of 'imbalance and bias in the American stance'.[59]

Clark, who went on to serve as both National Security Advisor and Secretary of the Interior under Reagan, had travelled to London and Dublin in December 1981. Sean Donlon recalled of Clark:

> Bill was interested in Ireland, to the point where eventually he bought a house here in Dublin and he kept horses in Ireland and he bought paintings of Ireland … his ranch in California is actually called the Hibernia ranch. He was a very close confidant of Reagan … his influence on Ireland never faded, he was always, if the President really wanted to know what was happening on Ireland he would frequently phone Bill.[60]

[56] *NYT*, 15/12/1981; *IT*, 10/12/1981.
[57] *IT*, 17/12/1981. Carron visited anyway, along with Danny Morrison, and found himself deported to Canada, *IT*, 29/1/1982.
[58] *NYT*, 22/12/1981.
[59] *Washington Post*, 8/1/1982.
[60] Sean Donlon, interview with author, 24/2/2012.

During the latter leg of his 1981 trip, he had given a televised interview in which he said that, while there was no current initiative on Ireland, 'the hope, the prayer of all Americans [is] that this [process] will ultimately lead to reunification'.[61] It was this quote that had caught Paisley's attention. Clark added that the Reagan government would stand by Carter's pledge to promote investment in Ireland, a pledge that ultimately led to the creation of the International Fund for Ireland.[62]

Paisley's protests were in vain and he was not issued a new visa. Instead, he travelled to Canada and was replaced on the Operation USA tour by his wife Eileen. He would return to the United States later that year, however, after he was granted a visa to attend the funeral of Guy Weniger, the President of the Baptist Seminary in San Francisco. He again visited in the summer of 1983 to attend a religious conference at Bob Jones University in South Carolina, a university that awarded him an honorary doctorate, and one considered by the *Washington Post* to be full of 'religious bigots'.[63]

The Operation USA team was also missing the Reverend Robert Bradford, MP for Belfast South, who was killed by the IRA on 14 November 1981. A tribute to the noted firebrand politician featured in the Operation USA handbook, *Ulster: The Facts*.[64] Bradford was replaced on the trip by his wife Norah, who spoke to American audiences on the situation in Northern Ireland as a struggle between Communism and Christianity.[65] Also present on the tour were Official Unionist MEP John Taylor and Paisley's deputy in the Democratic Unionist Party (DUP), Peter Robinson.[66]

With two preachers as part of the original touring party and a trip that travelled across some of the major southern cities of the United States, Operation USA served to underline the religious dimension to the Northern Ireland conflict. Placing emphasis on this was perceived to be a useful strategy for Ulster Unionists, as it offered the prospects of engaging evangelical Protestants in the United States, perhaps the natural constituency for Ulster Unionist politics in the country. Michael Carroll has noted how nearly three-quarters of Irish Americans in

[61]   *NYT*, 9/12/1981.
[62]   *IT*, 8/12/1981.
[63]   *NYT*, 10/9/1982, 20/3/1983, 17/7/1983; *IT*, 20/1/1982; *Washington Post*, 19/1/1982.
[64]   Paisley et al., *Ulster: The Facts*, pp. 15–24.
[65]   *IT*, 11/1/1982.
[66]   *IT*, 5/1/1982.

the southern states are Protestant. This made the southern states a friendlier terrain for the unionist group. Important ties between the clergy and the Unionist Party were further emphasised by the fact that the Reverend Martin Smyth was chosen to replace Bradford as Belfast South MP in the March 1982 by-election. Smyth had similarly critical views of the role of the United States in the political situation in Northern Ireland, joining Ulster Unionist Party leader Jim Molyneaux and prominent MP Enoch Powell in claiming that the Pentagon and the Central Intelligence Agency had become involved in Northern Ireland. Smyth had previously suggested enlisting the help of the Soviet Union.[67]

Most significantly, the touring group was unable to secure any meetings with high-ranking US political figures, who were wary of engagement with the controversial preacher.[68] The tour passed without significant event and the speeches delivered by Eileen Paisley were described in the *Washington Post* as 'a mere hiccup compared with the thunders that shake the Free Presbyterian Church at Sunday night prayer services'.[69]

Political leaders in Dublin were, predictably, more welcome in the United States and the remainder of 1982 saw two different Taoisigh visit. The speed with which both Charles Haughey, who became Taoiseach in February, and Garret FitzGerald, who succeeded him in November, sought to travel to the United States spoke to the high priority that engagement with Washington retained for Dublin. Haughey attended the St Patrick's Day luncheon where he met 'the most influential American Irish voice in Washington', Bill Clark, later meeting a group of US financiers at the New York Economic Club where Haughey sought to encourage investment in Ireland.[70]

FitzGerald's visit saw him meet Vice-President George Bush, Bill Clark, and the Friends of Ireland group, and a reciprocal visit from Bush followed in July 1983.[71] Bush's decision to travel to Ireland drew scorn from Sean Cronin, writing in the *Irish Times*: 'George Bush knows no more about Ireland than what his State Department briefing tells him.

---

[67]   Carroll, M.P., 'How the Irish Became Protestant in America', *Religion and American Culture* 16(1) (2006), pp. 25–54; *IT*, 30/3/1982 and 15/12/1981.
[68]   *IT*, 21/1/1982.
[69]   *Washington Post*, 19/1/1982.
[70]   *IT*, 20/3/1982 and 25/3/1982.
[71]   *IT*, 15/9/1982 and 17/5/1983.

He has met Dr Garret FitzGerald "twice or three times in my office".
They have "common friends".[72] During the meeting, FitzGerald
told Bush of the concern of the Irish Government over US policy in
Central America. These were a particular issue for Tomas MacGiolla
of the Workers' Party who boycotted a reception for Bush in protest.[73]
FitzGerald and Bush also discussed developments in Northern Ireland
in the aftermath of the 1983 UK general election and his ambitions
for the New Ireland Forum. The re-election of Margaret Thatcher
saw renewed vigour in the Anglo-Irish process and Robert Armstrong,
now Secretary of the Cabinet, approached Mrs Thatcher to urge her
to 'get back on terms with the Republic'.[74] FitzGerald noted that the
normalisation of Anglo-Irish relations was essential for the success of
any US involvement, a reference to the financial support that took the
form of the International Fund for Ireland. The Taoiseach added that
'I don't think it is a good thing for the Northern Ireland situation to be
allowed to fester without movement'.[75] This was emphasised by Ceann
Comhairle Tom Fitzpatrick, chairperson, or speaker, of Dáil Éireann,
during a visit to the United States: 'we are convinced from our many
contacts in the Senate and House of Representatives that there is a real
appreciation that the problems of Northern Ireland cannot be allowed
simply to continue at the serious level of the last 14 troubled years'.[76]

With a view to resolving this stagnation, an idea that emerged was
one that became an integral part of President Bill Clinton's Northern
Ireland strategy in the late 1990s: the appointment of a special envoy
to Northern Ireland. The idea of the United States becoming an active
third party to the Northern Ireland situation was immediately resisted
in British circles. Nigel Sheinwald recalled: 'going back to the eighties
that was the sort of idea which we did not like because that was the
proposal of the [Irish] republican side of the argument, but of course
by the time you get to the nineties, the UK government of the day
was rather in favour of almost contractualising the American interest
through a figure of that kind'.[77] The idea of a Northern Ireland envoy
was debated during the 1984 primary contests and received support

[72]   *IT*, 4/7/1983.
[73]   *IT*, 5/7/1983.
[74]   Moore, C., *Margaret Thatcher at Her Zenith: In London, Washington and Moscow*
(New York: Knopf, 2016), p. 303.
[75]   *IT*, 6/7/1983.
[76]   *IT*, 29/7/1983.
[77]   Sir Nigel Sheinwald, interview with author, 26/4/2013.

from candidates such as former Vice-President Walter Mondale and Senator John Glenn, but was opposed by President Reagan. The idea itself marked a significant change in US attitudes towards its own role in Northern Ireland. That it featured during the election cycle was also significant; as the *New York Times* noted, in 1980, 'hardly a single word was uttered about Northern Ireland'.[78]

The New Ireland Forum represented another such attempt. Established by Taoiseach Garret FitzGerald and featuring Irish nationalist party members, it reported in May 1984 and suggested three possible solutions to the problems in Northern Ireland. The first solution was unification with the Republic of Ireland—probably no solution at all given the inevitable violent resistance from loyalists and Unionists. A second idea was the establishment of joint authority between the British and Irish governments, and the third was the creation of a federal or confederal state.[79] The report and its recommendations were popular in the United States, backed by both houses of Congress, and quickly endorsed by Tip O'Neill and Ted Kennedy.[80] FitzGerald had been heavily invested in the forum from the earliest days, and suggested that its failure would exacerbate problems in Northern Ireland.[81] Margaret Thatcher was rather less impressed. The three options were the subject of her famous 'out, out, out' speech. Thatcher's language in the November 1984 Press Conference following a meeting with FitzGerald, in the view of her biographer Charles Moore, was 'too eloquent not to provoke a frenzy of reaction'.[82] Thatcher commented:

> I have made it quite clear—and so did Mr. Prior when he was Secretary of State for Northern Ireland—that a unified Ireland was one solution that is out. A second solution was confederation of two states. That is out. A third solution was joint authority. That is out. That is a derogation from sovereignty. We made that quite clear when the Report was published.[83]

---

[78]   *NYT*, 19/11/1983.
[79]   *New Ireland Forum Report* (Dublin: The Stationery Office, 1984), available at https://cain.ulster.ac.uk/issues/politics/nifr.htm.
[80]   *NYT*, 3/5/1984.
[81]   *The Times*, 31/5/1983.
[82]   Moore, *Margaret Thatcher at Her Zenith*, p. 321.
[83]   Press Conference following Anglo-Irish Summit, 19/11/1984, available at www.margaretthatcher.org/document/105790.

Thatcher recalled, in her autobiography, her wariness at the possible weakening of the union had she supported these measures.[84] Her comments in the House of Commons at Prime Minister's Questions, on May 17, were somewhat more defiant: 'We try to work with the Republic of Ireland, because we believe that it is in the interests of the people of Northern Ireland to do so. The constitutional future of Northern Ireland is a matter for Northern Ireland and this Parliament, and for no one else'.[85] With Reagan due to visit the UK and Ireland, Irish-American groups looked instead to the President in the hope that he would press the significance of the New Ireland Forum report on Thatcher.

Reagan Visits Ireland; Adams Banned from USA

'Ronald Reagan, C.I.A., how many kids did you kill today?'[86]
Protester chant during Reagan visit to Ireland

Reagan's 1984 trip to Ireland was met with widespread protest at US foreign policy, including fifty nuns who spent his visit fasting in the Dublin Garden of Remembrance.[87] The *Irish Times* reported the view among Irish people that Reagan's re-election would have a negative impact on world peace.[88] In Galway, where Reagan received an honorary doctorate from the National University of Ireland, security was tight, with over 1,000 officers on duty.[89] Reagan's visit also upset locals in his ancestral hometown of Ballyporeen, in County Tipperary, where US media coverage was considered by one to be a 'bloody disgrace, and its very bad for Ballyporeen's cultural image'. A *New York Times* reporter commented, somewhat acerbically, that 'the locals do not like their village being called a one-street backwater, especially since they have two streets'. The town very clearly had its sights on establishing itself as a tourist destination with its association to a sitting President. One bar

[84] Thatcher, *Downing Street Years*, p. 396.
[85] House of Commons PQs, 17/5/1984, www.margaretthatcher.org/document/105683.
[86] *NYT*, 3/6/1984.
[87] *IT*, 28/5/1984 and 2/6/1984.
[88] *IT*, 31/5/1984.
[89] *NYT*, 3/6/1984.

had renamed itself 'The Ronald Reagan' and a Reagan lookalike from Cork, who claimed to be a distant relative of the President, had made the trip to Ballyporeen for the visit.[90]

Where President Kennedy had drawn huge crowds, the turnout for the Reagan visit was relatively low. There were 5,000 present in Galway and the expected crowd of 20,000 in Ballyporeen ended up at around 2,000. Reagan's visit stuck to a tight schedule and, as the *New York Times* observed, this might have served to limit both crowds and public protests.[91] The visit, predictably, had a lot more to do with reaching out to people in the United States than it did establishing relations with people in Ireland; where Reagan said that his time in Ballyporeen had 'given my soul a new contentment', a report in *New York Times* highlighted that 'Presidential aides have not even tried to conceal their delight over the resonance that today's visit is expected to have with millions of Irish-American voters at home'.[92] Reagan did, however, at least pay lip service to the problems of the land he was visiting, or returning to. Upon his arrival into Shannon airport, one of the President's first comments was a call for unity between Protestants and Catholics while emphasising that 'those who advocate violence or engage in terrorism in Northern Ireland will never be welcome in the United States'.[93]

During the Presidential banquet at Dublin Castle the Taoiseach informed the President that the Irish people wanted the problems of Central America to 'be resolved peacefully, by the people of the region themselves'. Reagan, in return, commented that he was hopeful the New Ireland Forum report would strengthen cooperation between London and Dublin and facilitate reconciliation in the North.[94] The following day Reagan again spoke with FitzGerald before addressing a joint session of the Oireachtas.[95] During his address Reagan commented, rather oddly, 'I know I cannot claim to be a better Irishman than anyone here, but I can perhaps claim to be an Irishman longer than most any of you here'.[96] As previously noted, Irish

[90]   *NYT*, 2/6/1984.
[91]   *NYT*, 5/6/1984.
[92]   *NYT*, 4/6/1984.
[93]   *IT*, 2/6/1984.
[94]   *NYT*, 4/6/1984.
[95]   *IT*, 4/6/1984.
[96]   Address by the President of the United States of America, Ronald Reagan, 4/6/1984, available at www.oireachtas.ie/viewdoc.asp?fn=/documents/addresses/04June1984.htm.

Ambassador to the United States, Sean Donlon, had informed Reagan of his Irish heritage soon before the 1980 Presidential election. The President continued to talk at great length about peace in Northern Ireland and the economic role of the United States in helping that goal before turning to the Cold War, the Soviet Union, and Nicaragua.[97] The latter part of his speech, in particular the section that focused on Central America, won little favour among Irish protesters. Librarian Julie O'Donoghue, interviewed by the *New York Times*, asked, 'do the American people realize that we're not falling in love with his love of the leprechaun nonsense? We are a Catholic country … what the Americans are doing in El Salvador and Nicaragua is just another form of tyranny'.[98]

Soon after Reagan concluded his visit to Ireland, the AOH invited Sinn Féin President and newly elected Belfast West MP Gerry Adams to address their national convention in Albany, New York. Despite his credentials as a newly elected representative, and the leader of a political party, Adams's associations with the IRA proved problematic. The *New York Times* headline summarised the situation that he found himself in: 'U.S. denies visa to IRA politician'.[99] He was later described as an 'I.R.A. Supporter', a description which Adams himself, who has famously persisted in the denial of his membership of the group, might have accepted. It was these ties to the IRA that allowed his visa to be blocked, and a highly symbolic battle over his visa ensued.

Early supporters of his cause included Congressman Mario Biaggi, who, along with fourteen of his colleagues, wrote to Secretary of State George Shultz in support of Adams.[100] The Belfast Consulate reasoned that 'in light of Provisional Sinn Féin's public support for the Provisional IRA's terrorist campaign in Northern Ireland and Mr Adams's own advocacy of violence he was found ineligible for a visa'.[101] In his absence, Nobel Laureate Sean MacBride addressed the AOH meeting and criticised the decision not to allow Adams into the country.[102] There was an element of reciprocity to this ban, with Noraid's Martin Galvin excluded from the UK following clashes with

[97]   Ibid.
[98]   *NYT*, 5/6/1984.
[99]   *NYT*, 10/7/1984.
[100] *IT*, 14/6/1984.
[101] *IT*, 10/7/1984.
[102] *IT*, 14/7/1984.

police during a 1983 trip to Belfast. The exclusion order for Galvin was
issued 'on the grounds his exclusion is conducive to the public good'.[103]
It was reported that a small group of Congressmen wrote to the UK
Ambassador in Washington to protest against the decision, but the ban
remained intact.[104] The following summer, Galvin decided to lead a
Noraid delegation to Ireland for a trip that included an eight-day visit
to Belfast to attend a series of rallies to mark the thirteenth anniversary
of internment without trial.[105]

   According to Sinn Féin, Galvin, along with 100 members of the
Noraid party, arrived in Dublin on 1 August and promptly went into
hiding.[106] The majority of the group travelled, without Galvin, to
Newry to stage a demonstration on 5 August.[107] Galvin reportedly
conducted a clandestine meeting with Martin McGuinness in Derry
on 9 August, crossing the border, posing for photographs, and
providing an interview to the *Derry Journal*. In it, he declared his
intention to travel to Belfast and boasted that evading the security
forces had been easy.[108] Given the close proximity of the Irish border
to the city of Derry, such appearances would prove markedly easier
to accomplish than a trip to Belfast, as was proven when, on 12
August, Galvin appeared at a rally at the Sinn Féin headquarters
on the Falls Road in Belfast with Gerry Adams.[109] The event was
heavily policed, as was typical for such gatherings, and as Galvin was
introduced to the crowd RUC officers charged and deployed plastic
bullets. One of these plastic bullets struck Sean Downes, killing
him. Two years later, the Reserve Constable who fired the bullet
was acquitted on manslaughter charges.[110] The heavy-handedness
of the police response and the fact that Galvin eluded capture later
prompted Secretary of State James Prior to admit that the decision
to ban him had been a 'bad mistake'.[111]

103   *NYT*, 29/7/1984.
104   *IT*, 3/8/1984.
105   *IT*, 30/7/1984.
106   *NYT*, 3/8/1984.
107   *IT*, 6/8/1984.
108   *IT*, 10/8/1984; Wilson, *Irish America*, 219.
109   *IT*, 14/6/1984.
110   McKittrick et al., *Lost Lives*, pp. 993–994; *NYT*, 13/8/1984.
111   *NYT*, 15/8/1984. Douglas Hurd replaced Prior as Northern Ireland Secretary
in September.

Extradition and the Anglo-Irish Agreement

During the late 1970s, the IRA acquired an M60 heavy machine gun from United States-based supporters. A unit, known as the M60 gang, began attacks on security force personnel in 1979 and, in May 1980, soon after killing an RUC officer in an ambush, attacked an SAS unit in North Belfast, killing Captain Herbert Westmacott.[112] The unit was arrested and charged with murder, but several members escaped custody and fled. They were convicted *in absentia* in June 1981. One of their number, Joe Doherty, travelled to the United States on a false passport and remained at large for two years until he was arrested whilst working in a bar in Manhattan in June 1983. On 13 December 1984, with Thatcher scheduled to visit newly re-elected President Reagan, Judge John E. Sprizzo of the Manhattan Federal District Court refused to extradite Doherty on the grounds that his offences were political in nature. There began a near-decade-long process on the part of the British government to extradite Doherty to the UK in order to serve his sentence.

The United States and United Kingdom had previously established new extradition arrangements in 1972, eventually ratified by the US Senate in June 1976. The emphasis on the issue of offences of a political nature appeared in Article V, which read:

> (1) Extradition shall not be granted if ... (c) (i) the offense for which extradition is requested is regarded by the requested Party as one of a political character; or ... (ii) the person sought proves that the request for his extradition has in fact been made with a view to try or punish him for an offense of a political character.[113]

This became known as the 'political offence exception'. The United States formulated a two-pronged political offence test: 'there must be an uprising or other violent political disturbance at the time of the charged offense', and the offence must be 'incidental to, in the course of, or in the

[112]   Dillon, M., *Killer In Clowntown: Joe Doherty, the IRA and the Special Relationship* (London: Arrow, 1992), pp. 64–82; McKittrick et al., *Lost Lives*, pp. 827–828.
[113]   Full text of the 1972 UK–USA Extradition Treaty, available at www.statewatch.org/news/2003/jul/22aUKUS1972.html, also available at http://internationalextraditionblog.files.wordpress.com/2011/03/gibraltar.pdf.

furtherance of the uprising'.[114] Ambivalence in terms of what constituted an uprising, as well as what actions could reasonably be considered to be 'incidental to, in the course of, or in the furtherance of' such an uprising, were integral to the situation that the UK and US governments found themselves in over the cases of Joe Doherty and three of his comrades: Peter McMullen, William Quinn, and Desmond Mackin.

The first of these extradition requests, chronologically, was that of former British soldier Peter McMullen. The request for his extradition was the first such warrant for an Irish political offender since 1903.[115] McMullen stood accused of attacks on British Army barracks in Belfast and Yorkshire. He had entered the United States in April 1978 under an assumed name, and upon his detention invoked the political offence exception, claiming that his crimes were political, and he was therefore exempt from extradition proceedings.[116] He also offered to share his knowledge of Provisional IRA activities in exchange for political asylum in the United States.[117] In 1979, Judge Frederick Woelflen ruled that McMullen should indeed be exempt from extradition proceedings. This was also the assertion of Judge Sprizzo, in the Doherty case, who considered that the killing of Westmacott was a political act and therefore fell outside the terms of the extradition treaty that existed between the United States and the United Kingdom. Sprizzo argued that Doherty presented 'the assertion of the political offense exception in its most classic form'.[118]

Doherty was certainly an Irish republican with strong political views. His views on the conflict tended towards the socialist side of republicanism, evident in his February 1986 publication, a brochure entitled *The Destruction and Revival of Irish Culture*, which described

---

[114]   *Quinn* v. *Robinson*, 783, F.2d 776, 797 (9th Cir. 1986), cited in Basso, 'The 1985 U.S.–U.K. Supplementary Extradition Treaty', pp. 308–309.

[115]   McElrath, K., *Unsafe Haven: The United States, the IRA and Political Prisoners* (London: Pluto Press, 2000), p. 47. See also Farrell, M., *Sheltering the Fugitive? The Extradition of Irish Political Offenders* (Cork: Mercier Press, 1985).

[116]   McMullen was eventually extradited and tried for the crime in 1996; see *Independent*, 8/11/1996.

[117]   *NYT*, 13/1/1992; Justia, US Law, Case Law, Federal Courts, Courts of Appeal, Ninth Circuit Court, 1981, *Peter Gabriel John McMullen, Petitioner* v. *Immigration and Naturalization Service, Respondent*, 658 F.2d 1312 (9th Cir. 1981) Argued and Submitted 13/5/1981, Decided 13/10/1981, available at http://law.justia.com/cases/federal/appellate-courts/F2/658/1312/50826/.

[118]   *NYT*, 14/12/1984.

'The Irish natives under a harsh, brutal occupation, the native Celtic nation subjected to slavery, poverty, starvation, and murder, were weakening, and as time went by, were forced by physical and economic measures to accept, reluctantly, the Anglo-Saxon culture', continuing to draw analogy between the civil rights marches in either nation.[119] He was also quite comfortable with the brutality of his actions. In a 1988 interview, Doherty described the killing of Westmacott as 'an operation that was typical of all operations where we set up an ambush of a British military convoy ... it is a war and this was a military action'.[120] Sprizzo concurred with this assessment, stating that the death 'occurred in the context of an attempted ambush of a British Army patrol'. He continued:

> Had this conduct occurred during the course of more traditional military hostilities, there could be little doubt that it would fall within the political offense exception ... The only issue remaining therefore is does the political exception become inapplicable because the Provisional Irish Republican Army is engaged in a more sporadic and informal mode of warfare ... while it may be a radical offshoot of the traditional Irish Republican Army, has both an organization, discipline and command structure that distinguishes it from more amorphous groups such as the Black Liberation Army or the Red Brigade.[121]

Sprizzo's view was that 'it was the British Army's response to [the ambush] that gave rise' to the death of Westmacott.[122] Given the fact that the IRA unit was using the heavy M60 machine gun, it is unclear what Sprizzo's view as to the purpose of the IRA ambush actually was, other than to kill as many soldiers as possible.

Doherty's was the fourth successive request by the UK government for the extradition of an IRA fugitive that had been rejected by US courts on these grounds. It prompted British Foreign Secretary Geoffrey Howe to suggest that the existing extradition treaty between the two

[119]   Doherty, J., *The Destruction and Revival of Irish Culture* (February 1986), available in Irish Republicanism Collection, AIA 22, Box 5 Series B: Prisoners, Tamiment Library, NYU.
[120]   *NYT*, 4/7/1988.
[121]   *NYT*, 14/12/1984.
[122]   Ibid.

nations be amended. In a memorandum, the State Department alluded to their own frustrations at the ability of such fugitives to invoke the political offence exception.[123] Sprizzo delivered his verdict nine days before Thatcher and Reagan met at Camp David, and the short time frame meant that meaningful exchanges between the two leaders on the situation were not possible.[124] Reagan had been under pressure to encourage Thatcher to push forward on Northern Ireland and there was concern within the NSC that British intransigence could impact the bipartisan support that his Northern Irish policy had enjoyed.[125] Thatcher assured Reagan that she enjoyed a positive working relationship with Taoiseach FitzGerald and this cooperative working relationship was reflected across the British and Irish negotiating teams; Lord Armstrong, a key negotiator on the British side, fondly recalled working with Sean Donlon, Michael Lillis, and Dermot Nally on the Irish side.[126] This relationship would ultimately help to bring about the 1985 Anglo-Irish Agreement.[127]

Thatcher returned to the United States in February 1985 to address a joint session of Congress. Ahead of this visit, Congressman Mario Biaggi continued to protest against the State Department's refusal to issue a visa for Gerry Adams. Biaggi, through his ad hoc Congressional Committee on Irish Affairs, invited Adams to address his group on the same day that Margaret Thatcher was scheduled to address Congress. Setting up a competing event was an obvious ploy to draw some attention from Thatcher, but it seems unlikely that many members of Congress would have skipped a joint address from the British Prime Minister to attend Biaggi's event. In any case, Adams, by now also under an exclusion order from Great Britain, was denied a US visa.[128]

---

[123] US State Department briefing on Doherty Case, Reagan Library, European and Soviet Directorate NSC (Thatcher Visit, December 1984), available at http://margaretthatcher.org/document/109404.

[124] No. 10 briefing cards, 'Talks with President Reagan' (undated), THCR 1/10/73/f27, available at http://margaretthatcher.org/document/136415.

[125] US State Department brief (Thatcher visit) (undated), Reagan Library: European & Soviet Affairs Directorate NSC, available at http://margaretthatcher.org/document/109416.

[126] Lord Armstrong, interview with author, 9/10/2013.

[127] Memorandum of Conversation, Meeting with British Prime Minister Margaret Thatcher, Camp David, 28/12/1984, NSC Records, European and Soviet Directorate NSC, Reagan Library, available at www.margaretthatcher.org/archive/displaydocument.asp?docid=109185.

[128] *IT*, 18/2/1985.

Media coverage had softened, though, and Adams was now depicted as the 'Sinn Féin Chief', rather than the 'IRA politician'.[129] His trip, however, would have to wait.[130]

In lieu of an address by Adams, the AOH, Noraid, the Irish American Unity Conference (IAUC), and the Irish-American Labour Coalition organised demonstrations in front of the Capitol building.[131] Some 1,500 people turned out to protest against the Thatcher address, led by Martin Galvin, Mario Biaggi, and Paul O'Dwyer.[132] Inside, Thatcher's talk focused on Cold War issues. She did, however, comment on the progress that had been made on Northern Ireland, particularly in terms of Anglo-Irish relations. Thatcher made a point of underlining the principle of consent and drew an analogy with the Constitution of the United States. She emphasised:

> There is no disagreement on this principle between the United Kingdom Government and the Government of the Republic of Ireland. Indeed, the four constitutional nationalist parties of Ireland, north and south, who came together to issue the New Ireland Forum Report, made clear that any new arrangements could only come about by consent, and I welcome too their outright condemnation and total rejection of terrorism and all its works.

This interpretation of the New Ireland Forum was somewhat more generous than the 'out, out, out' analysis of a few months earlier. Her comments also alluded to the progress that would be made on some form of cooperation between the British and Irish governments over the administration of Northern Ireland throughout 1985, enshrined in the Anglo-Irish Agreement. She criticised the Provisional IRA as well as Americans who 'may be misled into making contributions to seemingly innocuous groups', adding that 'that money buys the killing and wounding even of American citizens visiting our country'. Finally, Thatcher again

[129] *NYT*, 10/7/1984 and 17/2/1985.
[130] A review of the State Department's policy towards granting visas to Northern Irish figures was conducted by Richard Lugar in 1986 and, in April 1988, the State Department introduced a new law which eased the granting of visas to political persons entering the US for lectures, but stated that it did not apply to Gerry Adams. See *IT*, 29/9/1986 and 28/4/1988.
[131] *IT*, 19/2/1985.
[132] *Washington Post*, 21/2/1985.

paid tribute to the Irish Taoiseach.[133] Within four months of Thatcher's address to Congress, a new extradition treaty was in place, although the process of it passing through Congress itself proved slightly trickier.

In June 1985, the United Kingdom and United States agreed upon a Supplementary Extradition Treaty. Later accounts report that Thatcher had warned the Reagan Administration that the continued failure of the United States to extradite wanted IRA members was becoming a major issue between the two nations.[134] It was noted in the media that 'State and Justice officials said that it was an embarrassment that U.S. courts in recent years have denied extradition for four alleged IRA terrorists'.[135] Once the treaty itself had been agreed upon, the significantly more complicated process of achieving the necessary two-thirds approval from the Senate began.

The Senate Foreign Relations Committee held hearings on the Supplementary Extradition Treaty in August, September, and October of 1985.[136] Early in proceedings, Senator Paul Trible emphasised that the existing arrangements allowed people 'accused of violent crimes, such as murder and kidnapping' to avoid extradition. Senator Joseph Biden was less supportive, questioning the legality of the Northern Irish court system that depended on Diplock Courts. Diplock Courts were created in 1973 to protect citizens from jury intimidation during paramilitary cases. In September, DePaul Law Professor and State Department adviser M. Cherif Bassiouni gave evidence. Bassiouni emphasised the inconsistencies that perturbed the British government over the application of the political offence exception. In 140 years, the political offence exception had been applied for seventy-six times, only four successfully. British governments had issued at least sixty-four extradition warrants to the United States in a twenty-year period and all but three were upheld, in each case members of the IRA who had invoked the political offence exception.[137] The political status of

[133]   Speech to Joint Houses of Congress, 20/2/1985, www.margaretthatcher.org/document/105968.
[134]   *NYT*, 13/1/1992.
[135]   *Los Angeles Daily*, 13/6/1986.
[136]   United States and United Kingdom Supplementary Extradition Treaty, Hearings before the Committee on Foreign Relations, United States Senate, Ninety-Ninth Congress, First Session S. Hrg. 99–703 (Washington, DC: US Government Printing Office, 1986), especially pp. 1, 12–14, 18, 20, 39, 51, 97, 110.
[137]   Bassiouni, M.C., *Testimonial Statement to Senate Foreign Relations Committee, 99th Congress, First Session, Hearings of September 18, 1985*, 276–305.

IRA prisoners, and the political purpose of the IRA campaign itself, had been at the core of the prison protests in Northern Ireland that ultimately led to the 1980 and 1981 hunger strikes. Previous to 1976, special category status had been afforded to paramilitary prisoners, tacit acceptance that they were not ordinary criminals. The election of Bobby Sands had driven this point home to many. As hunger-striker Gerard Hodgins later pointed out: 'on one hand the government is saying "Bobby Sands you are a criminal, you are not a political prisoner", on the other hand he's getting 30,000 votes that say, "you are political, you're an MP". You don't get any more political than that'.[138] The difference in the cases of Doherty, McMullen, Mackin, and Quinn was that it was the perception of the US judicial and legislative branches that would be decisive.

Nigel Sheinwald, then First Secretary in the Embassy, wrote to Peter Sommer, the Director for European and Soviet Affairs at the NSC:

> We see this new Treaty as a significant, practical contri-
> bution to the fight against international terrorism. Stable and
> reliable extradition arrangements have long been regarded
> by the Western democracies as an important part of our
> defence against terrorists. Unfortunately in recent years terrorist
> fugitives from UK justice have been able to find safe haven in
> the United States. There have been four such cases, all involving
> members of the Provisional IRA convicted of or wanted for
> murder or attempted murder. Three of the four cases involved
> the death of or injury to civilians. Yet the courts accepted that,
> under the present UK–US Extradition Treaty, the offences were
> 'political' and that individuals concerned should not therefore
> be extradited.[139]

Sheinwald was very clear on the fact that the United States still retained significant veto power over extradition requests, with the requirement of a minimum twelve-month sentence for conviction of the same crime in the United States established as mandatory. The argument that crimes committed against the police or armed forces were political was, however, dismissed, Sheinwald noting that 'we

---

[138]   Gerard Hodgins, interview with author, Belfast, 25/3/2010.
[139]   Letter from Nigel Sheinwald to Peter Sommer, 6/9/1985, CA Peter Sommer Files, RAC Box 2, 3, Box 3, Reagan Library. The NSC is the National Security Council.

cannot accept that innocent men and women may be regarded as legitimate targets for terrorists simply because they wear a uniform'.[140] Sheinwald, who went on to serve as British Ambassador to the United States between 2007 and 2012, later recalled:

> One big thing that I dealt with in my time in Washington in the eighties was that we had negotiated a new extradition treaty, a supplemental extradition treaty, primarily to deal with the problem that we couldn't get any of the people suspected of terrorist crimes extradited from America back to the UK. They were exploiting this thing called the political offence exception and we changed the basis of the treaty to bring it up to date because obviously times had moved on in Europe, and since then. It was very difficult to get that through because of the bad image of Northern Ireland, the feeling that there was still political prisoners. Joe Biden, at that stage and very early in his career on the Foreign Relations committee, was an opponent of that treaty. The two people who were helpful in getting that through were Senator Luger, then the chairman of that committee, and Senator Eagleton, a very senior senator on the Democratic side, both members of the committee, and they shepherded this through and made some compromises, dealt with Senator Biden and others and eventually it went through, but it was a long, long delay before we were able to get it.[141]

In the words of Assistant Attorney General Stephen Trott:

> The Supplemental Treaty does not abolish the political offense exception. Rather, it would remove from the purview of the political offense exception certain crimes that are terroristic in nature. For example, airplane hijackers, hostage takers, murderers, and bombers would no longer be able to avoid extradition merely by claiming that their heinous acts were political offenses entitling them to some special protection from the laws that govern civilized people.[142]

[140] Ibid.
[141] Sir Nigel Sheinwald, interview with author, 26/4/2013.
[142] Letter from Stephen S. Trott, Assistant Attorney General, Criminal Division to Richard McEldowney, Supreme Sir Knight, Knights of Equity, 4/12/1985, WHORM Subject File CO167 United Kingdom, Box 214, Reagan Library.

The issue in the United States was not necessarily just about whether or not the four IRA men deserved political status; rather it was about the potential for a significant constitutional change that would alter the way the state viewed political offences internationally. For Kathleen Basso, 'the Reagan Administration became concerned about the United States' role in protecting such activities'.[143] This concern was shared by Democratic opponents to the treaty within Congress, who were 'concerned to avoid the charge of being soft on terrorism', though this concern proved insufficient to prevent the delay of the ratification of the treaty.[144] Karen McElrath has emphasised that it was common for the United States to seek to narrow the political offence exception in treaties with its close allies, even if 'modifications to the US–UK extradition treaty in 1986 reflected the most substantial change ever to US extradition law'.[145] These substantial changes were, for Basso, the effective negation of the political offence exception by 'stripping the political character away from an entire schedule of offenses that are normally associated with political revolution'. She also noted that it created a unique extradition relationship between the United States and the United Kingdom; no such arrangements existed with any other countries.[146]

The final Senate Foreign Relations Committee hearings on 22 October 1985 were scheduled to coincide with Judiciary Committee hearings, but the latter were cancelled indefinitely, reportedly at the request of the Irish Ambassador to the United States, Padraig McKernan.[147] By the end of the month it had become clear that the Foreign Relations Committee was unlikely to send the treaty to the Senate for ratification before the end of the year.[148] Thatcher and Reagan met in October, with the British hopeful that pressure on Reagan could help press Congress to secure ratification of the treaty.

---

[143] Basso, K., 'The 1985 U.S.–U.K. Supplementary Extradition Treaty: A Superfluous Effort?', *Boston College International and Comparative Law Review* 12(1) (1989), Article 11, pp. 301–333, at p. 302. Also Parry, J.T., 'No Appeal: The U.S.–U.K. Supplementary Extradition Treaty's Effort to Create Federal Jurisdiction', in 25 *Loyola of Los Angeles International and Comparative Law Review* 543 (2003), pp. 543–580, at p. 551.

[144] Telegram from UK Embassy Washington to FCO, 17/10/1985, PREM 19/1660, TNA.

[145] McElrath, *Unsafe Haven*, p. 51.

[146] Basso, 'The 1985 U.S.–U.K. Supplementary Extradition Treaty', pp. 313, 315.

[147] *IT*, 16/10/1985.

[148] *IT*, 31/10/1985.

Progress on the Anglo-Irish process was also thought to be important to help secure the extradition treaty. Thatcher had repeatedly spoken of her good working relationship with FitzGerald, particularly when speaking to an American audience, and President Reagan was a strong supporter of what became the Anglo-Irish Agreement.[149] Those involved were acutely aware of the importance of the success of the Agreement. Robert Armstrong recalled:

> I was never conscious of any American involvement in the process of negotiation or any expression by the American government of pressure or advice for a particular feature in the negotiations. I would have said that they left it to the British government to conduct the negotiations, but equally I've no doubt that President Reagan made it clear to Mrs Thatcher that he wanted to see a successful outcome from the negotiations; he didn't want them to break down. Mrs Thatcher was a very cautious participant in the process and there's no doubt she wanted an agreement, but one of the reasons for wanting an agreement was that the President of the United States wanted a successful outcome.[150]

The Anglo-Irish Agreement was duly signed on 15 November 1985. With it began a period of negotiation during which the fates of the extradition treaty, and what became the Anglo-Irish Agreement Support Act, would be decided. The Agreement itself drew significant protests from Unionists, angry at the copper-fastening of Irish influence over the future of Northern Ireland. It was reported that three-quarters of Northern Irish Protestants opposed the deal.[151] The images of a huge crowd gathered outside Belfast City Hall, unified in protest, spoke to this. Thatcher had earlier reached out to both Ian Paisley and James Molyneaux in October in an attempt to reassure them that 'there is no threat whatsoever to the Union'.[152] The three met in London on 30 October with the Unionists hoping to convince Thatcher to put any agreement to a referendum and expressing concern over the US

---

[149]   UK Embassy Washington to FCO, 'UK–US Supplementary Treaty', 17/10/1985, PREM 19/1660, TNA.
[150]   Lord Armstrong, interview with author, 9/10/2013.
[151]   *Sunday Times*, 24/11/1985.
[152]   Letter to Ian Paisley from Margaret Thatcher, 14/10/1985, CENT/3/37A, PRONI.

dimension to the agreement.[153] The British government was conscious
that a new agreement was necessary to improve the image of both
Northern Ireland and the UK internationally.[154] For Thatcher:

> I could never understand why leading Unionists—apparently
> sincerely—suggested that in my dealings with the South and
> above all in the Anglo-Irish Agreement ... I was contemplating
> selling them out to the Republic ... It was not perfect from
> either side's point of view. Article 1 of the agreement affirmed
> that any change in the status of Northern Ireland would only
> come about with the consent of a majority of the people of
> Northern Ireland and recognized that the present wish of that
> majority was for no change in the status of the province. I
> believed that this major concession by the Irish would reassure
> the Unionists that the Union itself was not in doubt. I thought
> that given my own well-known attitude towards Irish terrorism
> they would have confidence in my intentions. I was wrong
> about that.[155]

Robert Armstrong, a key architect of the agreement on the British side,
recalled:

> We tried to craft an agreement ... which they couldn't wreck
> or that would be very difficult for them to wreck and we didn't
> talk to Unionists at all. I don't know how much they knew about
> what was going on, I don't know what Mrs Thatcher told Ian
> Gow or what Ian Gow told the Unionists but those of us who
> were conducting the negotiations ... had to work out ... how far
> we might be able to go without causing the Unionists to wreck
> the agreement. On balance I think we succeeded. They didn't
> like it, they objected to it, there was nothing in it with which
> they could refuse to cooperate.[156]

There was, however, immediate and strong support from the
international political community, with French President François
Mitterrand and German Chancellor Helmut Kohl quick to offer

[153] *IT*, 28/10/1985.
[154] Note of points made during PUS's meeting with NI Permanent Secretaries,
19/9/1985, CENT/3/36A, PRONI.
[155] Thatcher, *Downing Street Years*, pp. 385, 402.
[156] Lord Armstrong, interview with author, 9/10/2013.

congratulations.[157] In the United States, the Agreement evidently pleased both Reagan, who issued a lengthy statement praising what he termed a 'promise of peace and a new dawn for the troubled communities of Northern Ireland',[158] and Tip O'Neill, who, when asked if he supported aid to Northern Ireland, stated firmly 'absolutely, all the way, and I'll lead the fight'.[159] Speaker O'Neill had, earlier that summer, hosted a breakfast for a visiting Oireachtas delegation and he pledged to use all his influence to support the agreement.[160] O'Neill's support included a pledge to increase the financial incentives, previously offered by Jimmy Carter, during a March visit to Ireland.[161] Soon after the agreement was signed, Tánaiste Dick Spring travelled to the United States.[162] Spring's goal was to secure US financial backing for the agreement, but the British had more complicated objectives in the aftermath of the signing.

On 14 January 1986, meetings were held in Washington between representatives of all three governments in order to discuss the implementation of US aid. Both chambers of Congress had offered their support in December, but faced the challenge of making a significant contribution in the midst of a cut in government spending.[163] Reagan's budget cut some $38 billion from the deficit in early February, but raised questions about to what extent the United States could genuinely afford to contribute to Ireland. Secretary of State George Shulz offered assurance to the British and Irish parties that the money for Ireland would be found.[164] Two months later, Reagan proposed the Northern Ireland and Ireland Assistance Act, a five-year, $250 million aid programme. The President urged Congress to approve the programme immediately, and the House Foreign Affairs Committee obliged only two days later.[165] Securing Senate ratification was more problematic, given the Senate had yet to

[157] Joint Press Conference with French President (François Mitterrand), 18/11/1985, available at http://margaretthatcher.org/document/109416; Joint Press Conference with West German Chancellor (Helmut Kohl), 27/11/1985, available at http://margaretthatcher.org/document/106183.
[158] *IT*, 16/11/1985.
[159] *IT*, 4/12/1985.
[160] *IT*, 24/7/1985.
[161] *IT*, 19/3/1985.
[162] *IT*, 23/11/1985.
[163] *IT*, 14/1/1986 and 31/1/1986.
[164] *IT*, 6/2/1986.
[165] *NYT*, 5/3/1986 and 7/3/1986.

complete ratification of the new Supplementary Extradition Treaty. Richard Lugar, in his position as Chair of the Senate Foreign Relations Committee, warned that the aid programme could not be approved until the extradition treaty was ratified.[166] Ted Kennedy had hoped to secure a quick vote on the aid bill to enable Reagan to sign it on St Patrick's Day in the presence of the Taoiseach, but Lugar, much to the relief of the British government, was insistent that the Foreign Relations Committee must give the bill a full hearing and investigation and it could not be expedited past other foreign aid requests that were awaiting ratification from the Senate.[167] Among the outstanding business for the committee was the extradition treaty. Resistance from Senate Democrats such as Joe Biden, John Kerry, and Christopher Dodd posed problems for Lugar, who needed to secure a two-thirds majority in the Senate to pass the extradition treaty, whereas the aid bill required only a simple majority. Lugar made the decision to pair the two issues together, a move that seemed likely to expedite their concurrent approval.[168]

Garret FitzGerald travelled to the United States for St Patrick's Day where he attended the Washington parade before meeting with Reagan and members of Congress. There was, regrettably for many in the US government, no bill ready for the President's signature. Of further regret to many in Irish America, Tip O'Neill had announced his decision to retire from public service in 1986, and FitzGerald attended a dinner in O'Neill's honour.[169] One week later FitzGerald wrote in the *New York Times* to express his optimism in the future of Northern Ireland, praising 'a genuine attempt to alleviate the inequalities felt by the nationalist community without in any way depriving the Unionists of their rights and their sense of belonging to the United Kingdom'.[170]

The Anglo-Irish Agreement Support Act and the 1986 Supplementary Extradition Treaty still remained outstanding, however, and Senator Lugar sought to amend the extradition treaty with a view to easing its

---

[166] *IT*, 15/2/1986.
[167] *IT*, 13/3/1986.
[168] *IT*, 2/5/1986. The Republican members of the committee at the time were Richard Lugar, Jesse Helms, Charles Mathias, Nancy Kassebaum, Rudy Boschwitz, Larry Pressler, Frank Murkowski, Paul Trible, and Daniel Evans, whilst the Democrats featured Claiborn Pell, Joe Biden, Paul Sarbanes, Edward Zorinsky, Alan Cranston, Christopher Dodd, Thomas Eagleton, and John Kerry.
[169] *IT*, 15/3/1986. Ian Paisley referred to the fund as a retirement package for O'Neill; see *IT*, 8/5/1986.
[170] *NYT*, 24/3/1986.

passage through Congress. He noted that certain offences specified in the treaty lacked a clear counterpart in US law and that some language was ambiguous and vague. There were concerns that the standard of proof should satisfy a US magistrate.[171] Reagan, predictably keen to see the extradition treaty passed, wrote to Lugar and Bob Dole, the Senate Majority Leader:

> As Great Britain demonstrated once again last week, she is our staunchest Ally in the battle against international terrorism. Rejection of the [Supplementary] Treaty would be viewed by the British—and the world at large—as a weakening of U.S. resolve. This must not happen. Indeed, we see Senate ratification of this Supplemental Treaty as a key element of our wider efforts to promote greater international cooperation.[172]

This demonstration of loyalty, namely British support for the US bombings of the Gaddafi regime in Tripoli, was not necessarily a simple matter of assisting a historical ally in their response to the bombing of a Berlin disco which killed two US servicemen. There was significant pressure from London over this issue, as evident in a letter from then-Private Secretary to the Permanent Under-Secretary of State Sherard Cowper-Coles to Assistant United States Attorney Otto Obermaier. Obermaier was informed that 'The Prime Minister believes you owe us this one. She allowed your Government to use our territory for your F-111s when they were on their way to Libya'.[173]

Diplomats from all three states were therefore faced with a tricky situation: the International Fund, with near-universal support, could not be approved until the Extradition Treaty passed and Britain had already sacrificed a bargaining chip by allowing US bombers to use UK air bases for their sorties into Libya. Further, some commentators have suggested that Thatcher's endorsement of the Anglo-Irish Agreement was designed to appease the Americans so that they would

[171]   *IT*, 4/6/1986.
[172]   President's Letter to the Chairman of the Senate Foreign Relations Committee and the Senate Majority Leader, 22 Weekly Comp. Pres. Doc. 524, 28/4/1986.
[173]   Sherard Cowper Coles to Otto Obermaier, quoted in Pyle, *Extradition, Politics and Human Rights*, p. 197. Other authors emphasise the Libyan dimension to the treaty: Cronin, S., *Washington's Irish Policy 1916–1986* (Dublin: Anvil Books, 1987); Dillon, *Killer in Clowntown*; Kelly, J.T., 'The Empire Strikes Back: The Taking of Joe Doherty', *Fordham Law Review* 61 (1992), pp. 317–399.

agree to the new treaty.[174] In order to achieve a compromise, and to resolve the two issues, something would have to give. In mid-May, Thatcher and Reagan again met at a summit in Tokyo with Reagan seeking wider support for his hard-line approach to Libya. Thatcher was less concerned with Libya, however, and reportedly commented to Reagan that there was little point in declaring war on international terrorism if the United States would not ratify the treaty.[175] It was pointed out to Reagan that had the Brighton bombers, who had come so close to killing Thatcher in 1984, escaped to the United States, the political offence exception would have precluded the United States from extraditing them.[176] With the 1986 midterm elections approaching, however, Thatcher's ability to force Reagan's hand over intransigence from the Senate was limited.

Reports emerged in late May that Kerry, Dodd, and Biden had convinced Senator Jesse Helms, a conservative Republican from North Carolina, to join their opposition to the treaty, leaving the treaty with a majority of opponents in the Foreign Relations Committee. Sean Cronin posited that Helms's opposition was probably a product of his desire to prevent any foreign power from exerting influence over the US legal system, though later it was suggested that Helms had become concerned that anti-Communists would be open to extradition if it were agreed.[177] This concern was the focus of discussions in the Senate Foreign Relations Committee, which met again in June to find a compromise that would protect those seeking political sanctuary in the United States but that would also enable the United States to extradite suspected terrorists to the UK.[178]

One week later, the committee finally voted on the treaty, with fifteen in favour, only two opposing, and passed it to the Senate.[179] The Senate duly ratified the treaty by a vote of eighty-seven to ten. D'Amato

---

[174]   Ogden, C., *Maggie: The Portrait of a Woman in Power* (New York: Simon & Schuster, 1990). Andrew Wilson has noted how Reagan's influence on Thatcher helped bring about the Agreement; see Wilson, *Irish America*, pp. 243–245.
[175]   *IT*, 6/5/1986 and 7/5/1986.
[176]   Poindexter to President Reagan, 'Letters to Senators Lugar and Dole, United Kingdom, 1986, 21/4/1986, 24/4/1986', Box 90901, Peter Sommer Files, Reagan Library.
[177]   *IT*, 19/5/1986 and 2/6/1986.
[178]   *IT*, 7/6/1986.
[179]   *IT*, 13/6/1986. The new language had won over Helms, Kerry, Biden, and Dodd.

had proposed an amendment to the treaty that would have prevented it from applying retroactively, namely in the cases of Joe Doherty, William Quinn, and Peter McMullen, but this was defeated sixty-five to thirty-three.[180] The UK and US governments were finally free to revisit the three outstanding extradition cases that had prompted the change in legislation, Desmond Mackin having been deported to Ireland in December 1981.[181]

In February 1986, William Quinn's case had been sent to the Ninth Circuit Court of Appeals where the cases divided the three judges: Judge Betty Fletcher accepted that Quinn's activities in England were part of the Ulster conflict, but Judges Stephen Reinhardt and Ben Duniway disagreed and supported the extradition request.[182] Reinhardt's justification for this view was important, based as it was on the grounds that the political offence exception could only be applied to acts in furtherance of an uprising within the boundaries of one's own land: 'it does not cover terrorism or criminal conduct exported to other locations'. Reinhardt added that 'although an uprising existed in Northern Ireland at the time the charged offenses were committed, there was no uprising in England'.[183] Further complicating his case, Quinn had used an inconsistent line of defence throughout his trial, claiming both not to be the killer but also that 'the killing was a political act and that he therefore could not be extradited'.[184] Quinn received financial support from Noraid, who covered all his legal costs throughout the extradition process, but the new treaty had closed off all legal avenues of appeal and Quinn was duly extradited to the UK on 20 October 1986 aboard a Royal Air Force plane.[185] In February 1988 he was sentenced to life imprisonment for the murder of Constable Tibble. The judge told him: 'you shot repeatedly and at point-blank range a man who was in fact a police officer, though you could not have known he was other than an ordinary member of the public'.[186] He was released from prison in April 1999 under the terms of the Good Friday Agreement. Quinn was the only one of the three to be extradited under the terms of the new treaty.

[180]   *IT*, 18/7/1986.
[181]   *NYT*, 1/1/1982.
[182]   Wilson, *Irish America*, p. 259.
[183]   *Los Angeles Times*, 18/2/1986.
[184]   *NYT*, 21/10/1986.
[185]   Ibid.; *Glasgow Herald*, 17/2/1988.
[186]   McKittrick, *Lost Lives*, p. 521; *IT*, 17/2/1988.

The resolution of the Quinn case had no effect on the Doherty or McMullen cases, so specific were the appeals processes that each was involved in. Doherty dropped his legal efforts to seek asylum in the hope that he could be deported to the Republic of Ireland, though given the British and Irish governments had also recently come to new extradition arrangements it was likely that in the event of his deportation to Ireland he would subsequently be extradited to the UK.[187] US Attorney General Edwin Meese III duly issued this deportation order in June 1988. The decision to deport was significant as it meant that Doherty was not subject to the newly signed extradition treaty and therefore could not argue that he had been unfairly targeted by its creation. Doherty's deportation order was on the grounds of his illegal entry to the United States. Crucially, Meese refused Doherty's request to be extradited to the Republic of Ireland, where he faced only a ten-year prison sentence compared to a life sentence in the United Kingdom.[188] A new appeals process duly began although it was noted that 'despite Mr Meese's decision today, Mr. Doherty … will not face deportation for some time. Court appeals in the case could take months, and Mr. Doherty has moved separately for a new court hearing on his request for political asylum'.[189] Doherty's appeal process would drag into the 1990s.

Meanwhile, in light of the revised treaty, McMullen was arrested in Salt Lake City in December 1986 and held for deportation to the Republic of Ireland.[190] Again, the decision to deport was significant, as was the decision to deport to the Republic of Ireland; these bypassed a range of legal obstacles, as McMullen would come to argue in his defence that the new extradition treaty was unconstitutional on the grounds that it targeted him specifically.[191] His appeal process would also drag on until 1992 when the United States Court of Appeals for the Second Circuit upheld a District Court ruling that the 1986 Supplementary Extradition Treaty was being used to punish Peter McMullen, Joe Doherty, and Desmond Mackin.[192] This effectively ruled that the treaty unlawfully singled these men out for punishment. The court considered that McMullen's extradition would mean 'almost certain incarceration

[187]   *NYT*, 16/1/1992.
[188]   Basso, 'The 1985 U.S.–U.K. Supplementary Extradition Treaty', p. 325.
[189]   *NYT*, 15/6/1988.
[190]   *IT*, 18/12/1986.
[191]   *Glasgow Herald*, 5/8/1996.
[192]   *NYT*, 13/1/1992.

in British prisons, where he will likely face torture and death from either the British, his former compatriots, or both'. It did, however, rule that he was eligible for deportation to Ireland.[193] McMullen eventually gave up his appeal and returned to the UK in March 1996.[194] The lengthy diplomatic process that had resulted in the Supplementary Extradition Treaty had yielded only a single extradition.

The Northern Ireland and Ireland Assistance Act also passed—with significant ease when compared with the extradition treaty—and on 18 September the US and UK governments signed an agreement which saw £36 million, roughly $50 million at 1986 exchange rates, donated to the International Fund for Ireland (IFI) by the US government.[195] The ever-grateful Ian Paisley described the donation as 'a mere pittance', claiming that it would be used to boost Irish republicanism rather than cross-community employment.[196] Charles Brett, a Belfast solicitor and former member of the Northern Ireland Labour Party, was appointed as chairman-designate of the fund.[197] The philanthropic dimension to the US role in Northern Ireland was exemplified on St Patrick's Day 1987, with the first round of IFI funding received, and a merger of the American Irish Foundation (founded in 1963 by Eamon de Valera and John F. Kennedy) and The Ireland Fund (founded in 1976 by Anthony O'Reilly and Dan Rooney) producing the American Ireland Fund.

The Ireland Fund maintained an annual gala which raised hundreds of thousands of dollars for Irish causes each year. Rooney recalled that the organisation, by the time of the merger, had established itself as a credible alternative to Noraid. This had not been easy, however, despite Rooney's status as the President of the Pittsburgh Steelers: 'we often had to explain that we were not raising money for bombs'.[198] This misunderstanding captured so much about the lack of awareness about the situation in Northern Ireland within the United States and indeed much of Irish America, with the idea that anyone raising money for Irish causes in the United States could only be doing so in the name of the IRA clearly persuasive. Both men were very private about their

[193] Ibid.
[194] *IT*, 8/11/1996.
[195] *NYT*, 7/3/1986; *IT*, 18/9/1986.
[196] *IT*, 19/9/1986.
[197] *IT*, 2/10/1986.
[198] Dan Rooney, interview with author, 21/10/2013.

political affiliations, but Tony O'Reilly felt moved, in a 1988 *New York Times* feature, to state that he favoured 'constitutional nationalism'. O'Reilly also took the opportunity to declare that the Ireland Fund was raising, on average, $4 million a year.[199] In 1981, the Ireland Fund gala took place amidst the tension of the hunger strike. Security was tight at the Waldorf Astoria hotel and Dan Rooney went outside to talk to the picketers, but could not quell one nun who wandered in to the dinner and seized the microphone to denounce British rule in Ireland.[200]

The merger was significant for the purposes of creating a single philanthropic strategy for Irish America. As Rooney recalled, 'many Americans confused this organization with our Ireland Fund. I believed we could have a greater impact if we merged with the American Irish Foundation. One big organization would be more effective than two smaller ones'.[201] The merger also brought Loretta Brennan Glucksman into the fold. Glucksman was, for Rooney, decisive in pushing the organisation forward, providing the necessary energy. Along with her husband Louis, Glucksman became very active in Irish issues during the late 1980s. Perhaps the most visible contribution was the opening of Glucksman Ireland House at New York University in 1993, but the Glucksmans were particularly active in the American Ireland Fund and Loretta served as the Chairperson of the fund until 2014.[202]

Shoot to Kill and the End of the O'Neill Era

Tip O'Neill stepped down as the Speaker of the US House of Representatives in January 1987. He was the only Speaker to serve for five complete consecutive Congresses. It had been speculated when O'Neill announced his retirement that Joseph P. Kennedy II, the eldest son of Robert, would seek to replace him in the House. The seat had once been held by Joseph's uncle, John, and O'Neill endorsed Kennedy as his replacement in September 1986.[203] Kennedy had a mixed record

[199]	*NYT*, 8/5/1988.
[200]	Rooney, *My 75 Years*, pp. 177–178.
[201]	Ibid., p. 178.
[202]	Glucksman Ireland House NYU, Center for Irish and Irish-American Studies, History, available at http://as.nyu.edu/irelandhouse/about/history.html; The Ireland Funds 'The American Ireland Fund Chairman', available at https://web.archive.org/web/20150316163421/www.theirelandfunds.org/aif-chairman.
[203]	*IT*, 5/12/1985.

on Irish issues, and while he supported both the MacBride principles and the Anglo-Irish Agreement, he once suggested that the Irish Government should be allowed to police nationalist areas in Northern Ireland, a quite radical breach of sovereignty.[204] Kennedy then chose to join the Mario Biaggi-led Ad Hoc Committee for Irish Affairs rather than the Congressional Friends of Ireland group, which his uncle Ted had established in 1981.[205]

Joseph P. Kennedy II was a guest of the British Embassy in Washington on 16 March 1988, speaking alongside figures such as Martin Luther King III, the Reverend Joseph Lowery, and Congressman John Lewis. Kennedy declared that 'what we face in Northern Ireland is discrimination as great as what we faced here in the 1960s'. What the other speakers might have thought of the analogy remains unclear, but Lewis avoided repeating it when invited to Ireland to deliver the fourth Iveagh House commemorative lecture in Dublin in 2014.[206] During the 1988 event, Kennedy met with Ambassador Sir Anthony Acland, requesting he deliver a letter to Thatcher which accused British security forces of taking on 'the character of death squads in Central America, with the enthusiastic support of your government'.[207] This was a reference to the actions of the SAS, who had been active against the IRA in the May 1987 Loughgall ambush, and during Operation Flavius on Gibraltar ten days before Kennedy's speech.

A month later, Kennedy travelled to Ireland and made a three-day stop in Northern Ireland. He visited Belfast City Hall, meeting the Lord Mayor and Official Unionist MP William Ross. Peter Robinson was invited to join the group but boycotted the meeting. DUP press officer Sammy Wilson commented that Robinson would not meet 'Joey, the Republican parrot', adding that 'when it became obvious that [Kennedy] had come here with all his prejudices parcelled up with

[204] *IT*, 15/9/1986.
[205] *IT*, 25/3/1987. Biaggi's time in Congress was coming to an end, and he had been significantly quieter on Irish issues. A series of bribery allegations that had led to a federal investigation, which led to his indictment in June 1987. Biaggi was sentenced to eight years in prison in November 1988; see *IT*, 4/6/1987 and 19/11/1988.
[206] Representative John Lewis, First Douglass/O'Connell Speech, Iveagh/ Dublin, 25/4/2014, transcript available at https://www.dfa.ie/media/dfa/ alldfawebsitemedia/ourrolesandpolicies/ourwork/congressmanlewis/John-Lewis-speech.pdf.
[207] *IT*, 19/3/1988.

him, we just felt that it was not worth wasting time'.[208] Robin Renwick, later appointed as British Ambassador to the United States, recalled that 'Unionist suspicions were thoroughly justified in the case of … the insufferable Joseph Kennedy Jr'.[209]

During his time in Belfast, Kennedy visited the family of Thomas McErlean, who had been shot dead during a loyalist attack on a republican funeral. Upon leaving the McErlean home in the Divis Flats complex in the lower Falls area, Kennedy's car was stopped and searched by soldiers. Kennedy became involved in an altercation with a soldier, the two men reportedly telling each other to go back to their own country.[210] He later reflected on the incident: 'it was just a disappointment and an eye-opener in terms of the basic attitude that … British troops seem to have for the Irish Catholics'. He then travelled to Dublin and met with the Taoiseach before a visit to his family homestead of New Ross in County Wexford.[211] In Wexford, Kennedy continued to comment on the 'absolute despair' of the people of West Belfast and the 'overbearing arrogance' of British soldiers, adding, 'you know as well as I do that the British have no right occupying the North of Ireland'.[212]

Northern Ireland continued to be plagued by violence throughout 1987, and as the third anniversary of the Anglo-Irish Agreement arrived, the need to expedite its full implementation was apparent to all parties. Thatcher had paid outgoing President Reagan a visit in November 1988, but Northern Ireland was absent from the agenda for their meeting.[213] Thatcher was asked about the Agreement during a press conference, and suggested that bureaucracy was to blame for the slow process in implementing key provisions. She added that because the Agreement 'gave fresh hope for the Nationalist Republican tradition in Northern Ireland that their particular concerns would also be met'; it was 'a very well balanced Agreement really offering more opportunities for reconciliation in Northern Ireland at the same time as making the Unionists fully conscious that there would be no

[208] *IT*, 8/4/1988.
[209] Lord Renwick, unpublished memoir; copy obtained from Lord Renwick, p. 226.
[210] *IT*, 6/4/1988 and 8/4/1988.
[211] *IT*, 9/4/1988.
[212] *IT*, 11/4/1988.
[213] President Reagan briefing cards for Margaret Thatcher visit, 15/11/1988, WHORM Subject File CO167 United Kingdom, Box 606691, Reagan Library.

change without their consent'.[214] Thatcher would work with Reagan's successor, Vice-President George H.W. Bush, to try and achieve some of these goals.

Northern Ireland was far from the dominant international narrative of the Reagan years, though it did represent a significant domestic issue for both Thatcher and Reagan. Charles Powell served as Private Secretary to Mrs Thatcher from 1984 until 1990, and then for another year in the same role to John Major, working principally as an adviser on foreign policy.[215] He recalled: 'in fact, Northern Ireland took up, I should think, for the most part of the eight or nine years I was in No. 10, four percent of my time, possibly five'.[216] Powell's comments emphasise the role of 'behind-the-scenes' figures in the accomplishments that took place in the Northern Ireland peace process during the 1980s.

Throughout the Ronald Reagan presidency, the United States was a strong supporter of Margaret Thatcher's Northern Ireland agenda. The new extradition treaty might only have led to the extradition of one IRA fugitive, but the efforts that the administration, and supporters of the treaty, went to in order to secure its ratification spoke to the importance of the US–UK relationship and the power that Thatcher wielded when it came to Northern Ireland policy. The resistance that was evident to the new extradition arrangements, particularly within the wider Democratic Party, reflected a deeper tendency that ultimately facilitated the interventions of President Clinton. Reagan frequently found himself caught between Thatcher and the powerful House–Senate combination of Speaker Tip O'Neill and Senator Edward Kennedy on Irish issues. For Sean Donlon:

> the Speaker was clearly the more interventionist on Ireland and probably nudged the President into adopting somewhat tougher positions with the British than he might otherwise have done. This is particularly likely to have been the case in the autumn of 1984 when, within a few weeks of her 'out, out, out' rejection of the Report of the New Ireland Forum, Prime Minister Thatcher was somehow prevailed on to move into a more constructive mode.[217]

---

[214] Press Conference in Washington, 17/11/1988, available at http://margaret thatcher.org/document/107386; also *IT*, 18/11/1988.
[215] Thatcher, *Downing Street Years*, pp. 461, 473, 557, 747–748, 816–817, 843–844.
[216] Lord Powell, interview with author, 25/4/2013.
[217] *IT*, 14/1/1989.

CHAPTER FIVE

The Bush Administration
and Northern Ireland as a
Local Political Issue

> What does President Bush have to fear from the debate
> and dialogue of Gerry Adams? Could it be he is afraid
> Irish-Americans will be angered over U.S. indifference and
> collaboration and its terrible cost?[1]
>
> Irish Northern Aid 'America's Irish War' (undated)

The 1988 Democratic National Convention saw Arkansas Governor
Bill Clinton deliver the nomination speech for Michael Dukakis, the
party's candidate for the 1988 Presidential election. The speech was
not well received; accounts from the time recorded the highlight of
the speech being when Clinton said, 'in closing …'.[2] Clinton would,
only four years later, offer a strong line on Ireland as part of his
Presidential campaign but Irish issues lacked resonance in national
affairs and consequently played little role in the 1988 Presidential
election. Where both the Italian-American Foundation and the Jewish
Anti-Defamation League could secure both Presidential candidates at
events, only Dukakis attended the Irish American Presidential Forum
in New York in April.[3] Dukakis pledged to press for Irish issues and
offered his support to the International Fund for Ireland and the
MacBride Principles.[4]

---

[1]   Durkan Papers, AIA 008, Box 1, Folder 29, Irish Northern Aid Organization
Info: Communication (incl. 1989 split), Archives of Irish America, Tamiment
Library, New York University (hereafter Tamiment Library, NYU).
[2]   *NYT*, 21/7/1988.
[3]   *IT*, 3/11/1988.
[4]   *IT*, 11/4/1988.

The issue of the MacBride Principles had featured during campaigning ahead of the election. These were nine fair employment principles devised by the former Irish Minister for External Affairs, and a veteran republican, Sean MacBride, in 1984, and proposed as the corporate code of conduct for US companies doing business in Northern Ireland. During the 1988 Presidential election, both candidates supported the principles. Bush argued that: 'I believe that job discrimination must cease. I do not think that they alone will solve the problem ... if the Irish can bring about certainty, predictability and safety to themselves, then the climate for investment both foreign and domestic will be greatly improved'.[5] Dukakis also stated his support, though not going as far as Reverend Jesse Jackson, another contender for the Democratic Party nomination, who pledged to sign them into law.[6]

Bush's victory in the 1988 Presidential election was well received in Downing Street, understandably so given that it provided continuity with the Reagan administration and predictability to Anglo-American relations for the subsequent four years. Robin Renwick reported that the Prime Minister had 'breathed a sigh of relief' when Bush was elected, even though Bush, along with his Secretary of State James Baker, tended to view Germany as the key US partner in Europe.[7] As Sean Cronin pointed out in the *Irish Times*, 'in his varied political career, Mr Bush has had little to do with Ireland'.[8] He would continue to have relatively little to do with Ireland during his single term as President.

Where Irish issues lacked resonance at the national level, they still played an important role in local politics during the late 1980s. During campaigning ahead of the 1989 New York Mayoral election, both candidates sought to engage Irish voters, and drew the attention of British political figures in doing so. Ed Koch, the incumbent Mayor, had decided to skip the 1988 Democratic National Committee (DNC) to accompany Cardinal John O'Connor on a pilgrimage to Ireland. It was an unusual decision to make, particularly in an election year, and Koch received criticism from Irish-American figures like Niall O'Dowd. For Mary Holland, though, the trip was, in part, to 'impress

5   *IT*, 22/3/1988.
6   *IT*, 22/3/1988.
7   Renwick, *A Journey with Margaret Thatcher*, p. 160.
8   *IT*, 24/1/1989.

Irish-American voters who make up 12 per cent of the electorate in New York' ahead of the Mayoral election the following year.[9] The Irish vote, apparently, still meant something in New York politics.

For someone who saw more political value in a trip to Ireland than attending the DNC, Ed Koch had an oddly inconsistent position on Ireland. At various points, he considered that the British Government had 'concluded that Northern Ireland is its Vietnam', advocated for British withdrawal from Northern Ireland, and also argued that British troops in Northern Ireland were not an occupying force.[10] The last statement saw *Irish America* magazine remove Koch from its list of top 100 Irish Americans. Koch quickly retracted his statement and apologised: 'I'm sorry for the pain my unfortunate use of language may have inflicted on my friends, supporters and fellow New Yorkers of Irish descent. I hope they will accept my apology and understand that I am with them as I have been for the past 25 years. I always will be'.[11]

This retraction prompted Conservative Party members in London to condemn Koch as a 'weak-kneed politician' who had 'no principles, no morals, no guts'. Peter King, then Comptroller of Nassau County, dismissed the apology as damage control.[12] Nonetheless, Koch took part in the 1989 St Patrick's Day parade, his twelfth as Mayor and the first to feature a female grand marshal, Dorothy Hayden Cudahy. Interviewed following the parade, Koch stated his commitment to liberalising immigration laws and freeing Joe Doherty, the latter of which would have done little to warm the views of the UK Conservative party.[13] Koch ultimately lost his bid for the Democratic nomination for the Mayoral election to David Dinkins, the Manhattan Borough President. Dinkins, in turn, defeated US Attorney Rudolph Giuliani in the mayoral election. Among those working on the Dinkins campaign was George Harrison, the former IRA gunrunner.[14]

---

[9]   *IT*, 3/8/1988.
[10] *IT*, 24/9/1981; *NYT*, 14/3/1989.
[11] *IT*, 1/8/1988.
[12] Ibid.
[13] *NYT*, 7/1/1989 and 18/3/1989.
[14] Letter from Jack Holland to George Harrison, 28/9/1989, AIA 9: The Papers of George Harrison, Box 1, Series A, Personal Papers, Tamiment Library, NYU; see also *Philadelphia Inquirer*, 27/9/1989; *Irish Republican News*, 15/10/2004.

Mayor Dinkins, The New York St Patrick's Day Marches, and Ireland

David Dinkins began his term as Mayor of New York City on 1 January 1990 and led his first St Patrick's Day parade in March, marching alongside 125,000 others, carrying a black shillelagh and wearing a 'Free Joe Doherty' badge upon his green jacket, evoking comparison with then-Presidential candidate Jimmy Carter who paraded wearing a badge that read 'England get out of Ireland' in 1976. Former Mayor Ed Koch also took part, and was reportedly well received by crowds.[15] During Dinkins's term in office, the St Patrick's Day parade became increasingly politicised. By the time of his second parade, in March 1991, Dinkins decided to march with the Irish Lesbian and Gay Organization (ILGO), 'for reasons we all understand'.[16] The Manhattan chapter of the AOH had refused to allow the ILGO to take part in their parade, so Dinkins joined their parade which took place two hours after the traditional event. The conservative nature of the AOH reflected Irish law, which did not decriminalise homosexual activity until 1993.[17] In 1992, Dinkins chose the New York state chapter of the AOH, rather than the national organisation, to sponsor the parade in the hope that this would persuade the group to allow the ILGO to take part. It was to no avail; the Order banned the gay rights activists, condemning them for 'outrageous behavior'.[18] This time, the Mayor did not march at all and rescinded the AOH permit to hold the march. The ensuing legal case saw Federal Judge Kevin Thomas Duffy rule that Dinkins's insistence that the ILGO be included in the parade was unconstitutional. Judge Duffy returned control of the parade to the AOH.[19]

At this point, Dinkins completely changed tack on the ILGO and the St Patrick's Day parade, deciding to block the group from staging its own march in 1993. This was a gamble that some believed was designed to try to win Dinkins some favour from conservative Irish-American voters in the 1993 Mayoral election.[20] To what extent it was necessary

---

[15] *NYT*, 18/3/1990.

[16] *NYT*, 16/3/1991.

[17] This was five years after Senator David Norris had brought a case to the European Convention on Human Rights which found that Irish law violated Article 8 of the Convention.

[18] *NYT*, 23/1/1992.

[19] *NYT*, 10/1/1992, 11/2/1993, 1/3/1993.

[20] *NYT*, 21/3/1993.

to appeal to Irish voters in the New York mayoral election was unclear. Dinkins had only received 18 per cent of white Catholic votes in 1989 and the Irish presence in New York city was visibly dwindling, with only 350,000 in attendance for the 1992 parade compared with millions that lined the streets in previous years. In 1989, Dinkins had, however, gained with homosexual voters, who accounted for between 10 per cent and 15 per cent of the electorate.[21] This made the decision to antagonise the ILGO all the more puzzling. He decided to boycott the parade in 1993, unlike Police Commissioner Raymond W. Kelly, who marched despite his previous statements in favour of including gay people in the parade.[22]

As was evident from the badge on his jacket on St Patrick's Day 1990, Dinkins supported the cause of Joe Doherty, something of a cause célèbre during the early 1990s. The street corner outside the Metropolitan Correctional Center in lower Manhattan where Doherty was held was renamed Joe Doherty Corner, with the approval of New York City Council, in June 1990.[23] Dinkins met Doherty twice, in April 1991 and again in 1992, on the latter occasion travelling to the Federal prison in Lewisburg, Pennsylvania, where Doherty was awaiting deportation.[24] Dinkins later, during his campaign for re-election, declared his intention to visit Doherty in Maze prison in Northern Ireland.[25] The British Consul General in New York, Alistair Hunter, wrote to Dinkins to tell him that he was 'surprised and disappointed' at these comments, 'particularly in the light of this city's current preoccupation with terrorist incidents', a reference to the Al Qaeda bombing of the World Trade Center in February 1993. Hunter argued that 'by offering support to Mr Doherty in this way, and by making public your wish to see him, you are undermining our joint efforts to combat the terrorist threat'.[26] Dinkins responded with a lengthy letter that detailed his dissatisfaction with the drawn-out British campaign to have Doherty sent back to Northern Ireland, arguing that the US government had

[21]   *NYT*, 1/3/1993.
[22]   *NYT*, 4/3/1993.
[23]   *Victoria Advocate*, 3/6/1990.
[24]   *NYT*, 10/2/1992.
[25]   Letter from HM Consul-General Alistair Hunter to Mayor Dinkins *c*.May 1993. Re Dinkins comments at Shannon Airport, AIA 9: The Papers of George Harrison, Box 5, Series B: Prisoners, Tamiment Library, NYU.
[26]   Letter from HM Consul-General Alistair Hunter to Mayor Dinkins *c*.May 1993. Re Dinkins comments at Shannon Airport, Irish Republicanism Collection, AIA 22, Box 5 Series B: Prisoners, Tamiment Library, NYU. Also *IT*, 19/8/1993.

'adopted its aggressive posture in Mr Doherty's case in order to further the interest of your government ... I believe that Mr Doherty suffered a terrible injustice in this country'. He concluded that 'It is unfortunate that, often, when Americans speak out about the situation in Northern Ireland they are accused of supporting violence'.[27]

David Dinkins lost the 1993 New York Mayoral election to Republican candidate Rudolf Giuliani. A few days after the new Mayor arrived in office, Gerry Adams arrived in New York and a year later Giuliani would present the Sinn Féin President with the Crystal Apple, an award extended to foreign dignitaries by the Mayor of the city.[28]

Joe Doherty

Receiving Mayor Dinkins in early 1992, Joe Doherty was at the end of his long campaign against his removal to the United Kingdom, where he would face a life sentence for his part in the murder of Captain Westmacott. Doherty's campaign had appeared to be over when, in June of 1988, Attorney General Edwin Meese ordered his deportation, but Meese was forced to resign in July amidst a scandal over the awarding of government contracts.[29] His replacement, former Pennsylvania Governor Richard Thornburgh, decided to launch a review into the Doherty case in February 1989, and asked the Immigration and Naturalization Service, who supported deportation, and Doherty's legal team, who sought to claim asylum for their client, to resubmit arguments.[30]

Thornburgh had the support of figures such as Delaware Senator Joseph Biden in this decision; Biden was of the view that Doherty might have been denied due process and questioned objections to Doherty's desire to be deported to Ireland.[31] The review ultimately

[27]   Letter from Mayor David Dinkins to the Honorable Alistair Hunter, HM Consul-General, 10/8/1993, Irish Republicanism Collection, AIA 22, Box 5 Series B: Prisoners, Tamiment Library, NYU.

[28]   *NYT*, 29/9/1994.

[29]   *Los Angeles Times*, 5/7/1988.

[30]   *NYT*, 15/6/1988 and 26/2/1989.

[31]   Letter from Joseph Biden to Thornburgh, 19/12/1988, Box 759, Folder 11, Cases and investigations: Doherty, Joseph (deportation) 1989–1991, Dick Thornburgh Papers AIS 1998.30, Archives Service Center, University of Pittsburgh.

complete, Thornburgh followed the lead of his predecessor and ruled in favour of deportation, stating, 'in my discretion, I would not grant the respondent asylum ... it is the policy of the United States that those who commit acts of violence against a democratic state should receive prompt and lawful punishment'.[32] Biden was one of 137 members of Congress who signed a resolution seeking Doherty's release.[33] Sherard Cowper-Coles, now in the British Embassy in Washington as the First Secretary, wrote to John Harris in the Justice Department to express British concerns that if Doherty were released on bail he would abscond.[34]

The appeals process ultimately escalated the INS v. Doherty case to the United States Supreme Court in January 1992, a full eight-and-a-half years since he was originally arrested in a Manhattan bar, and eleven-and-a-half years since the killing of Herbert Westmacott. Chief Justice William H. Rehnquist authored a five to three decision which upheld Attorney General Thornburgh's decision and ruled that Doherty was not entitled to a new hearing in his prolonged legal struggle to avoid deportation.[35] Justices Antonin Scalia, John Paul Stevens, and David H. Souter all disagreed with the decision, writing in their dissent that denying Doherty's right to reopen the case 'takes on a particularly capricious coloration when one compares it with the considerable indulgence accorded to the INS's procedural defaults in the same proceeding'.[36]

On 19 February 1992, Joe Doherty was flown to an American airbase in England and was returned to Belfast. Nassau County Comptroller Peter King described the decision as 'an absolute disgrace'.[37] Doherty was imprisoned in Maze prison, and immediately set about an appeal to have the nine years he spent in jail in the

---

[32]   *NYT*, 1/7/1989.

[33]   *People*, 6/1/1991.

[34]   Letter from Sherard Cowper-Coles, British Embassy, to John Harris, Department of Justice, 24/9/1990, Box 759, Folder 11, Cases and investigations: Doherty, Joseph (deportation) 1989–1991, Dick Thornburgh Papers AIS 1998.30, Archives Service Center, University of Pittsburgh.

[35]   *NYT*, 30/6/1990 and 16/1/1992.

[36]   *Philadelphia Inquirer*, 31/1/1992. See also *Immigration and Naturalization Service, Petitioner* v. *Joseph Patrick Doherty*, 502 U.S. 314 (112 S.Ct. 719, 116 L.Ed.2d 823), Argued Oct. 16, 1991, Decided Jan. 15, 1992, available at https://www.law.cornell.edu/supremecourt/text/502/314.

[37]   *NYT*, 20/2/1992.

United States taken into consideration for his application for parole.[38] Reflecting on the Doherty saga in an undated newsletter entitled 'America's Irish War', the Irish Northern Aid Committee contended that the British media campaign in the United States had been as 'masterful as it was malicious'. Noraid's frustration with the wider Irish-American community was also obvious: 'Irish-Americans were now more status conscious than morally conscious and generally unaware of Britain's history of deceit in Ireland', concluding that 'Goebbels couldn't have done better!'[39] As Marian Price later reflected on the overall Irish republican campaign against the British, 'We're not designed for a long war; we're designed for a short sharp hit and then retreat'.[40] The Doherty extradition campaign had in itself been a long war, one that exhausted the resources and will of many supporters who found themselves unable to fight the complicated legal framework of the so-called 'special relationship' between the United States and the United Kingdom.

Doherty's deportation was the end of an era for Irish America, representing the last broad-based movement of the conflict. Doherty had fought for nearly a decade with unwavering support from Irish America, but eventually exhausted his legal options. It was also the last time Irish America would unify behind the Irish republican cause. The Doherty campaign, symbolic of the perceived legitimacy of the IRA campaign, had brought together all factions of Irish America: politicians, diplomats, community leaders, and ordinary members of society. With the new extradition treaty in place, it would, theoretically at least, be the last time an IRA volunteer could seek asylum from prosecution in the United States.

Interviewed two decades after his return to Belfast, Doherty noted that he regularly walked past the site of the Westmacott killing on his way to his local supermarket: 'I stop and do a prayer for him. For his soul. It's all I can do'.[41]

---

[38]   *IT*, 1/2/1994.

[39]   Irish Northern Aid Committee America's Irish War (undated), AIA 008, Durkan Papers, Box 1 Folder 29, Irish Northern Aid Organization Info: Communication (incl. 1989 split), Tamiment Library, NYU.

[40]   Marian Price, interview with author, 1/7/2010.

[41]   'Troubles militant Joe Doherty look back 20 years on with regret', Irish Central, 21/7/2015, available at www.irishcentral.com/news/troubles-militant-joe-doherty-look-back-20-years-on-with-regret-video.

Irish America during the Bush Years

The late 1980s saw Irish America riven with factionalism. Noraid had suffered a split in 1986 when founder Michael Flannery left the organisation in protest at the decision to end Sinn Féin's policy of abstention from the Irish Dáil. Along with veteran republicans like George Harrison and Joe Stynes, Flannery formed Cumann na Saoirse, the Irish Freedom Committee. This mirrored the split that took place in Ireland, with Ruairí Ó Brádaigh leading a breakaway group called Republican Sinn Féin. The US split became bitter and Flannery labelled the Sinn Féin leadership, 'Free Staters'. In response, others, including Joe Doherty, denounced Flannery. Flannery's group aligned with Ó Brádaigh's, whilst Martin Galvin pledged Noraid's 'unequivocal moral and political support for Sinn Féin'.[42] Further division followed in 1989 when a group led by former INAC chair Pat O'Connell led a new group calling itself the Friends of Irish Freedom.[43]

Publicly, Sinn Féin attempted to spin the split in Noraid as cordial, but letters to Noraid members revealed a series of allegations about the misappropriation of funds and strategic disagreements.[44] In an attempt to reaffirm control over the situation, Noraid launched its 'Homefront' campaign in late 1990. Gerry Adams wrote to American supporters of the Irish republican cause 'under circumstances of dire emergency', calling upon them to 'enlist in the Irish Northern Aid Home Front'. He praised the 'creation of Green Cross and An Cumann Cabhrach to accept and distribute your donations from America—so critical to our success', before asking for more:

> Your Homefront membership dues will establish a nation-wide outreach, education, and political action campaign. Through your membership dues, you will sustain the counterattack on

[42] *Sunday Press*, 11/1/1987, cited in Wilson, *Irish America*, p. 278. Martin Galvin, interview with author, 15/5/2012.

[43] Wilson, *Irish America*, p. 280.

[44] Letter from Sinn Féin to all National Executive Members, 4/7/1989; and Letter from Sinn Féin to Members and Supporters Irish Northern Aid Committee, 29/8/1989; Letter from James Maunsell, National Chairman to Robert Smith, National Secretary, An Cumann Cabhrach July 1990; Letter from Bob Smith, Chairperson, An Cumann Cabhrach to All Friends of Irish Political Prisoners and their Dependants, all from AIA 008, Durkan Papers, Box 1 Folder 29, Irish Northern Aid Organization Info: Communication (incl. 1989 split), Tamiment Library, NYU.

British propaganda in America. You will subsidize the offensive against U.S. policy that denies visas to our spokespeople. You will underwrite the creation and distribution of educational material to schools, libraries, community organizations … You will support the Homefront's computerized fundraising, merchandising, and 1-800-IRELAND campaigns. You will establish the Homefront's national book and video club. You will champion our political action strike forces.[45]

This was surprisingly defiant rhetoric and spoke to the belief that Sinn Féin retained in its US branch. Despite Adams's claim that 'Our successes in Ireland have come in the face of British partition, internment, assassination, torture, constant surveillance, harassment, and censorship', the British were quite aware that Irish America was an increasingly insignificant source of weaponry and financial backing for Irish republicans:

We can no longer produce alibis like 'it's coming out of Irish America'. The majority is raised by criminal means North and South of the Border, the majority of it in the North. We have been working very hard with the Irish-American community in the US, and there are now four or five beneficent vehicles under which Irish-Americans are contributing to the whole of Ireland.[46]

Adams later reflected on the period, noting the role of Irish-American politicians in undermining support for the Irish republican movement: 'A lot of the work in the political establishment in the upper echelons of Irish America was seen, I think quite rightly, as being … anti-Irish Republican'.[47] It was this pressure that had driven groups like Noraid and the Irish National Caucus to the fringes, squeezed from prominence by Congressional groups like the Friends of Ireland and even the Ad Hoc Congressional Committee, which could at least claim to have some domestic mandate within Irish America and a legitimate platform from which to espouse Irish causes. Newly appointed UK Ambassador to the United States, Lord Renwick, later recalled his first St Patrick's Day experience in Boston where 'a million dollars were raised … for

[45] Letter from Gerry Adams for distribution in USA, AIA 008, Durkan Papers, Box 1 Folder 29, Irish Northern Aid Organization Info: Communication (incl. 1989 split), Tamiment Library, NYU.
[46] *IT*, 12/10/1990.
[47] Edward M. Kennedy Institute, Oral History, 'Interview with Gerry Adams', available at https://www.emkinstitute.org/resources/gerry-adams.

worthwhile causes on both sides of the border'.[48] These were now the causes that the majority in Irish America worked for.

There were still events and issues around which a more radical faction of Irish Americans could coalesce. One notable cause was the campaign to secure what became the 1990 Immigration Act, which brought about nearly 50,000 new visas for Irish citizens. This act had congressional support from Senator Ted Kennedy, who introduced it to the Senate in February 1989, and Congressman Bruce Morrison, who was the House author.[49] Kennedy also secured bipartisan co-sponsorship from Democrats Daniel Moynihan and Chris Dodd and Republicans Alan Simpson and Alfonse D'Amato.

Another issue of transnational significance was that of the campaign in support of the MacBride principles. During this period, the campaign in the United States grew from strength to strength. The New York Assembly had, in 1986, voted 136 to eight in favour of using the MacBride Principles to set the standard for state investment in companies that do business in Northern Ireland. The bill was signed by Governor Cuomo in May, and New York state joined Massachusetts in endorsing the principles.[50] A total of eighteen states passed legislation related to MacBride, whilst four other states endorsed the principles. Several other companies and international organisations had also endorsed the principles, and they were part of the Omnibus Appropriations Act of 1998, setting the Congressional standard for economic relations with Northern Ireland. As part of the 1998 act, the Anglo Irish Agreement Support Act of 1986 was amended to include the line:

> United States contributions should be used in a manner that effectively increases employment opportunities in communities with rates of unemployment higher than the local or urban average of unemployment in Northern Ireland. In addition, such contributions should be used to benefit individuals residing in such communities.[51]

[48]   Renwick, unpublished memoir, p. 225.
[49]   101st Congress (1989–1990), S. 358 Immigration Act of 1990, available at https://www.congress.gov/bill/101st-congress/senate-bill/358.
[50]   *NYT*, 25/5/1986. Florida renounced the MacBride principals in 2015; see *Irish Echo*, 22/5/2015.
[51]   H.R. 4328 Omnibus Consolidated and Emergency Supplemental Appropriations Act, 1999, available at https://www.congress.gov/bill/105th-congress/house-bill/4328/text.

It also added clarification in terms of the 'banning of provocative sectarian or political emblems from the workplace', 'all job openings be[ing] advertised publicly and providing that special recruitment efforts be made to attract applicants from underrepresented religious groups', 'providing that layoff, recall, and termination procedures do not favor a particular religious group', and 'abolishing job reservations, apprenticeship restrictions, and differential employment criteria which discriminate on the basis of religion'.

Passing as a bill in a state legislature in the United States did not, however, provide any guarantee of successful implementation in Northern Ireland. Particularly problematic was the fact that the UK's 1976 Fair Employment Act prohibited 'reverse discrimination'. US Ambassador to the UK Charles Price argued that while employment discrimination was 'unacceptable … the MacBride Principles are wrong because they can do incalculable harm'. The Ford Motor company, one of several US corporations that had set up facilities in Northern Ireland, was found guilty of anti-Catholic discrimination at its Belfast plant in 1985 by the Fair Employment Agency.[52] A decade later, a long-tenured employee at the plant in Finaghy, west Belfast, was awarded £40,000 as a result of religious discrimination on the part of Ford. The Fair Employment Tribunal found that Tom Irvine, a Catholic, had been overlooked for a promotion in favour of Protestant candidates who were judged to be inferior.[53] The following year, Gerry Adams was excluded from a Ford motors luncheon for newly elected officials who represent constituencies with Ford plants. Adams noted 'it has not been a happy relationship with the people of West Belfast'.[54]

In late 1991, a congressional delegation led by Speaker Tom Foley travelled to Northern Ireland and visited west and north Belfast to explore areas supported by the International Fund for Ireland. They also met with Secretary of State Peter Brooke, who considered that he had established 'a valuable basis for further dialogue' in Northern Ireland. The delegation assured concerned spectators that the US government would not speak to Sinn Féin until it had repudiated IRA violence.[55] The importance of this line was emphasised in an address delivered

[52]   *NYT*, 4/9/1986.
[53]   *IT*, 5/6/1996.
[54]   *An Phoblacht*, 21/8/1997.
[55]   *IT*, 5/9/1991.

by the Irish Ambassador to the United States, Dermot Gallagher, at a black-tie dinner at the Willard Hotel in Washington.[56]

Changes in government in both London and Dublin altered the dynamics of the Northern Ireland peace process over the early weeks of 1992. Margaret Thatcher resigned as Prime Minister in November 1991 and was replaced by her Chancellor, John Major. As Major settled into office in early 1992, he found a new counterpart in Dublin following the resignation of Charles Haughey. Albert Reynolds arrived as Fianna Fáil leader and Taoiseach on 6 February 1992. As Roger MacGinty has noted, Reynolds had no ideological interest in Northern Ireland and was prepared to take risks in order to achieve progress in the peace process.[57] In an interview with the Edward M. Kennedy institute, Gerry Adams recalled Reynolds's positive attitude on the issue of Northern Ireland:

> When Albert came in, Albert moved. Haughey was very cautious. You also have to remember, in fairness to him, that the atmosphere at that time was entirely in support of British policy and strategy. I mean, they're all in the same cradle. The Irish government would have put it in different terms, but all of the bad things that happened in terms of censorship, denial of people's rights, internment, shoot to kill. The Irish government was mute in all of those issues because it had bought into the defeat of terrorism, as it was described. It would have been a big thing for Haughey to have broken that cycle ... However, Albert came in, looked at it in a very practical way, saw there was a chance, and then went looking for that.[58]

Political change was coming, too, for Sinn Féin. In the 1992 UK general election, Sinn Féin's President lost his Belfast West seat to Dr Joe Hendron of the SDLP. The day after the election, 10 April, the IRA planted a bomb at the Baltic Exchange killing three people. It was claimed this bomb caused £800 million worth of damage, an enormous figure when it was estimated that the damage sustained by the whole of Northern Ireland since the outset of the conflict was £615m.

---

[56]   *IT*, 31/10/1991.
[57]   MacGinty, R., 'American Influences on the Northern Ireland Peace Process', *Journal of Conflict Studies* 17(2) (1997).
[58]   Edward M. Kennedy Institute, Oral History, 'Interview with Gerry Adams', available at https://www.emkinstitute.org/resources/gerry-adams.

Enter Clinton

With Adams now out of elected office, Sinn Féin needed support from Irish America more than ever. It was this base that was, for Adrian Guelke, highly influential in bringing the party leadership round to the idea that a ceasefire was essential to ensure progress in Northern Ireland. Central to this was a group that became known as Americans for a New Irish Agenda. This group, originally Irish-Americans for Clinton, was formed in 1991 by Niall O'Dowd, a leading figure in the Irish Immigration Reform Movement and the publisher of the *Irish Voice* newspaper, along with former Congressman Bruce Morrison.[59] Morrison, a former law school classmate of Arkansas Governor Bill Clinton, had been active on the Ad Hoc Committee for Irish Affairs during his time in office but had retired to run for Governor of Connecticut in 1990.[60] In March 1992, Morrison wrote to Clinton, who had announced his candidacy for President in October 1991:

> I have been trying to be of help to your campaign financially and otherwise … however, I believe that there are things that I could be doing of a more substantial nature, given the opportunity … [in particular] my ability to be of help to you in the Irish American community, especially as it may relate to the New York primary. As you may know, as Chairman of the House Immigration Subcommittee, I was instrumental in creating new immigration opportunities for the Irish, which has resulted in my achieving special prominence and recognition in the Irish American community over the past two years. I would like to use this access and standing on your behalf.[61]

The 1992 Presidential election was a pivotal moment for the Northern Ireland conflict. Clinton's ultimate success brought in a President with a keen interest in working towards a solution to a conflict that was now well into its third decade. Joseph O'Grady has noted that

[59]   Guelke, A., 'The United States, Irish Americans and the Northern Ireland Peace Process', *International Affairs* 72(3) (1996), pp. 521–536, at p. 523.
[60]   *IT*, 23/8/1994.
[61]   Letter from Morrison to Clinton, 19/3/1992, Correspondence in the Irish Americans for Clinton–Gore subseries of Series VIII: Ireland, Archives & Special Collections at the Thomas J. Dodd Research Center, University of Connecticut Libraries, Bruce A. Morrison Papers, MS 1991.0021 (hereafter Morrison Papers, UConn Library).

neither Clinton nor Jerry Brown, the former Governor of California and Clinton's leading opponent in the Democratic primary contests, had shown much interest in Ireland prior to the Connecticut primary on 24 March. Brown's narrow victory there, where he carried the majority of white Catholic voters, prompted a rethink on the part of the Clinton campaign, with the potentially pivotal New York primary only two weeks away.[62] Clinton himself recalled, in his memoir, 'I first got involved in the Irish issue because of the politics of New York, but it became one of the great passions of my presidency'.[63] It would become a major bilateral issue for the United States in its relationship with the United Kingdom, as John Major would later reflect: after Clinton came to office, 'there were two issues on which Britain and America took different views: Bosnia and Northern Ireland'.[64]

Arriving relatively late to the Irish question, Clinton could formulate his own perspective on the conflict free from any historical or ideological affiliation. On 5 April, he gave a speech to the American-Irish Presidential Forum in New York. Here, he laid out his platform on Irish issues: reversing the ban on Gerry Adams entering the USA; support of the MacBride principles; and a commitment to appoint a peace envoy to Northern Ireland. The importance of these issues for an Irish audience in New York was underlined by the fact that Jerry Brown made the same commitments.[65] Brown's commitment to these issues must remain a matter of conjecture, but Clinton's ability to last the course on Irish issues was, as noted by Roger MacGinty, thanks in part to key Irish-American actors such as Bruce Morrison, Niall O'Dowd, Mutual of America President Bill Flynn, and Charles 'Chuck' Feeney, the Chairman of General Atlantic Corporation and founder of Atlantic Philanthropies.[66] Gerry Adams has also cited the influence of John Dearie, a State Assemblyman representing the Bronx, and a prominent lawyer:

> John organized a conference in New York to which he invited the Presidential hopefuls. He asked them—or he and others in the audience asked them—would they support an end to

[62]   O'Grady, J., 'An Irish Policy Born in the U.S.A.: Clinton's Break with the Past', *Foreign Affairs* 75(3) (1993), pp. 2–7, at p. 3.
[63]   Clinton, B., *My Life* (London: Hutchinson, 2004), p. 401.
[64]   Major, *The Autobiography*, p. 497.
[65]   *IT*, 7/4/1992.
[66]   MacGinty, 'American Influences on the Northern Ireland Peace Process'.

discrimination here, would they support measures to highlight collusion between British forces and lawyers, would they support a visa for me, and other issues? And Bill Clinton said 'Yes'. So Niall [O'Dowd] and a few friends then came together and formed a group that eventually came to be called Americans for a New Irish Agenda.[67]

The group, which became known as Irish-Americans for Clinton/Gore following the Democratic National Convention, was deeply critical of the Bush Administration for being 'locked in a blindly pro-British policy concerning the north of Ireland that virtually ensures the continuation of anti-Irish violence and human rights violations'.[68] Branches of Irish-Americans for Clinton sprang up across the country, notably in Boston and New York but also Connecticut, New Jersey, Chicago, Michigan, Southern California, Virginia, and Florida, and Clinton continued to engage with Irish issues as his campaign advanced towards the November election.[69]

The notoriously private Feeney was one of the key players in this group and yet, as discussed at length by Conor O'Clery in his book *The Billionaire Who Wasn't*, his existence was barely acknowledged outside of the very close circles he kept. It was Morrison who began the process of bringing Feeney into the fold in July 1992 by inviting him to a $50,000 dinner party on 9 August as well as a larger-scale meeting with Irish-American business, political, and community leaders.[70] A year later, Feeney sat in a Dublin coffee shop with O'Dowd, Morrison, and Bill Flynn reflecting on the IRA ceasefire that the group had helped to bring about. O'Clery described the scene: 'Ireland was at peace, if

[67]   Edward M. Kennedy Institute, Oral History, 'Interview with Gerry Adams', available at https://www.emkinstitute.org/resources/gerry-adams.

[68]   Tennessee Senator Al Gore was chosen as Clinton's running mate in July; see *NYT*, 10/7/1992; Irish Central, 'The Irish and the Clintons: A Love Affair', 20/1/2014, available at www.irishcentral.com/news/politics/The-Irish-and-the-Clintons-A-love-affair.html; Irish Americans for Clinton–Gore newsletter, in General Correspondence, Series VIII: Ireland in Morrison Papers, UConn Library.

[69]   Letter from O'Kennedy to Morrison, 28/9/1992, in General Correspondence, Series VIII: Ireland in Morrison Papers, UConn Library; Memorandum from Morrison to Christopher Hyland, 30/10/1992, General Correspondence, 1992–1996, Morrison Papers, UConn Library.

[70]   Letter from Morrison to Feeney, 27/7/1992, in General Correspondence, Series VIII: Ireland in Morrison Papers, UConn Library.

only for a few days, and it had been achieved by the four guys in the coffee shop'.[71]

Clinton first met Feeney at an event in New Jersey on 30 September. Morrison briefed the candidate ahead of the meeting, emphasising that the man, 'universally known as Chuck', was 'aggressively interested in improving economic and social conditions in both Ireland and the United States'. Feeney was also 'extremely concerned that the Clinton administration harness the potential of corporate America by defining a vision which calls actively on corporations and their leadership to contribute much more broadly to the solving of economic and social problems in their communities'. The memo included a two-page explanation of Feeney's philosophy about the philanthropic strategies that corporations should adopt.[72] Feeney was quickly on board with Clinton's strategy and soon made two substantial donations: $20,000 to the DNC Federal Account and $30,000 to the DNC Non-Federal Account.[73]

In October, Clinton visited the Eire Irish bar in Dorchester, Boston. The visit recalled that of Ronald Reagan, who had visited the same bar in 1983 during his campaign for re-election, a re-election he won quite successfully thanks in part to the votes of working-class Irish Democrats. Boston Mayor Raymond Flynn suggested that the so-called Reagan Democrats were now ready to return to the Democratic Party.[74] He also paid attention to Clinton–Gore's commitment to 'move intelligently on the foreign policy front to maintain America's role as the world's peacemaker [which is] a cherished part of America's heritage', adding that 'I would like to see it applied more even-handedly in regard to Northern Ireland'. Flynn had been critical of Bush for his failure 'to contribute in a meaningful way to the search for peace in Northern Ireland. [His] laissez faire approach to Northern Ireland is hardly neutral, for it relies on the British Government for advice, as demonstrated in the Joe Doherty extradition case'. He went on to suggest that the recent electoral failure of former Attorney

[71] O'Clery, C., *The Billionaire Who Wasn't: How Chuck Feeney Made and Gave Away a Fortune* (New York: Public Affairs, 2007), p. 188.

[72] Memorandum from Morrison to Clinton, 25/9/1992, 'Briefing on Chuck Feeney for September 30th New Jersey Event', in General Correspondence, Series VIII: Ireland in Morrison Papers, UConn Library.

[73] Letter from Morrison to Hyland, 5/10/1992, in General Correspondence, Series VIII: Ireland in Morrison Papers, UConn Library.

[74] *IT*, 1/10/1992.

General Richard Thornburgh was because 'the voters in Pennsylvania remembered Thornburgh's shabby treatment of Joe Doherty and they ousted him from public office'.[75]

Clinton wrote to Morrison, citing 'the lasting contributions of the Irish-American community', which 'are what have helped make this country strong ... Senator Gore and I share the goal of all Irish-Americans for peace in Northern Ireland. We believe that the United States must reflect this concern more effectively in its foreign policy'.[76] He also pledged that:

> A Clinton Administration will take a more active role in working with the leaders in these nations to achieve a just and lasting settlement of the conflict. A permanent and peaceful solution to the crisis in Northern Ireland can only be achieved if the underlying causes of the strife and instability are dealt with vigorously, fairly and within a time-frame that guarantees genuine, substantial, and steady process. I believe the appointment of a U.S. special envoy to Northern Ireland could be a catalyst in the efforts to secure a lasting peace.[77]

The need for this catalyst was becoming ever more obvious to the parties in London and Dublin. Peace talks that were led by Peter Brooke and Sir Patrick Mayhew had stalled on Strand One, the section that focused on the institutions of Northern Ireland, so moved on to Strands Two and Three; the 'north-south' dimension of the relationship between Northern Ireland and the Republic, and the 'east-west' dimension of Irish-British relations, respectively. These three strands were the major tenets of the 1998 Good Friday Agreement. The involvement of the Dublin government angered Ulster Unionists, and in September DUP leaders Ian Paisley and Peter Robinson walked out of talks on Strand Two, the two still aggrieved at the retention of an Irish dimension to the peace process

---

[75]   Statement of Raymond L. Flynn, Mayor of Boston, 28/10/1992, AIA 008, Durkan Papers, Box 1 Folder 8, Meeting at White House, Correspondence and Press, July–Dec. 1996, Tamiment Library, NYU.

[76]   Letter from Clinton to Morrison, 23/10/1992, Correspondence in the Irish Americans for Clinton–Gore subseries of Series VIII: Ireland, in Morrison Papers, UConn Library.

[77]   Ibid. The special envoy promise echoed a pledge made whilst campaigning in California in October; see *IT*, 28/10/1992.

two decades after Sunningdale.[78] Political talks began to stall over late 1992 and Unionists were frustrated by Secretary of State Patrick Mayhew referring to a united Ireland as a 'legitimate' aspiration. Peter Robinson branded these remarks controversial, though Mayhew later reflected on his own comments:

> Nothing of substance in that speech had not been said by my distinguished predecessor at least two years ago. There was nothing in my remarks concerning the Union to occasion surprise to anyone. I said that as long as the greater number of people living in Northern Ireland wanted to continue being a part of the United Kingdom, that would be warmly, solemnly and sincerely respected and upheld. If, on the other hand, the day should come when the majority wanted some other citizenship, the British Government would not stand in the way. I find it difficult to see any point of principle that would be supported in the House which would lead to a contrary conclusion.[79]

The speech, in the context of Brooke's earlier comments that Britain had no 'selfish economic or strategic interest' in Northern Ireland, provided further indication that the British government were prepared to work with the aspirations of nationalists and republicans in Northern Ireland as they pushed towards a peaceful resolution of the conflict. The engagement of Irish nationalists and republicans was integral to any realistic effort at restoring peace to Northern Ireland, and Unionist resistance had to be overcome to achieve this. This was where Bill Clinton could play a significant role. Unbeholden to Ulster Unionist groups, and willing to push the British and Irish governments on the tempo of political progress in Northern Ireland, the only restraint on Clinton's actions was the long-standing US policy of non-intervention in Northern Ireland, and the established protocol of following the lead of the British government. The British, perhaps

---

[78] Bloomfield, D., *Developing Dialogue in Northern Ireland: The Mayhew Talks 1992* (Basingstoke: Palgrave, 2001), p. 80; *Independent*, 11/8/1992; Edward M. Kennedy Institute, Oral History, 'Interview with Edward M. Kennedy, 27/2/2006' available at https://www.emkinstitute.org/resources/edward-m-kennedy-2-27-2006.

[79] Political Initiatives, The Secretary of State for Northern Ireland (Sir Patrick Mayhew), Hansard, HC vol 217, cols 482–485 (21 January 1993), available at https://api.parliament.uk/historic-hansard/commons/1993/jan/21/political-initiatives.

unintentionally, provided Clinton with some justification for adopting a more aggressive stance on Northern Ireland, when it was revealed that the Conservative Party had instructed British officials to search Home Office records for evidence of Clinton's anti-Vietnam activities during his time at Oxford, for the purposes of aiding President Bush in the election campaign. A significant rift between Clinton and the newly re-elected government of John Major was created.[80] The US Ambassador in London, Raymond Seitz, recalled that, 'as far as he was concerned, the Tory Party had done its best to prevent his election. His coterie of score-keeping advisers was even more embittered'.[81]

In October, President Bush spoke on Clinton's time as a Rhodes Scholar at Oxford: 'You know, Governor Clinton is already talking about pulling together the best and the brightest, all the lobbyists, economists, lawyers, all those guys, liberal guys that were hanging out with him in Oxford when some of you were over there [in Vietnam] fighting, and have them solve all of America's problems'.[82] Bush had some assistance from both the British media and the British Government in emphasising this point to the American electorate. Clinton had arrived in Oxford in October 1968 shortly after completing his undergraduate degree at Georgetown. A report in the *Independent* newspaper quoted one of Clinton's fellow Rhodes scholars, lawyer Doug Eakley, who recalled the relief at 'getting out of the US and out of the extraordinary pressure cooker that the US represented in the 1960s'. It also interviewed another solicitor, Katherine Gieve, who reportedly dated President Clinton in 1969:

> Politics, as taught in Oxford then, was about ideas. It was very distant from actual experience. But Bill was thinking about people. He made a relationship between abstract ideas and the meaning of people's experiences. That was true for all of the Americans at Oxford then. Because of the Vietnam war, demands were being made of the state that were crucial to the way they lived their own ideas.

---

[80] Wallace, W., 'Foreign Policy' in Kavanagh, D. and Selden, A. (eds), *The Major Effect* (London: Macmillan, 1994), pp. 295–296. The allegations were effectively confirmed by John Major in his autobiography, though he noted the actions of junior party officials were 'not with my knowledge nor at my bidding'. See Major, *The Autobiography*, p. 498.
[81] Seitz, R., *Over Here* (London: Weidenfeld & Nicolson, 1998), p. 321.
[82] *Independent*, 10/10/1992.

Novelist Sara Maitland, another former classmate, recalled 'Bill said that feeling bad wasn't good enough', emphasising Clinton's anti-war sensibilities, which a letter from Clinton about Frank Aller, who committed suicide in 1971, also alluded to. Clinton described Aller as 'a draft resister … he is one of the bravest, best men I know'.[83]

On Tuesday, 3 November 1998, Arkansas Governor Bill Clinton was elected as the forty-second President of the United States. The Bush years had been very much 'more of the same' from the United States as it pertained to Northern Ireland. The Clinton years could scarcely have been further from that.

---

[83]   Ibid.

CHAPTER SIX

Bill Clinton and the Path to Good Friday

Dear Irish-American Leader, please find herewith a set of recommendations to President Bill Clinton from the Irish community in the United States. These recommendations have been gathered and shaped from the opinions of Irish-Americans and Americans of good will throughout the United States, and represent the critical ways in which American policy can have a constructive impact on improving the political, social, and economic landscape in the Republic of Ireland and Northern Ireland.[1]

Draft letter from Irish-Americans for Clinton–Gore, 1992

Graduating alongside Bill Clinton and Hillary Rodham in Yale Law School's class of 1973, Bruce Morrison was part of a class that also featured future Secretary of Labor Robert Reich. Nearly a decade after graduating with his Juris Doctor, Morrison was elected to Congress for Connecticut's 3rd district. He served on the House Banking Committee and the House Judiciary Committee before coauthoring the Immigration Act of 1990. This bill included a provision that permitted increased migration from countries such as Ireland which were considered to have lost out thanks to per-country limits to migration in the 1965 Immigration and Nationality Act. The 1965 bill had received support from Ted Kennedy, despite its impact on Ireland, and Kennedy's involvement as the Senate author of the 1990 act would go some way to

---

[1]   Irish-Americans for Clinton–Gore draft letter, Box 1 Folder 1, Series I: Americans for a New Irish Agenda: Irish-Americans for Clinton–Gore (Recommendations), AIA 008, Durkan Papers, Tamiment Library, NYU.

rectifying this. Morrison went on to run for Governor of Connecticut but finished behind third party candidate Lowell Weicker and Republican John Rowland. Disillusioned with politics, and the divided Connecticut Democrats, Morrison returned to legal practice and set up his own firm, returning to politics to support Clinton's bid for the Presidency.

Morrison was also familiar with Ireland and Irish issues, having visited Derry in August 1987 where he found himself held at gunpoint by the RUC.[2] Six years on, Morrison and his Irish-Americans for Clinton–Gore co-chair, Boston Mayor Raymond Flynn, issued the organisation's statement of purpose. It cited the Clinton letter of 23 October and the five steps that he pledged to make to assist with the resolution of the Northern Ireland conflict: the appointment of a special envoy, attention to human rights abuses in Northern Ireland, continuing visa opportunities for Irish citizens, supporting the MacBride Principles, and eliminating foreign interference in the US Judicial system.[3] These five items became the focus of Irish America during the early years of the Clinton administration, buoyed by the new President's commitment to help resolve the situation in Northern Ireland and yet frustrated at the apparently slow pace that he actually sought to implement this commitment. This was a concern of the AOH, who met in December 1992 to celebrate Clinton's win. Shortly afterwards, Jim Gallagher of the AOH wrote to attendees of the meeting to warn them that 'it would be naïve to assume that the Clinton Administration will undertake the full spectrum of the five tasks that we identified without our continued support or urging'.[4]

Making Good on Campaign Promises

There was significant pressure on Clinton from both the UK and Northern Ireland not to intervene in the ways he had pledged. In February 1992, a group of four church leaders from Northern Ireland visited the United States. These were Cardinal Daly, Archbishop

---

[2]   Rhodeen, P., *Peacerunner: The True Story of How an ex-Congressman Helped End the Centuries of War in Ireland* (Dallas, TX: BenBella Books, 2016), p. 1.

[3]   Irish-Americans for Clinton–Gore, Statement of Purpose, General Correspondence, 1992–1996, Morrison Papers, UConn Library.

[4]   Letter from Jim Gallagher to AOH meeting attendees (undated) (*c.*13/12/1992), General Correspondence, Morrison Papers, UConn Library.

Eames, Methodist Reverend Ritchie, and Presbyterian Moderator Dr Dunlop, with Eames scheduled to speak against the appointment of a special envoy, and the others against the MacBride Principles.[5] This trip drew concern from within Irish America that Clinton would not make good on his promises. Bruce Morrison fielded communication from the IAUC and the AOH expressing concern at the situation, with Bob Linnon of the IAUC noting that 'our troops are getting very restless … people are talking about going out on their own'.[6] This concern was rooted in the perception within Irish America that Clinton was employing what the *Irish Independent* newspaper had referred to as the 'Kennedy method', namely he would express concern at Irish affairs throughout the election campaign, but ultimately abandon the cause once in office.[7] Once in office, of course, Clinton had to deal with an enormous range of issues, both domestic and international, not least the 1993 World Trade Center bombing.

Two days before the attack, Clinton met British Prime Minister John Major, and leading congressional figures like Ted Kennedy, John Kerry, and Chris Dodd pleaded with him to raise the subject of Northern Ireland. The group was particularly concerned about the 'deeply troubling … human rights abuses of the British security forces', notably allegations that British troops were operating shoot-to-kill operations as well as colluding with loyalist paramilitaries.[8] Clinton, pressed on the issue of the special envoy during questioning, responded: 'If the United States can in some way make a constructive contribution to a political settlement, of course, we'd be interested in doing that. But that is not a subject we have discussed in any way so far'. Clinton also wryly commented that 'I told the Prime Minister today that I was just grateful that I got through this whole campaign with most of my time in England still classified'. Major was, predictably, rather more serious in his remarks:

[5]   Memorandum from Father Des Wilson's Office, General Correspondence, Morrison Papers, UConn Library.
[6]   Letter from Jim Gallagher to Morrison, 23/2/1992 and Fax from Bob Linnon to Morrison, 25/2/1992, both General Correspondence, 1992–1994, Morrison Papers, UConn Library.
[7]   *Irish Independent*, 25/2/1962. Sherrill has contested that Ted Kennedy, much like his brother, was trying to enhance his reputation as an internationalist. Sherrill, *The Last Kennedy*, p. 36.
[8]   Letter to the President, 22/2/1993, Correspondence related to Americans for a New Irish Agenda Morrison Papers, UConn Library.

I think from time to time distinguished visitors from the United States in Northern Ireland have come back to the United States, and they have actually explained the remarkable changes that have taken part in Belfast. There was a delegation that was there recently. And the reality is that anyone who knew the place 10 years ago and knows the place today will see there is an absolute and total sea change. And I think the fact that there is a great knowledge about the willful peace amongst people in Northern Ireland and especially the ordinary people of Northern Ireland of both sides of the sectarian divide, the more that is understood, the better. And what is actually needed in Northern Ireland to help speed that is more understanding of the process, more support for the talks, more investment for job creation, and less money to fund terrorism. And the more people know about that, the nearer we come to a solution.[9]

These were all commitments that the government of the United States was prepared to make, both in the White House and in Congress. The Congressional Friends of Ireland remained powerful throughout the Clinton presidency, with the dominant figure of Ted Kennedy consistently engaged with Irish affairs throughout the administration. On a more informal level, the Ad Hoc Committee for Irish Affairs, established by Mario Biaggi in 1977, was now co-chaired by Hamilton Fish, Tom Manton, and Ben Gilman, and counted five senators and eighty-seven members of Congress among its numbers. Predominantly male, it did feature Representatives Helen Bentley, Rosa DeLauro, Marcy Kaptur, Barbara Kennealy, Carolyn Maloney, Constance Morella, Patricia Schroeder, and Louise Slaughter.[10]

In addition to these groups, Irish-Americans for Clinton–Gore evolved into Americans for a New Irish Agenda (ANIA). This group issued a statement, drafted by Morrison and Flynn, which criticised the 'annual St. Patrick's Day admonishment instructing Americans not to contribute to terrorism [as] an outdated way of framing the Irish discussion'. Their view was that 'a policy of political and economic

---

[9] The President's News Conference with Prime Minister John Major of the United Kingdom, 24/2/1993, the American Presidency Project, available at https://www.presidency.ucsb.edu/documents/the-presidents-news-conference-with-prime-minister-john-major-the-united-kingdom-0.

[10] Ad Hoc Committee for Irish Affairs, 1/3/1993, General Correspondence, 1992–1994, Morrison Papers, UConn Library.

incentives which satisfies the entire Northern Ireland community and leads to peace' was the optimal solution and that 'an envoy appointed by President Clinton can be a catalyst to develop these incentives'. It was also felt that empowering the Ambassador in Dublin and Consul General in Belfast to work together would help facilitate the peace process.[11] This was problematic, given, at the time, Clinton had yet to nominate his Ambassador to Ireland. William FitzGerald, appointed by President Bush to succeed Richard Moore, officially remained in the position until June 1993 while the new President sought a replacement.

One of the leading figures in ANIA, reclusive billionaire Chuck Feeney, wrote to Clinton shortly after the election to express his concern that the Ambassador post not be left open for too long. He suggested that Elizabeth Shannon, whose husband William had served in the role from 1977 to 1981, be considered for it.[12] William Shannon passed away in 1988, but his wife retained a prominent position within the Irish-American community, notably through the establishment of the Shannon Fellowship which brought Irish students to Boston University to study.[13] Elizabeth Shannon later recalled that she had conveyed her interest in the Ambassador's position and had received support from Tip O'Neill and the *Boston Globe*. She claimed to have spoken to Ted Kennedy about her candidacy but found that the Senator was going to support his sister Jean Kennedy Smith instead. Shannon recalled 'I was miffed by that … she went off to Ireland instead of me and she was there a long time. I know she found it very difficult at first, but eventually got into the rhythm of it and then got very involved in Northern Ireland'.[14]

Jean Kennedy Smith was appointed as the US Ambassador to Ireland on St Patrick's Day 1993. Clinton planned to allow Kennedy Smith time to arrive and settle into her role in Dublin before deciding what Washington's role in Northern Ireland should be.[15] She was confirmed in the role in June and arrived in Dublin shortly afterwards

[11] 'The United States can help find peace in Northern Ireland'. Statement by Morrison and Flynn, General Correspondence, 1992–1994, Morrison Papers, UConn Library.
[12] Letter from Feeney to Morrison, 9/11/1992, General Correspondence, 1992–1996, Morrison Papers, UConn Library.
[13] Edward M. Kennedy Institute, Oral History, 'Interview with Elizabeth Shannon', available at https://www.emkinstitute.org/resources/elizabeth-shannon.
[14] *Boston Globe*, 6/1/1993.
[15] *NYT*, 18/3/1993.

to begin what would be five years of service.[16] At the same time, Clinton appointed Boston Mayor Raymond Flynn as his Ambassador to the Holy See. Flynn's departure saw Bruce Morrison assume the leading role in Americans for a New Irish Agenda and Morrison immediately wrote to Clinton requesting a meeting between the President and a group of Irish-American community leaders.[17] Christopher Hyland from the Presidential transition team asked for more information; the President was concerned that 'the entire agenda [would] be centered on helping a foreign nation'.[18]

Clinton's decision to appoint National Security Council Staff Director Nancy Soderberg as the person responsible for Irish issues in the White House drew criticism because of Soderberg's perceived lack of experience.[19] One of her first acts in this role was to schedule a meeting on St Patrick's Day with Bruce Morrison, where the two reviewed Clinton's five commitments to Northern Ireland. She assured Morrison that the Special Envoy appointment was still being actively considered but that the decision would be postponed until after local elections had taken place. There had been concern at a report in the *New York Times* that Anthony Lake, the National Security Advisor and Soderberg's boss, was set to 'walk the President back from the [envoy] commitment'.[20]

The official launch of Americans for a New Irish Agenda took place in late 1993. In December, as Clinton approached a year in office, Morrison wrote to the President to advise him of the transition and to offer a statement of purpose for the new organisation:

> Americans for a New Irish Agenda (ANIA) is a broad coalition of Irish-Americans and others deeply committed to the United States playing an active and constructive role in helping secure a just, lasting and peaceful resolution of the troubles in Northern Ireland. ANIA was formed in order to promote

[16] *NYT*, 25/6/1993.
[17] Letter from Morrison to Hyland, 1/12/1992, General Correspondence, 1992–1996, Morrison Papers, UConn Library.
[18] Memorandum for Morrison, *c.*December 1992, General Correspondence, 1992–1996, Morrison Papers, UConn Library.
[19] Lynch, T.J., *Turf War: The Clinton Administration and Northern Ireland* (Aldershot: Ashgate, 2004), p. 91.
[20] *NYT*, 21/3/1993.

the implementation of the agenda which you presented to the Irish-American community while campaigning for President in 1992.[21]

Reminding Clinton of his commitments to Northern Ireland and pressuring him to honour them was not as easy as those within Irish America might have hoped, but the issues that ANIA focused on gave some indication of their priorities. The immediate concern of the group was the establishment of a special envoy, which they described as 'one aspect of a greater effort to formulate a U.S. policy toward Northern Ireland that is constructive and positive'. As Bruce Morrison travelled to Ireland in 1993, ANIA published an additional position paper on the topic of the special envoy which declared its strong intention 'to deliver a special envoy to Ireland on behalf of the Clinton administration'. They saw their own visit as stage one; the 'endgame' was the appointment of former President Jimmy Carter as the special envoy. Carter was already responsible for 'a conflict resolution program in Atlanta which is considered a world role model. Short of Carter we would wish to see someone like his protégé, Andrew Young, former U.S. Ambassador to the U.N.' Significantly, the Carter Center had actually written the envoy plank, which was presented to the Clinton team by Irish-Americans for Clinton–Gore.[22] As it happened, the special envoy would not materialise until late in Clinton's first term in office. Clinton would, however, make a bold move in early 1994, when, fulfilling one of the promises he delivered in New York ahead of the 1992 Democratic primary, he allowed Gerry Adams into the United States.

The Gerry Adams Visa

Gerry Adams lost his Belfast West seat in the 1992 UK general election to Dr Joe Hendron of the SDLP. The loss deprived Adams of the international legitimacy that Nancy Soderberg felt was required to allow

---

[21] Letter from Bruce Morrison, Chair Americans for a New Irish Agenda, to Clinton, 7/12/1993, Morrison Papers, UConn Library.
[22] Position Paper: US Envoy (undated), in Ireland Trip, 1993, September, Documents related to the Northern Ireland peace process in Series VIII: Ireland in Morrison Papers, UConn Library.

President Clinton to offer Adams a US visitor's visa.[23] This seemed to put the prospects of bringing Adams to the United States in cold storage. The continuing IRA campaign, the group marking the new year with a series of firebomb attacks across Northern Ireland and in London, seemed to confirm this.

Better known for his time as the Chief of Staff to Prime Minister Tony Blair, Jonathan Powell's earlier career had taken him to the British Embassy in Washington during the early 1990s. There, he assumed the role of First Secretary, previously held by figures such as Nigel Sheinwald and Sherard Cowper-Coles. Those in the role of First Secretary had provided key insight to the UK government as to the issue of Northern Ireland in the United States, and one of the most significant events of Powell's time in the role of First Secretary was the decision to permit Gerry Adams into the United States in early 1994. It was arguably Clinton's definitive moment regarding Northern Ireland. Powell recalled his part in the affair:

> As soon as we got warning of the possibility [of it happening], we were mobilised into action to lobby. It was basically down to Robin Renwick, who was the Ambassador, and me, and we lobbied every single organ of state that we could get hold of: the Justice Department, the CIA, the FBI, the State Department, as much as we could in Congress—although that wasn't quite as significant because this was an executive decision—and the White House, the Chief of Staff and the National Security Advisor. We thought we had all the bases covered because all the organs of state and departments told us they were against the visa and they understood our argument against it [that we should] wait for the ceasefire.[24]

Renwick himself recalled:

> The decision to grant Adams a visa, in my view at least, was vindicated by subsequent events. While arguing strongly the British government's case, I could never entirely rid myself of the feeling that we did not have much of a track record when it came to Ireland and that, in some circumstances, it could actually

[23] Memorandum from Morrison to Americans for a New Irish Agenda, 31/3/1993, General Correspondence, 1992–1994, Morrison Papers, UConn Library.
[24] Jonathan Powell, interview with author, 16/1/2013.

be helpful to have some external involvement. The decision, nevertheless, was taken in the wrong way, and at least in part for the wrong reasons; and in John Major's mind it undoubtedly raised questions as to how far the President could be trusted.[25]

Gerry Adams had been denied entry to the United States for almost a decade at this point; the initial move to block him from the United States was made in 1984, shortly after his election as the MP for Belfast West.[26] A second attempt to bring Adams to the United States was made in 1985, and the State Department again denied the application because of his 'advocacy of violence in Ireland'.[27] In 1986, Adams, interviewed by Francis Clines in the *New York Times*, commented that 'I'm not a pacifist, but I would rather the business of taking life had passed'. Clines, describing Adams as 'more intellectual than revolutionary' in appearance, noted that Adams craved the opportunity to explain the complexities of his cause in the United States: 'He feels this is unjust because while he admits trying to escape from a British prison over a decade ago, he says that he was never convicted after a roundup in which habeas corpus was suspended and that he was released after charges of I.R.A. membership were ordered dropped in a court review'. Adams added that 'all the people in power in Dublin at the moment and those in opposition are the descendants of the terrorists of yesteryear'.[28] These efforts to humanise Adams were widespread, challenged in part by the UK's broadcast ban from 1988 to 1994 which prevented Adams, and other Irish republicans, from appearing on television and radio. Famously, most broadcasters used actors to dub the voice of anyone subject to the ban. Niall O'Dowd was one who considered the broadcast ban a foolish exercise and Adams later reflected that 'we were shifting our organization very significantly, and that came to the attention of some people in Irish America, mostly famously Niall O'Dowd'.[29] This shift, along with the support of figures like Jean Kennedy Smith and Father Alec Reid, a Redemptorist Priest based at Clonard Monastery in Belfast, helped persuade Clinton to shift from his stance that had seen

[25] Renwick, unpublished memoir, p. 230.
[26] *NYT*, 10/7/1984.
[27] *NYT*, 17/2/1985.
[28] *NYT*, 18/9/1986.
[29] Edward M. Kennedy Institute, Oral History, 'Interview with Gerry Adams', available at https://www.emkinstitute.org/resources/gerry-adams. Also *Washington Post*, 8/3/2018.

him deny Adams a visa on two occasions during his first year in office. Adams recalled:

> The head of the FBI, the head of the CIA, and three or four very senior officials all opposed the visa … When we put in for the visa, we made a formal request for a visa. We had just had this conference that Bill [Flynn] and his friends had organized, and Jean Kennedy Smith wrote a letter of endorsement, endorsing the visa, but senior officials in her department, in her office wrote objecting to the visa.[30]

The persistence of IRA violence continued to place an obstacle in Adams's path to a visa.[31] In late March 1993, the IRA exploded two bombs in a shopping centre in central Warrington, a town in north-west England. The bombs killed three-year-old Johnathan Ball and fatally wounded twelve-year-old Timothy Parry. It was the second time the IRA had attacked Warrington that year, raising significant questions about the utility of operations in a relatively small industrial town in England. Ball's father, who had been shopping with his son for a mother's day present, commented, 'a child of three years and ten months. He has done nothing to anybody. In my heart I don't think I can ever forgive them'.[32] Ball died in the initial explosion, whilst Parry ran from the first straight into the second.

The IRA statement claimed that 'responsibility for the tragic and deeply regrettable death and injuries caused in Warrington yesterday lies squarely at the door of those in the British authorities who deliberately failed to act on precise and adequate warnings', but Martin McGuinness would later comment that 'I feel badly about the Warrington bomb, badly about those children and badly about the effect. I believe that the republican struggle was damaged as a result. I do not believe that the people involved in that intended for that to happen'. And later still, 'the killing of Jonathan and Tim was wrong. It should not have happened and there is a responsibility on all of us to bring about a peace process'.[33]

---

[30]   Edward M. Kennedy Institute, Oral History, 'Interview with Gerry Adams', available at https://www.emkinstitute.org/resources/gerry-adams.

[31]   Friends of Ireland St Patrick's Day statement, March 1993, General Correspondence, 1992–1994, Morrison Papers, UConn Library.

[32]   Quoted in McKittrick et al., *Lost Lives*, pp. 1314–1315.

[33]   Quoted in English, *Armed Struggle*, p. 378 and Toolis, K., *Rebel Hearts* (London: Picador, 1995), p. 325.

The morality of the IRA campaign was rarely more questionable than after Warrington. A single bomb with precise warnings that enabled the evacuation of the area around the device was one thing, but a dual bomb attack could hardly be taken to have intended anything other than significant loss of life. It was a strategy the IRA had employed in the killing of eighteen soldiers at Warrenpoint in August 1979. Calculating that the soldiers they would target would take shelter from an initial explosion, the bombers planted a second device in the most likely refuge, and this second bomb tripled the number of fatalities. Utilising the same tactic against the general public, and ultimately killing two children, was a heinous act that brought widespread condemnation of the IRA. Outrage over Warrington reached the United States, with the *New York Times* commenting that 'it takes no courage to murder children and injure 50 people in a crowded shopping center. It is no less repellent for Protestant gunmen to play God by slaughtering still more civilians. One may justly conclude that the killing has become an end in itself'.[34] A protest group, called Peace 93, was set up in the aftermath of Warrington and held a huge rally in Dublin on 25 March that drew an estimated crowd of 20,000.[35] At the time of writing, Cheshire Police still have no suspects for the murders of Timothy Parry and Jonathan Ball.[36]

The Warrington bomb, rather than negatively impacting Adams's prospects of being admitted to the United States, emphasised to many of the key players the urgent need to bring Sinn Féin into the peace process. Later that year, Monaghan Councillor Caoimhghin Ó Caoiláin, a prominent member of the party who had no direct ties to the IRA, travelled to the United States in October 1993, in Adams's stead, to meet with several political figures. Among those meetings was one with David Dinkins to brief the New York Mayor on the peace initiatives that Gerry Adams had been working on with John Hume. Dinkins, who was fighting an ultimately unsuccessful campaign for re-election against former State Attorney Rudolf Giuliani, had written to President Clinton to urge him that the denial of a visa for Adams be overturned. Ó Caoiláin also met with Congressmen Peter King, Richard Neal, and James Walsh.[37]

[34]   *NYT*, 26/3/1993 and 29/3/1993.
[35]   *IT*, 26/3/1993 and 29/3/1993.
[36]   Cheshire Police, 'Historical and Unsolved Murders', available at https://www.cheshire.police.uk/media/1165/historical-and-unsolved-murders.doc.
[37]   *IT*, 29/10/1993.

King, newly elected to Congress in 1993, represented a strong voice in Adams's favour on the Republican side of the aisle. He enjoyed solid support for his stance on Irish issues from his constituents, dating back to his time as Comptroller of Nassau County on Long Island.[38] In 1985, King commented, 'If civilians are killed in an attack on a military installation, it is certainly regrettable, but I will not morally blame the I.R.A. for it'.[39] As late as 1993, he was still calling for 'diplomatic intervention by the United Nations in the north of Ireland'. The idea of UN intervention had largely been dismissed, given the strong resistance it met from the governments of the UK, Ireland, and the United States when it was discussed during the 1970s. King, however, argued that 'I truly believe by bringing the Irish issue to an international forum we will be better able to focus world attention on British oppression which is the root cause of the violence in the six counties'.[40]

King's first sponsored item was an item of legislation calling for UN intervention in Northern Ireland. He has sponsored or co-sponsored seventy-one pieces of legislation in his Congressional career to date. In his press release he cited 'the violent suppression of the civil rights movement, the numerous violations of international law and human rights as cited by the European Court of Human Rights, Amnesty International and the United Nations Human Rights Commission, and the repeated failure of Britain's so-called peace initiatives'. Unsurprisingly, the legislation did not make it past committee.[41] He would enjoy more success later that year as a supporter of a visitor visa for Gerry Adams.

[38] A heavily Irish area; see American Factfinder, Community Facts, Profile of General Population and Housing Characteristics: 2010, in 2010 Demographic Profile Data, available at https://factfinder.census.gov/faces/tableservices/jsf/pages/productview.xhtml?src=CF; and American Factfinder, Annual Estimates of the Resident Population: April 1, 2010 to July 1, 2014, available at https://factfinder.census.gov/faces/tableservices/jsf/pages/productview.xhtml?pid=PEP_2018_PEPANNRES&src=pt. The 2010 Census gives the population of Nassau at just over 1.3 million people.
[39] NYT, 8/3/2011.
[40] Letter from Peter King to Durkan, 6/5/1993, Box 4 Folder 8, Series III: Sinn Féin Gerry Adams US Visit, Feb. 1994, AIA 008, Durkan Papers, Tamiment Library, NYU.
[41] Congressman Pete King Press Release, 5/5/1993, Box 4 Folder 8, Series III: Sinn Féin Gerry Adams US Visit, Feb. 1994, AIA 008, Durkan Papers, Tamiment Library, NYU; Congressional Record Proceedings and Debates of the 103d Congress, First Session, vol. 139, Washington, Wednesday, May 5, 1993, No. 61. AIA 008, Durkan Papers, Tamiment Library, NYU.

In December, Taoiseach Albert Reynolds and Prime Minister John Major offered Adams a seat at the table for negotiations if he renounced the IRA. One month later, Adams renewed his application for a US visa.[42] With an event in New York planned for late January 1994, the Clinton Administration softened the US position on the issue, stating that Adams could enter the US if he renounced violence.[43] Pressure came from congressional figures like King, Hamilton Fish, and Nita Lowey, who had earlier written to Clinton, urging the President to 'end the State Department's efforts to prevent Mr. Adams from visiting the United States'.[44] Clinton maintained that he was concerned about not violating principles of free speech and political discourse but emphasised that his administration was in 'compliance with the Immigration and Nationality Act which specifically bars entry into the United States of those who have engaged in terrorist activity', adding that 'the State Department and the FBI concluded that Mr. Adams is ineligible for a visa under the terms of that act'.[45] For Adams:

> It was ridiculous that Irish Republicans couldn't visit the States. Not that we had any entitlement to visit the States, but as I've said many times, American citizens should have the right to hear information and then form an opinion. The British were there, the Irish government was there, the Unionists were there. The only people who were excluded was the Irish Republican cadre.[46]

Of course, as Ian Paisley had found out a few years earlier, only some Unionists were 'there' and in most cases they had no presence in the United States whatsoever.

House Speaker Tom Foley was clear that 'the visa ban on Gerry Adams should not be lifted until such time as Sinn Féin accepts the notion of abandoning violence, and the support for violence, as a manner of resolving problems in Ireland'.[47] Adams later claimed that Foley came

[42]   *NYT*, 16/1/1994.
[43]   *NYT*, 28/1/1994.
[44]   Letter to Clinton, 27/4/1993, Correspondence related to Americans for a New Irish Agenda, Morrison Papers, UConn Library.
[45]   Letter from Clinton to Hamilton Fish, 26/5/1993, Correspondence related to Americans for a New Irish Agenda, Morrison Papers, UConn Library.
[46]   Edward M. Kennedy Institute, Oral History, 'Interview with Gerry Adams', available at https://www.emkinstitute.org/resources/gerry-adams.
[47]   *NYT*, 27/1/1994.

to regret his stance on the issue.[48] The continuing IRA campaign at this time was seriously detrimental to Adams's credibility in the United States, particularly when it appeared as though Adams had no influence over the actions of the IRA. This lack of cohesion was rarely more evident than in late April 1993 when Gerry Adams and John Hume met to issue a joint statement that read: 'we accept that the most pressing issue facing the people of Ireland and Britain today is the question of lasting peace and how it can best be achieved'.[49] The day after the statement was issued, the IRA detonated a large bomb in Bishopsgate in central London.[50] This bombing, which killed a photographer, was typical of the IRA's late-campaign strategy: high-profile, low-collateral-damage attacks that were intended to underline the importance of engagement with Sinn Féin throughout peace talks and negotiations. Timing the bomb to coincide with the Hume–Adams statement rather undermined Adams's authority to speak in favour of peace on behalf of Irish republicans. One event that did yield a cessation of violence was an early September visit from a delegation of Irish-Americans, led by Bruce Morrison, to Belfast and Dublin. Others on the trip included Chuck Feeney, Bill Flynn, Niall O'Dowd, and Brian O'Dwyer.[51] The group published a position paper ahead of their trip that emphasised that 'A cessation during their visit would have the major effect of empowering them when they return to the U.S. and report to the Clinton White House on their visit'.[52]

Arriving in Dublin, the group met with US Ambassador Jean Kennedy Smith along with Irish figures such as Taoiseach Albert Reynolds, Tánaiste Dick Spring, and President Mary Robinson.[53]

[48]   Edward M. Kennedy Institute, Oral History, 'Interview with Gerry Adams', available at https://www.emkinstitute.org/resources/gerry-adams.
[49]   Sinn Féin, 'John Hume/Gerry Adams, Statement 23rd April 1993', available at www.sinnfein.ie/contents/15217.
[50]   *Independent*, 25/4/1993.
[51]   Letter from Morrison to Christopher Hyland, 23/8/1993, in Ireland Trip, 1993, September, Documents related to the Northern Ireland peace process in Series VIII: Ireland in Morrison Papers, UConn Library.
[52]   Position Paper: US Envoy (undated), in Ireland Trip, 1993, September, Documents related to the Northern Ireland peace process in Series VIII: Ireland in Morrison Papers, UConn Library.
[53]   Visit schedule (undated), in Ireland Trip, 1993, Letter from Dick Spring to Morrison, 1/9/1993 and Fax from Joseph Brennan, Deputy Secretary to the President, to Morrison, 3/9/1993 in Ireland Trip, 1993, September, Documents related to the Northern Ireland peace process in Series VIII: Ireland in Morrison Papers, UConn Library.

The meeting with Reynolds reportedly lasted over two hours.[54] The following day, the Morrison delegation met John Hume in Derry and then Gerry Adams in Belfast. Morrison again wrote to Clinton, urging him to make the appointment of the special envoy and to issue a visa to Gerry Adams. He also sought the President's assurance that the State Department's human rights report examined Northern Ireland in depth.[55]

The Morrison delegation was not well received by John Taylor, the Unionist MP for Strangford, who issued a statement about 'a group of interfering Americans' who 'hope to interfere in the affairs of Northern Ireland and have the audacity to suggest that the USA should appoint a PEACE ENVOY to Northern Ireland'. He added, 'Mr Morrison's group of visitors are the very type of people who have done and continue to do a disservice to the cause of peace in Northern Ireland. They continue to misinform the American people about the real facts in Northern Ireland'.[56] Taylor's anger may have been somewhat tempered by the lack of activity from the IRA during the visit. The *Irish Times* commented: 'How much more welcome would be the news that the IRA, its point made, now recognised the merits of more lasting restraint and was prepared to swap its weapons for a place in the history of reconstruction'.[57] That the visit of the Morrison group had prompted the IRA to go on ceasefire, even temporarily, was hugely significant, though they quickly returned to violence before the end of the month, exploding two large bombs in the centre of Belfast, causing significant damage but no fatalities. The ceasefire helped support Adams's claim to have influence over the IRA, but also provided evidence that his programme of engagement with Irish America was an attractive one to those in Ireland. It also put pressure on President Clinton to move on the issue of granting Adams a visa to visit the United States. Morrison wrote to the President in December, this time on behalf of Americans for a New Irish Agenda, to remind him of this:

54   *Irish Voice*, 7(38), Wednesday, 15 September–Tuesday, 21 September 1993.
55   Letter from Morrison to Clinton, 3/9/1993 and Letter from Clinton to Morrison, 20/9/1993, Correspondence related to Americans for a New Irish Agenda, Morrison Papers, UConn Library.
56   John Taylor Statement (undated), in Ireland Trip, 1993, September, Documents related to the Northern Ireland peace process in Series VIII: Ireland in Morrison Papers, UConn Library.
57   *IT*, 11/9/1993.

We took your campaign promises in the same serious way in which you made them. We have defended you against the charge that they were mere rhetoric to gather votes. The situation now demands that they be implemented, not to prove that you were sincere, but to achieve the beneficial effect of the actions which you promised to take. Please reaffirm our confidence in your leadership on this issue by signalling a willingness to grant a visa for Gerry Adams in the near future and by selecting a special envoy ready and willing to provide American assistance to the current opportunity for progress towards peace in Northern Ireland.[58]

Clinton again kept his cards close to his chest, responding only to thank Morrison and the ANIA for their interest in the issue.[59] Adams himself recalled the importance of the Morrison visit, which was notable in the context of his own discussions with John Hume:

John Hume and I had come up with what was called the Hume–Adams Agreement—we looked at this as the putting together of a jigsaw puzzle. So one part of the jigsaw clearly was Irish America, which now had the attention of the White House to some degree, and John Hume. We had the Irish government in the frame and we needed some sort of a program or a mission statement or a series of commitments. So we then spent some considerable time trying to negotiate that act. Out of those deliberations came the Downing Street Declaration.[60]

The Downing Street Declaration was built upon the foundations of the Anglo-Irish Agreement and, in turn, influenced the 1998 Good Friday Agreement. It was issued at a time when political progress was absolutely essential. The security situation had become precarious after the IRA bombing of Frizzell's fish shop on the Shankill Road. Ostensibly an attempt to kill the members of the Ulster Defence Association's commanding 'Inner Circle' who were known to convene

---

[58] Letter from Bruce Morrison, Chair Americans for a New Irish Agenda, to Clinton, 7/12/1993, Correspondence related to Americans for a New Irish Agenda in Morrison Papers, UConn Library.
[59] Letter from Clinton to Morrison, 6/1/1994, Correspondence related to Americans for a New Irish Agenda in Morrison Papers, UConn Library.
[60] Edward M. Kennedy Institute, Oral History, 'Interview with Gerry Adams', available at https://www.emkinstitute.org/resources/gerry-adams.

in offices above the shop, the attack instead killed nine civilians and one of the bombers. Reports since have suggested that Johnny Adair, the local UDA commander who many believe was the target of the attack, instructed his gunmen to launch gun attacks on Saturday night mass around the city. In an interview with historian Ian S. Wood, Adair confirmed, 'our boys drove over from the Shankill and out of Tigers Bay to do the hit. They were a good team, fully tooled up'.[61] Instead a different, but no less horrific, attack took place five days later when the Ulster Freedom Fighters launched a gun attack on the Rising Sun bar in Greysteel, in County Derry, killing six Catholics and one Protestant. The gunmen later claimed that they had been given intelligence that senior IRA men drank in the Rising Sun bar.[62]

Between the morning of 23 October and the evening of 30 October, twenty-three people died in violence in Northern Ireland. A taxi driver was shot in the head as he delivered a Chinese meal to a fake address, an elderly Catholic widower was shot dead in his home, two Catholic civilians were killed in a gun attack on a cleaning depot, two Catholic brothers were shot dead in their home, along with the ten victims of the Shankill bomb and the seven victims at the Rising Sun. A peace rally the following weekend drew 3,000 protesters.

The need for a new government-led initiative was desperately apparent. It was reported in late November that the British government was talking directly to the republican movement, discussions that led the British into the Downing Street Declaration seeking 'to foster agreement and reconciliation, leading to a new political framework founded on consent and encompassing arrangements within Northern Ireland, for the whole island, and between these islands'.[63] This statement, in turn, prompted the National Committee on American Foreign Policy, a non-profit non-partisan activist organisation in New York, to develop a 'hastily organized' conference on Northern Ireland, to which 'representatives from all sides from the strife-torn region were invited to present their views in New York on February 1, 1994'.[64] Among those invited to appear was Gerry Adams. This invitation was made in early

[61]   Quote in Wood, *Crimes of Loyalty*, p. 172.
[62]   Wood, *Crimes of Loyalty*, p. 173.
[63]   Joint Declaration on Peace: The Downing Street Declaration, Wednesday, 15 December 1993, available at https://cain.ulster.ac.uk/events/peace/docs/dsd151293.htm.
[64]   O'Grady, 'An Irish Policy Born in the U.S.A.', p. 4.

January 1994, as Northern Ireland began the New Year amidst a series of firebomb and gun attacks.

Clinton received encouragement in the form of a letter signed by over forty members of Congress including Ted Kennedy, John Kerry, George Mitchell, Joseph Kennedy II, and Richard Neal, who all wrote in favour of allowing Adams to receive a visa. The letter argued that despite Adams's 'relationship with the Irish Republican Army and his refusal to disavow its campaign of violence ... we believe that granting a visa at this time will enhance, not undermine, the peace process'. It continued, 'While no one can be certain that a visa for Mr. Adams will result in the IRA's accepting the conditions established by Ireland and Great Britain for participation in the peace process, the United States cannot afford to ignore this possibility and miss this rare opportunity for our country to contribute to peace in Northern Ireland'.[65]

There were signs of a possible breakthrough for Adams on 27 January, when the White House issued a statement that 'we have instructed our embassy in Dublin to determine whether Mr Adams will publicly renounce violence and support the [Downing Street] Declaration. Our decision on whether to provide him with a visa will depend on his response'.[66] Adams met the US Consul General in Belfast, Valentino Martinez, the following day and the report that Martinez filed to the State Department stated that Adams had not significantly changed his view on IRA violence.[67] By 30 January, however, Adams was in possession of a visitor's visa to enter the United States and he duly arrived in New York on Monday, 31 January. The Clinton Administration cited 'newly conciliatory comments' by Adams as justification for their decision, whilst the British Embassy in Washington made an official statement that they considered the decision an internal American matter. Adams was not permitted to travel more than twenty-five miles from the conference site, the Waldorf Astoria hotel in New York, nor was he allowed to do any fundraising. Speaker Foley remained opposed to the issuance of the visa, whilst figures like Chris Dodd considered it a 'very positive signal at a very critical moment'.[68]

[65]   Letter to Clinton, 15/1/1994, AIA 008, Durkan Papers, Tamiment Library, NYU. See also *IT*, 17/1/1994.
[66]   *IT*, 28/1/1994.
[67]   *The Times*, 10/2/1995.
[68]   *NYT*, 31/1/1994.

In New York, Adams addressed the National Committee on American Foreign Policy, along with John Hume and Alliance Party leader John Alderdice. He also appeared on political talk show *Larry King Live* on CNN, but while US viewers could watch the show, the ongoing broadcast ban that Adams remained subject to meant that the appearance was not screened in Europe.[69] Adams argued that his appearance in the US was 'a small step ... But it's also a small victory for free speech'.[70] Before leaving, Adams pledged not to disappoint those who had expended political capital in order to help secure his visa. The *Washington Post* commented:

> Gerry Adams is no hero. The Belfast Catholic, who is the leader of Sinn Féin, the political arm of the Irish Republican Army, was granted a visa to enter the United States for 48 hours to attend a peace conference and do some speaking. The granting of a visa, after eight earlier denials, does not confer an honor, endorse IRA violence or indicate and change in US policy, which is aimed at encouraging a peaceful solution to the Irish troubles. But it does say something about this country and its new leadership that is commendable, namely that American borders are open to visitors who come to speak and not terrorists, even when the views expressed are likely to enrage and scandalize.[71]

The British government remained furious at the decision to allow Adams into the United States. Adams cited British attempts at interference as an important reason for his visa being issued: 'Had they never objected in the first place to me coming to the US and tried to interfere with the affairs of the US, when I came here no one would have noticed'.[72] This tension spilled over shortly after Adams returned with John Major and his Foreign Secretary Douglas Hurd throwing what the *New York Times* described as 'a fit': 'The US Ambassador to Britain was summoned to Downing Street for a harsh lecture ... Mr Adams made the most of British mistakes without expressing a single new thought'.[73] Most egregious for the British government, and Ulster Unionists, was the fact that the Adams visit took place without any evidence of a permanent cessation of IRA violence. Three carefully planned mortar attacks

[69]   *IT*, 1/2/1994.
[70]   *NYT*, 1/2/1994.
[71]   *Washington Post*, 2/2/1994.
[72]   *New York Post*, 3/2/1994.
[73]   *NYT*, 5/2/1994.

at Heathrow Airport, a popular destination for US airlines bringing passengers to the UK, took place in March, and the second of these occurred just before Queen Elizabeth landed at the airport aboard a Royal Air Force plane. This prompted Clinton to call on the IRA to disarm during his St Patrick's Day address.

Clinton later wrote to Morrison, in April 1994, long after the furore had quietened, to thank him for his input during the process, highlighting 'the interest and insights you bring to this issue'.[74] Similarly, Peter King wrote to Congress to reflect on 'an unforgettable 48 hours' during which Adams 'demonstrated to the American people that he is a true spokesman for the oppressed nationalists in the north of Ireland'. He acknowledged his own role in the effort to bring Adams to the United States, before adding, 'This was a massive defeat for the British government and a victory for free speech'.[75] Jonathan Powell recalled 'Peter King was actually quite supportive of keeping the IRA on the peaceful route because he had real credibility, particularly after 9/11, but also before'.[76] This was not a view shared by the Major government in 1994.

There was serious violence from loyalist paramilitaries around this time as well. The UVF had been actively pursuing a brazenly sectarian campaign over the spring of 1994, killing Catholic civilians throughout Northern Ireland in May and June, but the Loughinisland attacks of 18 June 1994 were particularly sinister. As locals watched the Republic of Ireland game against Italy during the 1994 World Cup in the United States, UVF gunmen burst into The Heights bar in the tiny village in County Down and shot six civilians dead, including eighty-seven-year-old Barney Green, the oldest victim of the conflict, wounding a further five people. It was later suggested in a documentary entitled 'Ceasefire Massacre', which aired as part of ESPN's *30 for 30: Soccer Stories* series, that Loughinisland had been deliberately chosen as a message to Bill Flynn, who had been instrumental in bringing Adams to the United States.[77] Flynn's father, William Sr., was originally from the town.

[74]   Letter from Clinton to Morrison, 7/4/1994, Correspondence related to Americans for a New Irish Agenda in Morrison Papers, UConn Library.
[75]   Letter from King to Congress, February 1994, AIA 008, Durkan Papers, Tamiment Library, NYU.
[76]   Jonathan Powell, interview with author, 16/1/2013.
[77]   Irish Central, 'ESPN Doc Uncovers Link between 1994 World Cup and Loyalist Massacre', 25/4/2014, available at www.irishcentral.com/culture/entertainment/ESPN-doc-uncovers-link-between-1994-World-Cup-and-Loyalist-massacre-VIDEO.html.

With loyalist paramilitaries plagued with allegations of collusion, there is also an implication that the British state might have had some influence over the attack. Indeed, the reasons that the UVF hit squad would have had for deliberately selecting a small town for an attack would far more likely have been based on the fact that it was a soft target. Loyalist paramilitaries typically lacked any strategic nuance, particularly during the 1990s when the vast majority of their operations were reactionary and directed at civilians. More likely is the explanation that the attack, along with those that took place the previous day, were a reaction to the INLA killing of two UVF men on 16 June in a gun attack on the Shankill Road. The IRA spent much of July and August on the offensive, planting bombs in loyalist bars, shooting dead three prominent loyalists, and launching mortar attacks on British military installations, but then announced a cessation of military operations on 31 August.

The August 1994 ceasefire would not last and the violent activities of a group calling themselves Direct Action Against Drugs, widely believed to have been IRA members using a cover name, suggest that it was not even observed. The timing of the ceasefire, however, was hugely significant. Sectarian, tit-for-tat violence had spread during the summer of 1994 and, once again, Northern Ireland appeared to be on the precipice. Avoiding further bloodshed, if only at this stage of the conflict, was a significant achievement on the part of those pressing for peace, and the role of figures from Americans for a New Irish Agenda must be acknowledged. In late August, a group, including Morrison, Chuck Feeney, Bill Flynn, and Niall O'Dowd travelled to Ireland at the invitation of Sinn Féin.[78] One particularly cynical comment, which has been attributed to *The Times*, was that 'it should be obvious that a visit by six dilettante Americans has no contribution whatsoever to make to this process'.[79] This attitude was ignorant of the fact that the previous visit had seen a short cessation by the IRA, and surely boded well for prospects of further progress. Adams, however, did not welcome such speculation: 'I will be meeting the US delegation later this week. I consider the meeting to be an important one. The media speculation that the IRA will declare a ceasefire to coincide with the visit is news to me and is unhelpful'.[80]

[78] *Hartford Courant*, 1/9/1994.
[79] This comment was only cited in *Hartford Courant*, 1/9/1994 and *Baltimore Sun*, 2/9/1994.
[80] Sinn Féin Press Release (undated), Documents related to the Northern Ireland peace process in Series VIII: Ireland in Morrison Papers, UConn Library.

The group met with Taoiseach Albert Reynolds and Tánaiste Dick Spring on Thursday, 25 August before travelling north, where they neglected to approach the perennially intransigent DUP leadership. Ian Paisley had publicly stated that any approach for such a meeting would be turned down whilst the Ulster Unionists were invited to meet the Morrison group but refused; a party spokesman said that the Americans had identified themselves with Irish republican groups and that a meeting would serve no useful purpose. Jim Wilson, the general secretary of the UUP, said that Unionists were 'not interested in phoney ceasefires. We're interested only in one ceasefire—a permanent ceasefire'.[81] Chris McGimpsey added that 'what the IRA are offering is, instead of murdering people in two weeks' time they'll murder them in 10 weeks' time'. Morrison noted that Paisley had 'indicated an official reluctance to meet', emphasising that 'anyone who meets with Sinn Féin can't meet with them'. Morrison joked, 'not meeting people is a great sport among Unionists'. There was also some hostility from the SDLP, with chairman Mark Durkan commenting that the organisation of the visit had been 'pretty shambolic' whilst Joe Hendron said that he did not think the delegation had any meaningful part to play. Durkan explained that the group had requested to meet John Hume, but that the request was only received two days in advance and at a time when Hume was in the United States.[82]

The criticism that the ANIA delegation faced from many sides of Northern Irish politics appears to have been somewhat misplaced. The group had clear influence over the IRA, influence reflected by the words of Bill Flynn, who argued that Gerry Adams was 'a man of peace and a man of honour … a man who is willing to go to the line in search of peace'.[83] Adams gained significant political capital from the IRA cessations, although his political opponents in Northern Ireland remained cynical. One of the suggestions that Adams made to the group was that veteran republican Joe Cahill should be issued a visa to travel to the United States, a suggestion that had the support of the Irish government. Cahill had been banned from the United States since 1971, when he landed only to find that his previously issued visa had been revoked whilst he was in transit. With the United States considering a reconstruction package for Northern Ireland of between

[81]   *IT*, 24/8/1994.
[82]   *IT*, 25/8/1994.
[83]   *IT*, 29/8/1994.

$120 million and $200 million, it was argued that Cahill could visit the US to help secure support from within Irish America for the final de-escalation of the IRA's campaign. Cahill was duly granted a visa to visit the United States on 30 August 1994.[84] This was the second time in a single year that the Clinton administration had granted a visa to someone associated with the IRA despite the protestations of the British government. The *Independent* newspaper noted, 'the Clinton administration has shown again that it has distinct views on Northern Ireland—unlike President Bush and President Reagan who almost entirely endorsed British policy'.[85] This was clearly an uncomfortable time for the British government, finding their previously strong ally now open to suggestion on the issue of the IRA and its role in Northern Ireland.

Adams later claimed that 'The issue of Joe Cahill's visa became a little test, although it was never intended to be the case', and emphasised the role of Ted Kennedy and Jean Kennedy Smith in helping to secure Cahill's visa. Asking for a visa for Cahill in particular, a man who had previously been excluded from the United States, seems most likely to have, in fact, been a 'little test' by Adams to assess how deep his influence ran in the United States. Adams contended that 'there was no better man to tell [Irish-American groups] what the story was than Joe Cahill, and no better example of proof that things had changed, that there was a new dispensation and everybody was going to be treated on that basis'.[86] Cahill was initially given a five-day visa to allow him to visit IRA supporters in Boston, Philadelphia, New York, and Chicago, but as the IRA ceasefire persisted this was extended for fifteen days to allow him to visit San Francisco, Los Angeles, and Florida.

A quid pro quo developed between the US government and the Sinn Féin leadership: continued inactivity on the part of the IRA would lead to regular access to the United States. Peter King emphasised this point, also noting that in these circumstances the British would no longer have exclusive access to US leaders.[87] The implication that Sinn Féin politicians now enjoyed equal footing with British government officials when it came to the United States would further exacerbate

[84] *IT*, 30/8/1994; *NYT*, 31/8/1994.
[85] *Independent*, 30/8/1994.
[86] Edward M. Kennedy Institute, Oral History, 'Interview with Gerry Adams', available at https://www.emkinstitute.org/resources/gerry-adams.
[87] *IT*, 5/9/1994.

British tension over the situation, but the IRA ceasefire duly arrived on 31 August:

> Recognising the potential of the current situation and in order to enhance the democratic process and underlying our definitive commitment to its success, the leadership of the IRA have decided that as of midnight, August 31, there will be a complete cessation of military operations. All our units have been instructed accordingly ... We believe that an opportunity to secure a just and lasting settlement has been created. We are therefore entering into a new situation in a spirit of determination and confidence, determined that the injustices which created this conflict will be removed and confident in the strength and justice of our struggle to achieve this.[88]

The IRA ceasefire was a pivotal moment in the Northern Ireland peace process. A loyalist paramilitary ceasefire followed shortly thereafter, announced by the Combined Loyalist Military Command, an umbrella body representing both the Ulster Volunteer Force and Ulster Defence Association, on 13 October. The UVF had earlier commented that they would react favourably to an IRA ceasefire, adding, 'there is a genuine desire within the UVF for peace'.[89] Journalist Suzanne Breen visited the Shankill Road, the heartland of Ulster loyalism, noting that the mood was 'of quiet confidence'. One interviewee commented that 'if there was anything to worry about our side wouldn't have called a ceasefire'.[90] Morrison's fingerprints appeared all over the IRA ceasefire, at least from the US perspective, and it was speculated that Morrison could be appointed to the role of US Special Envoy to Northern Ireland, once Clinton saw fit to create it. This would take well over a year.[91]

Adams returned to the United States in late September, a month after the ceasefire, at a time when the banning order that prevented him from visiting Britain remained intact.[92] He was met at Boston's Logan Airport by Ted Kennedy and travelled across the country for two weeks, collecting honours that included the Crystal Apple from New

[88]   Irish Republican Army Ceasefire Statement, 31/8/1994, available on https://cain.ulster.ac.uk/events/peace/docs/ira31894.htm.
[89]   *IT*, 27/8/1994.
[90]   *IT*, 14/10/1994.
[91]   *NYT*, 1/9/1994.
[92]   *IT*, 30/9/1994.

York Mayor Rudy Giuliani, who took the opportunity to encourage Clinton to meet the Sinn Féin leader.[93] The new goal became to secure a visit for Adams at the White House and Irish-American figures, including Ted Kennedy, began to campaign for such an invitation.[94] Upon his arrival in Washington, on Monday, 3 October, he was not admitted to the grounds of the White House, nor was he met by Lake nor Vice-President Gore.[95] Adams's arrival in DC coincided with the funeral of Michael Flannery in Queens, New York. Pointedly, Adams did not attend.[96]

The following day, however, Adams spent over an hour at the State Department, the office that had fought against his visa, with both State officials and figures from the Vice-Presidential staff. Anthony Lake, although not present at the meeting, did lift the US administration ban on contacts with Sinn Féin so that a direct dialogue could begin 'primarily through our embassy in Dublin and our consulate general in Belfast'.[97] Dialogue between the administration and Sinn Féin had, hitherto, been conducted primarily by Ciaran Staunton and Niall O'Dowd of ANIA.[98]

The Special Envoy and the Clinton Visit to Belfast

On 1 December 1994, George Mitchell was appointed Special Adviser to the President and Secretary of State for Economic Initiatives in Ireland. In everything but name, this was the US Special Envoy to Northern Ireland that Clinton had pledged to create two years previously. The appointment took place on the same day that it was announced that the British government and Sinn Féin would begin negotiations.[99] Mitchell was in the process of retiring from the Senate, where he had been Majority Leader, and was sworn in to his new post on 10 January 1995.

---

[93]   *NYT*, 29/9/1994.
[94]   *IT*, 1/10/1994.
[95]   Also in the USA at this time was Alliance Party leader John Alderdice who found himself in considerably less demand than Adams, unable to meet with any high-level official or representative; see *IT*, 3/10/1994.
[96]   *IT*, 8/10/1994.
[97]   *IT*, 5/10/1994.
[98]   *IT*, 8/10/1994.
[99]   *NYT*, 2/12/1994.

One of his first tasks was to coordinate a Clinton-backed investment conference on Ireland.[100]

There had been some 'alarm' building within Irish America, notably within ANIA, that 'promises made in your [Clinton's] presidential campaign for a new approach to the conflict in Ireland were going unfulfilled', as Bruce Morrison wrote to the President in early January 1995. 'Happily, as it turned out, your Administration was already taking steps to review the existing policy and to change course. The intervening year has been one of progress'.[101] Undoubtedly, the IRA ceasefire was the most significant event of 1994, but the Adams visa had been an important step towards the ceasefire, and the appointment of Mitchell represented the first step beyond the ceasefire into the even more complicated issue of copper-fastening peace and engaging in post-conflict resolution. During the announcement of Mitchell's appointment as Special Envoy, it was also announced that Adams would be invited to a meeting at the White House.[102]

Even though the ceasefire may have been the ultimate goal for many, the cessation of violence itself could only be the start of a new chapter for Northern Ireland. The full political engagement of all parties in the conflict was a crucial next step. From the perspective of the Clinton Administration, it also represented the start of a new chapter as the incumbent President began his campaign for re-election.

To this end, Clinton could rely on the Irish-Americans for Clinton–Gore once again and Morrison was quick to pledge the support of the ANIA group for the 1996 campaign. The Republican Party had made huge gains in the 1994 mid-term elections, seizing both houses of Congress. So great was the shift that even Ted Kennedy struggled to retain his seat. Morrison argued that these domestic setbacks only placed increased emphasis on the importance of Clinton's foreign policy legacy and noted that 'the peace process was slowed by the change in the Irish government coalition. More threateningly, the British government has not fully engaged in peacemaking'. The British were of course in a far trickier position. Full engagement could not come without the support of Ulster Unionists, who sought significantly more from Irish republicans before they would engage. Morrison was also perturbed by a delay to

[100]   *IT*, 11/1/1995.
[101]   Letter from Morrison to Clinton, 10/1/1995, Correspondence related to Americans for a New Irish Agenda in Morrison Papers, UConn Library.
[102]   *NYT*, 1/12/1994.

a proposed meeting between ANIA and the White House, which he considered was 'discouraging to your ardent supporters and is becoming an embarrassment'. Morrison noted that:

> It is important to maintain White House ascendancy in setting Irish policy. The NSC has played a powerful and progressive role. I know you are aware that I sought to maintain lines of communication with the NSC when the Irish-American peace delegation made its several trips to the North to talk with Sinn Féin. Resistance to your new policy remains strong in sections of the State Department, the Department of Justice, and the FBI. Ambassador Jean Kennedy Smith has played an outstanding role, but, for example, the Belfast Consul General's office has treated the Adams visa application in a shabby and humiliating way.[103]

This rhetoric, and the idea that the United States should be taking the lead in policy, would have been anathema to previous administrations, but four years into Clinton's time in office, one of his key advisers felt comfortable to express this directly to him and spoke to the influence that the NSC had over Northern Ireland policy. Clinton would continue to push the Northern Ireland peace process throughout his time in office. These efforts were led by the issuance of a multiple-entry visa to Gerry Adams, replete with fundraising rights in the United States, and the invitation to the White House's St Patrick's Day reception in March 1995.[104] The campaign to allow Adams fundraising rights in the United States had only been launched by Ted Kennedy on 14 February, and therefore enjoyed a quick turnaround.[105] Clinton justified the decision on the grounds that Sinn Féin was meeting expectations with regards to its commitments to peace. Sinn Féin representatives in New York, led by Friends of Sinn Féin, were quick to arrange a series of events for Adams, including a high-end $200-a-plate dinner at the Plaza Hotel. The first Sinn Féin fundraiser in the United States, however, was held in the Tower View Center in the Woodside area of Queens, attended by roughly 1,000,

---

[103] Letter from Morrison to Clinton, 10/1/1995, Correspondence related to Americans for a New Irish Agenda in Morrison Papers, UConn Library. This quote concurs with the assessment of Timothy J. Lynch, who suggests that the NSC drove Clinton's approach towards Ireland. See Lynch, *Turf War*.
[104] *NYT*, 10/3/1995; Letter from Morrison to Clinton, 9/3/1995, Correspondence related to Americans for a New Irish Agenda in Morrison Papers, UConn Library.
[105] *IT*, 14/2/1995.

who would, according to Friends of Sinn Féin president Larry Downes, 'be priced out of a $200-a-head luncheon'. The *New York Times* speculated that upwards of $20,000 was raised during the event. Not all those in attendance were supporters of Adams, though. One commented that 'he's left a legacy of a lot of broken families in Ireland'.[106]

The key political event on the trip was, of course, Adams's visit to the White House. Ahead of his arrival, John Major wrote to Clinton requesting that he put pressure on Adams to begin the process of IRA decommissioning. Major had endured a difficult time in office with regards to Northern Ireland. He was very much caught between the strong desire for peace and the necessity of not allowing Sinn Féin to dictate the terms of the peace process. He commented, 'I'm afraid that Sinn Féin are still directly associated with a fully formed terrorist organization'.[107] He was also, by now, acutely aware that he could not exert significant influence over Clinton's actions when it came to Northern Ireland.

Adams's appearance at the White House rather overshadowed that of new Taoiseach John Bruton, who was invited to attend the St Patrick's Day luncheon by Speaker of the House Newt Gingrich. Bruton argued that allowing Adams into the United States would accelerate the Northern Ireland peace process but emphasised that complete decommissioning would be necessary on all sides.[108] After the assembled media left the event, Adams approached Clinton and the two men shook hands, speaking for a few minutes.[109]

Adams, taking full advantage of his new status in the United States, returned again in May, arriving in Boston for a two-week tour that would culminate with the George Mitchell-led White House investment conference on Ireland. The changed circumstances of Irish republicans in the US was never more apparent than at the fundraising dinner at the Plaza hotel in New York, where a plate cost $1,000. Adams was expected to raise over a million dollars on this trip, triple what Noraid had accumulated in the six months following Bloody Sunday.[110] The trip also marked Adams's first meeting with British Secretary of State for Northern Ireland, Sir Patrick Mayhew. Mayhew described the meeting

[106] *NYT*, 13/3/1995.
[107] *NYT*, 14/3/1995.
[108] *NYT*, 20/3/1995.
[109] *NYT*, 17/3/1995.
[110] *IT*, 5/5/1995.

as 'civil', but added that 'I won't negotiate with a party associated with a paramilitary organization that won't give up its arms'.[111] Adams, interviewed later for the EMK Institute's oral history project, recalled:

> My first talk with a British official, which was Patrick Mayhew, who was the British Secretary of State for North Ireland, again happened in the States. That's again, I think, proof of the influence of the pressure that could be put when the White House was focused. I was visiting the States quite often, and increasingly by now we were able to fundraise. Irish Americans were able to come to events, and in many ways they became almost celebrations.[112]

Unionist politicians like Jim Molyneaux and Ian Paisley were not in attendance, but 300 businesspeople were and were presented with a major strategic overview of both Northern Ireland and the border counties. Businesses were encouraged to take advantage of access to the EU markets, strong supply of labour with good labour relations, relatively low pay, an English-speaking labour force, as well as investment incentives.[113] Clinton urged US companies to consider investment, also vowing to fight for a 60 percent increase to the US contribution to the International Fund for Ireland, despite pressure on his budget proposals from the Republican-dominated Congress. Clinton argued that Congress wanted 'to cut these programs which support peace'.[114] It was significant, therefore, that a US trade delegation visited Ireland in October 1995, including a business development mission headed by US assistant secretary of commerce for international economic policy Charles Meissner. His role was to complement that of commercial representative Joe White, who had already been appointed.[115]

The persistence of violence was problematic in the context of the planned economic development of Northern Ireland. In the relative vacuum of the ceasefire that persisted throughout 1995, however well-observed one considers it actually to have been, political and economic discussions could take place, but without any guarantees

[111] *NYT*, 25/5/1995.
[112] Edward M. Kennedy Institute, Oral History, 'Interview with Gerry Adams', available at https://www.emkinstitute.org/resources/gerry-adams.
[113] *IT*, 24/5/1995.
[114] *NYT*, 26/5/1995.
[115] *IT*, 3/10/1995.

about its durability it was unlikely that large corporations were likely to invest significantly in Northern Ireland. The political engagement necessary to achieve a lasting ceasefire had been sorely lacking from Northern Ireland for over twenty-five years at this point and the necessity of US mediators was all too apparent. Talks between government officials and Irish republicans continued to stumble over the issue of decommissioning, something the IRA branded 'a deliberate distraction and stalling tactic by a British government acting in bad faith'.[116] Decommissioning, namely the act of putting all the IRA's weapons beyond use, would remain a sticking point for the peace process for several years. At this point, however, it pushed peace discussions to breaking point and prompted a further request from Bruce Morrison to President Clinton for assistance.

Morrison urged Clinton to press three major tenets of what became the Good Friday Agreement in discussions, namely prisoner release, police reform, and repeal of 'repressive' legislation. He noted that 31 August marked the one-year anniversary of the IRA's ceasefire, but cautioned that 'many in Northern Ireland see little progress on the real issues that affect their lives'.[117] Clinton replied, noting that he considered decommissioning to be an 'essential component of this process'.[118] There were, however, obvious issues as to how useful the ANIA could be without Clinton's assistance and the question of whether or not Clinton's direct input was essential to moving the process forward. At this time, the British and Irish governments both wrote to the White House inviting Clinton to visit in late November.

The Clinton Visit

On 5 July 1995, it was agreed that Clinton would visit London, Belfast, and Dublin between 28 November and 2 December.[119] For Clinton:

[116] IRA Statement, 29/9/1995, in Decommissioning of IRA Weapons, 1995–1999, Materials related to the Northern Ireland peace process in Series VIII: Ireland in Morrison Papers, UConn Library.

[117] Letter from Morrison to Clinton, 22/6/1995, Correspondence related to Americans for a New Irish Agenda in Morrison Papers, UConn Library.

[118] Letter from Clinton to Morrison, 25/7/1995, Correspondence related to Americans for a New Irish Agenda in Morrison Papers, UConn Library.

[119] O'Clery, C., *The Greening of the White House* (Dublin: Gill & Macmillan, 1996), p. 218.

the goals of the trip include strengthening the transatlantic partnership in which the United Kingdom plays such a special role, nurturing our close ties of friendship and culture with Ireland, and underscoring the President's support for the joint efforts of the Irish and British governments and the people of Northern Ireland to achieve a lasting and peaceful settlement.[120]

As soon as this trip was confirmed, Morrison, O'Dowd, Flynn, Jameson, and Feeney immediately arranged a trip to Belfast and Dublin between 22 and 24 July. There, they would target meetings with Bruton and Dick Spring as well as John Hume, Seamus Mallon, Gerry Adams, Martin McGuinness, John Alderdice, Unionist Jeffrey Donaldson, and loyalists such as Gary McMichael, Billy Hutchinson, and Chris McGimpsey.[121] US figures had not tended to engage with loyalists throughout the process, so the significance of these meetings must be emphasised.

The Morrison group also met with Michael Ancram, Minister of State for Northern Ireland, who was reported to be 'a serious and attentive politician, unlike some others in high NIO positions and he seemed to wish to make progress in talks'. The 'brief sense of movement about overcoming the "decommissioning" logjam', had 'dissipated', but both Hume and Adams agreed on the need to move to all-party talks. It was noted that Bruton was 'not as comfortable playing the American card … [he] was concerned about danger of renewed strife in North on inward investment and economic recovery'. There was concern, too, in the north, where nationalists were emphasising to Bruton that the ongoing impasse could not continue. Clinton, who was 'not happy with the slow pace of peace process', was nonetheless reluctant to push the situation along in the absence of similar pressure from Dublin, so the ANIA group identified that:

the clear task is to step up Irish America grassroots political pressure, through 're-opened political channels' such as Dodd, Kennedy, Manton, DNC etc on the Administration that not all

[120] Press Release, 'President Clinton to visit United Kingdom and Ireland', 6/7/1995, in Ireland Trip, 1995, November, December, with President Clinton, in Documents related to the Northern Ireland peace process in Series VIII: Ireland in Morrison Papers, UConn Library.
[121] Fax from Morrison to Feeney, 19/7/1995, in Ireland Trip, 1995, November, December, with President Clinton, in Documents related to the Northern Ireland peace process in Series VIII: Ireland in Morrison Papers, UConn Library.

is rosy and the success of the peace process and the President's trip—and all the hoped for electoral benefits—are by no means assured. The White House is not getting enough Irish-American pressure.[122]

A statement from Clinton to mark the one-year anniversary of the IRA ceasefire noted that he was 'looking forward to visiting a peaceful Northern Ireland later this year and paying personal tribute to those who have worked so hard to bring about this new day'.[123] It is true that all parties were working hard, though the utility of that work in the wider context of advancing the peace process is highly questionable. Certainly, the prospect of all-party talks remained low. The largest Unionist group, the Ulster Unionist Party, and their leader David Trimble, remained intransigent over the issue of decommissioning, even though an international commission on decommissioning, headed by George Mitchell, was moving ahead.[124]

The inability of Unionists to coordinate some form of engagement was destructive to the short-term prospects of a new peace agreement, and also to the credibility of the then-dominant Ulster Unionist Party. Ian Paisley's Democratic Unionist Party was emerging as a hard-line alternative for Unionist voters, maintaining a consistently anti-republican line, whilst the popular desire for peace had to be channelled through the political necessity of each group coming out as 'the winners' of the power struggle: peace, but on one's own terms. The Clinton administration did make attempts fully to engage Unionists during this difficult period of negotiations. In late October, Ian Paisley visited the White House, followed by David Trimble on 1 November. Both men met with Gore and Lake and had Clinton participate in part of the meetings. Press releases reporting on the meetings seemed to suggest its explanatory quality, reassuring the Unionists that the intentions of the US government were directed at peace.[125]

---

[122] ANIA Meeting, 17/8/1995, Morrison trip to Ireland, 21–24 July, Box 1 Folder 4, ANIA Minutes and Correspondence 1995, AIA 008, Durkan Papers, Tamiment Library, NYU.

[123] Statement by the President on the first anniversary of the ceasefire in Northern Ireland, 30/8/1995, in IRA Ceasefire, 1994–1996 Materials related to the Northern Ireland peace process in Series VIII: Ireland in Morrison Papers, UConn Library.

[124] *IT*, 3/10/1995.

[125] Press Release, 27/10/1995 and Press Release, 1/11/1995, Ireland Trip, 1995, November, December, with President Clinton, in Documents related to the Northern Ireland peace process in Series VIII: Ireland in Morrison Papers, UConn Library.

Meanwhile, Adams continued to travel internationally, making the most of his newly acquired *persona grata* status in the United States, cultivating the image of an international statesman, and raising the profile of Sinn Féin in the process. In September 1995, he was again received at the White House where he met with Vice-President Gore and National Security Advisor Anthony Lake.[126] Both Gore and Lake emphasised their commitment to the twin-track proposals, but 'reiterated the importance of a serious discussion of decommissioning'.[127] Adams was followed to Washington by Dick Spring, who also met with Gore and Lake while Clinton dropped in on their meeting.

Peace talks were inching along, but the stop–start nature of talks frustrated Adams, who commented in November that 'the only dynamic for momentum is that inherent in the U.S. President'.[128] The President was, of course, also the most prominent figure with the least to lose if the talks did not proceed in a particular manner. Adams had a scheduled return trip to the United States, ahead of Clinton's Belfast visit, where he would meet with Anthony Lake and Nancy Soderberg.[129] He also maintained contact with Bruce Morrison, and warned the former Congressman that British demands for IRA disarmament were threatening the ceasefire. These demands were also described by Sean O hUiginn, who became Irish Ambassador to the United States in September 1997, as 'the single most serious mistake' made by any administration involved in the peace process.[130] Niall O'Dowd commented: 'people who look for nice and tidy solutions all wrapped up in a gift package will be disappointed. Making peace is a much more difficult proposition at this point than making war'.[131] This defined the necessarily slow process that built trust and ultimately led to decommissioning.[132]

[126] *NYT*, 18/9/1995.
[127] Press Release, 13/9/1995, in Ireland Trip, 1995, November, December, with President Clinton, in Documents related to the Northern Ireland peace process in Series VIII: Ireland in Morrison Papers, UConn Library.
[128] *NYT*, 4/11/1995.
[129] In the event, he only saw Lake; see Press Release, 15/11/1995, Ireland Trip, 1995, November, December, with President Clinton, in Documents related to the Northern Ireland peace process in Series VIII: Ireland in Morrison Papers, UConn Library.
[130] *IT*, 8/2/2016.
[131] *IT*, 23/8/1993.
[132] Devashree Gupta has argued for the importance of American actors in securing decommissioning whilst simultaneously pressuring the British to negotiate with Irish republicans; see Gupta, D., 'The Role of Licit and Illicit

The Presidential delegation included figures such as Bill Flynn, Tony O'Reilly, former Coca-Cola CEO Don Keough, and General Motors President John Smith. While Air Force One flew to London for a short meeting with British officials, they flew directly to Belfast from Andrews Air Force Base in Maryland.[133] The Clintons then arrived in Belfast on 30 November, making Clinton the first sitting US President to visit Northern Ireland.[134] News of progress met the delegation on arrival, with the British and Irish governments announcing that they had agreed to a 'twin-track' process on the decommissioning and all-party negotiations issues. The delegation all received a letter from Alexis Herman, one of the President's assistants, which described the trip in detail:

> As a guest of the President, you will travel via military aircraft to Belfast, Dublin and Western Ireland, where you will participate in a number of activities with the President and members of the President's Cabinet in an effort to bolster the peace process and encourage U.S. investment. Your presence, along with others, will help highlight the commitment of the American people to lasting peace and prosperity in the region … While you will be an official guest of the President, you will be responsible for the cost of airfare, ground transportation, accommodations, as well as all personal expenses. We expect the cost of airfare, ground transportation and accommodations to run approximately $3,500. We will be back in touch with you in the next day to confirm the exact cost and method of payment.[135]

President Clinton and the First Lady travelled to both Belfast and Derry, before switching on the Christmas lights in Belfast. The Belfast Christmas tree had been brought over from Tennessee, the home state of Vice-President Al Gore. Clinton also delivered a keynote address at Mackie's factory in West Belfast where he emphasised that 'we are

Transnational Networks during the Troubles', in White, T.J. (ed.), *Theories of International Relations and Northern Ireland* (Manchester: Manchester University Press, 2017), pp. 93–115.

[133]   *IT*, 10/11/1995.

[134]   *NYT*, 1/12/1995.

[135]   Letter from Alexis Herman, Assistant to the President to Brian O'Dwyer, 21/11/1995, Box 1 Folder 5, ANIA President Clinton's Irish Trip Nov. 29–Dec. 1 1995, AIA 008 Durkan Papers, Tamiment Library, NYU.

proud to support Northern Ireland ... we will stand with those who take risks for peace in Northern Ireland and around the world'.[136] The Clintons stayed in the Europa Hotel, one of the most frequently bombed hotels in Europe, before travelling to Dublin.[137]

Across the border, Clinton addressed the Dáil before meeting privately with Taoiseach Bruton and President Mary Robinson, meetings in which Hillary Clinton, in her role as First Lady, was present. Whilst the President was in Dublin, the British and Irish governments launched their twin-track process by sending invitations to the Northern Ireland political parties to attend preliminary talks. This justified the *New York Times* report that 'hopes have never been higher among ordinary people and officials for lasting peace'.[138] David Trimble, predictably, turned down the invitation.

Clinton reflected in his memoirs over 'two of the best days of my presidency' spent in Northern Ireland, highlighting his stop on the Shankill Road, where he visited the site of the IRA bombing of the previous year, and meeting Gerry Adams outside a bakery on the Falls Road. He recalled that he 'had the feeling that my trip had shifted the psychological balance in Ireland'.[139] From the British perspective, Alastair Campbell noted in his diary that 'Clinton was ... unfortunately going into overdrive in praise of Major', and added that Clinton and new Labour leader Tony Blair 'got on pretty well'.[140] Major's role in the peace process, often underappreciated, was clearly very apparent to President Clinton. Campbell, then a Blair spokesman and later his Press Secretary, emphasised that opposition leaders are often just 'something of an add on' when a President meets with a Prime Minister, but he later reflected that 'even if the meeting attracted little attention, it was an important encounter'.[141] It certainly was that, given the relationship the two men would enjoy after Blair's election as Prime Minister in 1997.

[136] Bill Clinton, 'Address to the Employees of the Mackie Metal Plant', 30/11/1995, Miller Center, University of Virginia, available at https://millercenter.org/the-presidency/presidential-speeches/november-30-1995-address-employees-mackie-metal-plant.
[137] Clinton, B., *My Life*, pp. 686–687.
[138] *NYT*, 5/12/1995.
[139] Clinton, B., *My Life*, pp. 686–688.
[140] Campbell, A., *The Irish Diaries, 1994–2003* (Dublin: Lilliput, 2013), p. 17.
[141] Ibid., p. 18.

Ireland and Clinton's Re-election Campaign

Writing to Morrison in August 1995, Brian O'Dwyer, son of famous Irish-American lawyer Paul O'Dwyer, argued that 'no President in the history of our Republic has done more to promote the cause of Irish freedom and nationalism than President Clinton'. O'Dwyer went on to lay out a strategy for Clinton's campaign for re-election and the useful role that Irish Americans could play in that.[142] Morrison would take a back seat, however, having been appointed the chair of the Federal Housing Finance Board in early 1996. He stepped down from his role in Americans for a New Irish Agenda and was replaced by Frank Durkan. In a press release, ANIA announced that it would 'continue to pressure for a continued US Government role in the Northern Ireland problem, particularly in view of the recent British rejection of the Mitchell Commission Report. It is the considered view of many of its members that only renewed intervention from Washington can bring about a change of attitude at Westminster', adding that Westminster's actions had 'only served to sabotage the Peace Process'.[143] Durkan wrote to Clinton in March, shortly after St Patrick's Day, to assure him that 'our best activists are already preparing to work with your 1996 re-election campaign to help you win the White House again in November'.[144] It would be a task complicated by the breakdown of the IRA ceasefire.

On 9 February, the IRA detonated a large lorry-bomb in the Docklands area of London, killing two people, before carrying out further acts of violence across London over subsequent weeks. It set the scene for George Mitchell's return to Belfast in late February. Mitchell, along with Canadian General John de Chastelain, and former Prime Minister of Finland Harri Holkeri, had published a report on decommissioning in January, which suggested that decommissioning should take place alongside all-party talks, not as a prerequisite for them, or as a

[142]   Memorandum from Brian O'Dwyer to Morrison, 4/8/1995, General Correspondence, 1992–1996, Morrison Papers, UConn Library.
[143]   Press Release, Frank Durkan Appointed Chairman of ANIA, Box 1 Folder 6, Minutes, Correspondence, Press, January 1996, AIA 008, Durkan Papers, Tamiment Library, NYU.
[144]   Letter from Durkan to Clinton, 19/3/1996, Box 1 Folder 6, Minutes, Correspondence, Press, January 1996 AIA 008, Durkan Papers, Tamiment Library, NYU.

result of them.[145] Gerry Adams was, at this time, seeking the renewal of his visitor visa to return to the United States for St Patrick's Day.[146] In light of the IRA's return to violence, decommissioning seemed an increasingly unlikely prospect and questions were raised about whether Adams should be allowed to return to the United States in light of the IRA's return to violence. Adams had raised an estimated $1.25 million in the United States since he was granted fundraising rights. Bruce Morrison was doubtful that Sinn Féin leaders would be denied entry to the United States for fundraising even in light of recent events, noting that 'what Sinn Féin does in the United States, so far as fund-raising and the like, is not governed by any prohibition in US law'.[147]

Clinton's statement on the Docklands bombing condemned 'in the strongest possible terms this cowardly action and hope those responsible are brought swiftly to justice … I am deeply concerned by reports that the Irish Republican Army has announced an end to the cease-fire'. He emphasised that 'the United States stands ready to assist the two governments in continuing their search for negotiations and peace'.[148] Adams took the opportunity of his own statement on the bombing to blame the British government:

> Our response to today's events is one of sadness. My sympathy and thoughts are with those injured today. I regret that an unprecedented opportunity for peace has floundered on the refusal of the British government and the Unionist leaders to enter into honest dialogue and substantive negotiations. I appeal for calm. Sinn Féin's peace strategy remains as the main function of our party. It is my personal priority. All those who made genuine efforts to build a peace process must keep our nerve in the face of predictable and hypocritical reaction from public representatives who have done nothing to encourage the risky search for a peace settlement. That search for peace must be redoubled.[149]

[145] See Report of the International Body on Arms Decommissioning, 22 January 1996, available at https://cain.ulster.ac.uk/events/peace/docs/gm24196.htm.
[146] *NYT*, 21/2/1996.
[147] *Belfast Telegraph*, 10/6/1996.
[148] Statement by the President, in IRA Ceasefire, 1994–1996, Materials related to the Northern Ireland peace process in Series VIII: Ireland in Morrison Papers, UConn Library.
[149] Gerry Adams remarks, Friends of Sinn Féin Press Release, 9/2/1996, Box 1 Folder 6, Minutes, Correspondence, Press, January 1996, AIA 008, Durkan Papers, Tamiment Library, NYU.

By this stage of the conflict, Adams had perfected his technique of delegating blame for IRA violence. Empowered by his credibility internationally, most notably in the United States, he felt assured in his perception as a political figure, not a military commander, and sought to score political points on the back of acts of violence that he would clearly have at least been aware of. The British government would seem to have little cause to risk a return to violence only seventeen months after the original IRA ceasefire. Where Adams derived the confidence to continue with this deflecting rhetoric from was clear from the ANIA statement that followed:

> There will be time enough for assigning blame for the end of the ceasefire. Two heroes in the struggle for a just and lasting peace have been weakened by the political effects of the bombing, John Hume and Gerry Adams. They fathered the Irish peace process. Our government must do all in its power to support these leaders in their work for a restored ceasefire, all-party talks, and a political settlement.[150]

Echoing the Adams statement, and following a meeting between the IRA leadership, Sinn Féin, and the SDLP, the IRA issued a statement that also blamed the British on their decision to recommence their campaign of violence:

> We pointed out to Mr Hume and Mr Adams that the failure of the British government to put in place inclusive negotiations free from preconditions, the abuse of the peace process by the British over 18 months and the absence of an effective and democratic approach capable of providing an irrevocable momentum towards a just and lasting peace in Ireland, were the critical elements which led to the failure, thus far, of the Irish peace process.[151]

Adams recalled the role that Ted Kennedy played at this crucial time, using his position to exert influence on both sides of the Atlantic to

---

[150] Americans for a New Irish Agenda, Press Release, 14/2/1996, Box 1 Folder 6, Minutes, Correspondence, Press, January 1996, AIA 008, Durkan Papers, Tamiment Library, NYU.
[151] IRA Statement, 29/2/1996, available at https://cain.ulster.ac.uk/events/peace/docs/ira290296.htm.

ensure that discussions did not cease.[152] Nevertheless, the IRA went back to war. Volunteers murdered Garda Jerry McCabe during an attempted robbery in Limerick in June, but the organisation also continued to focus its campaign on the British mainland and volunteer Edward O'Brien was killed when the bomb he was transporting exploded on a bus in central London.[153] The IRA then detonated a huge bomb in Manchester city centre, injuring 200. These attacks rather confirmed the view of Unionist leaders, who considered that the IRA's return to violence 'clearly and conclusively proves that there is no prospect of the republican movement becoming committed to exclusively peaceful means'. UUP leader David Trimble, later awarded a Nobel Prize for his efforts in the peace process, was also critical of the British for their role in the IRA's return to violence. He lampooned the British government, citing notorious serial killer Fred West, when he asked:

> What would have happened if John Bruton and John Major had been in charge of the investigation into Fred West? You can just imagine it. There they would have been, on the doorstep of number 25 Cromwell Street saying, 'Mr West, if you could just see your way to stop all this killing. And maybe if you could, we could make a deal to satisfy your needs in other ways'. And then imagine it if Fred turned round and said, 'OK, maybe I will not kill anybody for the time being, until I see what you will do for me'. And before you know it the two Johns would be inviting Fred West down to the station for a celebration together with all the fellow travellers of the so-called Anglo-Irish process.[154]

The IRA's return to violence also posed problems for Clinton as he headed into the 1996 election campaign. At the annual St Patrick's Day event on 15 March 1996, Clinton hosted a reception which was attended by Frank Durkan in his capacity as the chair of ANIA. Durkan wrote to Clinton after the reception, noting that 'the end

[152]   Edward M. Kennedy Institute, Oral History, 'Interview with Gerry Adams', available at https://www.emkinstitute.org/resources/gerry-adams.
[153]   A search of O'Brien's home uncovered significant amounts of semtex, timers, and detonators, McKittrick et al., *Lost Lives*, p. 1390.
[154]   Speech by David Trimble at the Annual General Meeting of the Ulster Unionist Council, 23/3/1996, available at https://cain.ulster.ac.uk/events/peace/docs/dt23396.htm.

of the ceasefire ... took away from what would have been a glorious holiday celebration of the impact your recent trip and your continuous leadership in the Irish peace process'.[155] The organisation also issued a statement:

> it's important to remember that 25 years of the 'politics of condemnation' did not produce an IRA ceasefire. Rather, it was the creation of a political path forward by Northern nationalism, Hume and Adams mainly, then joined by the Irish Government and by the US Administration, that cleared the way for the August 1994 ceasefire. Sadly, it was mainly the stupidity and complacency of the British government that squandered the subsequent 17 months of precious political opportunity.[156]

It was not difficult to assert the source of Adams's empowerment. The implication that all parties other than the British and Unionists had been working hard and the deaths and injuries of 1996, and those that followed in 1997, were the fault of the 'stupid' and 'complacent' British government. It is important to remember the similarities between the IRA's 1995 attacks and the 1993 Al Qaeda bombing of the World Trade Center in New York. This comparison was particularly important in late 2001 when commentators argued that the 9/11 attacks, also by Al Qaeda at the World Trade Center, had cost the IRA its international legitimacy. On this occasion, the United States decided against blocking Adams from returning to the United States, but he was stripped of his fund-raising privileges on his March trip.[157]

ANIA continued to engage the White House, mainly through direct communication from Durkan to the President. One letter argued that 'only increased US involvement can restore the peace process'.[158] Another sought to draw the President's attention to the

---

[155] Letter from Durkan to Clinton, 19/3/1996, Correspondence related to Americans for a New Irish Agenda in Morrison Papers, UConn Library.

[156] Americans for a New Irish Agenda, 23/5/1996, Talking Points, Box 1 Folder 7, ANIA meeting with White House, NSC May–June 1996, AIA 008, Durkan Papers, Tamiment Library, NYU.

[157] *Sun-Sentinel*, 21/2/1996; *Baltimore Sun*, 2/3/1996; *NYT*, 13/3/1996.

[158] Letter from Durkan to Clinton, 25/7/1996, Box 1 Folder 8, Meeting at White House, Correspondence and Press July–Dec. 1996, AIA 008, Durkan Papers, Tamiment Library, NYU.

protests that met the Orange Order during their annual parade in Portadown:

> I realize that the I.R.A.'s decision to call off the ceasefire has met with well-merited condemnation. I say this cognizant as I am of the way the British squandered opportunities for real peace in the 17-month period during which the ceasefire lasted … However, I think it is a mistake to hinge everything on the I.R.A.'s willingness to restore the ceasefire. A far more damaging event occurred in Ireland at a place called Drumcree where Loyalist members of the Orange order engaged in a full week of intimidation and lawlessness which has not merited the same opprobrium as the actions of the I.R.A.[159]

Durkan indulged here in the well-worn Northern Irish political pastime of 'whataboutery', seeking to draw analogy between two issues that were both harming the peace process. The level of influence Clinton was likely to have over the Drumcree Orangemen was minimal, but the expectation was that he could perhaps exert some influence over the British government to try and resolve the situation there. This complicated leadership role was discussed by Anthony Lake during an October address at Georgetown University. There, he emphasised that 'we can—and we must—continue to lead the way in bringing seemingly intractable conflicts to resolution. For often, peace is a prerequisite to long-term progress'. He added that:

> The President and the American people remain deeply outraged by the IRA's breach of the ceasefire, its vicious bomb attacks in London and Manchester, and its continuing attempts to main and kill innocent civilians. We were dismayed by the bitterness of this summer's marching season, by the rekindling of old hatreds and old fears on both sides.

Lake noted the importance of the talks to be both 'meaningful and comprehensive' and that it was crucial that 'their representatives to negotiate with tenacity and good faith—both essential to reaching an agreement as soon as possible that will benefit the whole community'. The administration remained committed, both to peace and to encouraging

[159] Letter from Durkan to Clinton, 18/9/1996, ibid.

US businesses to invest in Northern Ireland upon the achievement of peace.[160]

This commitment to the peace process and the determination to maintain engagement with Irish republicans drew criticism from Clinton's opponent in the 1996 Presidential election, Republican Senator Bob Dole, who sought to undermine Clinton's Northern Ireland credentials. In October, Dole commented that 'even though the President invited a terrorist to the White House it did not lead to peace in Ireland'. Dole's rhetoric might have been strong, but ignored the reality of him also having received Adams on Capitol Hill in his role as Senate Majority Leader. Dole reportedly told Adams that if he were elected President, Adams would be welcome in the White House. Nevertheless, this was the line pursued by Republicans throughout the 1996 campaign. Former Secretary of State James Baker, at the Republican convention in August, went so far as to call Clinton a 'representative of terrorism'.[161] Former US Ambassador to the UK Raymond Seitz, who later referred to Jean Kennedy Smith as an 'ardent IRA apologist', criticised the Clinton administration for allowing Gerry Adams into the US, arguing that as somewhere 'which had suffered so often at the hands of terrorists around the world, should have been the last place to offer a platform to Gerry Adams, but in the end this is what the President did'.[162]

Bruce Morrison returned to Northern Ireland in September along with Chuck Feeney, Niall O'Dowd, and Joe Jameson to conduct a series of meetings. Among the names on their agenda were those of Lord Alderdice, John Hume, David Trimble, and Gerry Adams.[163] Morrison may have taken a backseat in ANIA since his departure from the chair of the organisation, but he remained active in fundraising for Clinton, organising a big-ticket fundraising event for the re-election campaign.[164] Nancy Soderberg later recalled Morrison 'was so persistent and so responsible in how he presented issues. He would listen and he

---

[160]   Anthony Lake, Assistant to the President for National Security Affairs, Remarks to the Institute for the Study of Diplomacy, Georgetown University, Washington, DC, 8/10/1996, AIA 008, Durkan Papers, Box 1 Folder 8, Meeting at White House, Correspondence and Press, July–Dec. 1996, Tamiment Library, NYU.

[161]   *IT*, 4/10/1996.

[162]   *NYT*, 19/1/1998.

[163]   *Belfast Telegraph*, 20/9/1996.

[164]   Memorandum from Morrison to Senator Christopher Dodd, 20/8/1996, General Correspondence, 1992–1996, Morrison Papers, UConn Library.

understood the politics of it for the President ... He was a genius about orchestrating a yes out of Clinton'.[165] He was not part of a Belfast trip by ANIA in July 1997 following the restoration of the IRA's ceasefire, but did meet Northern Ireland Secretary Mo Mowlam in August 1997 and suggested that signals from the United States helped to persuade the IRA to restore its ceasefire: 'what they wanted from the States was clarity that Sinn Féin would once again achieve access to the States and to the White House, and ability to do fundraising—things that they had achieved in the first ceasefire'.[166]

With Clinton having made good on his pledges to provide a visa to Gerry Adams and create a special envoy, the focus of Irish-American groups shifted to the President's commitment to the MacBride Principles. This was perhaps the trickiest part of his five-part plan to adhere to, given serious resistance from both British and Northern Irish sources. There was also the problem of the American Overseas Interests Act of 1995. Versions of the act, which sought to make the next $19.6 million contribution to the International Fund for Ireland contingent on the adoption of the MacBride Principles, had passed in both houses of Congress but the bill ended up in a conference committee which decided not to make MacBride compliance mandatory. Instead:

> The Committee fully supports the increased levels of U.S. assistance to the IFI as requested by the Administration for [financial year] 96. This contribution is timely and necessary to support and advance the peace process at this important moment in Irish history ... Based on testimony before the Committee, it is evident that U.S. assistance should be carefully targeted at the areas of greatest need, based upon levels of unemployment and the changes incorporated in the Anglo-Irish Agreement of 1986, to accomplish that worthy goal ... In the Committee's opinion, the increased U.S. assistance and the clear need for targeted investment consistent with the principles of economic justice establish a need for greater involvement and oversight by the U.S. observer to the IFI ... In extending U.S. oversight to the IFI, the Committee does not intend to extend the other

[165] Quoted in Rhodeen, *Peacerunner*, p. 127.
[166] *Belfast Telegraph*, 5/8/1997.

restrictions and requirements of the Foreign Assistance Act to Funds activities.[167]

President Clinton vetoed the act, much to the 'deep disappointment' of the Irish National Caucus, who now warned that 'you cannot expect us to be silent as you continue to oppose one of our very top legislative issues. Furthermore, it would be unfair for us to criticize Democratic Senators, and not yourself, when they are simply following your lead in obstructing passage of the MacBride Principles'.[168] Such criticism of Clinton was met by figures like Frank Durkan and Niall O'Dowd. Durkan wrote to the *Irish Echo* asking them, 'We have developed a reputation for self-destruction in the face of historical crises and the events of this past week prove it is well merited. Must we bite the hand that has fed us?'[169] A coalition of eleven groups, including the AOH, wrote to the President criticising him for vetoing the bill. O'Dowd's *Irish Voice* newspaper criticised the group for 'insultingly' asking Mr Clinton to take his cue from Republicans.[170]

Further attempts to introduce legislation that incorporated MacBride included the MacBride Principles Economic Justice Act of 1996, which attempted to amend the 1986 Anglo-Irish Agreement Support Act by requiring US contributions to be distributed in accordance with the MacBride Principles. The bill was co-sponsored by a bipartisan yet predictable list of representatives, including Peter King, Jim Walsh, and Richard Neal.[171] It did not pass committee. Eventually, in October 1998, Clinton signed the Omnibus Consolidated and Emergency Supplemental Appropriations Act, 1999. The text of the act, in reference to the IFI, stated that financial support 'should be provided to individuals or entities in Northern Ireland which employ practices consistent with the principles of economic justice'.[172] By this time, the people of Northern

---

[167] 104th Congress, H. Rept 104-128—American Overseas Interests Act of 1995, available at https://www.congress.gov/congressional-report/104th-congress/house-report/128/1.

[168] Letter from Irish National Caucus to Clinton, 11/3/1996, Box 1 Folder 9, MacBride Principles: Clinton Veto, aftermath, March 1996–May 1997, AIA 008, Durkan Papers, Tamiment Library, NYU.

[169] *Irish Echo*, 24/4/1996.

[170] *IT*, 25/4/1996.

[171] 104th Congress, H.R.3621—MacBride Principles of Economic Justice Act of 1996, available at https://www.congress.gov/bill/104th-congress/house-bill/3621.

[172] 105th Congress, H.R.4328—Omnibus Consolidated and Emergency

Ireland had overwhelmingly voted in favour of the implementation of the Good Friday Agreement which had been signed, on 10 April 1998, after much encouragement from both British Prime Minister Tony Blair and President Clinton.

The Good Friday Agreement and the Second Clinton Visit

After the IRA restored its ceasefire in July 1997, the road to the Good Friday Agreement started to clear. It was removed from the State Department's list of foreign terrorist organisations, a process that began with an October 1997 review.[173] The State Department declared, upon its biennial review in 1999, that: 'The peace process in Northern Ireland continues, albeit not without obvious difficulties, and we have again determined that the IRA should not be designated at this time. We are, however, concerned over recent indications of increased terrorist activity in Northern Ireland, and we will continue to monitor closely the activities of all paramilitary groups'.[174]

IRA violence, though never rising to the level that might threaten its new non-terrorist organisation status in the United States, continued to pose problems in Northern Ireland. In early 1998, it was believed responsible for the murders of drug dealer Brendan Campbell and loyalist Bobby Dougan. Its members were also responsible for the murder of Andrew Kearney, who was badly beaten, shot three times, and left to die in a stairwell in the New Lodge area of North Belfast in July 1998. Kearney had intervened in a dispute between a young man and an older man, known to be an IRA commander in the area. Kearney and the IRA commander became involved in a fistfight and the IRA man was knocked unconscious. The killing was the IRA commander's revenge; Kearney's punishment was to bleed to death in that stairwell. To date, nobody has ever been charged with the murder and British indifference to the premeditated, brutal killing was exemplified in the comments of a British civil servant, who referred to

Supplemental Appropriations Act, 1999, available at https://www.congress.gov/bill/105th-congress/house-bill/4328/text.
[173]   *NYT*, 9/10/1997.
[174]   Foreign Terrorist Organizations, Designations by the Secretary of State, 8/10/1999, available at https://2001-2009.state.gov/s/ct/rls/rpt/fto/2682.htm.

the murder as 'internal housekeeping' on the part of the IRA.[175] This killing took place three months after the signing of the Good Friday Agreement: the unnamed civil servant's comments clear indication of the paramount importance of maintaining the agreement at all costs.

The Good Friday Agreement, also known as the Belfast Agreement, was signed on 10 April 1998, with a referendum on the agreement held on 22 May. The negotiations ran through the night of 9 April and required significant input from President Clinton, who called Gerry Adams three times, also speaking to David Trimble.[176] Clinton recalled, 'Good Friday … was one of the happiest days of my presidency', noting that George Mitchell had woken him at 5 a.m. to call Gerry Adams in order to help 'seal the deal'.[177] Three days after the signing of the agreement, Clinton announced his intention to visit Northern Ireland to help ensure its success. The visit would take place in September; a pre-referendum visit had been considered inadvisable because of concern that voters would 'not take kindly to being told how they should vote'. Writing in the *Irish Times*, Mary Holland noted:

> That is why it was decided that President Clinton should not visit the North in the run-up to the referendum. He was advised that Unionists would see his visit as part of a campaign orchestrated by the pan-nationalist front and that Dr Paisley would make hay of the occasion. There are others who think that this would have been a risk worth taking. Bertie Ahern in particular is known to have argued that a visit by President Clinton—and all the emotional razzamatazz surrounding it—would create a much-needed air of excitement around the referendums and thus increase the vote.[178]

[175]   *The Village*, 6/3/2004.
[176]   Powell, J., *Great Hatred, Little Room: Making Peace in Northern Ireland* (London: Bodley Head, 2008), pp. 90–119, especially pp. 101 and 104. In addition to this memoir from Powell in his role as Blair's Chief of Staff, other valuable accounts of the Good Friday process can be found in De Breadun, D., *The Far Side of Revenge: Making Peace in Northern Ireland* (Cork: Collins Press, 2008); Cox, M., Guelke, A., and Stephen, F. (eds), *A Farewell to Arms: Beyond the Good Friday Agreement*, 2nd edn (Manchester: Manchester University Press, 2006); Bew, P., *The Making and Remaking of the Good Friday Agreement* (Dublin: Liffey Press, 2007), and Mitchell, G., *The Negotiator: A Memoir* (New York: Simon & Schuster, 2015), among others.
[177]   Clinton, *My Life*, p. 784.
[178]   *IT*, 7/5/1998.

The referendum achieved 81 per cent turnout and 71 per cent of Northern Irish voters were in favour of the agreement. Still, the summer marching season, and the continuing protests at Drumcree, brought tension to Northern Ireland. Both sides of the community were united in a tragedy that took place on the night of 12 July, the traditional day that the Orange Order marches to celebrate the victory of King William of Orange at the Battle of the Boyne in 1690. The home of a Catholic family in Ballymoney was petrol bombed and the resultant blaze claimed the lives of three young boys, Richard, Mark, and Jason Quinn.

President Clinton wrote to Christine Quinn, the mother of the boys, to convey 'our deepest condolences'. In his letter, Clinton emphasised that 'your family's tragedy redoubles our determination to do all we can to make sure that others need not have to experience what you are so courageously facing'.[179] He also pledged to the surviving Quinn brother, Lee, that he would do all he could to bring peace to Northern Ireland. In May 1999, Thomas Garfield was convicted of the murders, receiving three life sentences for his role in driving the car that was used in the attack.[180] UVF members Johnny McKay, Raymond Parke, and Ivan Parke were named in court as being the others responsible for the attack but were never convicted thanks to lack of evidence.[181] There was further horror that summer after the Real IRA, a group that splintered from the Provisional IRA in 1997 in protest at the group's engagement with the peace process, bombed Omagh, a nationalist town in County Tyrone. The Omagh bomb, on 15 August 1998, claimed twenty-nine victims, including several children.

Speaker Newt Gingrich visited Ireland in August 1998, leading a bipartisan delegation as part of the revitalised US–Ireland Parliamentary Group.[182] During his week there, he 'researched his Irish roots, discussed the prospects for peace in Northern Ireland [and] even donned work gloves and blue jeans to help build a home in Belfast for a good-will project' in the Glencairn estate in north Belfast.[183] One of the political

[179] Letter from Clinton to Christine Quinn (undated), image available in Associated Press news report, 'N. Ireland: Mother of 3 Murdered Catholic Boys Speaks', 17/7/1998, available at www.aparchive.com/metadata/youtube/4deabc6 3d421c51135b132ef8b886959.
[180] *Irish Echo*, 5–11/5/1999.
[181] BBC World Service, 'Life for Quinn Boys' Murder', 29/10/1999, available at http://news.bbc.co.uk/2/hi/europe/493558.stm.
[182] *Orlando Sentinel*, 12/8/1998; *IT*, 4/5/1998.
[183] *NYT*, 3/2/2012; *IT*, 12/8/1998.

issues that the group sought to explore was the granting of 50,000 non-immigrant visas to young people from Ireland and Northern Ireland.[184]

Clinton followed this group over a few weeks later, arriving amidst a domestic political storm after allegations of an affair with White House intern and staffer Monica Lewinsky broke. These had brought about Congressional hearings in August and the Clinton–Lewinksy affair drew attention to the visit of First Lady Hillary Clinton, who also travelled to Belfast, her third visit to the province. She arrived a day ahead of the President to attend the 'Vital Voices: Women in Democracy' conference in Belfast.[185] Clinton delivered a speech to 'a rapt, applauding audience' at the Waterfront Hall.[186] She emphasised 'it is up to you, the women of Northern Ireland, speaking out whenever injustice arises, to point out opportunities, to face up to challenges, and to speak for those who are still voiceless'.[187] President Clinton arrived the following day and also addressed an audience at the Waterfront Hall. There, he spoke passionately, focusing on the idea that hope and peace might overcome the desperation of Omagh:

> The terror in Omagh was not the last bomb of the troubles; it was the opening shot of a vicious attack on the peace … So much more unites you than divides you: the values of faith and family, work and community, the same land and heritage, the same love of laughter and language. You aspire to the same things: to live in peace and security, to provide for your loved ones, to build a better life and pass on brighter possibilities to your children. These are not Catholic or Protestant dreams, these are human dreams, to be realised best together. The American people, as the Lord Mayor noted, know from our own experience about bigotry and violence rooted in race and religion. Still today, we struggle with the challenge of building one nation out of our increasing diversity. But it is worth the effort. We know we are

---

[184] *IT*, 8/8/1998. It later transpired that the trip was backed by Freddie Mac and Fannie Mae, two housing companies that Gingrich would later denounce as he sought the republican nomination for the 2012 Presidential election, *NYT*, 3/2/2012.

[185] Clinton, H.R., *Hard Choices* (New York: Simon & Schuster, 2014), p. 224.

[186] *Philadelphia Inquirer*, 3/9/1998.

[187] *Baltimore Sun*, 3/9/1998.

wiser, stronger, and happier when we stand on common ground. And we know you will be too.[188]

On 20 August, five days after the Omagh bomb, the US Navy launched Operation Infinite Reach. This was a pre-emptive strike on Al Qaeda bases in Afghanistan and the Al-Shifa pharmaceutical factory in Khartoum, Sudan. Mary Holland noted that the President had been accused of hypocrisy for visiting Omagh in light of the Sudanese factory attack, but added that 'there has been a tendency to write down his contribution' to Northern Ireland as a result.[189]

There was, however, significant and rapid progress following Clinton's visit. The extent to which this progress could be attributed to the Presidential visit rather than widespread horror at the destruction of Omagh is debateable, but a Real IRA ceasefire was announced on 7 September. Three days later, Trimble and Adams met, and the following day the first paramilitary prisoners were released on licence under the terms of the Good Friday Agreement. On 19 November, the Northern Ireland Act came into law. This provided for the implementation of the Good Friday Agreement. On 10 December, John Hume and David Trimble travelled to Norway to receive their jointly awarded Nobel Peace Prize.

Clinton made one further trip to Northern Ireland before leaving the White House. He returned in December 2000 with Senator-Elect Hillary Clinton. They spent the day in Dublin and Dundalk before travelling on to Belfast where the President met Tony Blair in the newly constructed Hilton Hotel near the city's Central Station.[190] They spent one night in Belfast, where both delivered speeches, and then travelled to England where Clinton stayed with Tony Blair at the Prime Minister's retreat at Chequers.[191] Throughout the trip Hillary Clinton was introduced as 'First Lady' rather than as senator-elect from New York, which was reported as being important to her staff who did not want to detract from the 'victory lap aspect' of President Clinton's visit. Taoiseach Bertie Ahern, with one eye on the future, noted that 'Hillary Clinton is a friend we know we will have in the U.S. Senate'. During

---

[188]   Bill Clinton, President of the USA, keynote address at the Waterfront Hall, Belfast, Thursday, 3 September 1998, available at https://cain.ulster.ac.uk/events/peace/docs/bc3998.htm.

[189]   *IT*, 3/9/1998.

[190]   *IT*, 13/12/2000.

[191]   *IT*, 12/12/2000.

her speech in Belfast Senator Clinton acknowledged the role of women in securing political stability in Ireland.[192]

Having won the seat vacated by the newly retired Daniel Patrick Moynihan, and having spent eight years in the Clinton White House where Northern Ireland was a major foreign policy success, Hillary Clinton engaged on Irish issues throughout her election campaign, conscious of maintaining the available support from within the Irish-American community in the state of New York. Her prominent role during Clinton's visits in support of the Good Friday Agreement also provided her with valuable foreign policy experience. One of her early moves was to march in the St Patrick's Day parade, an event that New York Democrats had tended to boycott since the David Dinkins Mayoralty because of its exclusion of gay and lesbian groups.[193] Clinton was confronted by the Gay and Lesbian Independent Democrats in Greenwich Village and during this confrontation she argued that 'I have worked very hard over the last six years or so in every way I could to further the peace process in Northern Ireland', adding that marching was 'one way of demonstrating that'.[194] She was joined by former Mayor Ed Koch before returning to the White House for a reception that included Bertie Ahern and Gerry Adams.[195]

The importance of the Clinton Presidency for the evolution of the Northern Ireland peace process has been well established. The two ceasefires on the part of the Provisional IRA, reciprocated by loyalist paramilitaries, effectively ended the widespread campaigns of violence and pushed the role of those who would seek to perpetuate acts of violence even deeper into the margins of society. The signing of the Good Friday Agreement provided legislative guidance for the coming years in Northern Ireland and firmly established a path out of the three-decade-long conflict. It is difficult to imagine this all taking place in essentially a four-year period without the strong backing that came from the White House during Bill Clinton's Presidency. Clinton pushed where his predecessors had been afraid, unwilling, or unable to push. He had engaged a significant section of Irish America in doing so and retained their engagement through a series of initiatives delivered throughout his administration.

---

[192]   *NYT*, 14/12/2000.
[193]   *NYT*, 10/12/1999.
[194]   *NYT*, 15/3/2000.
[195]   *NYT*, 18/3/2000.

In March 2011, Clinton was inducted into the Irish-American hall of fame.[196]

The broader context of the situation in Northern Ireland itself must not be ignored, however. The Provisional IRA had become war-weary and damaged by aggressive counter-insurgency and counter-terrorist operations on the part of British security forces—an IRA that had seen its legitimacy undermined by the duration of its war and a wider republican movement that became ever more committed to electoral politics with the rise of Sinn Féin and the political initiatives that became possible thanks to investment from the governments of the United Kingdom and the Republic of Ireland, as well as the United States.[197]

Labour leader from 1983 until 1992, Neil Kinnock summarised the events of the time as being 'made possible by an accumulation of experiences, developments and what—for brevity—I'll call "maturing" by people, leaders, communities and institutions', emphasising that 'it owed a huge amount to John Hume'.[198] In the United Kingdom, the government of Tony Blair has certainly taken much credit for the peace process in Northern Ireland, and Blair is very much tied to Clinton in the historiography of the Good Friday Agreement, but the efforts that were made by his predecessors in office must also be acknowledged. The same is true for Bertie Ahern's predecessors in Dublin.

There was, of course, significant work that remained for Clinton's successor. George W. Bush arrived in office with little debt to Irish America and little apparent interest in Northern Ireland. It was under his watch that the implementation of the Good Friday Agreement, and its political structures, would take place.

[196] *Irish America*, April/May 2016, available online at http://irishamerica.com/2016/03/bill-clinton-the-peacemaker/.
[197] Indeed, Lynch argues that Northern Ireland was 'actually more a peace process when Clinton became involved', *Turf War*, p. 55.
[198] Lord Kinnock, correspondence with author, 21/3/2012.

CHAPTER SEVEN

George W. Bush, Barack Obama, and Post-Conflict Northern Ireland

I told him I would like to be in a position to make a deal but that any deal must be fair, and it must address to my satisfaction and my electorate's satisfaction all the fundamental issues that have blocked progress for so long ... We told him that we must build a solid foundation in order to move forward ... We reminded the President of the fact that he would not have terrorists in his government and that we must be satisfied that IRA terrorism is over and cannot return.[1]

Ian Paisley on his conversation with President George W. Bush, *Irish Times*, 27 November 2004

Bill Clinton left office as Northern Ireland began to emerge from three decades of conflict. The Good Friday Agreement, which Clinton had been heavily invested in achieving, had provided the framework for peace but its full implementation would require continued and significant investment from political actors on either side of the Atlantic.

George W. Bush, the son of the forty-first President and a former Governor of Texas, narrowly won the 2000 Presidential election. Both parties had referred to Northern Ireland in their election platforms, but it was significant that the Republican Party made more of 'the historic reconciliation' there.[2] Vice-President Al Gore had sought to distance

---

[1]   *Irish Times*, 27/11/2004.
[2]   2000 Republican Party Political Platform, 31/7/2000, available at www.presidency.ucsb.edu/ws/index.php?pid=25849.

himself from Clinton during his campaign and had been marginal to Clinton's efforts in Northern Ireland in any case.[3]

Bush's election restored a more historically familiar pattern to US–NI relations. The most significant move was the transferral of the special envoy position from the White House, where Clinton had established it, to the State Department. Bush appointed Richard Haass, a career civil servant, to the role in early 2001. The work of the envoy shifted from creating and maintaining cessations of violence and encouraging political agreement to the equally tricky task of accomplishing decommissioning. The leading scholar of the George W. Bush administration's relationship with Northern Ireland, Mary Alice Clancy, has noted that 'the Bush administration has had a significant impact upon the politics of post-Agreement Northern Ireland, and ... this is due to the autonomy that the White House grants to its special envoys to Northern Ireland'.[4] She discussed the role that Haass played in achieving an initial round of IRA decommissioning through a tough line towards Sinn Féin, and how this process involved Dublin and an engagement with the DUP. She also noted the 'profound' contribution of Mitchell Reiss, who succeeded Haass in 2003. Reiss adopted an even tougher stance against Sinn Féin, which, Clancy argues convincingly, expedited decommissioning and Sinn Féin support for policing. Without these events, the Sinn Féin–DUP agreement to share power would not have been possible.[5]

Clancy's work demonstrates that President George W. Bush would follow his own path on Northern Ireland, despite the success enjoyed by Clinton. It was not, however, to the detriment of the peace process. Rather, it offered balance to the complicated process and countered the perception that Clinton had favoured Irish republicans by both engaging Unionists and pushing reciprocity from the republicans.[6]

---

[3]   *NYT*, 20/10/2000.

[4]   Clancy, M.A.C., 'The United States and Post-Agreement Northern Ireland, 2001–6', *Irish Studies in International Affairs* 18 (2007), pp. 155–173 at p. 155. Clancy also argued that Clinton's interventions were based on an erroneous understanding of the conflict in Northern Ireland, perceiving more commonality with racial divisions in the USA than was accurate; see Clancy, M.A.C., 'The Lessons of Third Party Intervention? The Curious Case of the United States in Northern Ireland', in White, T.J. (ed.), *Lessons from the Northern Ireland Peace Process* (Madison: University of Wisconsin Press, 2013), pp. 173–197.

[5]   Clancy, 'The United States and Post-Agreement Northern Ireland', p. 173.

[6]   Though Clancy notes that Haass enjoyed a friendlier relationship with Gerry Adams than he did with David Trimble. See Clancy, 'The Lessons of Third Party Intervention?', p. 182.

Clinton's influence meant that the British government now engaged Irish republicans, rather than seeking to coerce them into action by excluding them from discussions. Once Sinn Féin were seen to be included in the future of Northern Ireland, reflected in their participation in high-level discussions, by their presence on the global stage at high-profile events in the United States, and by election results, they became a more realistic vehicle for Irish republican aspirations and the role of the IRA diminished significantly. Sinn Féin grew from the fourth largest party in Northern Ireland in 1998 to the second largest by 2005.

Bush, as Clancy observes, redressed the balance in terms of US engagement with the parties in Northern Ireland. Bush saw significance in the special envoy role and retained it, simply moving it to the State Department where they worked under Secretaries Colin Powell and Condoleezza Rice. Attitudes towards the participants in the Northern Ireland conflict would also change. Where Clinton had reached out to republicans to engage them in the process, Bush punished them for dragging their heels over the implementation of the key aspects of the Good Friday Agreement.

9/11, Colombia, and the War on Terror

Writing in the *Irish Times* shortly after Bush's election, Steve King noted that the December 2000 visit by Clinton to Northern Ireland might mark the end of US interest in Northern Ireland. King argued that Bush's weak grasp of foreign policy would place him in the hands of his Atlanticist National Security Council advisers and that 'we can expect every effort to be made to rebuild the so-called special relationship between the US and the UK'.[7] Of course, examining the manner in which consecutive administrations had handled Northern Ireland, it was entirely predictable that a Republican President would revert back to a position on Northern Ireland that was more favourable to the British government. Bush's more conservative approach was perhaps inevitable even before the events of 11 September 2001, but the new US approach towards the Northern Ireland peace process was not necessarily to the detriment of the peace process.

The terror attacks that became known as 9/11 changed global understanding of terrorism and political violence. Only one month before

7   *IT*, 7/12/2000.

the attacks, three IRA volunteers were arrested at Bogota International Airport. Niall Connolly, James Monaghan, and Martin McCauley were charged with training Colombian FARC rebels and travelling on false passports. Found guilty only on the first charge, the three men fled Colombia whilst the prosecution appealed the second charge. By the time the appeal court overturned the second verdict in December 2004 and sentenced each man to seventeen years' imprisonment, they had already fled to Ireland. Both Monaghan and McCauley had close ties with the IRA, Monaghan having developed mortars for the IRA in the 1970s and McCauley regarded as a leading figure in the IRA's engineering department. Connolly, however, had ties to Sinn Féin as the party representative in Havana and was reported to have been organising a meeting between Gerry Adams and Fidel Castro. One political source commented to the *Observer* that the Colombian authorities had been tipped off by British sources eager to prove to Unionists that they were very much on top of continuing IRA activity. Also, by dealing Sinn Féin a slight blow, they would cause embarrassment but not something that would prove fatal to the peace process.[8]

The discovery of a Sinn Féin link in Havana was potentially troublesome for Sinn Féin's Irish-American lobby. Richard Haass, then the State Department's director of policy planning and President Bush's envoy on Northern Ireland, spoke directly to Sinn Féin to convey the concern of the White House at these links. Haass told Adams that 'this should not have happened, that is should cease immediately and that it should never happen again'.[9] Washington was furious at tangible links between Adams and Cuba, a nation that was still on very unfriendly terms with the United States at that time, as well as between Sinn Féin and FARC, a group on the State Department's list of foreign terrorist organisations. The latter in particular was highly inconsistent with the image of Adams as a partner for peace, an image he had carefully cultivated over a number of years. Pointedly, the *New York Times* carried a report of Haass's meeting with Adams in its 11 September 2001 edition.[10] Bill Flynn, a strong supporter of Adams in the past, made his position clear at the time: the IRA had to decommission, and the sooner the better.[11] Sinn Féin had lost the support of some of

[8]   *Observer*, 18/8/2001.
[9]   *NYT*, 19/11/2001.
[10] *NYT*, 11/9/2001.
[11] Moloney, *A Secret History of the IRA*, pp. 489–490.

its power brokers in the United States and would have to negotiate on less-favourable terms.

Political figures from Northern Ireland continued to visit Washington throughout the Bush years, and all party leaders were invited to attend the White House's St Patrick's Day events in 2002. Northern Ireland Secretary John Reid had travelled to Washington in February of that year to ask the Bush administration to help find a new way to engage Northern Irish protestants. Reid met with Haass, Colin Powell, and FBI director Robert Mueller.[12] There were foreseeable theatrics on St Patrick's Day when DUP leader Ian Paisley refused to share a platform with Gerry Adams while UUP leader David Trimble, though a willing participant, referred to the Republic of Ireland as a 'pathetic sectarian state'. For Richard Haass, this was 'exactly the sort of language that ought to be avoided'.[13] Trimble and SDLP leader Mark Durkan, the First and Deputy First Ministers, later mingled with guests at the American Ireland Fund annual dinner, at which Irish Taoiseach Bertie Ahern was honoured for his role in the peace process.[14]

The parties were forced to deal with a cut in US contributions to the International Fund for Ireland in 2003. President Clinton had increased the annual payment from its previous average of $19.6 million to $25 million in 2000, but the Bush administration sought to cut it by over half to only $8.5 million. The British and Irish governments would not find an opportunity to negotiate with Bush over the cuts, coming as they did shortly before the US invasion of Iraq. Taoiseach Bertie Ahern visited Bush in 2003, defying anti-war protestors in Ireland who called for him to cancel. Ahern insisted that it would have been an insult to do so. The annual White House St Patrick's Day reception was scheduled four days early because of an anticipated US-led attack on Iraq the following week. The US invasion of Iraq duly occurred on 20 March.[15]

Shortly after the invasion, Bush travelled to England where he met Prime Minister Tony Blair and the two discussed peace efforts in both

12   *IT*, 13/2/2002.
13   *IT*, 12/3/2002 and 14/3/2002.
14   *IT*, 14/3/2002. The American Ireland Fund, part of the Worldwide Ireland Funds, continues to contribute to projects in Ireland, raising well over $600 million for its current focus areas of education, supporting a shared future in Northern Ireland, promoting Irish Culture and Heritage, assisting the elderly 'forgotten Irish', assisting disadvantaged youth, and promoting philanthropy. For further details, see https://irelandfunds.org/about-us/.
15   *IT*, 12/3/2003.

Northern Ireland and the Middle East, as well as the war in Iraq.[16] The two then met with Taoiseach Bertie Ahern at Hillsborough Castle, the site of the signing of the 1985 Anglo-Irish Agreement, in an attempt to find common ground on the blueprint for the re-establishment of the Northern Ireland Assembly.[17] The relative lack of success in their conversations over Northern Ireland during this meeting will undoubtedly pale into historical insignificance alongside the decisions that were made regarding Iraq, but progress on the former was forthcoming the following year.

Richard Haass stepped down from the role of envoy in 2003 and was replaced by Mitchell Reiss. Right up to his final days in the role, Haass continued to negotiate with Gerry Adams and Martin McGuinness to try and secure a firm commitment from the IRA on the complete cessation of their activities.[18] Reiss continued this work, notably during 2004 talks at Leeds Castle, and developed a reputation for pushing Sinn Féin hard on key issues.[19] The talks at Leeds Castle made progress on military issues, particularly the touchy subject of decommissioning, but political issues, notably the accountability of ministers, remained outstanding.[20]

A key result from the talks was a direct call for IRA decommissioning from Sinn Féin, something approaching the firm commitment that Richard Haass had sought from Adams and McGuinness. Journalist Jack Holland commented that 'the message for Sinn Féin was very clear: it had to distance itself from terrorism or risk losing its support in the United States'. Adams claimed to have spoken to the IRA and suggested to the group that 'if it could make a groundbreaking move on the arms issue, that this could save the peace process from collapse and transform the situation'.[21] Why this had not been obvious after the United States denied Adams fundraising on an earlier visit was unclear. This was, however, a skilful move from Adams, a shrewd political operator throughout his career, refocusing attention on what had become an inevitable event. The Provisional IRA could not return to violence, now largely the purview of the so-called dissident republican groups, without completely

[16]   *NYT*, 5/4/2003.

[17]   *NYT*, 9/4/2003.

[18]   *NYT*, 12/4/2003; *IT*, 11/12/2003.

[19]   Guelke, A., 'The United States and the Peace Process', in Barton, B. and Roche, P.J. (eds), *The Northern Ireland Question: The Peace Process and the Belfast Agreement* (Basingstoke: Palgrave Macmillan, 2009), pp. 222–237, at p. 234.

[20]   BBC News, 'NI Talks End without a Deal', 18/9/2004, available at http://news.bbc.co.uk/2/hi/uk_news/northern_ireland/3667642.stm.

[21]   *NYT*, 23/10/2001.

undermining Sinn Féin, which had become the largest nationalist party in 2001. Ted Kennedy joined the calls for decommissioning, commenting, 'I hope the IRA will begin the actual decommissioning of weapons immediately', and Bill Flynn added his voice to the growing support for the immediate destruction of the IRA's arsenal.[22]

Kennedy's support for reconciliation in Ireland was steadfast during this period, and he made a significant gesture by refusing to meet Gerry Adams following the 2005 murder of Robert McCartney in Belfast. McCartney had been the victim of what appeared to have been a bar fight that escalated into a deliberate and brutal murder. A crowd of republicans, having returned from a Bloody Sunday commemoration in Derry, visited Magennis's Bar in the city centre where an argument broke out. Robert McCartney and his companion were attacked, before McCartney was dragged into the street and stabbed repeatedly. It was reported that members of Sinn Féin had been present and the subsequent suspensions of twelve party members and the expulsions of three IRA members have been tied to the murder.[23] None of the estimated seventy potential witnesses came forward to give evidence, however.[24]

Adams recalled, 'it became a cause célèbre for the British and for others, and Teddy Kennedy and other people in the White House, or other people in government, had met with the families. So when it came to my going there at some point, Teddy had made it clear that until this issue was resolved we wouldn't be meeting'.[25] Adams claimed 'the IRA were not involved. Individual Republicans, perhaps even IRA volunteers, may have been involved, but any suggestion that the IRA either conspired as an organization or as a unit or as a group, why they killed this man, why they needed to cover up his killing, was just wrong'. The likelihood of Adams not knowing, or at least not being able to find out, was clearly slim. Few, including Ted Kennedy, were convinced.

This murder took place shortly after thieves stole an estimated £26.5 million from the Northern Bank in central Belfast. It was believed that the IRA had, again, been responsible.[26] Mitchell Reiss stated that 'it's time for the IRA to go out of business' and the State Department

[22] Ibid.
[23] *Irish News*, 27/1/2006.
[24] *Guardian*, 9/7/2008.
[25] Edward M. Kennedy Institute, Oral History, 'Interview with Gerry Adams', available at https://www.emkinstitute.org/resources/gerry-adams.
[26] *Belfast Telegraph*, 19/12/2014.

banned Sinn Féin from fundraising in the United States.[27] To be sure
that Sinn Féin got the message, the White House cancelled the annual
St Patrick's Day invitations to the leaders of Northern Ireland's political
parties, instead inviting Robert McCartney's sisters Gemma, Donna,
Paula, Claire, and Catherine.[28] They met with President Bush and
Senator Ted Kennedy, whilst Adams travelled to Cincinnati. Adams
later spoke at the Council on Foreign Relations, and commented that he
believed Senator Kennedy to have 'been badly advised'. He was faced
with a deluge of criticism from US representatives who had previously
been strong advocates for Sinn Féin and the party's right to visit and
fundraise in the United States. Richard Neal, Peter King, and Jim Walsh
all noted their concern at IRA activity, King arguing that 'for the peace
process to go forward and for Sinn Féin to have the input that it deserves,
it is time for the IRA to stand down. There is no constructive purpose
being served at this time by the continued existence of the IRA'.[29]

This had also been Adams's message in Cincinnati, where he insisted
that 'we in Sinn Féin want to see the IRA ceasing to be'.[30] The loss of
US fundraising privileges might have been a blow but the loss of the
party's place at the top table in the United States hit deeper. Shunning
Adams on this occasion was a point of pride for Kennedy, to the extent
that it appeared on his personal website in a section that claimed his
'consistently tough message, coupled with a decision not to see Gerry
Adams on St. Patrick's Day in 2005, contributed to the decision of the
IRA to disarm in September of 2005'.[31]

On 28 July, the IRA ordered its volunteers to dump arms, emphasising:
'all Volunteers have been instructed to assist the development of purely
political and democratic programmes through exclusively peaceful
means. Volunteers must not engage in any other activities whatsoever'.[32]
It followed this up by completely dismantling its weaponry on
26 September 2005, releasing a statement: 'The leadership of Óglaigh na
hEireann announced on 28 July that we had authorised our representative

---

[27] *NYT*, 10/3/2005.
[28] *NYT*, 7/3/2005.
[29] *NYT*, 15/3/2005.
[30] *NYT*, 14/3/2005.
[31] Ted Kennedy, 'Providing a Leading Voice for Human Rights and Democracy
around the Globe', available at https://web.archive.org/web/20150908015201/
http://tedkennedy.org/service/item/foreign_policy/.
[32] Text of IRA statement on the ending of the armed campaign, 28/7/2005,
available at https://cain.ulster.ac.uk/othelem/organ/ira/ira280705.htm.

to engage with the IICD to complete the process to verifiably put arms beyond use. The IRA leadership can now confirm that the process of putting our arms verifiably beyond use has been completed'.[33] This effectively marked the end of the Provisional Irish Republican Army, at least in so far as the international community was concerned.

The State Department decided not to lift the fundraising ban in time for Martin McGuinness's visit to the United States in October, and the continuation of the ban prompted Gerry Adams to cancel his trip the following month completely. Adams had been scheduled to receive the William J. Flynn Initiative for Peace award at the National Committee for American Foreign Policy dinner. A $500-a-plate Friends of Sinn Féin dinner in New York was also cancelled. Adams commented, 'I am personally disappointed in the position that Mitchell Reiss has adopted on this'.[34] He was, however, able to visit Toronto, where no fundraising restrictions were in place. Adams remained critical of Reiss into the New Year, commenting, 'I don't have high regards for Mitchell Reiss's input into this process … if it is he who is advising the president, it's very very bad advice'. Reiss responded, 'we try very hard to be an honest broker … we try to keep our eye on the main objective here—which is moving the peace process forward and keeping the focus on the people of Northern Ireland'.[35]

Reiss's role throughout this episode was clearly not to pander to Irish republicans. Holding a firm line, his actions were, in retrospect, absolutely essential for the development of the peace process. Adams may not have enjoyed suddenly finding himself on the outside of events but the significant steps that were taken by Sinn Féin over the course of 2006 spoke to an organisation with a newly found motivation to expedite the peace process. These steps included the full endorsement of the Police Service of Northern Ireland in 2007, part of the St Andrews Agreement, which helped restore the Northern Ireland Assembly. It was clear that Reiss's strategy had panned out, and the Irish republicans had begun the process of fully committing to the institutions of post-conflict

[33]   Text of IRA Statement on putting arms beyond use, 26/9/2005, available at https://cain.ulster.ac.uk/othelem/organ/ira/ira260905.htm. The IICD is the Independent International Commission on Decommissioning. Violence associated with the PIRA continued well into the 2010s, notably the 2015 murders of Gerard Davison and Kevin McGuigan.
[34]   *IT*, 2/11/2005 and 8/11/2005.
[35]   BBC News, 'Adams Criticises Bush's NI envoy', 16/3/2006, available at http://news.bbc.co.uk/2/hi/uk_news/northern_ireland/4813758.stm.

Northern Ireland. These steps led to the May 2007 restoration of power to the Northern Ireland Assembly. Two months previously, the Stormont election had left the DUP and Sinn Féin as the two largest parties, with thirty-six and twenty-eight seats, respectively. The convention of the largest party nominating the First Minister, and the second largest party nominating the Deputy First Minister, left Ian Paisley and Martin McGuiness heading up the Northern Ireland Assembly. Historian Brian Feeney argued that 'the word historic has to be used … it was the only way it was ever going to work. The two leaders of the two traditions had to do the deal'.[36] It was significant that both John Hume and David Trimble had stepped down from office in 2005, and their parties suffered losses in the 2007 election. Paisley stepped into the role of First Minister at the age of eighty-one, with the union safe, an IRA ceasefire, and a Sinn Féin endorsement of the Police Service of Northern Ireland in his pocket, and could claim his place in the resolution of the Northern Ireland conflict. It was, of course, a conflict he had done so much to stoke at myriad junctures.

In early January 2007, it was announced that Reiss would end his tenure and was to be replaced by Under Secretary of State for Democracy and Global Affairs, Dr Paula Dobriansky, who began her role on 15 February. Reiss had played a pivotal role at a crucial stage of the peace process and his importance was clear from comments made after his departure by figures in the Irish government, notably those from Minister for Foreign Affairs Dermot Ahern:

> The ongoing support of the US Administration for the work of the two Governments has been crucial to our efforts since this process began. Mitchell has worked side by side with us since his appointment and in particular as our work with the parties intensified over the last year. We have greatly appreciated his support and valued his counsel.[37]

In an interview with BBC reporter John Ware, Reiss recalled the complicated relationships that existed between Irish republicans and the British government, as well as those within the British government

---

[36] *NYT*, 27/3/2007.
[37] Minister Ahern Pays Tribute to Ambassador Mitchell Reiss, US Special Envoy on Northern Ireland, Department of Foreign Affairs and Trade Press Release, 24/1/2007, available at https://web.archive.org/web/20070204091028/www.dfa.ie/home/index.aspx?id=27353.

itself. He noted 'some pretty violent' disagreements he had endured with the British government over how hard to push Sinn Féin on key issues, arguing that Sinn Féin had become too used to the benevolence of Downing Street.[38] Here, Reiss neatly summarised the strategy of the Bush administration vis-à-vis Northern Ireland: Irish republicans, whom many in Unionist circles felt had enjoyed too much support from both the United States and London, were now going to be expected to follow quid pro quo principles.

After Dobriansky arrived in the post, questions were raised as to the continued focus of the Bush administration on Northern Ireland. She arrived late in Bush's second term in office and was to continue in her role of Under Secretary for Democracy and Global Affairs. She was described in the *Irish Times* as 'a prominent neo-conservative intellectual' and her support for the Iraq war was also noted.[39] Sinn Féin was more positive about the appointment, Martin McGuinness commenting a few months later: 'the energy and drive that Paula has brought to her position is quite exciting and very convincing … she's really determined to do something'.[40] In the event, Dobriansky served until the appointment of Declan Kelly by Secretary of State Hillary Clinton in 2009. Kelly then served for two years as an economic envoy, working alongside organisations such as Invest NI and the Northern Ireland Chamber of Commerce.[41] After he resigned, the role was left vacant for three years until President Obama appointed Gary Hart to the role.

Upon Kelly's resignation on 11 May 2011, Secretary Clinton remarked that he had been appointed to 'use his considerable talents and entrepreneurial drive to help Northern Ireland grow and sustain the benefits of peace. He found eager and able partners not only there, but also throughout the region. This collective effort has opened up new and exciting opportunities for the people of Northern Ireland to share a more prosperous future'.[42] One important issue that Kelly had navigated

---

[38]   BBC News, 'The Price of Peace', 2/3/2008, available at http://news.bbc. co.uk/2/hi/uk_news/northern_ireland/7273611.stm.
[39]   *IT*, 20/1/2007.
[40]   *IT*, 3/7/2007.
[41]   BBC News, 'How Declan Kelly Helped Bring US Investment to NI', 11/5/2011, available at www.bbc.com/news/uk-northern-ireland-13359794.
[42]   Press Statement, Hillary Rodham Clinton, Washington, DC, 'Resignation of Economic Envoy for Northern Ireland Declan Kelly', US Department of State, available at https://2009-2017.state.gov/secretary/20092013clinton/rm/2011/05/162984.htm.

was a 2010 dispute over the devolution of policing and criminal justice powers to Belfast, where Unionist intransigence had stalled matters. Kelly reached out to former President Bush to intervene and Bush, along with Secretary Clinton, contacted Ulster Unionist leader Reg Empey. Bush's role in the matter was considered by one source quoted in the *Guardian* newspaper as 'the most active thing George W. Bush has done in his post-presidency period'. Another added, 'it is a general sign of how concerned people are in the US about what David Cameron is up to'.[43] There was a general sense of unease at British Prime Minister David Cameron's lack of fortitude in supporting the deal—so much so that the Congressional Friends of Ireland felt compelled to write to Downing Street and warn the Prime Minister about the implications of its failure.[44]

The USA and Northern Ireland after 2008

After losing control of Congress in 2006, the Republican Party prepared for the 2008 Presidential election with a relatively straightforward primary campaign. Former Massachusetts Governor Mitt Romney withdrew from the race in early 2008, leaving Arizona Senator John McCain as the presumed nominee. The Democratic race would be far more competitive, with Senator Hillary Clinton offering a strong challenge to eventual nominee Senator Barack Obama. Clinton retained an interest in Irish issues, and was involved in the ongoing issue of the undocumented Irish citizens who were living in the United States, the topic of a conversation between Taoiseach Bertie Ahern and President Bush on St Patrick's Day 2008.[45]

Northern Ireland featured as an issue throughout the primary campaigns. Connecticut Senator Christopher Dodd claimed that he was 'ready to be President' because he had 'helped to end wars in Central America and bring peace to Northern Ireland'.[46] Clinton's involvement in the peace process was a strong theme of her campaign, but it brought intense scrutiny on the role she performed as First Lady. During campaigning and in support of her credentials as a candidate who understood the complicated field of US foreign relations, Hillary

[43]   *Guardian*, 9/3/2010.
[44]   *Guardian*, 7/3/2010.
[45]   *IT*, 8/12/2007 and 15/3/2008.
[46]   Transcript of the Fourth Democratic Debate, *NYT*, 24/7/2007.

Clinton made much of her experience with Northern Ireland. Within the wider context of a speech at Rutgers University on the marginalisation of women, Clinton emphasised that with the creation of a power-sharing government there was evidence that seemingly intractable social problems could be resolved.[47]

As the campaign progressed, Clinton met with Secretary of State for Northern Ireland Shaun Woodward. No meeting took place with Senator Obama, despite his position as the chair of the Senate Foreign Relations Subcommittee on European Affairs. The Clinton campaign questioned Obama's commitment to Northern Ireland, asking for an explanation as to 'what Senator Obama did to advance peace in Northern Ireland'.[48] It was clear that Obama recognised that he could not compete with Senator Clinton on this issue, and perhaps had no interest in even trying, but his campaign did try to pick holes in Clinton's credentials as an important diplomatic partner to the Northern Ireland peace process.

These credentials became a matter of interest and the *New York Times* published an assessment of Hillary Clinton's duties as the First Lady. This report emphasised a meeting she hosted between Protestant and Catholic women in Northern Ireland, noting that 'it gave everybody a safe place to come together and start talking about what they had in common'.[49] Clinton received support from Martin McGuinness, who wrote in the *Irish Voice* citing the 'important part' that she had played, and emphasising her 'huge contribution towards lifting the esteem of women in our society'.[50] Clinton herself recalled her early interactions with Ian Paisley, citing them as evidence of her ability to learn. She noted that Paisley refused to shake her hand when they first met 'because I didn't understand how difficult the problems were that he faced'.[51] This may have been somewhat generous to Paisley.

Clinton continued to cite her experience in Northern Ireland in the final debates for the Democratic nomination once the field had narrowed to two. Clinton and Obama met for a debate in Cleveland, Ohio. Clinton

[47]   *NYT*, 10/4/2007 and 20/4/2007.
[48]   Press Release, Statement from Representatives Neal, McCarthy, and Crowley calling on Senator Obama to Address Northern Ireland, 17/3/2008, available at www.presidency.ucsb.edu/ws/?pid=96553.
[49]   *NYT*, 26/12/2007.
[50]   Cited in Press Release, 'Hillary Clinton: A Strong Partner for Northern Ireland', 15/3/2008, available at https://www.presidency.ucsb.edu/documents/press-release-hillary-clinton-strong-partner-for-northern-ireland.
[51]   *NYT*, 5/1/2008.

again pointed to her 'experience in foreign policy ... helping to support the peace process in Northern Ireland' which she argued stood in contrast to Obama, whom she considered lacked the requisite experience to serve as President.[52] Obama, for his part, alleged that Clinton merely 'had tea with' world leaders in her role as First Lady.[53]

These were the sorts of accusations from the Obama campaign that Clinton had to fend off throughout the campaign process. In March 2008, Greg Craig, a former adviser to Ted Kennedy and later Counsel to President Obama, wrote:

> It is a gross overstatement of the facts for her to claim even partial credit for bringing peace to Northern Ireland. She did travel to Northern Ireland, it is true. First Ladies often travel to places that are a focus of U.S. foreign policy. But at no time did she play any role in the critical negotiations that ultimately produced the peace. As the Associated Press recently reported, '[S]he was not directly involved in negotiating the Good Friday peace accord'. With regard to her main claim that she helped bring women together, she did participate in a meeting with women, but, according to those who know best, she did not play a pivotal role. The person in charge of the negotiations, former Senator George Mitchell, said that '[The First Lady] was one of many people who participated in encouraging women to get involved, not the only one'.

Craig continued to argue that Senator Clinton's claims had surprised many in Northern Ireland:

> News of Senator Clinton's claims has raised eyebrows across the ocean. Her reference to an important meeting at the Belfast town hall was debunked. Her only appearance at the Belfast City Hall was to see Christmas lights turned on. She also attended a 50-minute meeting which, according to the Belfast *Daily Telegraph*'s report at the time, '[was] a little bit stilted, a little prepared at times'. Brian Feeney, an Irish author and former politician, sums it up: 'The road to peace was carefully documented, and she wasn't on it'.[54]

[52]   Transcript in *NYT*, 26/2/2008.
[53]   *NYT*, 16/3/2015.
[54]   Craig, G., 'Senator Clinton's Claims of Foreign Policy Experience Are Exaggerated', *Real Clear Politics*, 11/3/2008, available at www.realclearpolitics. com/articles/2008/03/clintons_exaggerated_experienc.html.

Former UUP leader David Trimble commented that, 'I don't know there was much she did apart from accompanying Bill going around … being a cheerleader for something is slightly different from being a principal player'.[55] In response, State Department assistant secretary Jamie Rubin, when questioned by MSNBC journalist Andrea Mitchell, commented:

> David Trimble is a crankpot and what he said about her was demeaning. He said, 'Oh well, maybe she accompanied her husband on a couple of trips'. As a woman, Andrea, I would think you would recognise when somebody is trying to demean the activities of a woman. She was an important First Lady in foreign policy. I know. I was in that administration and we understood she was not serving tea and cookies, she played a significant role.[56]

Trimble retorted that 'I usually regard it when somebody resorts simply to vulgar abuse that's a sign that they know they've a weak argument', whilst the Clinton campaign attempted to distance itself from Rubin's remarks.[57] Clinton did receive support from Taoiseach Bertie Ahern, who described her as having been 'hugely helpful' in the peace process, emphasising that in her role as the First Lady she was by default an extension of any discussions that were ongoing at the time.[58] Representative Peter King, a Republican, also argued that Senator Clinton was 'actively involved … she was certainly more than just someone along for the ride'.[59] Senator Clinton withdrew from the race in June and Obama picked Senator Joseph Biden as his vice-Presidential candidate for the 2008 election. Biden had a long track record of support for Irish issues and a May 2013 article by Megan Smolenyak in *Irish America* magazine explored the roots of 'Joey from Scranton'.[60] Hillary Clinton would be one of President Obama's first appointees, taking on the role of Secretary of State.

There was also interest in Northern Ireland from the Republican party during their campaign. Nominee Senator John McCain, who

[55] *Daily Telegraph*, 8/3/2008.
[56] *Daily Telegraph*, 27/3/2008.
[57] *Daily Telegraph*, 28/3/2008.
[58] *NYT*, 22/3/2008.
[59] *Daily Telegraph*, 8/3/2008.
[60] *Irish America*, April/May 2013.

had been present to welcome the McCartney sisters to Washington in 2005, spoke to the Irish-American Presidential Forum in Scranton, Pennsylvania on 22 September. He noted that 'you are very kind to invite someone with a name like McCain, a Scots-Irish descendent whose family came to the New World some generations ago. I hope you won't hold it against us—I do try to get back to the island as often as possible'. McCain argued that his agenda would include increasing trade between the United States and Ireland. He also spoke of the 'inspirational' Northern Irish peace process: 'Many of those who saw decades of fighting in that proud and beautiful land thought that the day might never come when talking took the place of tanks, and ballots the place of bullets. But that day has dawned in Northern Ireland and we are all—Irish and Americans alike—better off for it'. He committed to retaining the Special Envoy, noting that 'I know Senator Obama has questioned whether that appointment is needed. I would urge him to reconsider'.[61] The issue made it to the Republican Party platform for the election but was pointedly absent from the Democratic platform.[62]

Obama had little interest in Ireland, though he would later visit Ireland and learn of his ancestors from Moneygall in County Offaly. He was, however, an astute political operator and recognised the importance of the Irish Ambassadorship to the Irish and Irish-American communities. In this role he appointed one of his most prominent supporters, the founder of the Ireland Funds, Dan Rooney. In 2001, Rooney had been present at the White House St Patrick's Day reception that hosted DUP leader Ian Paisley. This was Paisley's first visit to the White House and represented an important step in the engagement of Ulster Unionist politicians, often absent at events in the United States, in the peace process. Eight years on, Rooney celebrated the Pittsburgh Steelers' victory in Super Bowl XLIII with his appointment to Dublin and the Deerfield Residence mansion in Phoenix Park. Rooney had been absent during Obama's inauguration in January

[61] John McCain, Remarks at the Irish-American Presidential Forum, Scranton, PA, 22/9/2008, the American Presidency Project, available at https://www.presidency.ucsb.edu/documents/remarks-the-irish-american-presidential-forum-scranton-pennsylvania.
[62] See 2008 Republican Party Platform, 1/9/2008, available at https://www.presidency.ucsb.edu/documents/2008-republican-party-platform; and Democratic Party Platform, 25/8/2008 available at https://www.presidency.ucsb.edu/documents/2008-democratic-party-platform.

due to preparations for the Super Bowl, but the President used the occasion of his first St Patrick's Day in office to appoint Rooney to the role, describing him as 'an unwavering supporter of Irish peace, culture and education'.[63]

Writing in the *Irish Times*, Deaglan de Breadun described the role that Rooney played for Obama during the election. He considered that Rooney's invitation to Obama to come to Pittsburgh, where he was presented with a Steelers jersey, had helped him both contend the Democratic primary, although Clinton still won, as well as secure the state in the Presidential election. De Breadun noted that Rooney was in many aspects quite a conservative Catholic, but also noted his 'much-praised record of hiring African-Americans', which influenced the NFL's so-called 'Rooney Rule', which dictates that all teams must consider minority candidates for coaching and football operations jobs.[64]

Dennis Staunton added that the Ambassadorships in 'London, Paris and Dublin ... have long been reserved for fundraisers and other influential supporters'.[65] These were certainly criteria that fit Rooney. The American Ireland Fund, as it became in 1987, now has chapters in twelve US cities and twelve countries worldwide. It reports having raised over $500 million which has gone to over 3,000 'outstanding organizations'.[66] The 2015 annual gala raised $4.3 million alone.[67] Rooney reflected in his memoirs, with a sense of pride, 'it has accomplished much and has made a real difference'. Of particular importance to the success of the Fund, in Rooney's eyes, has been the ability to 'keep away from banners and flags and politics'.[68] Rooney noted that 'we gave a little to a lot of organisations, I think sixty percent went to peace organisations ... we felt getting kids involved in normal things was particularly important'.[69]

Rooney stepped down as Ambassador in 2012, his last day in office being 14 December, and was replaced by chargé d'affaires John Hennessey-Niland.[70] The fact that no replacement was announced for two years spoke to the level of interest in Northern Ireland from within

63   *NYT*, 17/3/2009.
64   *IT*, 28/1/2009.
65   *IT*, 30/5/2009.
66   The Ireland Funds, 'About Us', https://irelandfunds.org/about-us/.
67   *IT*, 9/5/2015.
68   Rooney, *My 75 Years*, p. 180.
69   Dan Rooney, interview with author, 21/10/2013.
70   *IT*, 14/12/2012.

the administration. Clinton stepped down as Secretary of State soon after, and despite her replacement, John Kerry, also having maintained some interest in Irish issues over his career, it was not until pressure from within Irish America, notably from the American Ireland Fund itself, to replace Rooney developed that former Federal Prosecutor Kevin O'Malley, a long-time supporter of President Obama, was confirmed in an otherwise straightforward vote in September 2014.[71] O'Malley, formerly a dual citizen, returned his Irish citizenship to serve as US Ambassador to Ireland.

Hillary Clinton had addressed the Northern Ireland Assembly in October 2009, pleading those present to continue their investment in the Northern Ireland peace process. Her speech was hailed by Martin McGuinness, the then Deputy First Minister, who observed that 'clearly, Secretary Clinton is intellectually, emotionally and politically engaged in the process'.[72] Nonetheless, she chose not to draw on her Northern Ireland credentials for her second campaign for the Presidency in 2016. Instead, she devoted a section of her website to her 'vision for advancing equity and opportunity for Irish Americans and immigrants of Irish descent'.[73] Northern Ireland was, by now, an issue of marginal interest even for those who had played a role in its peace process.

[71] *IT*, 23/9/2014.

[72] *NYT*, 12/10/2009.

[73] Hillary Clinton 'Growing Together', available at https://web.archive.org/web/20160318035524/https://www.hillaryclinton.com/briefing/factsheets/2016/03/05/growing-together-advancing-equity-opportunity-irish-americans-irish-descent/.

Conclusion

On 25 August 2009, Senator Ted Kennedy passed away after fighting a brain tumour for over a year. Kennedy had made his final visit to Ireland in May 2007 to mark the restoration of Stormont, the culmination of forty-five years of engagement with Irish issues.[1] His long-standing efforts against violence in Northern Ireland were recognised by the United Kingdom in March 2009 when Kennedy was awarded an honorary knighthood for his contribution to US–UK relations, as recommended by Prime Minister Gordon Brown. Brown announced the honour during a speech to Congress, in which he stated that 'Northern Ireland is today at peace, more Americans have health care, more children around the world are going to school, and for all those things we owe a great debt to the life and courage of Senator Edward Kennedy'.[2]

For many who served in the British government during the late twentieth century, Edward Kennedy personified what they perceived to be the unhelpful role of US figures in the Northern Ireland conflict. The United States, under President Nixon, had defined the conflict as a matter internal to the United Kingdom, a decision that would undoubtedly have been welcomed by those in London but one that met with resistance from figures in Congress. Kennedy was one of the earliest and most prominent figures to speak out against Britain's Northern Irish policies. Despite the considerable work he did later in his career to undermine American support networks for Irish republicans, work that most would consider to have been beneficial to British interests in Northern Ireland, he was unable to change the minds of many British

---

[1]   *Irish Echo*, 2–8/9/2009.
[2]   *London Evening Standard*, 4/3/2009.

politicians. Lord Tebbit, former Chairman of the Conservative Party, was highly critical of the decision to award Kennedy an honorary knighthood:

> Edward Kennedy may never have said outwardly he supported the IRA, but he certainly leaned towards extreme republicanism. He was certainly no friend of the UK. This honour is wholly inappropriate on the basis of the sleaze attached to him after the crash at Chappaquiddick, let alone his support for nationalism in Northern Ireland. It cheapens the whole honours system.[3]

Conservative elements within the British press were also critical of the decision. A blogger in the *Daily Telegraph* argued: 'I'm sure Kennedy was essentially a good man and a servant of his own country, but he was certainly no friend of ours'.[4] In the *Daily Mail*, it was maintained that the Kennedy 'family has nursed a deep resentment against the country that they blame for forcing them out of County Wexford … it is no exaggeration to say that Ted Kennedy did his damnedest to poison US–UK relations over Ulster during the long decades in which he has castigated successive UK governments'.[5]

Reporting Kennedy's passing, news reports were rather less critical: the front cover of the *Belfast Telegraph* reading 'Farewell to a peacemaker'[6]; the *Guardian* mentioned the Chappaquiddick incident twice but spoke little of his involvement in Northern Ireland; the *Daily Telegraph* also neglected to stray far from the facts of his political life; whilst the *Independent* offered a longer biography.[7] Gerry Adams reflected on his relationship with Ted Kennedy, in an interview for the EMK Institute:

> As Sinn Féin became more successful here, then the Irish government, some Irish governments, took a less benign view … In many ways, it was useful to get Teddy Kennedy to talk to

---

[3]   *Daily Mail*, 4/3/2009.
[4]   West, E., 'IRA Sympathiser Ted Kennedy Was No Friend of Britain', *Daily Telegraph* blogs, 26/8/2009, available at https://web.archive.org/web/20121028041411/http://blogs.telegraph.co.uk/news/edwest/100007596/ira-sympathiser-ted-kennedy-was-no-friend-of-britain/.
[5]   *Daily Mail*, 5/3/2009.
[6]   *Belfast Telegraph*, 27/8/2009.
[7]   *Guardian*, 26/8/2009; *Daily Telegraph*, 26/8/2009; *Independent*, 26/8/2009.

Irish government officials … at different times when there was turbulence here with the government in Dublin not pressing ahead, he was good … And it isn't always the big event or the big act … It's more the quiet briefings, keeping people up to date, the right signal being sent, having friends in court who when somebody is talking nonsense, they can very gently say, no, we're not; that's not the way. That's the role that Teddy Kennedy played for all of that period, from when I first met him in '94, right up until his death.[8]

Jonathan Powell, who did not encounter Kennedy with much regularity during his time in the Embassy in the 1990s, said of Kennedy:

I think there's a lot of misunderstanding. People say, oh Ted Kennedy, he was terrible, he was on the side of the IRA. The level of misunderstanding in America about Ireland is huge but the level of misunderstanding in Britain about Irish America is also huge … They were not paying a lot of attention. So people would talk about Ted Kennedy supporting the IRA, actually he was perhaps the driving force behind the Four Horsemen, along with Tip O'Neill. I think that what they did in switching position to one against violence really had a big impact on Irish America and it shifted the debate away from the extremes to a more moderate approach. I think what they did was really important. Tip O'Neill was slightly before my time. Tom Foley carried on that sort of line, although he was even more moderate than Ted Kennedy, he was really quite friendly, his staff were quite helpful and that was important. The more radical Congressmen from our point of view, like Bruce Morrison and later Peter King, there were others too, were pretty busy attacking us but also willing to talk and I built relationships with them which continue. I actually think it's clear that Irish-American influence on the conflict, particularly in the later years, was net positive … I think people in Britain misunderstand the positive aspect of Irish-America, after they'd turned against violence.[9]

Former Ambassador Peter Jay considered:

[8] Edward M. Kennedy Institute, Oral History, 'Interview with Gerry Adams', available at https://www.emkinstitute.org/resources/gerry-adams.
[9] Jonathan Powell, interview with author, 16/1/2013.

Kennedy was in a different class, in my opinion. He was in the same class as Jack Lynch and Hume and probably Garret FitzGerald. He became truly statesman-like, he was really very interested [in Irish affairs]. I had lunch with him, on a tray across his desk in his Senate office and he was really anxious to understand ... In my opinion, he wanted to make it work and in a way that prefigured Clinton's role in the 1990s, tried to use his influence, which was very considerable, to guide things in that sort of direction. I think he was helpful to what both Sean Donlon and I were trying to achieve. Yes, there were occasional frictions and difficulties and so on, but I think there was a good working collaboration which was in the long run helpful to the gradual reduction of tensions. It had ups and downs and took another twenty years to lead to what hopefully is—even now you could not be quite sure—a permanent end to old style violence, although there's still the occasional violent incident and the residual terrorists are so-minded. I have a lot of time for Ted Kennedy and I had quite a lot of time for Moynihan ... Tip O'Neill and Governor Carey were slightly further removed, they were slightly deeper in the great standard American politics, or Irish-American politics which is very distantly related to anything happening in Ireland.[10]

Meanwhile, Lord Renwick, who served as UK Ambassador to the United States between 1991 and 1995, crucial years for the peace process, also noted, 'while I had frequent disagreements over tactics with Teddy Kennedy, I never doubted his commitment to the goal of a more peaceful future for Northern Ireland'.[11] Renwick's comment captures the essence of the complicated but absolutely necessary role that Kennedy played for Northern Ireland throughout his political career. Working in Kennedy's office for many years, his former adviser Trina Vargo recalled the complicated nature of Irish affairs in the United States:

The hard thing in American politics, even to this day, there are people who get attention for views that shouldn't be supported but they're loud and they're noisy and they bother members of Congress and some people cave in to that. I remember going

10   Peter Jay, interview with author, 7/12/2011.
11   Renwick, unpublished memoir, p. 226.

to Boston with Kennedy in the early years and he would be picketed by the Noraid types and it was a handful of people—they're not Irish-Americans, they want people to think they represent Irish-America—they represent a very small portion which is sympathetic to the republican cause, they supported the IRA and they would annoy members of Congress who basically didn't do a lot of investigation into the issue, just said 'whatever they want, fine, put it out there'.[12]

This is consistent with the recollections of Sir Nigel Sheinwald, who served in the role of First Secretary in the British Embassy in Washington during the 1980s. This was a role, Sheinwald recalled, that 'involved a significant element of working on Northern Ireland. I was the Northern Ireland desk officer'. He continued:

I myself never had any doubt that those who were particularly vocal on the issue would have liked to disrupt the core of the UK–American relationship. I never really thought that was likely to happen given that our interests in relation to the United States are so significant and we were in the middle of the Cold War at the time and there was a very close political relationship between our government and the US government at that stage. That didn't seem to me to be a very realisable objective from the point of view of the other side.[13]

The United States of America had a long history of engagement with Northern Ireland, from the very earliest days of the territory variously referred to as a country, a province, and a region. From the visit of Arkansas Senator Joe Robinson in 1925, to various Congressional delegation trips, through the multiple trips that President Bill Clinton made during the 1990s, to the creation of The Senator George J. Mitchell Institute for Global Peace, Security and Justice at Queen's University Belfast in June 2016, US political figures have sought to engage with the people, the politicians, and the economy of Northern Ireland with varying degrees of utility and success.[14] This book has attempted to explore these engagements in a fuller context, detailing

---

[12]   Trina Vargo, interview with author, 2/5/2012.
[13]   Sir Nigel Sheinwald, interview with author, 26/4/2013.
[14]   *Belfast Telegraph*, 24/6/2016; see also https://web.archive.org/web/201707 01121600/www.qub.ac.uk/Discover/About-Queens/Global-research-institutes/ TheSenatorGeorgeJMitchellInstituteforGlobalPeaceSecurityandJustice/.

the historical relationships between the Executive and Legislative branches of the US government and Northern Ireland, examining the Anglo-Irish context to US interventions in Northern Ireland during the conflict, and assessing the subsequent roles of both Republican and Democratic Presidents in the form of George W. Bush and Barack Obama as Northern Ireland began its long transition to a post-conflict society.

The story of the interventions of US actors in Northern Ireland is one of credibility, political capital, and persistence, or, to borrow from Official IRA leader Cathal Goulding's 1990 comments, appreciating that you were 'right too soon' and having the patience to engage with those who were 'right too late' whilst disengaging from those who 'will never be fucking right'.[15] Many US figures appreciated the merits of creating a stable economy, with guaranteed equal opportunities, in Northern Ireland, from the early days of the conflict. Politically, SDLP leader John Hume's brand of constitutional nationalism was attractive to many, but lacked constituency until Hume met Senator Edward Kennedy. The Kennedy–Hume meeting, and the burgeoning relationship between the two, can be seen as a pivotal event in the history of US involvement in Northern Ireland.[16] Maurice Fitzpatrick considers that 'by bringing the United States into the frame, Hume achieved a very subtle but necessary change in Anglo-Irish relations', and that 'the British were much more bound to honour the [Good Friday] agreement' than they might otherwise have been, while Peter McLoughlin notes the role that Kennedy played in raising Hume's profile, and with it his credibility, in the United States.[17]

Kennedy continued to reference Hume's influence on his thinking with regard to Ireland and perhaps the most significant long-term consequence of their 1972 meeting was Kennedy's commitment to

---

[15]   *Observer*, 3/1/1999. Goulding refers to his own view of Irish republicanism as being 'too soon', Gerry Adams's as 'too late', and that of Ruairí Ó Brádaigh as 'never'.

[16]   Timothy White has argued that the role of the USA was important in the context of 'the complex pattern of mutual influence that made the Good Friday Agreement possible'. See White, T.J., 'American Diplomacy and Economic Aid in the Northern Ireland Peace Process: A Neoliberal Analysis', *Open Library of Humanities* 4(1) (2018), p. 3, https://olh.openlibhums.org/articles/10.16995/olh.255/.

[17]   Fitzpatrick, *John Hume in America*, p. 200; McLoughlin, P.J., *John Hume and the Revision of Irish Nationalism* (Manchester: Manchester University Press, 2010), pp. 108–110.

working against radical Irish-American groups. This commitment defined his role with both the so-called 'Four Horsemen', and later the Congressional Friends of Ireland group. It continued into his twilight years in Congress, typified by his refusal to meet Gerry Adams after the murder of Robert McCartney in 2005. Kennedy's nuanced but fully involved role was crucial throughout this period.

Hume's influence on Kennedy was particularly important given the relative inability of other Northern Irish figures to maintain a prominent profile, or significant credibility, in the United States throughout the period of the troubles. This was particularly true after Bernadette Devlin's 1969 visit. Few other Northern Irish visitors attracted quite as much attention as did Devlin, and certainly nobody from a Unionist party enjoyed very much in the way of favourable press. This was a sore point for Ulster Unionists, who had followed Devlin to the United States in 1969 in an attempt to put across their own perspective to American audiences. Unionist politicians in particular struggled to find a constituency in the United States, not least because they sought to deliver a message that was not identifiably different from that of the United Kingdom, at least from the perspective of those in the United States. In the context of the United States, Northern Ireland was an issue contested by the British state and Irish republicans, largely through the form of Irish-American organisations like Irish Northern Aid and the Irish National Caucus. The credibility that the UK government had with its long-time ally in Washington helped to establish the view within the executive branch of the US government, if not entirely so within the legislative branch, that Northern Ireland was an internal affair of the United Kingdom and should be treated as such.

This was the view adopted by President Richard Nixon, who had the advantage of succeeding a President, in Lyndon Johnson, who had little of the affection that his own predecessor, John F. Kennedy, possessed for Ireland. It seems highly improbable that President Kennedy, had he lived, would have remained impartial on Northern Ireland, particularly as the conflict developed in the early 1970s. Kennedy would, of course, have been out of office before the British Army deployed to Northern Ireland in August 1969, but his possible role in these circumstances can only ever be a matter of speculation. Johnson, on the other hand, remained disengaged and this disengagement allowed him to form his own policy towards the conflict, unaffected by the views of his predecessors. Nixon's appointment of leading figures to roles related to Northern Ireland was an indication of his concern that he should have immediate and reliable information on the situation there, if necessary, but also suggested that Northern Ireland might be a task delegated to those figures. Henry Kissinger and John Moore were among Nixon's most trusted advisers and maintained a steady flow of information on Northern Ireland to the White House. The presence of Moore in Ireland as the conflict developed gave Nixon direct access to the latest events there. Once Nixon left office, Gerald Ford did little to shift US policy in any way and, consequently, little changed under his administration. His own successor, former Governor of Georgia Jimmy Carter, did make a stand on Northern Ireland in the form of his August 1977 statement on the situation there. The Carter statement, relatively benign in content, was made in part because of pressure from within the Democratic Party and pressure from Congress. Its very existence helped to establish the foundations upon which groups like the Congressional Friends of Ireland, founded in 1981, could build. Carter himself reflected:

> Among my chief concerns as a candidate and as president were the peaceful resolution of conflicts and the restoration of human rights wherever such problems occurred in the world. Naturally, I agreed with the Democratic Party's position that the U.S. government needed to speak out against the violence and terror, discrimination, repression, and deprivation of rights that for so long had plagued the Irish people. In my August 1977 statement, I reaffirmed my commitment to those who sought peace and rejected violence in Northern Ireland.[18]

The Congressional Friends of Ireland, particularly Speaker Tip O'Neill, exerted powerful influence over Carter's successor Ronald Reagan. This pressure meant that even with Reagan's famously close relationship with British Prime Minister Margaret Thatcher, the US government could exert influence over the British to help ease them towards the signing of the 1985 Anglo-Irish Agreement. This agreement, even with strong Ulster Unionist opposition, re-established the Irish dimension of the Northern Ireland peace process, which was essential to the success of the 1998 Good Friday Agreement. Much as the Nixon to Ford transition had brought with it a predictable continuity in US policy towards Northern Ireland, the Reagan to Bush transition was similarly predictable. The election of Bill Clinton in 1992, however, changed the landscape of the US role in Northern Ireland.

---

[18]   President Jimmy Carter, correspondence with author, 1/5/2012.

Clinton arrived in office committed to a multifaceted engagement on Northern Ireland by his own campaign promises and influential backers, led by his law school classmate Bruce Morrison. His commitment to the Gerry Adams visa, and the significance of this visa and the act of opening up the United States to elected members of Sinn Féin, cannot be overstated in the context of the overall peace process. It is impossible to imagine a re-elected President Bush risking the ire of the British government to allow Adams into the United States. Clinton's bold move was rewarded with the first IRA ceasefire of August 1994.[19] Soon after, he made good on a further pre-election pledge, the role of the Special Envoy. Under George Mitchell's skilful stewardship, the Northern Ireland peace process became stronger and developed more rapidly. Years of negotiations between nationalists, Unionists, and the British and Irish governments had introduced many ideas that contributed to the agreement that was signed on Good Friday 1998, but they had to be brought together in a format that could be agreed upon by a majority in Northern Ireland itself. It was here that Mitchell, along with Clinton, played a decisive role, convincing the parties of Northern Ireland to sign the agreement and offer the people of Northern Ireland a future beyond the conflict that had plagued their towns and cities for almost thirty years.

Postscript: The 'Flag Protest' and George Mitchell at St Patrick's Day, 2016

Shortly after the 2012 Presidential election, Northern Ireland saw significant unrest following the Belfast City Council decision to end its policy of flying the flag of the United Kingdom over city hall every day. This unrest necessitated the interventions of US actors and saw former special envoy Richard Haass return to Ireland.[20] It was significant that, much as when Special Envoy Declan Kelly had reached out to former President Bush rather than anyone in the Obama administration, it

---

[19]   Timothy Lynch considers that 'Clinton could not lose in Northern Ireland, only gain', but this depended greatly on the compliance of the IRA leadership; had the foundations for the politicisation of the movement not been laid over a number of years under the leadership of Gerry Adams, particularly in light of any major terrorist attack on the USA, Clinton's 'victory' on Northern Ireland might have turned out rather differently. *Turf War*, p. 98.

[20]   For details, see, for example, *Guardian*, 3/12/2012; *IT*, 3/12/2014.

was a Bush Special Envoy who was tasked with the attempt to restore order to the peace process. Haass returned to Northern Ireland, along with Professor Meghan O'Sullivan, to lead all-party talks on the issues of flags, parades, and dealing with the past. The talks were ultimately unsuccessful, with the two sides unable to come to agreement on these important issues. The idea, however, that US figures could once again serve as an impartial broker to political impasse in Northern Ireland remained persuasive, but even this could not overcome the significant problems facing Stormont. This lack of cohesion was reflected in the collapse of the Northern Ireland Assembly in January 2017 and the failure of the parties to form a government following elections in early March. Significant in these elections was the fact that the DUP only won twenty-eight seats, a loss of eight seats. Dropping below thirty seats cost them their automatic 'petition of concern', a legislative tool that allowed the party to block a vote on any issue the party was opposed to.[21] Possible items for debate that had previously been blocked by the DUP included the introduction of same-sex marriage in Northern Ireland. The rest of the UK allowed same-sex marriages to occur in 2014, and the Republic of Ireland legalised these marriages in 2015.

In March 2016, former Senator and Special Envoy George Mitchell was chosen as the grand marshal for the New York St Patrick's Day parade. Mitchell served as Chancellor of Queen's University Belfast from 1999 until 2009, when he was appointed as the United States Special Envoy for Middle East Peace. He also served in prominent roles in the Disney Corporation and led an investigation into the use of performance-enhancing drugs in Major League Baseball.

New York Mayor Bill de Blasio also took part in the parade, the first time he had elected to do so, at his third opportunity. The Mayor marched alongside the Lavender and Green Alliance, an organisation of Irish lesbian, gay, bisexual, and transgender people, based in Astoria, New York.[22] Where David Dinkins had skipped the march, his successors Rudy Giuliani and Michael Bloomberg both participated. After de Blasio's election in 2013, however, the group OUT@NBCUniversal was permitted to take part: some progress on the ban of openly LGBT groups, but, given that the OUT@ group featured employees of the television network that broadcasts the parade, one might reasonably suggest that it did not represent significant progress.

21 *Belfast Telegraph*, 4/3/2017.
22 *NYT*, 11/1/2016 and 17/3/2016.

Mitchell, by now eighty-two years of age, agreed to serve as Grand Marshal after the organisers arranged to open the parade to all openly LGBT marchers. Former chairman of the St Patrick's Day parade and Celebration Committee John Dunleavy had left the role in November 2015 to be replaced by Quinnipiac University's John Lacey and took with him his 'unyielding' opposition to the participation of LGBT groups.[23] In his speech before the march, Mitchell called for 'peace, openness, inclusion … let's all work together for a better future for people, Irish-Americans, all Americans, all people'.[24]

Mitchell's time as the Middle Eastern Envoy had been frustrating, but highlighted the differences between the peace process there and that in Northern Ireland. As Jonathan Powell noted, 'You have to be careful about this: Northern Ireland is *sui generis*, the solution we came to is *sui generis*. You cannot take the Northern Ireland model and apply it somewhere else; it would be ridiculous to try and do that either militarily or in terms of what we did in terms of peace'.[25] Mitchell, whose mother was born in Lebanon and therefore lacked the strong pro-Israel credentials that many in the Israeli lobby sought, was acutely aware of this but nonetheless optimistic of capitalising on his previous experience in the region, and came with strong credentials as an objective emissary.[26] He commented, on the eve of his second visit to the region: 'we had 700 days of failure in Northern Ireland … and one day of success. I cannot guarantee you a result, but I can guarantee you an effort'.[27]

The Northern Ireland peace process badly needed the efforts of George Mitchell and the President who appointed him to the role of Special Envoy for Northern Ireland, Bill Clinton, but it was also a peace process geared towards resolving a conflict that involved participants far more ready for the sort of engagement Mitchell could facilitate than that in the Middle East. The work that Clinton and Mitchell could do on behalf of the United States in Northern Ireland was the culmination of almost three decades of multilateral discussions, negotiations, and agreement which sought to end a conflict that took over 3,500 lives and caused almost 50,000 injuries.

[23] Irish Central, 'New York St. Patrick's Day Parade Leaders Praise Grand Marshal George Mitchell', 15/1/2016, available at https://www.irishcentral.com/news/irishvoice/new-york-st-patricks-day-parade-grand-marshal-george-mitchell.
[24] *Bangor Daily News*, 17/3/2016.
[25] Jonathan Powell, interview with author, 8/3/2011.
[26] *NYT*, 21/1/2009.
[27] *Haaretz*, 22/2/2010.

In 2015, Mitchell published his memoir, *The Negotiator*. It covers his entire political career, with obvious focus on his time as the Special Envoy to Northern Ireland and obvious pride in his accomplishments there. In one striking exchange, Mitchell recalls an episode where he took his young son Andrew to the Northern Ireland debate chamber:

> A half hour passed; to me it seemed an instant, but not to Andrew. He leaned toward me and whispered, 'Dad, this is really boring. Can we go now?' I smiled, hugged him, and said, 'Of course'. As we stood I said to him, 'I know it's boring to you, but that's the point. To me, it was soothing, like music to my ears'.[28]

Mitchell's successes on Northern Ireland were, unfortunately, not shared by many of his successors. Reflecting on the 2012 talks, Richard Haass commented:

> It takes extraordinary leadership to overcome [issues of cultural identity], and we simply didn't have enough of it in Northern Ireland during my period … I thought, more than anything, it was lacking on the Unionist side, and that is not surprising because there was a feeling that change would disadvantage them. I think the republicans and nationalists were more willing to entertain the possibility of change but the two leading Unionist parties were not.[29]

The United States had proven a powerful ally when there were issues to resolve on the republican side of the political spectrum, but, even with the successes that Bush's administration had enjoyed in terms of engaging Ulster Unionists, particularly under the watch of Mitchell Reiss, Haass was unable to facilitate resolution. The twentieth anniversary of the Good Friday Agreement was observed on 10 April 2018. That day also marked 439 days since the Northern Ireland Assembly had last met.

---

[28] Mitchell, *The Negotiator*, p. 251.
[29] *Belfast Telegraph*, 30/12/2014.

Select Bibliography

Interviews and Correspondence

Lord Armstrong, London, 9/10/2013
President Jimmy Carter, correspondence, 1/5/2012
Sir Sherard Cowper-Coles, London, 29/4/2013
Sean Donlon, Dublin, 24/2/2012
Martin Galvin, New York, 15/5/2012
Lieutenant General Sir Alasdair Irwin, Aberlour, 16/2/2009
Peter Jay, Oxford, 7/12/2011
Lord Kinnock, correspondence, 21/3/2012
Rosemary O'Neill, Washington, DC, 3/5/2012
Thomas P. O'Neill, III, Boston, 10/5/2012
Richard O'Rawe, Belfast, 15/2/2010
Lord (Charles David) Powell, London, 25/4/2013
Jonathan Powell, London, 8/3/2011 and 16/1/2013
Marian Price, Belfast, 1/7/2010
Dan Rooney, Pittsburgh, 21/10/2013
Sir Nigel Sheinwald, London, 26/4/2013
Trina Vargo, Alexandria, VA, 2/5/2012

Archives

Archives & Special Collections at the Thomas J. Dodd Research Center, University of Connecticut Libraries, Storrs, CT
Archives of Irish America, Tamiment Library, New York University, New York, NY
Archives Service Center, University of Pittsburgh, Pittsburgh, PA
John J. Burns Library, Boston College, Boston, MA
Jimmy Carter Presidential Library, Atlanta, GA
Gerald R. Ford Presidential Library, Ann Arbor, MI
Lyndon B. Johnson Presidential Library, Austin, TX

Edward M. Kennedy Institute, Boston, MA
John F. Kennedy Presidential Library, Boston, MA
The Linen Hall Library, Belfast
The National Archives, Kew
National Archives and Records Administration, College Park, MD
National Archives of Ireland, Dublin
Richard Nixon Presidential Library, Yorba Linda, CA
Public Record Office of Northern Ireland, Belfast
Ronald Reagan Presidential Library, Simi Valley, CA

Newspapers and Periodicals

The Atlantic
Baltimore Sun
Bangor Daily News
Belfast Telegraph
Boston Globe
Chicago Tribune
Christian Science Monitor
Daily Mail
Daily Telegraph
The Economist
The Glasgow Herald
The Guardian
Haaretz
Harper's Magazine
Hartford Courant
Hibernia
The Independent
Irish America
Irish Echo
Irish Examiner
Irish Independent
The Irish People
Irish Press
The Irish Times
The Irish Voice
London Evening Standard
Los Angeles Times
Magill
The Morning Call
New Statesman
New York Daily News
The New York Times
Newsday

Le Nouvel Observateur
Orlando Sentinel
Philadelphia Inquirer
An Phoblacht
Sarasota Herald-Tribune
Scotsman
Sun-Sentinel
Sunday Independent
Sunday Life
Sunday Press
The Sunday Times
Time
The Victoria Advocate
The Village
Wall Street Journal
The Washington Post

Monographs and Other Sources

104th Congress, House Report 104–128—American Overseas Interests Act of 1995, available at https://www.congress.gov/congressional-report/104th-congress/house-report/128/1.

1996 Democratic Party Platform, 'Today's Democratic Party, Meeting American's Challenges, Protecting America's Values', 26/8/1996, available at https://www.presidency.ucsb.edu/documents/1996-democratic-party-platform.

2000 Republican Party Political Platform, 31/7/2000, available at https://www.presidency.ucsb.edu/documents/2000-republican-party-platform.

Address by the President of the United States of America Ronald Reagan, 4/6/1984, available at https://www.oireachtas.ie/en/debates/debate/seanad/1984-06-04/2/.

Akenson, D., *Conor: A Biography of Conor Cruise O'Brien* (Ithaca, NY: Cornell University Press, 1994).

Aldous, R., *Reagan and Thatcher* (London: Hutchinson, 2012).

Amnesty International, *Northern Ireland: Report of an Amnesty International Mission to Northern Ireland (28 November 1977–6 December 1977)* (London: Amnesty International, 1978).

Bassiouni, M.C., *Testimonial Statement to Senate Foreign Relations Committee, 99th Congress, First Session, Hearings of September 18, 1985*, 276–305.

Basso, K., 'The 1985 U.S.–U.K. Supplementary Extradition Treaty: A Superfluous Effort?', *Boston College International and Comparative Law Review* 12(1), pp. 301–333.

Bew, P., *The Making and Remaking of the Good Friday Agreement* (Dublin: Liffey Press, 2007).

The Bloody Sunday Inquiry, https://www.gov.uk/government/publications/report-of-the-bloody-sunday-inquiry.

Bloomfield, D., *Developing Dialogue in Northern Ireland: The Mayhew Talks 1992* (Basingstoke: Palgrave, 2001).

Bradlee, B.C., *Conversations with Kennedy* (New York: W.W. Norton & Company, 1975).

Campbell, A., *The Irish Diaries, 1994–2003* (Dublin: Lilliput, 2013).

Lord Carrington *Reflect on Things Past* (Glasgow: William Collins, 1988).

Casey, M., and Lee, J.J. (eds), *Making the Irish American: History and Heritage of the Irish in the United States* (New York: NYU Press, 2007).

Clancy, M.A.C., 'The United States and Post-Agreement Northern Ireland, 2001–6', *Irish Studies in International Affairs* 18 (2007), pp. 155–173.

Clinton, H.R., *Hard Choices* (New York: Simon & Schuster, 2014).

Clinton, William J. (Bill), 'Address to the Employees of the Mackie Metal Plant', 30/11/1995, Miller Center, University of Virginia, available at https://millercenter.org/the-presidency/presidential-speeches/november-30-1995-address-employees-mackie-metal-plant.

—— *My Life* (London: Hutchinson, 2004).

—— 'Remarks on Lighting the City Christmas Tree in Belfast', 30/11/1995, UCSB Presidency Project, available at https://www.presidency.ucsb.edu/documents/remarks-lighting-the-city-christmas-tree-belfast.

Cooper, J., *The Politics of Diplomacy: US Presidents and the Northern Ireland Conflict 1967–1998* (Edinburgh: Edinburgh University Press, 2017).

Cox, M., Guelke, A., and Stephen, F. (eds), *A Farewell to Arms: Beyond the Good Friday Agreement*, 2nd edn (Manchester: Manchester University Press, 2006).

Craig, G., 'Senator Clinton's Claims of Foreign Policy Experience are Exaggerated', *Real Clear Politics*, 11/3/2008, available at https://www.realclearpolitics.com/articles/2008/03/clintons_exaggerated_experienc.html.

Cronin, S., *Washington's Irish Policy 1916–1986* (Dublin: Anvil Books, 1987).

Cullen, K., and Murphy, S., *Whitey Bulger: America's Most Wanted Gangster and the Manhunt That Brought Him to Justice* (New York: Norton, 2013).

Culture Northern Ireland, 'The Industrial Heritage of West Belfast', 11/12/2008, available at https://www.culturenorthernireland.org/features/heritage/industrial-heritage-west-belfast.

—— 'The Story of Irish Linen', 6/4/2011, available at https://www.culturenorthernireland.org/features/heritage/story-irish-linen.

Davidson, J.W., *America's Allies and War: Kosovo, Afghanistan, and Iraq* (New York: Palgrave Macmillan, 2011).

Davies, N., *Ten-Thirty-Three: The Inside Story of Britain's Secret Killing Machine in Northern Ireland* (Edinburgh: Mainstream, 1999).

Davis, T.D., *Dublin's American Policy: Irish-American Diplomatic Relations, 1945–1952* (Washington, DC: Catholic University of America Press, 1998).

De Breadun, D., *The Far Side of Revenge: Making Peace in Northern Ireland* (Cork: Collins Press, 2008).

Democratic Party Platform, 1956, 13/8/1956, available at https://www.presidency.ucsb.edu/documents/1956-democratic-party-platform.

Dillon, M., *The Dirty War: Covert Strategies and Tactics Used in Political Conflicts* (London: Hutchinson, 1990).

—— *Killer In Clowntown: Joe Doherty, the IRA and the Special Relationship* (London: Arrow, 1992).

Doherty, J., *The Destruction and Revival of Irish Culture* (February 1986), available in Irish Republicanism Collection, AIA 22, Box 5 Series B: Prisoners, Tamiment Library, New York University.

Dolan, J.P., *The Irish Americans: A History* (New York: Bloomsbury Press, 2008).

Dooley, B., *Black and Green: The Fight for Civil Rights in Northern Ireland and Black America* (London: Pluto Press).

Doyle, D.N., 'The Remaking of Irish America, 1845–1880', pp. 213–252, in Lee, J.J., and Casey, M. (eds), *Making the Irish American: History and Heritage of the Irish in the United States* (New York: NYU Press, 2006).

Drudy, P.J. (ed.), *The Irish in America: Emigration, Assimilation, and Impact* (Cambridge: Cambridge University Press, 1985).

Dumbrell, J., *A Special Relationship: Anglo-American Relations in the Cold War and after* (Basingstoke: Macmillan, 2001).

Ellis, S., 'The Historical Significance of President Kennedy's Visit to Ireland in June 1963', *Irish Studies Review* 16(2) (2000), pp. 113–130.

—— 'Lyndon Johnson, Harold Wilson and the Vietnam War: A Not So Special Relationship', pp. 180–204, in Hollowell, J. (ed.), *Twentieth-Century Anglo-American Relations* (Basingstoke: Palgrave Macmillan, 2001).

English, R., *Armed Struggle: The History of the IRA* (London: Macmillan, 2003).

Executive Order 12170—Blocking Iranian Government property, 14/11/1979, 44 FR 65729, National Archives and Records Administration, https://www.archives.gov/federal-register/codification/executive-order/12170.html.

Fair, J.D., 'The Intellectual JFK: Lessons in Statesmanship from British History', *Diplomatic History* 30 (2006), pp. 119–142.

Farrell, M., *Sheltering the Fugitive? The Extradition of Irish Political Offenders* (Cork: Mercier Press, 1985).

Faulkner, B., *Memoirs of a Statesman* (London: Weidenfeld & Nicolson, 1978).

Fitzpatrick, M., *John Hume in America: From Derry to DC* (Newbridge: Irish Academic Press, 2017).

Flynn, B., *Soldiers of Folly: The IRA Border Campaign, 1956–1962* (Cork: Collins Press 2009).

The Foreign Assistance Act of 1961 (Public Law 87-195), Section 502B, available at https://legcounsel.house.gov/Comps/Foreign%20Assistance%20Act%20Of%201961.pdf.

Frampton, M., 'Agents and Ambushes: Britain's "Dirty War" in Northern Ireland', pp. 77–100, in Cohen, S. (ed.), *Democracies at War against Terrorism* (Basingstoke: Palgrave Macmillan, 2008).

Guelke, A., 'The United States and the Peace Process, pp. 222–237, in Barton, B., and Roche, P.J. (eds), *The Northern Ireland Question: The Peace Process and the Belfast Agreement* (Basingstoke: Palgrave Macmillan, 2009).

—— 'The United States, Irish Americans and the Northern Ireland Peace Process', *International Affairs* 72(3) (1996), pp. 521–536.

Henderson, N., *Mandarin: The Diaries of Nicholas Henderson* (London: Phoenix Press, 1994).

Holland, J., *The American Connection: U.S. Guns, Money and Influence in Northern Ireland* (Dublin: Poolbeg, 1989).

Holland, J., and McDonald, H., *INLA* (Dublin: Torc, 1994).

Irish Republican Army Ceasefire Statement, 31/8/1994, available at https://cain.ulster.ac.uk/events/peace/docs/ira31894.htm.

Joint Declaration on Peace: The Downing Street Declaration, Wednesday, 15 December 1993, available at https://cain.ulster.ac.uk/events/peace/docs/dsd151293.htm.

Keane, E., *An Irish Statesman and Revolutionary: The Nationalist and Internationalist Politics of Sean MacBride* (London: I.B. Tauris, 2006).

Kelly, J.T., 'The Empire Strikes Back: The Taking of Joe Doherty', *Fordham Law Review* 61 (1992), pp. 317–399.

Kenny, K., 'American-Irish Nationalism', pp. 289–301, in Lee, J.J., and Casey, M. (eds), *Making the Irish American: History and Heritage of the Irish in the United States* (New York: NYU Press, 2006).

Lynch, T.J., *Turf War: The Clinton Administration and Northern Ireland* (Aldershot: Ashgate, 2004).

McCaffrey, L.J., *The Irish Catholic Diaspora in America* (Washington, DC: Catholic University of America Press, 1997).

—— *The Irish Diaspora in America* (Bloomington: Indiana University Press, 1976).

McCleery, M., *Operation Demetrius and its Aftermath: A New History of the Use of Internment Without Trial in Northern Ireland 1971–1975* (Manchester: Manchester University Press, 2015).

McDonald, H., *Gunsmoke and Mirrors: How Sinn Fein Dressed up Defeat as Victory* (Dublin: Gill & Macmillan, 2009).

McElrath, K., *Unsafe Haven: The United States, the IRA and Political Prisoners* (London: Pluto Press, 2000).

McEvoy, J., *The Politics of Northern Ireland* (Edinburgh: Edinburgh University Press, 2008).

MacGinty, R., 'American Influences on the Northern Ireland Peace Process', *Journal of Conflict Studies* 17(2) (1997).

McKittrick, D., Kelters, S., Feeney, B., Thornton, C., and McVea, D., *Lost Lives: The Stories of the Men, Women and Children Who Died as a Result of the Northern Ireland Troubles* (Edinburgh: Mainstream, 1999).

MacLeod, A., *International Politics and the Northern Ireland Conflict: The USA, Diplomacy and the Troubles* (London: I.B. Tauris, 2016).

McManus, S., *My American Struggle for Justice in Northern Ireland* (Cork: Collins Press, 2011).

Major, J., *The Autobiography* (London: HarperCollins, 2000).

Meagher, T.J., *Inventing Irish America: Generation, Class, and Ethnic Identity in a New England City, 1880–1928* (South Bend, IN: University of Notre Dame Press, 2001).

Miller, K.A., *Emigrants and Exiles: Ireland and the Irish Exodus to North America* (Oxford: Oxford University Press, 1988).

—— *Ireland and Irish America: Culture, Class, and Transatlantic Migration* (Dublin: Field Day Publications, 2008).

Mitchell, G., *The Negotiator: A Memoir* (New York: Simon & Schuster, 2015).

Moloney, E., *A Secret History of the IRA* (London: Penguin, 2003).

—— *Voices from the Grave: Two Men's War in Ireland* (London: Faber & Faber, 2010).

Moody, T.W., 'Irish-American Nationalism', *Irish Historical Studies* 15(60) (1967), pp. 438–445.

Moore, C., *Margaret Thatcher: The Authorized Biography*, vol. 2, *Everything She Wants* (London: Allen Lane, 2015).

Mount, G., *895 Days that Changed the World: The Presidency of Gerald Ford* (Montreal: Black Rose Books, 2006).

Mulvenna, G., *Tartan Gangs and Paramilitaries: The Loyalist Backlash* (Liverpool: Liverpool University Press, 2016).

New Ireland Forum Report (Dublin: The Stationery Office, 1984), available at https://cain.ulster.ac.uk/issues/politics/nifr.htm.

Northern Ireland (Emergency Provisions) Act 1978 (Continuance) (No. 2) Order 1978, Hansard, HL vol. 397, cols 826–837 (14 December 1978), https://api.parliament.uk/historic-hansard/lords/1978/dec/14/northern-ireland-emergency-provisions#S5LV0397P0_19781214_HOL_218.

O'Clery, C., *The Billionaire Who Wasn't: How Chuck Feeney Made and Gave Away a Fortune* (New York: Public Affairs, 2007).

—— *The Greening of the White House* (Dublin: Gill & Macmillan, 1996).

O'Grady, J., 'An Irish Policy Born in the U.S.A.: Clinton's Break with the Past', *Foreign Affairs* 75(3) (1993), pp. 2–7.

Offences Against the State (Amendment) Act, 1972, available at www.irishstatutebook.ie/eli/1972/act/26/enacted/en/html.

Ogden, C., *Maggie: The Portrait of a Woman in Power* (New York: Simon & Schuster, 1990).

Oppenheimer, J., *The Other Mrs. Kennedy; Ethel Skakel Kennedy: An American Drama of Power, Privilege, and Politics* (New York: St Martin's Press, 1995).

Owen, A.E., *The Anglo Irish Agreement: The First Three Years* (Cardiff: University of Wales Press, 1994).

Paisley, I.R.K., Robinson, P.D., and Taylor, J.D., *Ulster: The Facts* (Belfast: Crown Publishing, 1982).

Parry, J.T., 'No Appeal: The U.S.–U.K. Supplementary Extradition Treaty's Effort to Create Federal Jurisdiction', *Loyola of Los Angeles International and Comparative Law Review* 25 (2003), pp. 543–580.

Peter Gabriel John McMullen, Petitioner v. *Immigration and Naturalization Service, Respondent*, US Court of Appeals for the Ninth Circuit, 658 F.2d 1312 (9th Cir. 1981), argued and submitted 13/5/1981, decided 13/10/1981, available at http://law.justia.com/cases/federal/appellate-courts/F2/658/1312/50826/.

Powell, J., *Great Hatred, Little Room: Making Peace in Northern Ireland* (London: Bodley Head, 2008).

Prince, S., *Northern Ireland's '68: Civil Rights, Global Revolt and the Origins of the Troubles* (Dublin: Irish Academic Press, 2007).

Pyle, C., *Extradition, Politics and Human Rights* (Philadelphia: Temple University Press, 2001).

Reagan, R., with Brinkley, D., *The Reagan Diaries* (New York: HarperCollins, 2007).

Renwick, R., *A Journey with Margaret Thatcher: Foreign Policy under the Iron Lady* (London: Biteback, 2013).

Report of the Committee of Inquiry into Police Interrogation Procedures in Northern Ireland, Presented to Parliament by the Secretary of State for Northern Ireland by Command of Her Majesty March 1979 (London: HMSO, 1979).

Report of the Enquiry into Allegations against the Security Forces of Physical Brutality in Northern Ireland Arising out of Events on the 9th August, 1971 (London: HMSO, 1971).

Report of the Patrick Finucane Review, The Rt. Hon. Sir Desmond de Silva, December 2012, https://www.gov.uk/government/uploads/system/uploads/attachment_data/file/246867/0802.pdf.

Report of the Tribunal Appointed to Inquire into the Events on Sunday, 30th January 1972, https://cain.ulster.ac.uk/hmso/widgery.htm.

Rhodeen, P., *Peacerunner: The True Story of How an Ex-Congressman Helped End the Centuries of War in Ireland* (Dallas, TX: BenBella Books, 2016).

Rolston, B., 'An Effective Mask for Terror: Democracy, Death Squads and Northern Ireland', *Crime, Law and Social Change* 44(2) (2005), pp. 181–203.

Rooney, D., *My 75 Years with the Pittsburgh Steelers and the NFL* (Philadelphia: Da Capo, 2007).

Ross, F.S., *Smashing H Block: The Popular Campaign against Criminalization and the Irish Hunger Strikes, 1976–1982* (Liverpool: Liverpool University Press, 2011).

Rowthorn, B., and Wayne, N., *Northern Ireland: The Political Economy of Conflict* (Cambridge: Polity Press, 1988).

Rubin, M., 'Who is Responsible for the Taliban?', *Middle East Review of International Affairs* 6(1) (2002).

Sanders, A., *Inside the IRA: Dissident Republicans and the War for Legitimacy* (Edinburgh: Edinburgh University Press, 2011).

—— 'Landing Rights in Dublin: Relations between Ireland and the United States 1945–72', *Irish Studies in International Affairs* 28 (2017), pp. 147–171.

—— 'The Role of Northern Ireland in Modern Anglo-American Relations: The US Department of State and the Royal Ulster Constabulary, 1979', *Journal of Transatlantic Studies* 12(2) (2014), pp. 163–181.

Sanders, A., and Wood, I.S., *Times of Troubles: Britain's War in Northern Ireland* (Edinburgh: Edinburgh University Press, 2012).

Schlesinger, A., *Robert Kennedy and His Times* (New York: Houghton Mifflin, 2002).

Seitz, R., *Over Here* (London: Weidenfeld & Nicolson, 1998).

Smith, R.C., *John F. Kennedy, Barack Obama and the Politics of Ethnic Incorporation and Avoidance* (Albany: SUNY Press, 2013).

Steele, J., McBride, S., Kelly, J., Dearden, C., and Rocke, L., 'Plastic Bullet Injuries in Northern Ireland: Experiences during a Week of Civil Disturbance', *Journal of Trauma: Injury, Infection and Critical Care* 46(4) (1999), pp. 711–714.

Stevens Enquiry: Overview and Recommendations, 17 April 2003, Sir John Stevens QPM, DL, Commissioner of the Metropolitan Police Service, available at https://cain.ulster.ac.uk/issues/collusion/stevens3/stevens3summary.htm.

Thatcher, M., *The Downing Street Years* (London: HarperCollins, 1993).

Thompson, J.E., *American Policy and Northern Ireland: A Saga of Peacebuilding* (Westport, CT: Praeger, 2001).

Toolis, K., *Rebel Hearts* (London: Picador, 1995).

Tubridy, R., *JFK in Ireland: Four Days that Changed a President* (London: HarperCollins, 2010).

US House of Representatives, H.R. 224 To Require Certain Entities Receiving United States Funds from the International Fund for Ireland to Comply with the MacBride Principles, Introduced 4/1/1995, available at https://www.congress.gov/bill/104th-congress/house-bill/244/text.

—— H.R. 4328 Omnibus Consolidated and Emergency Supplemental Appropriations Act, 1999, available at https://www.congress.gov/bill/105th-congress/house-bill/4328/text.

Walker, G., *A History of the Ulster Unionist Party: Protest, Pragmatism and Pessimism* (Manchester: Manchester University Press, 2004).

—— 'Northern Ireland, British–Irish Relations and American Concerns, 1942–1956', *Twentieth Century British History* 18(2) (2007), pp. 194–218.

Wallace, W., 'Foreign Policy', in Kavanagh, D., and Selden, A. (eds), *The Major Effect* (London: Macmillan, 1994).

Ward, K., 'Ulster Terrorism: The US Network News Coverage of Northern Ireland, 1968–1979', in Alexander, Y., and O'Day, A. (eds), *Terrorism in Ireland* (London, 1984).

Weller, Cecil, E., Jr., *Joe T. Robinson: Always a Loyal Democrat* (Fayetteville: University of Arkansas Press, 1998).

Wharton, K., *Wasted Years, Wasted Lives Volume 1: The British Army in Northern Ireland 1975–1977* (Solihull: Helion, 2013).

White House, 'St Patrick's Day and Irish Heritage in American History', 14/3/2018, available at https://www.whitehouse.gov/articles/st-patricks-day-irish-heritage-american-history/.

Wilson, A.J., *Irish America and the Ulster Conflict 1968–1995* (Belfast: Blackstaff Press, 1995).

Wittke, C.F., *The Irish in America* (Baton Rouge: Louisiana State University Press, 1956).

Wood, I.S., *Crimes of Loyalty: A History of the UDA* (Edinburgh: Edinburgh University Press, 2006).

Index

Adams, Gerry
  and John Hume 222
  fundraising rights in the United
    States 233
  meets Clinton (Washington DC)
    234
  US visitor visa 214, 215, 224
Ad Hoc Congressional Committee
  on Irish Affairs 105–106, 125,
  210
  1977 foundation 109
  1985 invitation to Gerry Adams
    165
  Joseph P. Kennedy II joins 181
  view of Gerry Adams 194
Agate, Jeffrey 94–96, 138
Ahern, Bertie 252, 255, 256, 257
  2008 meeting with George W.
    Bush 270
  and Hillary Clinton 273
  Hillsborough Castle talks 264
  honoured by American Ireland
    Fund 263
American Congress for Irish
  Freedom 28, 34, 55
American Irish Foundation
  founding 17
  merger with Ireland Fund 179
Americans for a New Irish Agenda
  and the Special Envoy Role 213

five goals for Northern Ireland
  208
formation 198
re-election campaign 232
St Patrick's Day Statement 210
views on Northern Ireland 200,
  207
Ancient Order of Hibernians 109,
  111, 209, 250
  1984 invitation to Gerry Adams
    160, 166
  New York St Patrick's Day Parade
    188, 208
Anglo-Irish Agreement 111, 156,
  165, 171–172, 181, 182, 222, 249,
  264, 284
  Anglo-Irish Agreement Support
    Act 174–175, 195, 250
  Lord Armstrong 137
Armstrong, Robert
  1970 visit of Richard Nixon 45–46
  Anglo-Irish Agreement 156, 165,
    171–172
  Thatcher and Carter relationship
    137

B Specials *see* Ulster Special
  Constabulary
Balcombe Street Gang 79, 81
Behan, Brendan

and George Harrison 14
and JFK 12
Belfast
    flag protest 285–286
    investment in 4, 9, 22, 23, 113
    Peace Walls constructed 43
    President Clinton visit to 3,
        231–241
    twentieth century industry 2
    US Consulate General 33, 34,
        44, 63
    US visitors to 116, 161, 181, 220,
        237, 240
    Vital Voices: Women in
        Democracy conference 254
Biaggi, Mario 49–50
    1975 meeting with Irish
        republican leaders 116
    1978 visit to Ireland 115–116
    1980 comments on hunger strike
        137
    Ad Hoc Congressional Committee
        on Irish Affairs 105, 109, 181,
        210
    and 1980 Presidential election 131
    Gerry Adams visa 160, 165
    letter exchange with Jack Lynch
        106–107
    protest at Margaret Thatcher visit
        165–166
    RUC gun issue 123, 125, 127,
        129, 133, 145, 146
Biden, Joseph
    Extradition Treaty 167, 169, 174,
        176, 190
    resolution to release Joe Doherty
        191
    Vice President 273
Blair, Anthony (Tony) 214
    and Bill Clinton 241, 251, 255,
        257
    and George W. Bush 263
Boundary Commission 7

Brookeborough, Viscount (Basil
    Brooke)
    and internment 13
    Northern Ireland Prime Minister
        16
    United States visit 8–9, 16–17
Brown, Gordon 277
Burntollet 34
Bush, George H.W. 183, 200
    1983 meeting with Garret
        FitzGerald 155–156
    1988 Presidential election 186
    1992 Presidential election 204
    and Northern Ireland 201, 229
Bush, George W. 257, 282
    2000 Presidential election 260
    2005 meeting with McCartney
        sisters 266
    and Northern Ireland 260–261,
        270, 285
    and Special Envoys 262, 269
    Ian Paisley views on 259
    International Fund for Ireland
        263
    September 11 attacks 261
    visits from Irish figures 263

Cahill, Joe
    1971 detention in United States
        53–54
    1975 meeting with Mario Biaggo
        116
    1994 visit to United States and
        visa issues 228–229
    Noraid remittances 54
Callaghan, James
    1968 meeting with Brian Faulkner
        30
    1979 vote of no confidence 121
    relations with Jimmy Carter 99,
        102–103, 108, 137
Campaign for Social Justice 25, 28
Carey, Hugh 54, 100, 112, 280

1978 comments on Mario Biaggi
115
1981 hunger strike 149
Four Horsemen 138, 147
Carrington, Lord Peter
RUC gun embargo 130, 133–134
views on Ronald Reagan 141
Carter, Jimmy 29, 284
1976 election campaign 86, 87,
89, 91
1976 St Patrick's Day parade
87–88
1977 statement on Northern
Ireland 99–102, 110
1978 meeting with Callaghan 108
1979 meeting with Margaret
Thatcher 131
1980 Presidential election
130–131, 136
and James Callaghan 102
and Margaret Thatcher 137–138,
141
and Special Envoy role 213
concerns from Northern Ireland
office 103
inaugural address 94
investment in Ireland 154, 173
knowledge of Northern Ireland
128–129
letter of apology to Garret
FitzGerald 88
Neil Kinnock view of 138
Peter Jay view of 108
RUC gun sale issue 129, 131
Central Intelligence Agency (CIA)
228
Chichester-Clark, James
1969 planned visit to United
States 43
1971 planned visit to United
States 48
mobilises Ulster Special
Constabulary 38

resignation 50
succeeds O'Neill 36
Clark, William (Bill) 153–155
Clinton, Hillary Rodham
2008 Presidential campaign
270–273
address to Northern Ireland
Assembly 276
and Bertie Ahern 273
and Declan Kelly 269
elected Senator 256
New York St Patrick's Day Parade
256
Obama campaign comments 272
Special Envoy 269
Clinton, William (Bill) 1
1992 Democratic primary
campaign 198, 199
1995 visit 3, 236–241
1996 election campaign 242, 248
1998 visit 252, 254
2000 visit 255
and Bruce Morrison 198, 202,
207, 208, 212, 221, 226, 236,
285
and Chuck Feeney 201
and Frank Durkan 245, 250
and John Major 204, 209, 234
and MacBride Principles 249
and the 1988 DNC speech 185
and the International Fund for
Ireland 263
and the Special Envoy role 156,
213, 221, 230, 231
and Tony Blair 241
and Ulster Unionists 238
appointment of Nancy Soderberg
212
Gerry Adams visa 214, 217, 219,
221, 224
Good Friday negotiations 252
inducted into Irish-American hall
of fame 257

IRA Docklands bomb statement
    243
Joe Cahill visa 229
Mackie's speech 3, 240
nomination of Jean Kennedy
    Smith 211
peace process 4
time at Oxford University 204,
    205
United States investment in
    Northern Ireland 235
writes to Christine Quinn 253
Corrigan, Mairead 85, 104, 120
Cosgrave, Liam 73, 83, 100n55
Craig, Gregory
    comments on Hillary Clinton 272
Curragh internment camp 13
Currie, Austin
    Caledon protest 27

Democratic Party 9, 12, 24, 31n7, 57,
    110, 169
    1976 primary elections 87, 99
    1988 primary elections 185, 186
    1992 primary elections 199, 213
    2008 primary elections 270–275
    and 1985 extradition treaty 170,
        183
    and MacBride Principles 250
    British concerns over Democratic
        President 86
    divisions within 130
    Reagan Democrats 201
Democratic Unionist Party
    Good Friday negotiations 238
    Operation USA 154
Derry/Londonderry 32, 50
    1968 civil rights march 6, 27
    1981 hunger strike 151
    1984 Martin Galvin visit 161
    1987 Bruce Morrison visit 208
    1993 Morrison meeting with
        Hume 221

1993 Rising Sun massacre 223
1995 Bill Clinton visit 240
Bloody Sunday 57–60
DuPont chemicals 34, 95, 138
IRA Derry Brigade 97
New Year 1969 march 33
De Valera, Eamon
    1962 meeting with Eisenhower 10
    1963 meeting with JFK 16, 17
    1970 meeting with Nixon 47
    1972 meeting with Reagan 67
    American Irish Foundation 17,
        37, 179
Devlin, Bernadette
    1969 visit to United States 40–45,
        295
    elected 36
Dobriansky, Paula 268–269
Doherty, Joseph
    and David Dinkins 188–190
    and Michael Flannery 193
    arrested 162
    extradition case 163, 177, 178,
        187, 190–192, 201, 202
Donlon, Sean
    1978 Jack Lynch visit to United
        States 111–112
    1979 Jack Lynch visit to United
        States 128, 135
    1979 visit of Tip O'Neill to
        Ireland 118
    and Bill Clark 153
    and Peter Jay 114, 280
    and Ronald Reagan 139–142, 160
    and Tip O'Neill 183
    Anglo-Irish Agreement 165
    attempts to replace as
        Ambassador 113, 136
    British views of 113–114
    deployment of SAS to Northern
        Ireland 82
    Jack Lynch remarks on Northern
        Ireland 105

views of Ted Kennedy 65
Douglas-Home, Alec
    1967 meeting with Richard Nixon
      31
    1972 burning of United Kingdom
      Embassy in Dublin 58–59
    1972 meeting with Richard Nixon
      68, 70
Downing Street Declaration
    222–224
Dukakis, Michael 185, 186
DuPont chemicals
    investment in Derry 22, 23, 101,
      138
    Jeffrey Agate murder 95
Durkan, Frank
    Americans for a New Irish
      Agenda 242
    and Bill Clinton 245–247
    and Joe Cahill 53

Eisenhower, Dwight
    1956 election 9
    1959 visit from Sean T. O'Kelly
      10
    1962 visit to Ireland 10
    Queen's University 9
Europa Hotel 4, 241
European Court of Human Rights
    52, 104, 218
extradition treaty 79, 162–164,
    167–171, 174–179, 183, 192

Falls Curfew 45
Faulkner, Brian
    1968 meeting with Harold Wilson
      30
    1971 meeting with Edward Heath
      54
    ban on parades 57
    comments on Ted Kennedy 55
    internment 51
    murder of Jeffrey Agate 95

Northern Ireland Minister of
    Commerce 22, 34, 95
Northern Ireland Prime Minister
    50, 76
Federal Bureau of Investigation (FBI)
    Gerry Adams visa 214, 216, 219,
      233
    Noraid report 74
    Robert Mueller meeting with
      John Reid 263
Feeney, Charles (Chuck) 199, 200
    1993 visit to Ireland 220
    1994 visit to Ireland 227
    1995 visit to Ireland 237
    1996 visit to Ireland 248
    letter to Clinton 211
    meets Clinton 201
Fianna Fáil 39, 45, 93, 197
    1978 Ard Fheis 111
    Northern Ireland Office concerns
      103
    role of Sean Donlon 114
Fine Gael 73, 75
FitzGerald, Garret
    1973 meeting with Congress 75
    1974 meeting with Gerald Ford 77
    1975 visit to United States 78
    1976 Carter letter to FitzGerald
      88
    1983 meeting with George H.W.
      Bush 156
    1984 meeting with Ronald
      Reagan 159
    1986 visit to United States 174
    becomes Taoiseach 155
    John Moore comments on 73
    New Ireland Forum 157
    Peter Jay comments on 280
    Thatcher comments on 165, 171
    views on Congressional hearings
      110
Flannery, Michael
    forms Noraid 53

funeral 231
Noraid split 193
Flynn, Raymond 201, 208, 210
    Ambassador to the Holy See 212
Flynn, William (Bill) 199, 200, 216,
    227, 228
    1993 visit to Ireland 220
    1994 Loughinisland massacre 226
    1995 visits to Ireland 237, 240
    and IRA decommissioning 262,
        265, 267
Ford, Gerald 71, 284
    1975 meeting with Garret
        FitzGerald 78
    1975 meeting with Harold Wilson
        78
    1976 communique with Taoiseach
        83
    1976 letter from Paul O'Dwyer 85
    becomes President 77
Ford Motor Company 196

Galvin, Martin
    1985 protesting Thatcher visit 166
    Noraid support for Sinn Féin 193
    visit to Belfast 161
Gingrich, Newt 234, 253–254
Giuliani, Rudolf
    1989 New York Mayoral election
        187
    1993 New York Mayoral election
        190
    encourages Clinton to meet Gerry
        Adams 231
    New York St Patrick's Day parade
        286
    presents Gerry Adams with
        Crystal Apple 190
Good Friday Agreement 75, 202,
    222, 284, 285, 288
    Bruce Morrison role 236
    George W. Bush and implemen-
        tation 259

Hillary Clinton 256, 272
negotiations 251, 252
prisoner release 81n210, 126, 177,
    255
Goulding, Cathal
    appointed IRA Chief of Staff 13

Haass, Richard
    2002 meeting John Reid 263
    appointed Special Envoy 260
    concern over Sinn Féin links in
        Cuba 262
    flag protest 285–286, 288
    steps down as Envoy 264
Haig, Alexander 48, 65, 67, 70, 150
Hamilton-Fairley, Gordon
    murder of 80
Harland and Wolff 1, 2, 99, 117
Harrison, George
    migration to New York 14
    split in Irish Northern Aid 193
    work on Dinkins campaign for
        Mayor 187
Haughey, Charles
    1971 meeting with Ted Kennedy
        56–57
    arms trial 44–45
    becomes Taoiseach 93, 135–136
    resignation 197
    views of British officials on 136
    views on Congressional Friends of
        Ireland 147
    visits to United States 155
Heath, Edward (Ted)
    1970 meeting with Richard Nixon
        45–46
    1971 meeting with Jack Lynch 54
    1971 meeting with Richard Nixon
        64
    1972 Congressional hearings on
        Northern Ireland 61
    1972 meeting with Richard Nixon
        72

1972 meeting with Senate Foreign
  Relations Committee 72–73
and Ted Kennedy 55
Henderson, Nicholas
  1979 Margaret Thatcher visit to
    United States 131
  1981 Tip O'Neill letter 151
  and Mario Biaggi 131
  arrives as Ambassador 124
  RUC gun embargo 130, 145, 146
  freezing of Iranian assets 133, 134
Hillery, Patrick
  1969 visit to New York 39
  1970 meeting with Richard Nixon
    47
  1971 requests for US intervention
    49
  1972 visits to New York 57–59,
    62–63, 69–70
  and Falls Curfew 45
  replaced by Brian Lenihan 72
Hume, John
  Americans for a New Irish
    Agenda 244, 246
  and Bruce Morrison 221, 237, 248
  and Gerry Adams 217, 220, 222,
    237
  and Sean Donlon 136
  and Ted Kennedy 65–66, 84, 282
  and Tip O'Neill 153
  National Committee on American
    Foreign Policy 225
  Neil Kinnock view of 257
  Nobel Peace Prize 255
  Peter Jay view of 280

internment without trial
  1971 introduction 50, 51
  calls for 49
  during Border Campaign 13
  during World War II 13
  protests in Northern Ireland 57
  State Department view of 52, 58

Ted Kennedy view of 60
investment in Ireland 3, 4, 10, 22,
  23, 43, 50, 61, 62, 71, 72, 78, 83,
  101, 111, 113, 117, 128, 154, 155,
  186, 195, 210, 232, 234, 235, 237,
  240, 249
Iran 131–134
Iraq 263–264, 269
Irish-Americans for Clinton-Gore
  see Americans for a New Irish
  Agenda
Irish National Caucus 93, 102, 113,
  136, 138, 194, 283
  1976 event for Jimmy Carter 87
  Congressional hearings 108, 110
  fundraising 106
  MacBride Principles 150
Irish National Liberation Army 227
  1981 hunger strike 151
  assassination of Airey Neave 118,
    142
Irish Northern Aid Committee
  (Noraid) 26, 93, 102, 138, 146,
  185, 234, 283
  1981 hunger strike 150
  1984 delegation to Ireland
    160–161
  1985 protest at Thatcher visit 166
  Charles Haughey attempts to
    connect with 136
  formation 53
  fundraising 74, 81, 142, 150
  Gerry Adams view on 194
  Harold Wilson comments on 81,
    83
  Ireland Fund as an alternative to
    179
  Irish People newspaper 87
  Joe Cahill 54
  Joe Doherty 192
  Liam Cosgrave comments on 83
  Split and Homefront campaign
    193

Ted Kennedy office and dealing with 281
William Quinn 177
Irish Republican Army (pre-1969)
  Border Campaign 12, 13
  international support 14, 26
Irish Republican Army, Provisional (1969–2007)
  1969 split 44
  1971 internment without trial 51
  1981 hunger strikes 147–148
  1992 London bombing 197
  1994 ceasefire 200, 227, 228, 230, 285
  1996 bombing campaign 242–247
  1997 ceasefire 249, 251, 257
  Balcombe Street Gang 79–82
  Colombia Three 262
  decommissioning 234, 236, 239, 260, 261, 264, 267
  economic campaign 4
  extradition 163–168, 170, 183, 192
  former members in government 32
  inclusion in talks 219–220, 221
  international support 42, 73, 75, 78–79, 84, 135, 150, 179
  new cell structure 92–94
  post-ceasefire violence 251–252, 265, 266
  pre-ceasefire violence 214, 216, 222, 223
  response of Dublin government 50, 71, 104
  Ted Kennedy view on 67
  the M60 gang 162–165
  threat to Caroline Kennedy 80
  views of British figures 146, 166, 278, 279
  views of United States figures 52, 76, 85, 119, 125, 127, 151, 166, 196, 224, 226, 281
  violence in Northern Ireland 49,
      91, 95–99, 107, 117, 126, 138, 139, 154
  visits to the United States 53, 68–69, 72, 160, 225, 229
  Warrington bomb 216–217
Irish Republican Army, Real (post-1997) 253, 255

Jay, Peter
  1977 Carter statement 101
  and Hugh Carey 115
  and Sean Donlon 113–114
  IRA fundraising 109
  relationship between Jimmy Carter and James Callaghan 102
  RUC gun embargo 112–113, 124–125
  succeeded by Nicholas Henderson 124
  views on Jimmy Carter 108
  views on United States figures 280
Johnson, Lyndon Baines
  1968 meeting with Jack Lynch 25
  1968 Presidential election 24
  and Terence O'Neill 20–22
  becomes President 19

Kelly, Declan 269, 285
Kennedy, Caroline
  IRA bomb attack 80
Kennedy, Edward
  1962 visit to Ireland 15
  1963 meeting with Sean Lemass 19
  1970 visit to Ireland 54–55
  1971 resolution on Northern Ireland 54
  1974 visit to London 74–75
  1977 Ireland Fund dinner 84
  1977 visit to the UK 99
  1981 hunger strikes 147
  1990 Immigration Act 195

1993 meeting with John Major
  209
1994 midterm elections 232
and attempts to remove Donlon
  136
and Ian Paisley visa 153
and International Fund for
  Ireland 174
and IRA decommissioning 265
and Jean Kennedy Smith 211
and Jimmy Carter 130, 138
and John Hume 66, 282, 283
and New Ireland Forum 157
and Roy Mason 103, 106
and the Carter Statement 102,
  103
and Tip O'Neill 30, 93
commemorations 277–281
Congressional Friends of Ireland
  142, 147
Congressional hearings on
  Northern Ireland 56, 57, 59–61
Gerry Adams visa 224, 230, 233
honorary knighthood 277
Joe Cahill visa 229
La Mon bombing comments 107
letter to Nixon 63–64
McCartney sisters 266
resolution on the Ulster Defence
  Association 152
Sean Donlon on 65–66
Four Horsemen 99, 100
Kennedy, John F.
  1954 Friendly Sons of St Patrick
    dinner 11
  1960 election 10
  1963 European trip 14–19
  Algerian conflict 12
  and Brendan Behan 12
  and Terence O'Neill 20–23
  athletics stadium named for 10
  family history 11
  St Patrick's Day traditions 15

Kennedy, Joseph P.
  1988 event at British Embassy 181
  1988 visit to Ireland 181–182
  Gerry Adams visa 224
  replacing Tip O'Neill 180
Kennedy, Robert 24–25
Kennedy Smith, Jean
  1993 meeting with Bruce
    Morrison delegation 220
  contrast with Belfast Consulate
    233
  critical comments from Raymond
    Seitz 248
  Joe Cahill visa 229
  nomination as Ambassador 211
  support for Gerry Adams visa
    215–216
Kerry, John
  1993 meeting with Clinton 209
  extradition treaty 174, 176
  secretary of State 176
  support for Gerry Adams visa 224
King, Peter 187, 217
  and Gerry Adams 218, 226, 229
  and Hillary Clinton 273
  and IRA activity 266
  and Joe Doherty 191
  Jonathan Powell view of 279
  MacBride Principles 250
Kinnock, Neil
  Labour Party and Ronald Reagan
    138
  views on Jimmy Carter 137–138
  views on peace process 257
Kissinger, Henry
  1970 visit to Ireland 45–46
  appointed National Security
    Adviser 29
  comments on situation in Ireland
    37, 54, 68, 73, 76–77, 284
Koch, Edward 186–188, 256

La Mon House Hotel bombing 107

Lake, Anthony 212, 231, 238, 239, 247
Lemass, Sean
　1962 meeting with Eisenhower 10
　1963 visit to United States 18, 19, 21
　economic reforms 8
Lenihan, Brian 84
Lynch, Jack
　1968 meeting with Harold Wilson 28
　1970 planned trip to United States 43
　1971 meeting with Edward Heath and Brian Faulkner 54
　1971 visit to United States 47–49
　1972 cancelled visit to United States 59
　1973 general election 73
　1973 visit to United States 71–72
　1977 general election 103
　1978 appearance on RTE 104–105
　1978 visit to United States 111–112
　1979 visit to United States 128–129
　comments at Dublin Castle on Tip O'Neill 119
　exchange with Mario Biaggi 105–107
　Peter Jay comments on 280
　receiving Nixon 47
　resignation 135
　RFK funeral 25
　view of Henry Kissinger 46
　visit of Ted Kennedy 55

McAliskey, Bernadette see Devlin, Bernadette
MacBride, Sean
　and Gerry Adams visa 160
　the MacBride Principles 3, 181, 185, 186, 195, 196, 199, 208, 209, 249, 250
McCain, John
　2008 Presidential election 270, 273–274
　Irish American Presidential Forum 274
McCartney, Robert
　2005 murder 265
　sisters visit United States 266, 274, 283
McGuinness, Martin
　1984 meeting with Martin Galvin 161
　1995 meeting with Americans for a New Irish Agenda 237
　2005 visit to United States 267
　and Hillary Clinton 271, 276
　and Paula Dobriansky 269
　and Richard Haass 264
　Warrington bomb comments 216
Mackie International 2, 3, 240, 241
McManus, Sean 110
Major, John
　and Bill Clinton 204, 209, 210
Mason, Roy 99, 100, 101
　1977 visit to United States 103–104, 106
　1979 meeting with Michael O'Kennedy 117–118
Meese, Edwin 178, 190
Mills, W. Stratton
　debate with Bernadette Devlin 42
　visit to United States 41
Mitchell, George
　2016 St Patrick's Day parade 286
　and decommissioning 238
　and Gerry Adams visa 224
　and Queen's University, Belfast 281, 286
　memoir 288
　Special Envoy 4, 231–234, 238, 242, 252, 272, 285, 287

Moore, John D.J.
  1970 Richard Nixon visit to
    Ireland 47
  appointed Ambassador 36
  comments on situation in Ireland
    44, 46, 48, 71, 284
  on Garret FitzGerald 73
Moore, Richard
  appointed Ambassador 211
Morrison, Bruce
  1990 Immigration Act 195
  1993 visit to Ireland 213, 220–222
  1994 visit to Ireland 227
  1996 visit to Ireland 248
  Americans for a New Irish
    Agenda 210, 212
  and Bill Clinton 198, 201, 202,
    207, 208, 226, 232–233, 236,
    242, 285
  and Chuck Feeney 200
  and Ian Paisley 228
  and Special Envoy 230
  MacBride Principles 209
Moynihan, Daniel Patrick
  1976 Presidential election 86–87
  1978 meeting with Jack Lynch 112
  1990 Immigration Act 195
  Four Horsemen 100, 119, 138,
    147, 149, 153
  succeeded by Hillary Clinton 256
  views of Peter Jay 280
Mueller, Robert
  meeting with John Reid 263

Neal, Richard 217, 224, 250, 266
Needham, Richard 3
New York City
  1969 visit of Bernadette Devlin 40
  1969 visit of Patrick Hillery 39
  1971 planned visit of James
    Chichester Clark 48
  1972 visits of Patrick Hillery 57,
    69

1976 Liam Cosgrave visit 83
1976 Stanley Orme visit 82
1978 proposed summit 115
1978 Tip O'Neill address 121
1981 hunger strike impact 149
1988 Irish American Presidential
  Forum 185
1989 Mayoral election 186–190
1992 Irish American Presidential
  Forum 199
1994 National Committee on
  American Foreign Policy event
  223
1994 visit of Gerry Adams 225
1994 visit of Joe Cahill 229
Arms for the Irish Republican
  Army 14
borough of Queen's 74, 231, 233
borough of the Bronx 49
protest of Brookeborough 9
Sinn Féin fundraising in 233, 234,
  267
St Patrick's Day parade 24, 87,
  88, 188–189, 286
Nixon, Richard
  1969 meeting with Harold Wilson
    39
  1970 visit to Europe 45–46
  1970 visit to Ireland 47
  1971 meeting with Jack Lynch
    49
  1971 proposed visit from James
    Chichester Clark 48
  1972 meeting with Alec
    Douglas-Home 68
  1972 meeting with Patrick Hillery
    70
  1972 Presidential election
    campaign 67
  1973 meetings with Heath and
    Lynch 71–73
  and the American Congress for
    Irish Freedom 34

and the American Irish
    Foundation 37
appoints Henry Kissinger 29
discussions with British 64
establishing United States policy
    towards Northern Ireland
    30
Irish ancestry 31
sends Ronald Reagan to Ireland
    140
transition to Gerald Ford 77
views on situation in Northern
    Ireland 283–284
Northern Ireland Assembly
    2007 election 268, 277
Northern Ireland Civil Rights
    Association (NICRA)
    formation 26
    involvement of communists 33
    marches 27, 31
Northern Ireland Labour Party 27,
    68, 76n191, 179

Ó Brádaigh, Ruairí
    1973 visit to Capitol Hill 73–74
    1975 meeting with Mario Biaggi
        116
    1986 split in Sinn Féin 193
    denial of visa 109
O'Donnell, Kirk 118, 129
O'Dowd, Niall 186
    1993 visit to Ireland 220
    1994 visit to Ireland 227
    1995 visit to Ireland 237
    1998 visit to Ireland 248
    Americans for a New Irish
        Agenda 231
    broadcast ban 215
    Irish Americans for Clinton-Gore
        198–200
    views on peace process 239
O'Kelly, Sean T.
    1959 visit to United States 10

O'Kennedy, Michael 105, 111, 115,
    117
O'Neill, Terence
    1968 meeting in London 30
    becomes Northern Ireland Prime
        Minister 16
    Burntollet March 34
    critical of Lemass 19
    meeting with Harold Wilson 28
    meeting with Jackie Kennedy 22
    meeting with Lyndon Johnson 21,
        48
    praise for DuPont investment 23
    reform package 32, 33
    resigns as Northern Ireland Prime
        Minister 36
    Ulster at the cross roads 32
    visit to White House 20
O'Neill, Thomas P. 'Tip'
    1977 meeting with Roy Mason
        99, 100, 103–104
    1978 Ireland Fund dinner in
        honour of 84
    1979 meeting with Ian Paisley 153
    1979 meeting with Margaret
        Thatcher 132
    1979 visit to Ireland 119–121
    1981 hunger strikes 147, 149–151
    1985 Anglo-Irish Agreement 173
    and Jack Lynch 135
    and Ronald Reagan 141
    attempted removal of Donlon 136
    comments on Mountbatten
        killing and Warrenpoint attack
        126–127
    Congressional Friends of Ireland
        142
    Jonathan Powell comments on 279
    letter from Nixon assistant 37
    meets Ruairí Ó Brádaigh 73–74
    meets with Ulster Political
        Research Group 118
    New Ireland Forum report 157

on Congressional hearings 112
on Lynch criticism of Mario
    Biaggi 106
Peter Jay comments on 280
political football comments
    120–121
retirement 180
Royal Ulster Constabulary
    122–125, 127, 129, 132, 145
support for Elizabeth Shannon
    211
Obama, Barack 282, 285
2008 Presidential election
    270–273
and Dan Rooney 274–275
and Special Envoy role 269, 274
Orange Order 38, 247, 253

Paisley, Reverend Ian K.
    1969 visit to United States 42
    1995 visit to White House 238
    2001 visit to White House 274
    2002 visit to United States 263
    2007 Northern Ireland Executive
        268
    and Bernadette Devlin 42
    and George W. Bush 259
    and Hillary Clinton 271
    and the RUC arms issue 126
    Anglo-Irish Agreement 171
    Burntollet march 34
    Good Friday negotiations 202
    International Fund for Ireland 179
    Operation USA 152–154
    release from prison 36
    Ulster Constitution Defence
        Committee 32
    United Unionist Action Council
        99
    views of United States officials on
        76, 228
Parliament of Northern Ireland
    1969 election 28

Cabinet Security Committee 38
    collapse 76, 77, 99
    SDLP withdraws 51
Peace People 85, 104, 120
Penberthy, Grover
    United States Consulate General
        Belfast 80–81
People's Democracy
    1969 New Year's Day march 33
    Bernadette Devlin election 36
Police Service of Northern Ireland
    2007 Sinn Féin endorsement 267,
        268
Powell, Charles
    1972 Widgery visit to United
        States 68
    role of Northern Ireland for
        Thatcher 183
    Thatcher and Carter relationship
        137, 141
Powell, Jonathan
    First Secretary in Washington
        214
    Gerry Adams visa 214
    model of Northern Ireland peace
        process 287
    role of Peter King 226
    role of Ted Kennedy 279
Price, Marian 1
    and IRA kidnappings 99
    IRA campaign 92
    the long war 1

Queen's University Belfast 9, 281,
    286
Quinn brothers 253
Quinn, William
    extradition process 163, 168, 177
    murder of Stephen Tibble 79

Reagan, Ronald
    1972 visit to Ireland 67
    1980 Presidential election 137

1981 St Patrick's Day comments
    147
1983 visit to Eire Irish bar 201
1984 meeting with Margaret
    Thatcher 165
1984 visit to Ireland 158–160
1985 extradition treaty 167,
    170–171, 175–176
1988 meeting with Margaret
    Thatcher 182
and Bill Clark 153–154
and Margaret Thatcher 141, 143,
    183
and Mario Biaggi 146
and Tip O'Neill 149, 151, 284
Neil Kinnock comments on 138
Northern Ireland and Ireland
    Assistance Act 173–174
Northern Ireland envoy role 157
Sean Donlon comments on
    139–141
Reiss, Mitchell
    criticism from Gerry Adams 267
    IRA comments 265
    Special Envoy 260, 264, 288
Renwick, Robin
    election of George H.W. Bush
        186
    Gerry Adams visa 214–215
    St Patrick's Day experience 194
    UK view of Reagan pre-election
        141
    Unionist view of Joseph Kennedy
        182
    view of Ted Kennedy 280
Republican Party 9, 174n168, 259,
    261, 282
    1980 Presidential election 93, 137
    1994 midterm elections 232, 235
    2008 Democratic Party primary
        election 273
    2008 Presidential election 270,
        274

and 1985 extradition treaty 176
and 1993 New York Mayoral
    election 190
and Gerry Adams visa 218, 248
resolutions on Ireland 11, 195
Reynolds, Albert 197, 219, 220–221,
    228
Ribicoff, Abraham 54, 56, 59, 61,
    66
Robinson, Joe (Senator from
    Alabama)
    visit to Northern Ireland 7–8
Rogers, William 58, 59, 61, 70
    1972 meetings with Patrick
        Hillery 62, 69
Rooney, Dan
    1987 merger with American Irish
        Foundation 179–180
    2001 White House St Patrick's
        Day reception 274
    2009 appointed Ambassador
        274–275
    and Barack Obama 275
    founds Ireland Fund 84
    steps down as Ambassador 276
    Superbowl wins 84, 274
Royal Ulster Constabulary 39, 57,
    107, 208
    gun embargo 121–127, 130, 131,
        132, 134, 144–146
    United States officials view of 69
    violence involving 27, 38, 44, 93,
        94, 161, 162
Russell, Sean 12

Sands, Robert (Bobby) 147–148, 168
Scarman Report 38
Shannon Airport 17, 19, 47, 159, 189
Shannon, Elizabeth 211
Sheinwald, Nigel 139, 156, 168–169,
    214, 281
Sinn Féin 32
    1970 split 44

1984 Martin Galvin visit
161
1986 split 193
1992 UK general election 197
and Mitchell Reiss 260, 269
and Robert McCartney murder
265–266
and the Colombia Three 262
electoral success 261, 265, 268
fundraising in the United States
233, 234, 249, 267
Homefront campaign 194
IRA violence 220, 260, 264
views of US officials on 75, 160,
196, 217, 219, 225, 228, 231,
233, 243
Social Democratic and Labour Party
1971 withdrawal from Stormont
51
1996 meeting with Sinn Féin and
IRA 244
Bruce Morrison and 228
international appeal 67
Joe Hendron wins Belfast West
197, 213
John Hume and 282
Mark Durkan 263
negotiations with Brian Faulkner
76
Paddy Devlin on IRA murders of
business people 97
Soderberg, Nancy
and Bruce Morrison 248
appointed to National Security
Council 212
Gerry Adams visa 213–214, 239
Sonnenfeldt, Helmut (Kissinger aide)
44, 70
Special Powers Act (Northern
Ireland) 13
Stormont Parliament Buildings see
Parliament of Northern Ireland
Sunningdale Agreement 75, 203

Thant, U
1969 meeting with Bernadette
Devlin 41
and Northern Ireland 39, 40,
Thatcher, Margaret
1967 visit to United States 143
1979 United Kingdom general
election 93, 121
1979 visit to United States 129,
131, 132–133
1983 United Kingdom general
glection 156
1984 visit to United States 162,
165–167
1985 meeting with Ronald
Reagan 170–171
1988 meeting with Reagan 182
and Airey Neave 118–119, 142
and Charles Haughey 135, 149
and Jimmy Carter 137, 141
and Ronald Reagan 141, 143, 167,
183
and the Congressional Friends of
Ireland 148, 149, 284
Anglo-Irish Agreement 172, 175
extradition treaty 176
invitation to discuss Northern
Ireland with Hugh Carey
115–116
New Ireland Forum 157–158
resignation 197
role of Northern Ireland 183
RUC gun embargo 121, 127, 134,
146
Thornburgh, Richard 190, 191, 202
Trimble, David 238
1995 refusal to meet Bill Clinton
241
2002 invitation to United States
263
and Hillary Clinton 273
Gerry Adams visa 245
Good Friday Agreement 252

Morrison attempts to meet 248
Nobel Peace Prize 255
Trinity College, Dublin 17, 54, 55
Truman, Harry
  and St Patrick's Day 15

Ulster Defence Association 152, 222,
  230
Ulster Political Research Group 118,
  152
Ulster Special Constabulary
  B Specials disbanded 38, 76
  Burtollet 34
  mobilised by James
    Chichester-Clark 38
Ulster Unionist Party
  1972 Darlington Conference 68
  and Bill Clinton 238
  and Bruce Morrison 228
  and George W. Bush 270
  Brian Faulkner resignation 76
  Operation USA 154–155
  United States of America 9
Ulster Volunteer Force
  1966 murders 23, 29
  ceasefire 230
  Dublin and Monaghan bombs
    77n195
  visa applications 69
United Nations 39
  1969 visit of Bernadette Devlin 41
  intervention sought in Northern
    Ireland 35, 56, 57, 69, 137, 218

Irish commitments to 47
United States Consulate General,
  Belfast 33, 34, 44, 63, 68, 160,
  224, 233
United States Embassy, Dublin
  communication on situation in
    Ireland 50, 52, 56, 57, 70, 72,
    82, 147, 231
  Eisenhower visits 10
  planned construction of new
    building 16
  threats made on 54
United States Embassy, Tehran
  130 134

Warrington bomb 217
Williams, Betty 85, 104
Wilson, Harold
  1967 meeting with Richard Nixon
    31
  1968 meeting with Brian Faulkner
    30
  1968 meeting with Jack Lynch
    28
  1969 meeting with Richard Nixon
    39
  1974 meeting with Gerald Ford
    78
  1974 meeting with Ted Kennedy
    74–75
  comments on Noraid 81–82
  Constitutional Convention 136
Wolff, Lester 108, 118, 137